Bethesda and Surrounding Communities

BETHESDA
and Surrounding Communities

Rick Warwick

Williamson County Historian

Marcia P. Fraser, Editor

Special Collections Librarian
Williamson County Public Library

Williamson County Historical Society • Franklin, Tennessee

©2023

Bethesda and Surrounding Communities
Copyright ©2023, Williamson County Historical Society (Tennessee). All rights reserved.
ISBN: 979-8-9863055-1-6
Library of Congress Control Number: 2023915250
2nd Printing

Cover Design by Peg Raciti
Photo Editing by Peg Raciti

Interior Layout and Design by Marcia Fraser

Powered by Pressbooks

Printed in the United States of America
by IngramSpark, La Vergne, Tennessee

Front Cover Image: Civil War Map of the Bethesda Area
Back Cover Photo: The One Gallus Fox Hunters Association

Williamson County Historical Society
112 Bridge Street
Franklin, Tennessee 37064
www.williamsoncountyhistory.com

Contents

Dedication ix
Introduction x

Bethesda History

William S. Webb's Historical Account of Bethesda 2

The Military Line 7

Duplex, Harpeth, Callie, and Cross Keys 10

Churches 17

Fraternal Orders 26

Physicians 30

Country Stores 32

Schools 36

Old Homes and Sites 66

Notable Homes 89

Notable Homes No Longer Standing 94

Who's Who in Williamson County

Mattie Sue Ware Alexander (Mrs. C.E.), 1886-1959 100

Frank M. Anderson, 1883-1955 106

Sam F. Anderson, 1879-1944 111

Walter Anderson, 1868-1958 115

James W. Bond, Jr., 1906-1967 119

T.P. Crafton, 1873-1952 124

Fannie Daniel and Nannie Mai Daniel 129

Samuel Perkins Edgmon, 1871-1943 134

Miss Addie Eggleston, 1894-1979 137

Howard Hood, Sr., 1893-1974 140

Alice Alexander Irvin, 1855-1944 144

Brown Jefferson, 1889-1984 148

Herbert McCall, 1904-1984 153

Tennie Lavender McCord, 1851-1940 158

Ellie Clayton Morton Millard, 1858-1941 162

Marion Grigsby Warren, 1913-1996 165

Richard P. Waddey, 1877-1962 170

Lifestyles of the Past and Present in Bethesda

Introduction 175

Billy Alexander, 1922-2008 177

Franklin Bond, 1924-2007 190

Leo Grigsby Bond, 1905-1997 198

Lola Reed Glenn Bowersox 1918-2016 211

Cleo Grigsby, 1905-2003 224

Agnes Hargrove, 1905-2005 232

Annie Lou Reed McCord 1896-1998 247

Bessie Taylor Mosley, 1905-2004 256

Lester Mosley, 1919-2007 268

Jean Gary Sanders, 1926-2010 280

Willie Ruth Veach Taylor 1925-2014 295

James Trice, 1918-1999 304

Jerry Watkins, 1909-1997 314

Bill Wiley 1910-2005 319

Reflections of Joyce Smith 329
Reflections of Jessie Trice Bennett 332
Brief Biography of Hugh Keedy 335
In Miss Jessie's Footprints, by William T. Byrd 338
Faces of the Past 340
Index 352

DEDICATION

James and Judy Hayes

Judy Grigsby Hayes, daughter of Leonard Booker and Annie Lou Barker Grigsby, is a lifelong resident of the Burwood community, with deep roots in Bethesda, being a descendant of several pioneer families of the old 12th Civil District. She was a successful Williamson County teacher, popular County Commissioner, helpmate to a radio executive, as well as wife of the late Jim Hayes. She co-chaired the Tennessee and Williamson County Bicentennial Committee from 1995 to 2000 with me. She has been a leader in the Williamson County Chamber of Commerce for decades. Judy is recognized across Williamson County for her devotion to the improvement of schools, parks, and county services. She is a role model for community service.

When Judy heard about the Bethesda and Surrounding Communities project, she responded, "How can I help?" She has offered not only moral support but also provided seed money for publishing the book. Judy is my model for the biblical cheerful giver.

A great admirer and friend,
Rick Warwick, Williamson County Historian

INTRODUCTION

Overlook of the village of Bethesda from P.D. Scales home

Rick Warwick

In February 2023, William Byrd invited me to speak to the Bethesda Senior Citizens group and partake in lunch with them. In my opening remarks, I mentioned that Bethesda and Grassland were the last two major communities not having a written history. To my surprise, Joyce Smith spoke up saying, "I think we do have a history written by Hugh Keedy and Jessie Bennett back in the mid-1990s." Upon further inquiry, William Byrd found a copy of *Lifestyles of the Past and Present in Bethesda: Interviews with Long-time Residents of Bethesda*, in the Bethesda Library. Also, with the help of Marcia Fraser, a copy was found in the Special Collections Department of Williamson County Public Library. Very few copies were printed since only five copies have been found to date.

RICK WARWICK

Unbeknownst to Judy Grigsby Hayes and me, who were Williamson County co-chairs of the Tennessee and Williamson County Bicentennial Committee (1995-2000), Hugh and Jessie made these interviews Bethesda's Tennessee 200 Bicentennial Celebration project. This Bethesda project provides the reader today an insight into what life was like growing up in the Bethesda community in the first half of the twentieth century as told by those who lived it. Unfortunately, the informative interviews were not accompanied by period photos, which would have enriched the stories even more.

With a phone call to Judy Grigsby Hayes and William Byrd, I was encouraged to take up the mantle to spearhead this project that would give Bethesda and surrounding communities a written history. First, I asked Marcia Fraser, Special Collections Librarian, to scan the 1995 interviews, converting them to a Microsoft Word document, so that photographs from the Williamson County Historical Society Flickr site could be added. Additional photos were copied from the Bethesda Museum files along with contributions from the good folks of Bethesda. I then began writing brief histories of the schools, churches, physicians, postmasters, country stores, and fraternal orders of the area. I found an article written by William S. Webb in *The Review-Appeal* (June 16, 1938) entitled "Bethesda Community" which provides a timely synopsis of the subject. Also, seventeen interviews of Bethesda folks taken from Jane Owen's "Who's Who in Williamson County" series found in *The Review-Appeal* are included which provide information about the community found nowhere else. Then, eleven articles taken from Virginia McDaniel Bowman's *Historic Williamson County: Old Homes and Sites*, written in 1971, were added which provide a history and genealogy of Bethesda's pioneer families and their homes. The article on the Callie community was borrowed from Lyn Sullivan Pewitt's *Back Home in Williamson County*, (1996).

Lastly, an old newspaper article entitled "The Military Line" from *The Review-Appeal* (April 18, 1901) was included which relates how the heirs to Dr. Joseph Blythe's 4,800-acre North Carolina land grant became the pioneer families of Bethesda. This article was originally shared by Charles Grigsby in October 1994 when he spoke to the Williamson County Historical Society in the Bethesda School cafeteria about his youthful days growing up in Bethesda. His talk left a great impression on me to discover more about this part of Williamson County.

Special thanks to Judy Hayes, Marcia Fraser, Peg Raciti, Leslie Crowder, William Byrd, Jon Harris, Mike Hoover, and the Bethesda Senior Citizens for their help in producing this book. I hope my attempt at recording this history will be informative and well-received.

Rick Warwick,
Williamson County Historian

BETHESDA HISTORY

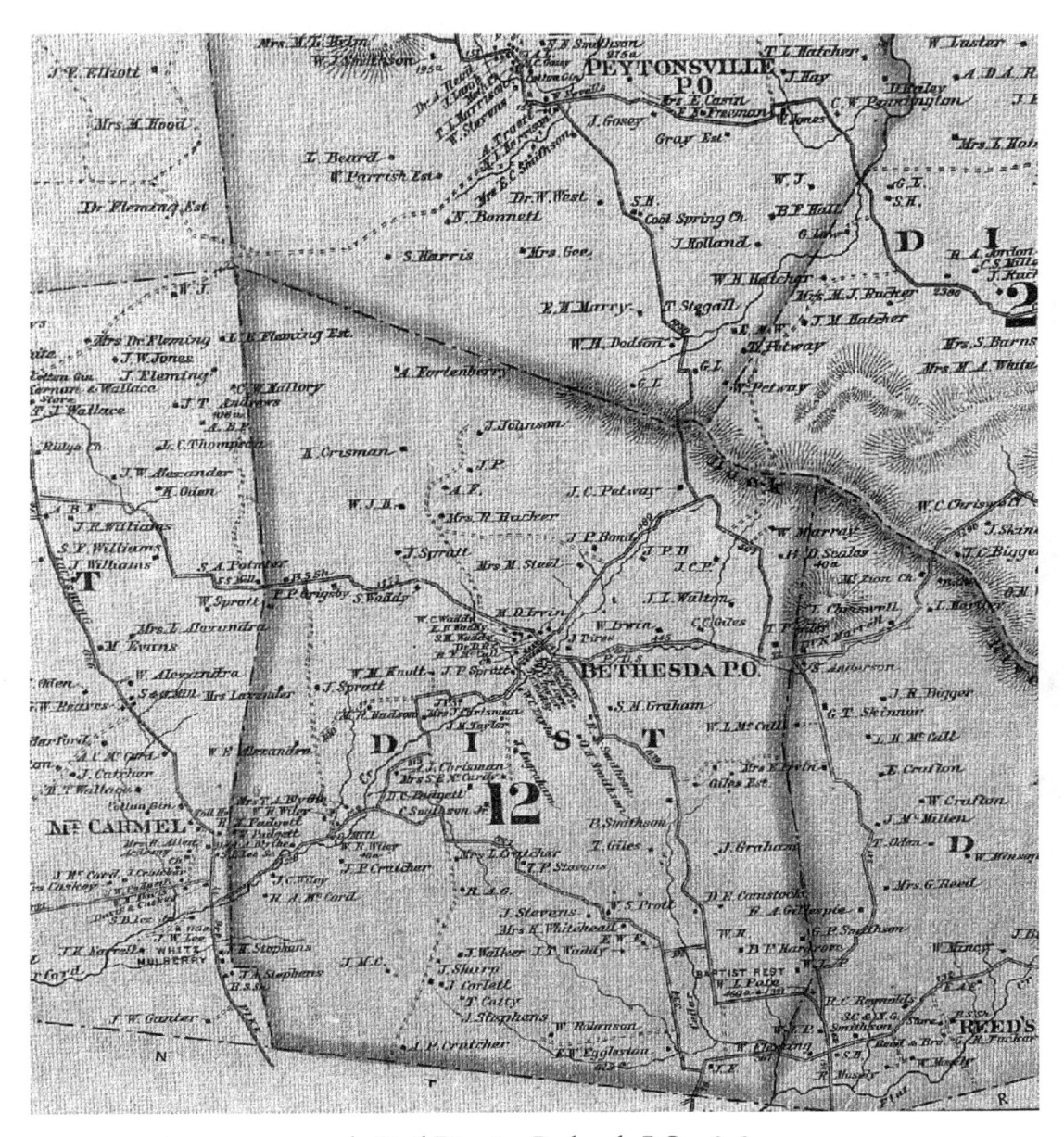

12th Civil District, Bethesda P.O., 1878

WILLIAM S. WEBB'S HISTORICAL ACCOUNT OF BETHESDA

The Review-Appeal, June 16, 1938
By William S. Webb

Bethesda is noted for its hospitable Christian people and its two churches – Methodist and Presbyterian.

Bethesda Methodist Church 1870-1961, also served as Bethesda Masonic Lodge No. 201

A Methodist church was erected here at the close of the Civil War. Two ministers have gone from this congregation, Rev. Thaddeus Hudson, of Pulaski, and Rev. Glenn Grigsby, of Bethesda, son of Mr. and Mrs. O.T. Grigsby.

The Rev. E.D. Trout is pastor of the Methodist church now, and the official board of stewards are O.T. Grigsby, A.B. Alexander, and Sam Gillespie. M.F. Clendenen is the Sunday School Superintendent. Sunday School teachers are L.P. Bond, T.R. Beasley, Mrs. J.E. Crafton, Prof. W.P. Scales, Miss Frances Hatcher, Misses Marion and Cleo Grigsby, Miss Mattie Sue Crafton, and Glenn Grigsby. There is a Methodist Woman's Missionary Society here. Rev. Trout preaches the second and fourth Sunday of each month at this church.

The Bethesda Presbyterian Church was established in 1879 and the beloved Rev. M.W. Millard, who died a few years ago was its pastor for over fifty years. He has a son, Rev. John Millard, pastor of the Presbyterian Church in Greensboro, N.C. Another son, Rev. Ernest Millard, died while studying for the ministry in college in South Carolina. The Rev. W.L. Smith is the present pastor of the Presbyterian church, and the board of elders are T.C. and

J.W. Bond, J.W. Stowers, and Joe Eggleston. Deacons are Gordon McCord, Bill Eggleston, and James Bond who is also the church treasurer. T.C. Bond is Sunday School superintendent. Teachers are J.W. Bond, Mrs. Mary Gary, Miss Lorene Bond, Mrs. W.L. Smith, and Misses Addie and Julia Eggleston. Officers of the Presbyterian Ladies Auxiliary are Mrs. Claude Lee, president; Miss Lorene Bond, secretary; and Mrs. W.L. Smith. The society meets monthly at the church. Rev. Smith preaches the first and third Sunday of each month.

Bethesda is located fifteen miles south of Franklin in the 12th civil district of Williamson County, in a rich farming and dairying section; chief sources of cash income are general farming, dairying, and beef cattle raising.

Besides the Methodist and Presbyterian churches, the village has one general merchandise store, a sawmill and planing mill, and a four-year high school.

Bethesda Presbyterian Church, est. 1879

The magistrates in this district are J.O. Grigsby, a member of the Williamson County School Board, and Herbert McCall, both prominent farmers.

The first settlers in this community were Philip Chapman, and Moses Steele, who came here from Campbell County, Virginia, in the early part of the last century.

The next family of early settlers who came to this community from Virginia was the Irvin family, who came across the mountains in covered wagons taking two weeks to make the trip. The original Irvin home is still occupied but has been moved from its first location one mile and this house was moved by sixty yoke of oxen.

There was once located here a chair and bed factory, and the [Benjamin Waddey] chairs which were manufactured were in great demand.

Another industry formerly located at Bethesda in its early history was a stove foundry. Thomas Russell, H.M. and William Steele, Charles Hatcher, and Carl Owen operated a flour mill for many years. Two cotton gins were once operated here, and Bob McCall operated a saddle factory.

Bethesda once had a post office and the first postmaster was P.D. Scales. Mail was brought from Franklin to this office on horseback by Frank Tomlin, Tom Walters, and Bill Taylor. Bethesda now receives its mail on Allisona, Tenn. R.F.D. 1. Url Smithson of Allisona, has been the popular carrier for many years.

Bethesda once had a male and female school and later a public school was built on the James Bennett farm.

The present Bethesda High School building which is a concrete-block building was completed two years ago at a cost of approximately $15,000. This building consists of eight classrooms, a basement, an auditorium, a library, and an office, and is modernly equipped with steam heat, electricity, and running water. The school has an enrollment of two hundred and twenty-five students in the grammar and high school departments. This is an accredited B-grade high school and offers the following courses of study: Shop Work, Home Economics, History, English, Geography, and Economics. Miss Helen Williams was editor of the senior class annual this year.

Members of the high and grammar school faculty for the past school year were: Prof. and Mrs. Charles Oliver, Prof. W.P. Scales, and Misses Julia and Addie Eggleston. Grammar school teachers were Misses Cleo and Marion Grigsby and Frances Hatcher. There has been a Parent-Teacher Association here for the past 8 years. The present officers are Mrs. J.E. Crafton, president; Mrs. A.B. Alexander, vice president, and Miss Lois Hurt, secretary. This year, the P.T.A. received a certificate of honor for its work in the field of health from the State Parent-Teacher Convention held in Nashville recently. The organization was instrumental in helping build the high school gymnasium four years ago; it pays janitor expenses, purchases instruments for the rhythm band, and has helped equip the school library with a thousand books or more, approved by the Tennessee Education Department in Nashville. The P.T.A. meets on the second Tuesday night of each month at the school building.

A Community Club was organized here about a year ago and the officers are A.B. Alexander, president; James Bond, first vice-president; Miss Marion Grigsby, second vice-president; and Mrs. Charles Oliver, secretary-treasurer. The purpose of this club is for a better understanding of farm conditions, better health conditions, and various cultural topics. This club has sixty-five or seventy members and meets the third Monday night of each month at the school building when supper is served.

A Masonic Lodge was organized here over fifty years ago and has been a powerful influence for moral good in the community. Its officers now are Marvin McCord, worshipful master; Wade McGee, senior warden; Blythe Poteete, junior warden; O.R. Stoddard, treasurer; Prof. W.P. Scales, secretary; Bill Eggleston, senior deacon; Reese Tomlin, junior deacon; and Tom Beasley, tyler.

Bethesda Chapter No. 341, Order of the Eastern Star was organized here on August 3, 1929. Its present officers are Mrs. Robert Eggleston, worthy matron; Walter E. Beasley, Sr., worthy patron; Miss Sara Beasley, associate matron; Robert Eggleston, associate patron; Miss Mildred Beasley, conductress; Miss Eunice Chrisman, associate conductress; H.M. Pantall, secretary; Mrs. Floy Pantall, treasurer; Mrs. Stella Chrisman, chaplain; Mrs. Mary McCord, marshal; Mrs. Alice Beasley, warden; Tom Beasley, sentinel; Miss Cleo Grigsby, Adah; Mrs. Fannie Anderson, Ruth; Mrs. Nina Beasley, Esther; Miss Addie Eggleston, Martha; Miss Julia Eggleston, Electra.

This community is the home of M.F. Clendenen, retired merchant at Cross Keys, near here, farmer, and present representative of Williamson County in the State Legislature at Nashville.

Bethesda Post Office and Scales Grocery. Pleasant D. Scales, postmaster, is seen here on the porch. Tom Bizzell, Charlie Grigsby, and John and Sam McCall are pictured on the roof.

Bethesda was the home of the late Dr. Jonathan Blythe Core who died a few years ago and who was greatly beloved by the people of this community where he practiced medicine for over 50 years.

Sam Anderson, one of the Williamson County Road Commissioners, lived here.

Many of Franklin's and Nashville's most prominent businessmen came from this area.

WILLIAM S. WEBB'S HISTORICAL ACCOUNT OF BETHESDA

BETHESDA POSTMASTERS	EFFECTIVE DATE
James G. Henderson	July 10, 1841
Thomas Banks	October 21, 1852
Robert F. McCaul	April 21, 1857
Napoleon B. Hartley	June 27, 1866
Richard F. Russell	September 4, 1866
Charles Smithson	December 17, 1868
William A. Hudson	March 22, 1870
Robert L. McCall	April 3, 1873
Pleasant D. Scales	January 19, 1880
John S. Irvin	November 25, 1914
Moved to Thompson's Station	December 31, 1917

DUPLEX POSTMASTERS	EFFECTIVE DATE
William M. Davis	January 8, 1883
George T. Caskey	June 6, 1884
Thomas Wiley	July 26, 1894
Thomas Knott	December 21, 1896
William B. Sampson	May 4, 1898
James T. Wiley	September 11, 1906
Moved to Spring Hill	January 2, 1907

HARPETH POSTMASTERS	EFFECTIVE DATE
William S. Webb	April 10, 1815
William E. Keith	April 1, 1816
William S. Webb	April 11, 1819
Samuel Webb	June 3, 1846
Discontinued	June 28, 1847
Thomas J. Wallace	May 3, 1880
Samuel M. Fleming	July 20, 1895
Millard F. Fleming	December 27, 1901
Moved to Franklin	December 14, 1903

THE MILITARY LINE

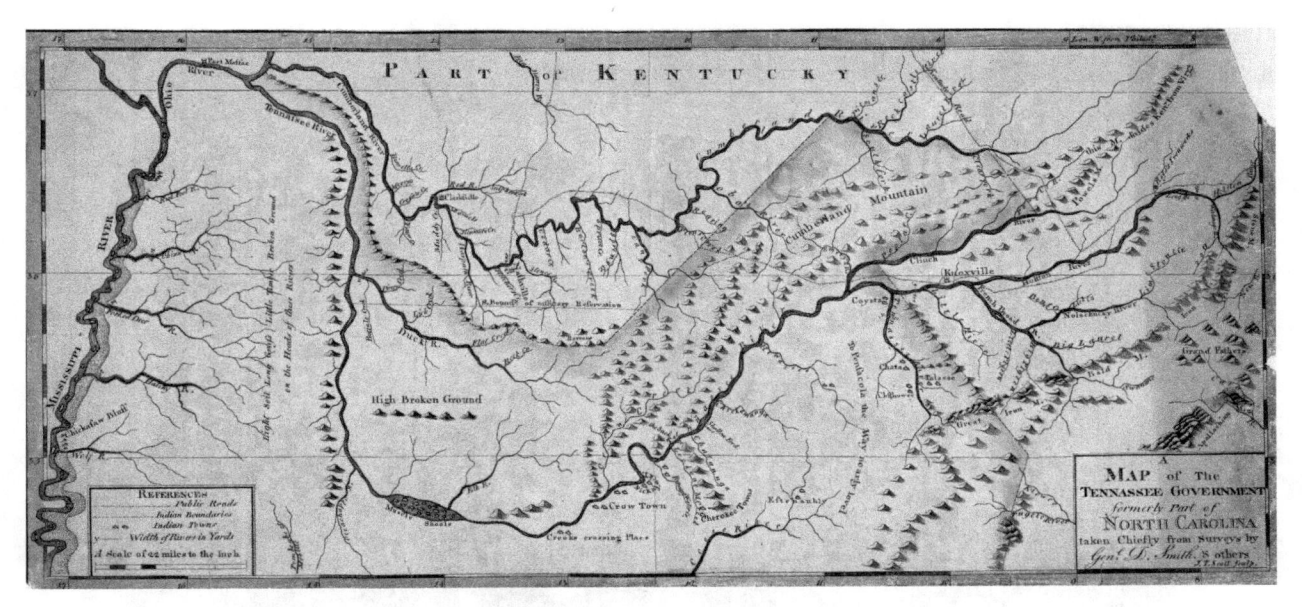

Matthew Carey's 1795 Map of Tennessee showing the Military Line

THE REVIEW-APPEAL, FRANKLIN, TENNESSEE, APRIL 18, 1901

The first (1783) survey was made from the Creek line (now the Alabama line) and extended 55 miles north from said line, the north boundary line running parallel to the Creek line, and passing through Williamson County, east and west about four miles south of Franklin, or about Douglas Church on the Lewisburg Pike.

Dissatisfaction had arisen among the Continental soldiers in regard to the location of that survey, so the Legislature of the Old North State [North Carolina] decreed the Reservation should be laid off in the northern part of the western domain and along the side of the Virginia line (then the Kentucky line). In obedience to this act, Commissioners were appointed, who, with a party of surveyors, laid off the military "preemptions."

The history of the survey enables us, with the use of instruments, to designate the point at which it began. It was on the Virginia (Ky) line, directly south of the present town of Adairville, Kentucky, and from that point, the first line, which was a baseline, ran south by the Bluff (Nashville) and through Williamson County at Mt. Pisgah, a short distance east of

Bethesda. Here the party of surveyors separated, Gen. Rutherford, the principal surveyor, and his party running the south boundary line west to the Tennessee River, thence with said river to the Virginia (Ky) line; thence with said line to the point where the Cumberland River crosses the same. The other party ran the line east to Caney Fork, in Warren County thence north to the Cumberland crossing. From this survey, we learn that the south boundary line of the Military Reservation boundary is identical to "The Military Line," to which reference has been made.

A view of Mt. Pisgah, a landmark located midway between Bethesda and Cross Keys, was used by Gen. Rutherford's surveyors to establish the military line in 1783.

In conclusion, I give a short sketch of the family history associated with the generous donation of our Mother State. Dr. Joe Blythe, a soldier and surgeon in the Continental Army, received his "preemption" in the northern part of what is now the Twelfth District of Williamson County; the allotment we know from his rank, which entitled him to 4,800 acres. His survey began at the "double poplars," the northwest corner of the farm now owned by Porter Epps, running south through or by the farms now belonging to S.F. Williams, John Cathey, Gus Evans, J. Wallis Alexander, Milton McCord, W.T. Alexander, William Wiley, and Mrs. Elizabeth Alexander to the Military Line; thence east with said line to Mt. Pisgah, on W.D. Irvin's farm; thence north with Gen. Rutherford's "baseline" to the Duck River Ridge; thence west to the beginning. Dr. Blythe died soon after the survey was made and leaving no family, his lands descended to his nearest heirs, the Sprott children.

These heirs came from North Carolina in carts and wagons, the tires on which being hickory withes bent and nailed to the spokes. Blythe Sprott settled on, or about, the Porter Epps farm; Andrew Sprott, on the J.C. Chrisman farm, or on the A.C. Lavender place, but soon sold it to the father of Thomas A. Craine, deceased, for a horse and a rifle and went back to North Carolina; John Sprott on the William Rucker place, but sold out and went back; Samuel Sprott on a farm in the southern part, but sold and removed to Marion County, Alabama; Joseph Sprott settled near Bethesda; William Sprott on Spencer Waddey's place; Catherine [Sprott] Allen, a sister, on the William Knott place; Betsy [Sprott] Hudson near a farm east of Bethesda, another sister on the Faulkenberry place. Billy O'Connor, a brother-in-law, settled on the Sam Pratt farm.

As there was a considerable depression on this farm, and a corresponding elevation, under which a cave, Andrew Sprott, a humor poet, said to the other heirs:

"Give O'Connor, the Irishman scholar;
A good share with the rest;
For he gets a hole in a hollow,
Where he can build his nest.

On a hill where now stands the house of M.J. Ferguson, lived one Willis Crutcher, who had a small distillery. Andrew frequently sent his jug, on which was a tag reading as follows:

"Willis Crutcher on the hill,
I send to you my jug to fill.
Fill it full–deny me not,
And charge the same to Andrew Sprott.

DUPLEX, HARPETH, CALLIE, AND CROSS KEYS

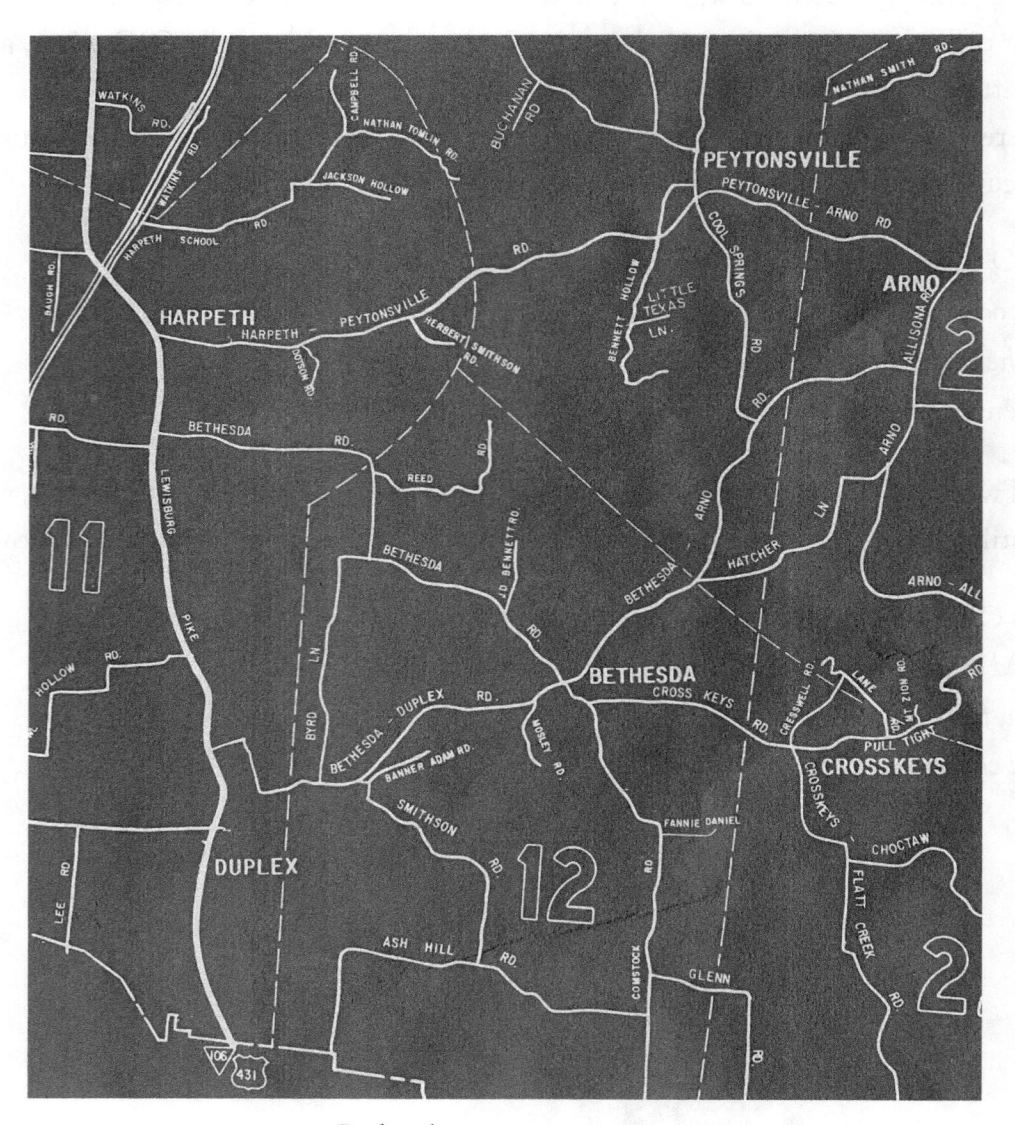

Bethesda area communities

History of Duplex

The Review-Appeal, April 11, 1901, supplied a brief history of the Duplex community, which is worthy of reprinting here.

Duplex, drawn by Robert Dickey for the Horse Review. Courtesy of the Harness Racing Museum and Hall of Fame in Goshen, N.Y.

Possibly, many of our readers are not aware that the once famous racer, Duplex, that made the world's record, is still living. His present owner is, or was, Mack Campbell, near Spring Hill, Maury County. He is now in his nineteenth year. The manner in which Duplex came into the possession of its fortunate owner, Mr. John W. Lee, is purely accidental. Wanting to buy a jack and hearing that W.S. Coffin, of Marshall County, had what he wanted, he went there accompanied by Mr. Tom Blair. He was well pleased with the jack and offered a price for him. Mr. Coffin refused to sell the jack unless he sold a three-year-old horse (Duplex) with him. He wanted $800 for the two. Mr. Lee started home without either, not wishing the horse at all as he had a fine one at home, but on the way home he sold his stallion. He then concluded he would return and buy the two, giving $800 for them. He had not ridden far on his young horse when he discovered that he owned a very fine horse. Within twelve months he sold the jack for $1,000 and had turned the young racer which he had named after the post office, "Duplex," over to the famous Nashville trainer Ed "Pop" Geers. In 1887 Duplex made his first record, realizing to his owner, $2,300. This year a Franklin man offered $3,000 for him without seeing him, another $4,000, then he refused $5,000 for half interest. Mr. Lee, before parting with his property, realized about $15,000 for half interest. He was very generous to Mr. Geers, his trainer, giving him $2,000 for his services.

Mr. Lee realized handsome profits from three other transactions in stock. He gave $15 for a jack colt that was so poor he could carry him on his shoulders. He finally sold him for $300. On another occasion he was persuaded, against his will, to buy a jennet and jack colt, for which he gave $18. They brought him $2,000. Another jennet and young jack for which he gave $250 realized him $2,000. All of this stock he bought against his own judgment, but the result proved the old adage of the fickleness of Dame Fortune.

Duplex Community

Though Duplex is outside the 12th Civil District, it is a neighborhood to the west with close ties to Bethesda. Originally known as Mt. Carmel, the community obtained its own post office, dubbed Duplex, from January 8, 1883, until January 2, 1907. The following served in succession as postmasters: William M. Davis, George T. Caskey, Thomas Wiley, Thomas Knott, William B. Sampson, and James T. Wiley. The famous racehorse took its name from the post office. Besides Mt. Carmel Cumberland Presbyterian Church and School, the community was served by Clinton C. Thompson's store, located at the crossroads of Lewisburg Pike (Hwy 431) and Duplex-Spring Hill Road. A modern grocery at the crossroads replaced two old wooden-framed buildings in the 1960s.

Mt. Carmel Cumberland Presbyterian Church, org. 1827

The C.C. Thompson Store and Duplex post office

One of the outstanding farms in southern Williamson County is owned by the John Lee family today. The 604-acre farm, known as Maplewood Farm, was acquired by Samuel Lee (1768-1865) as early as 1819; and has remained in the family to the present.

Samuel married Susan Napier in 1837, and with this came an interest in the iron manufacturing business. Their sons Samuel Brown, Jr., Charles, and John Wills Napier, Sr. carried the family business of growing tobacco and raising livestock. A son, John Wills Napier Lee, II. started Rock City Construction in 1913, the second licensed construction company in Tennessee. The company rose to fame with the extensive remodeling of the historic Tennessee Capitol building in the 1950s.

Maplewood, home of Samuel B. Lee, started in 1860 and completed in 1865

Samuel B. Lee, Jr. 1842-1910    John W.N. Lee, 1844-1921    John W.N. III & Martha Lee    John IV, Mona, Laura, Jack

Since the 12th civil district didn't have a school for black students, those students had to travel to Lee-Buckner School on Duplex Road or Cedar Hill School on Harpeth-Peytonsville Road. Cedar Hill closed in 1953 and Lee-Buckner students and teachers were transferred to Evergreen School, west of Thompson Station, in 1965. The Black students in southern Williamson County had little choice until county schools were integrated in September of 1967.

Harpeth Community

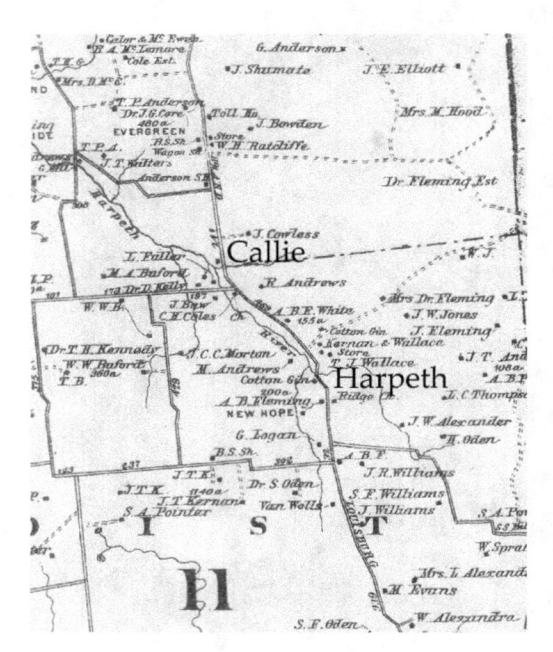

Callie and Harpeth communities in 1878

The Harpeth community is located on Lewisburg Pike (Hwy 431) northwest of Bethesda, north of Duplex, and east of West Harpeth. The heart of the community centers around Cowles Chapel United Methodist Church, Ridge Meeting Church, a new congregation that took over the New Hope Presbyterian Church building, the Exxon Convenience Center, and a Hispanic congregation, Esperanza Church, located on the old Harpeth School property. The biggest attraction to the community is The Graystone Quarry, located on Harpeth School Road, which brings thousands of attendees to concerts. Upon this road once lived the Tomlin, Poteete, Deason, Watkins, Veach, Mosley, and Jackson families. Notable families that have called Harpeth home were Baugh, Fleming, Wallace, Andrews, Cowles, Reams, Stone, Dodson, Lavender, Marlin, and Thompson. Few of these historic names are present here today. Only tombstones found in family cemeteries bear their names for modern-day readers. The infamous outlaw of the early 19th century, John A. Murrell (1806-1844) also called Harpeth his boyhood home. In 1825, Murrell was placed in the stocks in the Franklin courthouse yard, and branded HT on his thumb for stealing a horse. He is known in history as the "Great Western Land Pirate."

Callie Community

BACK HOME IN WILLIAMSON COUNTY, BY LYN SULLIVAN PEWITT, ©1986

The community of Callie, located about six miles south of Franklin just off Lewisburg Pike, was named for Callie McMillan, the youngest daughter of Jim McMillan, who ran the general store from 1893 to 1902. The store also served as a local post office, with Dee Page as one of the Franklin mailmen who took the mail to the Callie Store. People had to travel to the store to get their mail before the days of mail routes. The postmasters at Callie were James K. McMillan (1892-1903) and Mack Waddey (1903-1904). The Callie Post Office closed on January 30, 1904, and transferred to Franklin. In 1907, Sam Edgmon moved the store about 150 yards down the road and continued to operate it as a general store. Besides the post office, the store also housed the community blacksmith shop, and at one time, the store was the scene of community dances with Howard Hood, Sr. playing the fiddle and Bert Guffee accompanying him on another instrument.

There were no schools in the Callie community. Students went through the first eight grades at either the Douglas School on Henpeck Lane or Harpeth School on Lewisburg Pike.

Like most major roads in the county, Lewisburg Pike was once a turnpike, with the tollgate first located a mile south of Franklin. It was moved to the O.R. Stoddard farm, a mile past Callie, then moved again to a location across from the Cowles Chapel Church. Logan Hood ran a tollgate at the Cowles Chapel location. Beale Lane came into the Callie community from Peytonsville Road but ceased to exist around 1900.

At one time there was a spring on the west side of the road near the Callie Store. A pipe ran under Highway 431 from the spring to a watering trough on the east side of the road. When Lewisburg Pike was widened in the 1940s, the pipe was still there and the spring still running. When plans were first made for Interstate 65, it was intended to run right through the Callie Store, but plans were changed to its present location.

Susie and Oliver Stoddard

Families in the Callie community included Hood, Core, Stoddard, McMillan, and Edgmon. At one time, there were twenty Hoods on Route 2. The Callie community was a small portion of Williamson County, with only a few families making up the entire community.

Horace Edgmon

Howard Hood III

Thomas Stoddard US Navy WWII

THE CALLIE GIANT

In 1845, on the W.J. Shumate farm, in what is today the Callie community, the bones of a giant were found which led to an infamous hoax that brought much interest to Williamson County. The accompanying article was found in the *Nashville Republican Banner* on December 12, 1845.

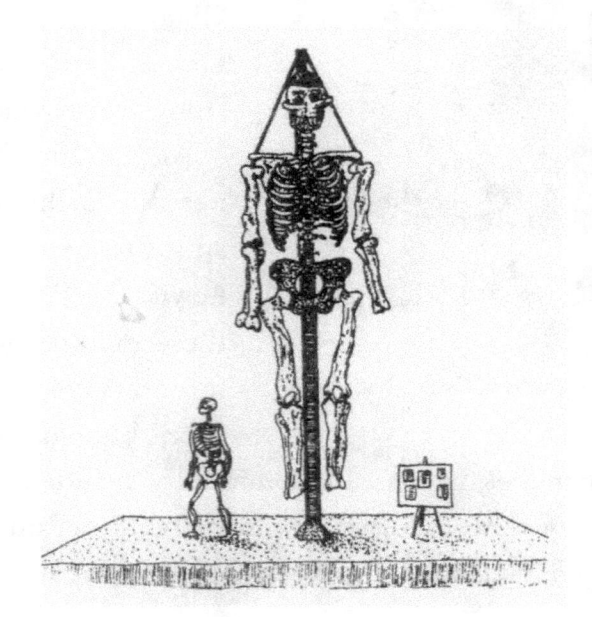

After touring across the United States, thousands viewed the giant skeleton only to be told by a professor of the Louisiana Medical College that the bones were not human but were the bones of a young mastodon.

Bones of the Williamson County Giant, W.J. Shumate farm, 1845

CROSS KEYS

The Cross Keys community is located southeast of Bethesda at the base of Pull Tight Hill. Revolutionary veteran Laban Hartley (1742-1842) appears on the county tax rolls in 1821. Hartley has the honor of being the last living Revolutionary veteran in the county. The community took its name from the Hartley Tavern which had a sign – Cross Keys – over the door. Other notable families in the community were Biggers, Bennett, Creswell, Anderson, Trice, Giles, Hargrove, McCall, and Crafton.

CHURCHES

Bethesda United Methodist Church

The present-day Bethesda United Methodist Church building

Bethesda Methodist itself dates back to 1832, but the present building on Bethesda Road was constructed in 1960 and 1961 on one and one-half acres of land given by sisters, Cleo Grigsby and Vivienne Watson. This is Bethesda Methodist's fourth church house and third site.

The first was a crude log building on land deeded in 1839 by Henry C. Horton and Mark Andrews and was on Rutherford Creek which often overflowed; the second and third were on a new site and were brick and frame, respectively. The third building had two stories and the upper floor was used by the Masonic Lodge – Harmony Lodge 201 Bethesda.

The second Methodist Church building

The third Methodist Church building

Mt. Carmel Cumberland Presbyterian Church

Mt. Carmel Cumberland Presbyterian Church and Congregation, 1913

The Mt. Carmel Cumberland Presbyterian Church dates back to 1913, but the congregation itself is the oldest Cumberland Presbyterian Church in the county, having been established between 1824 and 1827.

Mt. Carmel is located on the west side of Lewisburg Pike in the Duplex community on the waters of Rutherford Creek. There is a cemetery at the church.

On October 16, 1827, Allen Bugg made a deed of gift of 3½ acres to trustees Thomas E. Kirkpatrick, Clement Wall, Newton Ball, and William W. Bond; a meeting house was already there.

Members were to have free use of the spring. Before the first building, the grounds had been used as a campground.

The first building served as their meeting house until it was burned by Union soldiers. R.C. Thompson wrote that the second building stood until a storm in 1913 turned it around. It had to be completely rebuilt. Today, the main part of this building stands much as it did then.

Mt. Carmel Cumberland Presbyterian Church

Bethesda Presbyterian Church

By order of the Presbytery of Nashville, Rev. J.W. Hoyte, Rev. R. Wilson, Elder R. Blythe, Seth Elliot, and H.B. Lincoln met on the fifth Sunday of November 1879 in the Bethesda Methodist Episcopal Church, Williamson County, Tennessee, and proceeded to organize the Bethesda Presbyterian Church with the election of Elders and Deacons, installing them in their respective offices along with their Minister, the Rev. R.W. Wilson. On August 26th, 1889, the Rev. G.E. Thompson was called as Minister and served till October 1892. Rev. M.W. Millard was the next pastor called to the pulpit.

Bethesda Presbyterian Church

This church is an offspring of the New Hope Presbyterian Church on Lewisburg Pike. The land was given for a new structure by the Irvin heirs. Elders C.C. Bond, H.M. Steele, and W.A. Steele were appointed as trustees of the property for the congregation in July 1880. The Manse was owned by Rev. R.W. Wilson and sold to the two churches, New Hope and Bethesda, and is located in Bethesda. It was remodeled in 1931 and totally rebuilt in 1965.

CROSS KEYS BAPTIST CHAPEL

The Cross Keys Baptist Church was organized in 1954 by the work and prayers of the King, Jackson, Smithson, and Newcomb families. They began with a tent revival to see if the interest necessitated a new denomination within the local area.

The first place of worship was a storehouse across the road from Leslie Creswell. During this period, the Inglewood Baptist Church became aware of the need for a mission at Cross Keys. Under the direction of Harvey LaFollette, the Inglewood Church, and the community, an acre of land was purchased from Grover Trice and construction was begun.

Cross Keys Baptist Church

MT. ZION METHODIST EPISCOPAL CHURCH

Mt. Zion Methodist Church

At the foot of Pull Tight Hill in the Cross Keys community stands Mt. Zion. Originally, the church was organized as early as 1869 as a Methodist Episcopal Church, not affiliated with the Tennessee Conference Methodist Episcopal South until the merger in 1938. Laban Creswell donated an acre for the first location higher up the hill. In 1911, the church was moved nearer to Cross Keys crossroads on land donated by W.L. Crafton to church trustees J.C. Reed, R.T. Graham, W.L. Hartley, L.C. Hartley, and Sam F. Anderson. In the 1970s, the congregation withdrew from the Tennessee Conference and remained an independent church for a few years. Presently, the white clapboard country church stands unused.

Ash Hill Cumberland Presbyterian Church

Ash Hill Cumberland Presbyterian Church and Congregation, 1900

Ash Hill Cumberland Presbyterian Church, 1954

In April of 1881, the Ash Hill congregation was organized as a branch of Mount Carmel Church. The first sermon was delivered on the first Sunday in April by Rev. W.T. Dale under a brush arbor. John Stephens gave enough land on which to build the Ash Hill Cumberland Presbyterian Church. W.B. Cathey donated the lumber. On the first Sunday in September 1883, a meeting was held in the church, which included 15 members. Over the years, notable families have included Walker, Cathey, Roberson, Woodside, Smith, Hargrove, Stephens, Taylor, Wiley, Tomlin, Henson, Sharp, Neal, Crutcher, McCord, Gillespie, Stem, Hazelwood,

Ingram, Stevenson, Rummage, Skinner, Ketchum, Giles, Warren, Smithson, and Reynolds.

In 1887, Ash Hill became a member of the Richland Presbytery. In April 1954, the congregation moved into the present church building.

New Hope Presbyterian Church

New Hope Presbyterian Church

Rev. Duncan Brown organized the Presbyterians in the Duck River Ridge region in 1806. The first log church, called Ridge Meeting House, was erected one mile south of here four years later.; this was the first church south of Franklin in Williamson County. The congregation moved into a new frame building in 1829 and possibly changed the name to New Hope Presbyterian, then. The third and present church was built in 1869. This church and the Bethesda congregation often shared ministers. In 2022, due to a decline in members, the church was closed by the Nashville Presbytery and the building is being used by a non-denominational congregation known as Ridge Meeting House once again.

COWLES CHAPEL UNITED METHODIST CHURCH

Cowles Chapel United Methodist Church

Cowles Chapel United Methodist Church is located on the banks of the West Harpeth River at the intersection of Lewisburg Pike and Critz Lane. In 1827, Henry Reams gave land for a Methodist church and school in the Harpeth community known as Prospect Methodist Church. In 1871, John Cowles gave the land for the present church, which was renamed Cowles Chapel. The handsome, white-framed church was built with the traditional two-front doors, one for women and one for men, but separate seating is no longer practiced today. The present-day congregation is small but remains active in a changing community.

Esperanza Church occupies the old Harpeth School building on Lewisburg Pike at Harpeth.

Esperanza Church

Rather new to the Harpeth community is Esperanza Church, a Hispanic congregation making their home in the old Harpeth School. As Williamson County grows in leaps and bounds, our population is more diverse no longer just Methodist, Presbyterian, Baptist, or Church of Christ. We are no longer a rural, agricultural county, but we are transforming into a largely suburban community inching toward a cosmopolitan society.

FRATERNAL ORDERS

Members of Bethesda Lodge No. 193 I.O.O.F. Odd Fellows

L.H. McCall

L.G. McMillan

W. A. Hudson

W.J.S. Graham

J.E. Crafton

J.J. Taylor

C.C. Graham

C.C. Smithson

C.C. Curtis

G.P. Smithson

W.H. Gillespie

Thomas J. Giles

J.W. Simmons

John F. Graham

W.C. Taylor

Robert Graham

T.S. Biggers

Robert L. McCall

John Bell Walker

Dr. W.Y. Bennett

FRATERNAL ORDERS

L.G. Thompson et al of Bethesda Masonic Lodge No. 201 of F & A Masons

To] Deed, Bethesda Lodge No. 193 of I.O.O.F.

Registered Feby 7, 1877

Source: Williamson County, Tennessee, Deed Book vol. 6, page 59

The first Bethesda School and I.O.O.F. Lodge Hall, located in the village at the crossroads

Know all men by these present that we L.G. Thompson, Worshipful Master; W.G. Irvin, Senior Warden; J.L. Walton, Junior Warden, of Bethesda Lodge No. 201 F & A Masons and acting on behalf of said Lodge for and in consideration of the sum of One Hundred and Fifty dollars to us in hand paid, for said Lodge, the receipt of which and in behalf of said Lodge, do acknowledge, hath this day bargained, sold, and conveyed to C.C. Smithson N.G. and L.H. McCall, V.G. of Bethesda Lodge No 193 of I.O.O.F and this succession in office, to be held for said Bethesda Lodge No. 193 of I.O.O.F. all the right, title claims and interest that Bethesda Lodge No. 201 of Free and Accepted Masons and have in and to a certain House and lot lying and being in the village of Bethesda, 12th Civil District of Williamson County, Tennessee, Lot known as the Academy Lot and bounded as follows: Beginning P.D. Scales N.E. corner running from thence East 125/8 [poles] to Franklin Road, thence south 12 5/8 poles to J.D. Core's corner, thence West 12 5/8 poles to Core's corner thence North with Spring Hill Road 12 5/8 poles to the beginning, containing by estimation one acre together with all said Hall building and egress and ingress by the community for a school the improvements and privileges, hereditaments there unto attached. The covenant with the said Bethesda Lodge No 193 of I.O.O.F. through their officers C.C. Smithson, N.G., and L.H. McCall, V.G., that are lawfully seized of the same and have a good right to convey it, and will forever warrant the title of the same against all persons whomsoever in testamentary of which we have signed our names as Officers of the Lodge, and affixed the seal of the Lodge, on this the 27th of January 1876.

Lemuel G. Thompson, W.M.   *W.D. Irvin, S.W.*   *J.L. Walton, J.W.*

Bethesda Free and Accepted Masonic Lodge No. 201

The present Bethesda F.&A.M. Lodge No. 201 overlooking Bethesda Cemetery

The Bethesda F.&A.M. Lodge No. 201 was organized in 1850 with Dr. William Y. Bennett as the first Worshipful Master. It appears that Lodge 201 built the first school located at the crossroads. This is supported by a deed dated January 27, 1876, where L.G. Thompson, Worshipful Master; W.D. Irvin, Senior Warden; and J.L. Walton, Junior Warden, convey a lodge hall and the old academy lot containing one acre to C.C. Smithson, Noble Grand, and L.H. McCall, Vice Grand, officers of the Bethesda Lodge 193 of I.O.O.F. (Odd Fellows) for one hundred and fifty dollars. This act corresponds with the construction of the Bethesda Methodist new two-story framed building at the present site of the Masonic Lodge.

In 2023, Larry Giles is serving as the Worshipful Master and reports the lodge is functioning in proper order. Stated meetings are held every 3rd Monday at 6 p.m.

PHYSICIANS

The noble county doctors who delivered the babies and administered them to the sick at all hours of the day were often poorly paid. Dr. Jonathan Blythe Core was mentioned with fondness in the interviews with Bethesda senior citizens. Living in the center of Bethesda, next to the Grigsby and Irvin stores and school, Dr. Core would have been the first to call when an emergency arose. In the following list is taken from *Physicians of Williamson County: A Legacy of Healing, 1797-1997* by Hudson Alexander, we find these physicians who also served Bethesda and surrounding communities.

DR. RICHARD ANDERSON BLYTHE, 1815-1902

DR. JESS GILLIS CORE, SR., 1820-1883

DR. W.Y. BENNETT, 1822-1881

DR. JONATHAN DICKERSON CORE, 1839-1894

DR. WILLIAM CORE, 1851-1878

DR. JESS GILLIS CORE, JR., 1854-1888

DR. WALTER W. GRAHAM, 1868-1928

DR. JONATHAN BLYTHE CORE, 1870-1934

DR. PLEASANT ABLE CRESWELL, 1873-1943

DR. WILLIAM CLYDE EGGLESTON, 1880-1947

Dr. W.Y. Bennett

Dr. W.W. Graham

Dr. P.A. Creswell

Doctor's horse and medicine bag waiting for a call

Dr. J.B. Core

Dr. W.C. Eggleston

COUNTRY STORES

Ruth Thompson operated the store after her father's death in 1952.

It seems every crossroads in Williamson County had at some time a country store. These stores were really the nerve center of their community. The local merchant was usually the most popular member of the community. The store also served as a place to gather at lunchtime for a bologna sandwich along with some crackers and cheese. Old men, or loafers as they were called, spent the after-supper time sitting around the pot-bellied stove, sharing gossip, arguing the Bible, politics, and current events. Young folks after school liked to stop at the store for a cold drink and a moon pie. Sadly, only a few family-owned general stores still operate in the county, having been replaced with convenience stores.

The Irvin Store beside the Scales-Grigsby Store before the fire of 1928.

We should start at the crossroads in the village of Bethesda where at the turn of the 20th century we would find two stores side-by-side. Between the old Bethesda School, which sat at the intersection of Bethesda-Cross Keys Road and the Bethesda-Duplex Road, and Dr. J. Blythe Core's house, later Tom Beasley's house, we would find the Irvin Store and the Scales-Grigsby Store. Of course, ownership of these two stores changed hands many times until they both were consumed in a fire as described in Lester Mosley's interview. Later, in this location, Tom Beasley and John W. Beasley operated a store, which burned under Morris Williams's ownership.

The accompanying aerial photograph reveals the Morris Williams Store where, today, Mike Patel carries on the tradition of providing groceries, fuel, and a place to gather for breakfast, lunch, or supper. The historic Bethesda crossroads remains the nerve center of the village, though probably not as prominent as in times past.

The village of Cross Keys has had several general stores over the years. Agnes Hargrove mentions in her interview the merchants who carried on business at the crossroads leading back to Bethesda, towards Pull Tight Hill, or going south to Flat Creek. The impressive list included Hartley, Turner, Trice, Clendenen, Grigsby, Williams, Marlin, Giles, Hargrove, Hawkins, and Flippen. Robert A. Flippen was credited with taking down the old two-story store and building the one seen in this 1980 aerial photograph. Today, there is no sign of a country store at Cross Keys, only the ghosts of stores past haunt the crossroads.

At the intersection of Flat Creek Road and Comstock Road stands the vacant store building of J.W. and Mattie Sue Cathey Hazelwood. Its location was handy for those traveling from the Flat Creek community from the east or the Ash Hill community to the north. The Hazelwood Store offered groceries, fuel, and animal feed. The next to the last merchant here was David King, who came from the Kingfield community to marry a girl from the Comstock clan.

A legendary merchant of the Duplex community was C.C. Thompson, whose store was located at the intersection of Duplex Road and Lewisburg Pike (Hwy 431). Most likely, William M. Davis and George T. Caskey were the first to open a store at this intersection, as they both served, respectively, as postmasters for Duplex in 1883 and 1884. In 1906, C.C. Thompson purchased the store and operated it until his death in 1952. His daughter, Ruth carried on the business, and in the 1960s, moved to a larger brick building facing Lewisburg Pike built by her brother James.

The old Thompson Store was placed on the National Register of Historic Places in 1988 and removed in 2022; when the building was torn down. C.C. Thompson is also noted for building Thompson Lake on Mud Creek at the old Nelson Lavender homeplace, which was enjoyed by local fishermen for many years.

C.C. Thompson Store

To the north of Duplex on Lewisburg Pike at the intersection of the Harpeth-Peytonsville Road, we find the Harpeth community. In the 19th century, a store at this intersection was operated by Tom Wallace. After Wallace was elected as Williamson County Court Clerk, his brother-in-law, Samuel M. Fleming took over the store, granary, and cotton gin. When Fleming moved to Franklin in 1905, the store was operated by H.W. Lavender. Today, this intersection is home to a modern convenience store that serves the Harpeth community and the busy traffic along Highway 431.

Left: The Morris Williams Store in 1980 enjoyed being in the village of Bethesda at the crossroads.
Right: The Robert A. Flippen Store replaced the old two-story store in Cross Keys.

Left: The J.W. Hazelwood Store at the intersection of Flat Creek Road and Comstock Road in 1980.

Right: A 1985 view of the new Thompson Store built by son James Thompson and the old store on the right.

Left: The A & D Store at Harpeth was operated by Allen Brown and Dorothy Marlin.

Right: The Wallace-Fleming-Lavender Store, Lewisburg Pike, and Harpeth-Peytonsville Road at Harpeth

SCHOOLS

The first Bethesda School and I.O.O.F. Lodge Hall, located in the village at the crossroads

Schools are the institutions that define a community. Bethesda School, being the oldest and largest school in the southern part of Williamson County, was located in the old Twelfth Civil District. According to Williamson County School Board minutes, it appears to have been in operation at the village crossroads by 1871. The school was housed on the first floor of the Odd Fellows Lodge, having been purchased from the Bethesda Masonic Lodge in that year with mention that it was located on the academy lot. It is uncertain when the school moved to a new two-story building, but an old photograph with the dates 1900-1927 may lead one to conclude that the old lodge was replaced by 1900.

This remarkable photograph shows the old Bethesda School (1900-1927) at the corner of the crossroads with the Irvin and Scales Stores on the road to Duplex. As seen here, the schoolhouse and the school lot were not large enough to accommodate the elementary and high school students. Bethesda School remained at the crossroads until a new school was built on the hill in 1928. From the interviews of the older citizens found in this book, we are told that in May of

Old Bethesda School, 1900-1927

1935, this building was destroyed by a blaze that originated in the Delco lighting plant and spread to the school. The gymnasium was spared.

The 1936 building stood on the site of the 1928 school. This building was in use until a new school was constructed at the bottom of the hill beyond the ballfields in 1990. The 1930s-era gymnasium, cafeteria, agricultural, and shop buildings still stand.

Bethesda School, 1936-1990

Bethesda School (1928-1935) was built on the hill and purchased by the school board from Charles F. Grigsby. The gymnasium was built on a half acre of land also purchased from Charles Grigsby and constructed by the community, After the 1935 fire, classes were held in the Methodist and Presbyterian churches and teacherage.

Bethesda School 1936-1990 was the pride and joy of the community for 54 years. After the present school was built in 1990, the old campus became home to the Community Center, the Bethesda Rescue Squad, the Bethesda Public Library which opened in 1991, and the Bethesda Museum, founded by Hugh Keedy and Jessie Bennett.

Bethesda School, 1904

Bethesda School, 1904

1st row: ___ Carson, Jim Eggleston, Blythe Trice, Lawrence Bond, Leonard Bond, John Mack Taylor, Will Taylor, Lee Alexander, Buford Reed, John Hatcher, Andrew Eggleston

2nd row: Jack Walton, Willie Hatcher, ___ Johnson, Annie Lou Reed, Debbie Core, Naoma Alexander, Elise Core, Rebecca Core, ___ Carson, Clara Crafton, Jessie Walton, Ruth Giles, Hannah Daniel

3rd row: Robert Carson, Jim "Buck" Hatcher, Joe Eggleston, Annie Millard, Johnnie Alexander, Sara Alexander, Mary Millard, Mary Chrisman, Stella Ingram, Frank Core, Hawkins Giles, Will Johnson, Grover Trice, Allen Roop

4th row: Jim Carson, Jim Byrd, Ewing Crafton, Miss Mary Smithson – teacher, William "Toby" Crafton, Tommie Lou Daniel, Mary Walton, Mary Roop, Miss Irene Steele – teacher, Lizzie Chrisman, Willie Irvin

Bethesda School, 1906

Teachers: Charley Moss, Mary Smithson, Irene Steele Bond

1st row: Jim Eggleston, Ernest Millard, unknown, Lawrence Bond, Howard Bond

2nd row: Leonard Bond, Clara Crafton, Naoma Alexander, Ruth Reed, Eunice McMillan, (Pete) Louise Alexander, Lucille Bond, unknown, Debbie Core, Ethel Grigsby, Lorene Bond

3rd row: Mr. Charley Moss, Elise Core, Mary Irvin, Rebecca Core, Willie Hatcher, ___ Eggleston, Will Johnson, Miss Irene Steele (Bond), Jack Walton, unknown

4th row: Mary Waldon, Johnnie Alexander, Annie Millard (McCord), Liz Chrisman, Jim Chrisman, Annie McMillan, Mary Chrisman, Lizzie Smithson, Willie Irvin

BETHESDA SCHOOL, 1913

1st row: Mary Irvin, Carry Byrd, Jessie Irvin, John Bond, Harvey Chrisman, Albert Hartley, Leslie Irvin, Bill Eggleston, Howard Hargrove, Irvin Johnson, J.T. Irvin, Floyd Reed; 2nd row: Mrs. R.C. Landis, Blythe Eggleston, Lucille Bond, Margaret Evans, Scales Grigsby, Frank Williams, Milburn Lavender, ___ Byrd, ___ Johnson, Ernest Millard, James Bond, unknown; 3rd row: Louise Alexander, Louise Bond, Cleo Grigsby, Julia Eggleston, Minnie Irvin, Frances Hatcher, Allie Lavender, Leo Grigsby, Nettie Lavender, Howard Bond, Thomas Evans, Hugh Williams, Herbert McCall, Roy Hargrove, Edwin Glenn; 4th row: Ruth Giles, Addie Landis, Hannah Daniel, Lou Ellen Tomlin, Gladys Bond, Myrtle Hargrove, Mary Walton, Mary Millard, Eunice McMillan, Addie Eggleston, Debbie Core, Lorene Bond, Ethel Grigsby, Jessie Walton, Mr. R.C. Landis; 5th row: Bee Chrisman, Bertha Williams, Vivienne Grigsby, Mary Bond, Willie Lavender, Marvin Bond, Chub Hargrove, ___ Lavender, Joe Deason, Shannon Byrd, Blake Byrd; 6th row: Elizabeth Evans, Naoma Alexander, Elise Core, Rebecca Core, Johnnie Alexander, John Hatcher, Tommy Smith, Leonard Bond, Charley Williams, Lawrence Bond, Carl Glenn

Bethesda School, 1917

Mr. G.C. Wright, Principal; Mr. Marvin Clendenen, and Mrs. Mary Gooch, teachers

1st row: Barnett Beasley, Nettie Bond, Ella Frances Grigsby, Erlene Hargrove, unknown, Fronie Ingram, ___ Ingram, Bessie Mae Crafton, unknown, Preston Wylie, Watson Giles, Robert Irvin, Ottie McMillan, J.T. Irvin, unknown, unknown

2nd row: Herbert McCall, John Bond, Monroe Chrisman, unknown, unknown, Fern Chrisman, Bill Eggleston, ___ Mosely, Thomas Evans, ___ Ingram, Roy Wylie, unknown, unknown, unknown

3rd row: Lera Beasley, Willie Alice Reed, unknown, Bessie Taylor, Nora Wylie, Leo Grigsby, Hershel Reed, unknown, Kit Giles, unknown, unknown, Mr. G.C. Wright

4th row: Mrs. Mary Gooch, Myrtle Hargrove, Minnie Irvin, Cleo Grigsby, unknown, Mary Irvin, Bess Chrisman, Mebane Grigsby, Willie Mae Poteete, Jimmy Mathis, Mr. Marvin Clendenen, Scales Grigsby, Burney Glenn

BETHESDA SCHOOL, 1921

Mr. Wingo, Principal

1st row: Farrar Chrisman, Bill Eggleston, Frances Chrisman Young, Earlene Hargrove, Martin Smithson Kinnard, Jessie Grigsby, Mattie Sue Crafton Stanfield, Agnes Mathis, Katherine Hargrove, Herman Smithson, Braden Mathis, Charles Grigsby

2nd row: Mr. Wingo, Cleo Grigsby, Ella Frances Grigsby Webb, James William Bond, Jr., Murrey Hardison, Dewees Ghee, Leonard Grigsby, Dora Wiley, Willie Alice Reed Mosley, Bessie Taylor Mosley, Julia Woods, Robert Rice

3rd row: Leo Grigsby Bond, Mattie Bond Glenn, Bessie Mae Crafton Lamb, Lera McCall Biggers, Nelle Smithson Mosley, unknown, Rebecca Wiley Crutcher, Fred Griggs, John Ed Crafton, Howard Hargrove

Bethesda School, ca. 1930

Miss Foster Swan, teacher

1st row: Mary Crafton, Joe Howard Crafton, Ruby Hargrove, Emma Trice, Alexine Trice, Miriam Grigsby, Jessie McCord, unknown, Martha Beth Crafton

2nd row: Mattie Sue Taylor, Glenn Grigsby, Fannie Bell Crafton, Will Wiley, Joe Trice, Barnett Beasley, Lera Reed, Zack Beasley, Lizzie Scott

3rd row: Miss Foster Swan, Marion Grigsby, Donald Core Walton, unknown, Rainey McCall, unknown, Millard Smithson, John Dale Chrisman, Frank Hargrove, Everett Reed

BETHESDA SCHOOL, 1934-1935

Bethesda School, 1st, 2nd, 3rd Grades: Miss Leo Grigsby (Bond), Teacher

1st row: Leon Reed, Robert Overton, Elizabeth Beard, Mildred Taylor, Evelyn Beard, Willis Chunn, Howard Giles, Terry H. Reed, Dan Johnson, Thomas Irvin

2nd row: Morgan Hood, J.C. Giles, Robert Williams, Robert Kincaid, Gore English, Billy McCord

3rd row: Donald Trice, Clifton Ladd, Johnny Beard, Annie Bell Tansil, Charlotte Beard, Martha Frances Bond, Daisy Bennett, Thomas Wiley, Jessie Mae Creswell

4th row: Paul Kincaid, Leonard Giles, Roy Dale McCord, J.W. Wiley, Jim Stephenson, James W. Stephens, Odell Johnson, Elizabeth, Mary "Bunny" Beasley, Betty Ruth Parker

BETHESDA HIGH SCHOOL, 1937-38

Bethesda High School

1st row: Fenton Warren, ___ Dodd, C.W. Stephens, Lester Mosley, Homer Williams, George Ryan, Jake Elliott, Walter Taylor, Leon Hayes, James "Jake" Smithson, Miss Julia Eggleston

2nd row: Fronie Culberson, Laura Crafton, Beulah Beasley, Annelle Anderson, Mary McCord, Martha Ware, Helen Williams, Dorothy Trice, Sara A. Williams, Elizabeth Elliott, Ned Eggleston, Herbert Crunk, Mrs. Jessie Oliver

3rd row: Llewellyn "Boo" McCord, Musie Gillespie, Thelma Smithson, Lois Hunt, Stella Prince, Margaret James Brumbach, Virginia Childress, Elizabeth McCord, Lola Reed, Katherine Grigsby, Hugh Williams, Charles Oliver, Principal

4th row: Jim Jaynes Jordan, J.E. Gillespie, Harry Grigsby, Herman Anderson, Alma Giles, Gracie Buchanan, Woodard Smithson, Fred Lee Williams, Joe Smithson, Eugene Crunk, John Lee Beasley

BETHESDA SCHOOL, 1937

Bethesda School, 1937, 7th and 8th grades – Miss Addie Eggleston, teacher

1st row: Thomas Edgar Beasley, James McGee, J.T. Hood, John Hartley, Marvin Wallace

2nd row: Miss Addie Eggleston, Julia Grigsby (Barnett), Mary Amy Lillard, Dorothy McCord (Ryan)

3rd row: Willie Lee Taylor (Hamm), Glyndon Reed, Mary Ryan, Jewell Bennett (Denny), Kitty Margaret Waddey (Johnson), Judy Watkins (Hargrove), Sara Margaret Trice, Frances Hartley

Bethesda 1937-38 Girls Basketball – 1st row; Dorothy McCord (center), Willie Lee Taylor (guard), Sara Beasley (forward), Alma Reed (center captain), Beulah Beasley (guard), Glyndon Reed (forward) 2nd row: Martha Ware (guard, Kitty Waddey (guard), Agnes Smithson (center, Ann Murphy (center), Jewell Bennett (guard), Mary Ryan (forward, Sara Trice (center)

Bethesda 1937-38 Boys Basketball – 1st row: John Hamm (guard), George Ryan (guard), Walter Taylor (forward), John Lee Beasley (center), Fenton Warren (forward) 2nd row: Billy Alexander (guard), J.E. Gillespie (center), Fred Buchanan (guard, Earnest McCord (forward), James Adams (forward), Rodney McCord (forward), Richard F. Waddey (forward), Charles Oliver (coach)

Bethesda High School Principals, 1931-1975

Charlie Oliver, 1931-1938

W.B. Jones, 1938-1944

J.B. Sykes, 1944-1945

Fenton Warren, 1945-1946

H.F. Srygley, 1946-1948

J.M Walker, 1948-1951

Nelson Jones, 1951-1959

Carl Owen, 1959-1962

Charlie Shipley, 1962-1970

Bill Sawyer, 1970-1975

BETHESDA

BETHESDA ELEMENTARY SCHOOL TEACHERS OF NOTE

Betsy Beasley	Bessie Bond	Katie Lou Gatlin	Lola Glenn
Cleo Grigsby	Frances Hatcher	Elizabeth Houser	Dorothy Jackson
Ann York Roberson	Gladys Sullivan	Jim Watson	Vivienne Watson

SCHOOLS

BETHESDA HIGH SCHOOL TEACHERS OF NOTE

Clyde Adams

George Anderson

Joyce Calvert

James Donnelly

Margaret Farris

Tom Harris

Marie Pearce

James Ringstaff

Thelma Scales

Bob Vaden

Sharon Whittaker

James Wright

Bethesda

Faculty and Staff

Bethesda Faculty 1937-38 1st row: Frances Hatcher, Addie Eggleston, Leo Grigsby, Marion Grigsby, Julia Eggleston; standing: W.P. Scales, Jessie Oliver, Mrs. R.M. Lea, and Charles Oliver

Jean Gary Sanders, Bethesda School Secretary

Jean Gary Sanders, Bethesda School Secretary

Ellie Marshall Beasley, Bethesda School secretary

SCHOOLS

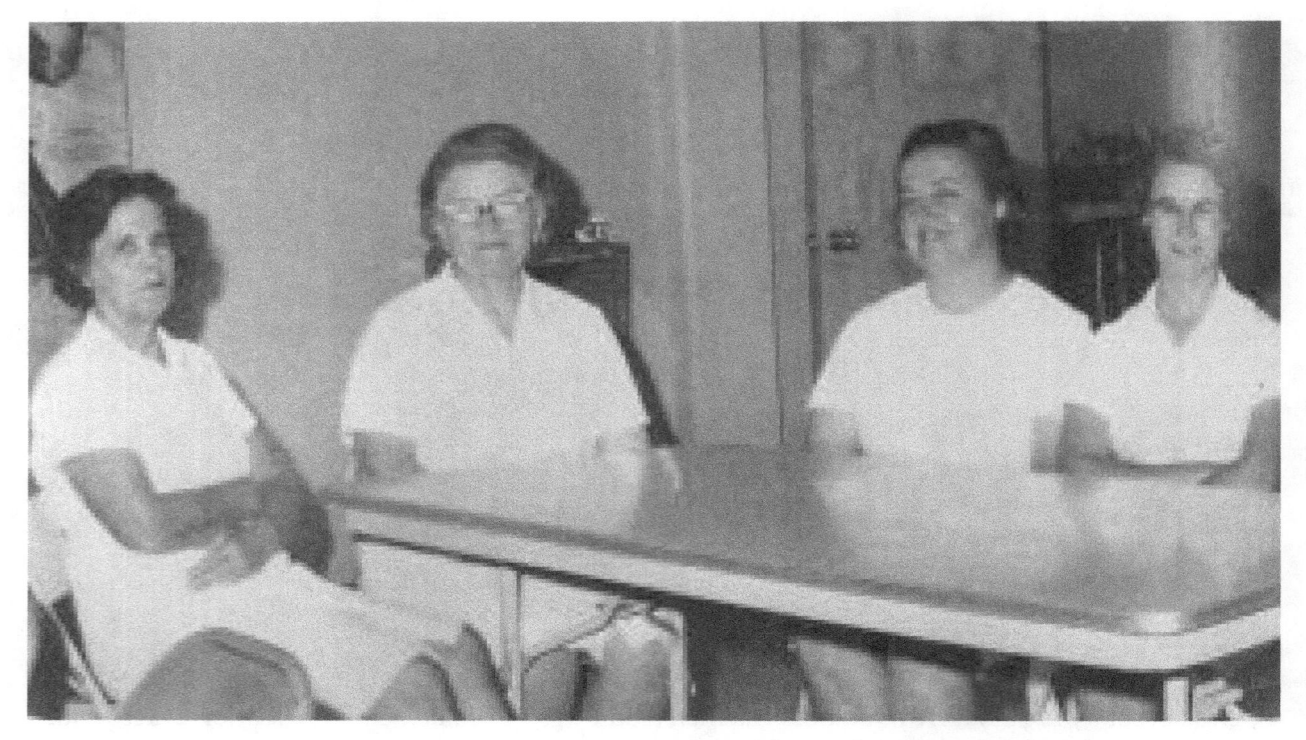

Bethesda School Cooks: Irene Clark, Bernice Lillard, Mary Stem, and Olly Burrow

Bethesda School cooks, 1957, Ethel Williams, Bernice Lillard, and Carrie Trice

BETHESDA

Buford and Evelyn Stephens, custodians

Mr. and Mrs. Ross Giles, custodians

Bill Lillard, custodian

Bethesda school bus drivers: ____ York, Frank Bond, B. Wiley, Bill Alexander, ____ Glenn

SCHOOLS

Bethesda's first automobile-modified bus was purchased from Franklin car dealer, Marshall Cook, a brother-in-law of Principal Charles Oliver.

In 1975, Page High School was built on Arno Road to combine the students from College Grove and Bethesda which relieved overcrowding of the two schools and provided broader curriculums and greater athletic opportunities.

For many years, Bethesda High School received the eighth-grade graduates of Choctaw, Ash Hill, Harpeth, and Peytonsville schools for their high school experience. In 1947, the school board closed Choctaw and Ash Hill and the elementary grades were added to Bethesda. In 1951, Mt. Carmel School on Lewisburg Pike was closed, and the students transferred to Bethesda or Thompson Station. In 1961, Peytonsville students and teachers were transferred to Bethesda. Students from Harpeth School were transferred to Bethesda in 1963, leaving the building for the County Special Education Center.

The faculty at Bethesda had a history of maintaining a high educational standard with many long-term members who were products of the school. An impressive list of those mentioned above included: Cleo Grigsby, Vivienne Grigsby Watson, Leo Grigsby Bond, Frances Hatcher, Bessie Chrisman Bond, Lola Reed Glenn, Ann York Roberson, Jim Watson, and Betsy Beasley. Accompanying a dedicated faculty, Bethesda was led by a list of competent principals. The mid-20th century and forward saw the likes of Charles Oliver, W.B. Jones, James Sykes, Fenton Warren, H.F. Srygley, J.M. Walker, Nelson Jones, Carl Owen, Charlie Shipley, Bill Sawyer, Michael Harris, and Steven Fisher.

Bethesda School, 1980 aerial

Choctaw School

Choctaw School was located south of Cross Keys at a site once known as McCall's Corner. The one-room framed school was situated next to Choctaw Road with little room for a playground. Closing in 1947, the building stood abandoned and forlorn for many years. Lola Glenn remembered her early teaching years here with fondness but with small compensation at thirty dollars a month. Water for the students had to be obtained from the well at the adjoining farm. The following school photographs show the sagging building and students and teachers of the early to mid-20th century.

SCHOOLS

Choctaw School closed in 1947 and remained a sad landmark until it rotted and fell to the ground.

Choctaw School – Miss Sallie Arnold, teacher

1st row: Ruth Creswell, Classie Reed, Birdie Creswell, unknown, unknown, ___ Edmonson, unknown, Grace Edmonson, ___ Hargrove; 2nd row: Miss Sallie Arnold, Ease Reed, Odeline Crafton, Birdie Creswell, Lunnie Victory, Bessie Creswell, Louise Creswell, Louise Trice, Clyde Edmonson, Herbert Hargrove; 3rd row: Annie Core Hargrove, Kimmie Lou Crafton, Mary Blythe Trice, Mary Lizzie Victory, Claude Edmonson, John Newt Sampson, Roy Creswell.

BETHESDA

Choctaw School – Mrs. Lola Reed Glenn, teacher

1st row: Leslie Smithson, LC. Reed, Raymond Crafton, Ross Dalton, Babe Hartley, O.C. Farrar, Thomas Beard, Robert Green

2nd row: Glothine Dalton, Maxine Dalton, Sue Trice, Robbie Jean Newcomb

3rd row: Jessie Trice, Nellie Smithson, Evelyn Newcomb, Frances Creswell, Nadine Beard, Johnny Trice, Mildred Glenn, Irene Newcomb

4th row: Hershel Hartley, Mildred Newcomb, Bill Green, Frank Reed, Mrs. Lola Reed Glenn, Jewell Beard, Junior Beard, Coolidge Dalton

SCHOOLS

The Review-Appeal (no publication date), Choctaw School – Geneva Anne McCall Bolton of 615 Nickajack Road in Mableton, Georgia, recently submitted this photograph to *The Review-Appeal*. "This is a photo of the pupils at Choctaw School in Bethesda, Tennessee, which was made during the period of 1906 or 1907 when my father, Jim McCall, was 6 or 7 years old."

[As originally printed] Top row, from left: Billy Bryant Trice, Charlie Trice, Wallace Trice, Alice Crafton, (M), Hawkins H. Giles, Eunice Reed, Bessie McCall, (M), James Murrey Hurt

2nd row, from left: Grover Trice, (M), Carrie Obera McCall, Eula Crafton, (M) Grover Trice, Stella Scales, (M), Jim Wallace, teacher Cora Reed, (M) White, Ode Reed, (M), Leonard Strickland White, Mary Beth Hartley, (M), Monrow Victory, Gusty Reed, (M), Pierce

3rd row, from left: Joe Crafton, Minnie Irvin, Bessie Slaughter, Bessie Mincy, Jimmie Lou Crafton, (M), W. Blythe Trice, Clarisa Turner, Myrtle Crafton, (M), Culberson, Elsie Graham, (M), Buddy Hargrove, (M), Owen Farrar, Bessie Lee Hargrove, Jody Crafton, (M), 1st Potts, (M), 2nd Ladd, Mary Blythe Trice

Bottom row, from left, Buford Edmonson, Luther Edmondson, Claude Edmonson, __ Irvin, Buddy Hargrove, Jim McCall, (M), Nannie T. Graham, Rich Turner, John Newt Sampson, (M), Naola Mae Skinner, W. Blythe Trice, Roy Crafton, (M), Nellie Jane White

Ash Hill School

Ash Hill School, 1924, Miss Luddie Sherfield, teacher

1st row: Willie Mai Skinner, Alda Smithson, Eunice Skinner, Addie Wiley, Elizabeth McCord, Irene Wiley, Buford Cathey, Louise Culberson, Fronie Culberson

2nd row: Miss Luddie Sherfield, Bill Woodside, Annie Roberson, Lera Roberson, Effie Roberson, Dee Cathey, Eva Woodside, Willie Lee Sharp

3rd row: Effie Mai Skinner, Mary Lee Roberson, Howard Roberson, Susie Wiley, James Culberson, Willie Wiley, Claiborne Culberson, Willie Mai Roberson, Fort Glenn, and Louise Wiley

Mt. Carmel School

Mt. Carmel School was located on Lewisburg Pike at the entrance of the Mt. Carmel Cumberland Presbyterian Church. For many years, Professor J.A. McCord was a schoolmaster at Mt. Carmel with a successful record of turning out fine scholars. After the eighth grade, students could go to Bethesda for their high school years. The one-room framed schoolhouse was under the direction of Miss Eva Lois Hurt for many years. The last year the school was open, Miss Jean Woody had the honor of closing the door for good in 1951.

Mt. Carmel School under the tutelage of Professor J.A. McCord who taught in the county for 42 years.

BETHESDA

Mt. Carmel School, 1913. Miss Annie Lee Harmon, teacher

1st row: Roy Sprott, Leslie Stephens, Clyde Stephens, Murry Jim Reynolds, Ludie Williams, Clara Stephens, Murry Harmon, Clyde McCord, Lawrence Stephens, and Charlie Harmon

2nd row: Roy Harmon, Roy Thompson, Joe M. Marlin, Joyce Stephens, Mitchell Reynolds, Ruth Thompson, Annie Margaret, Lorene McCord

3rd row: Clifton McCord, Annie Margaret Reynolds, Alcenia Stephens, Miss Annie Lee Harmon, Elmer Jordan, Pauline McCord, Gracie Thompson, and Susie May Sprott

SCHOOLS

HARPETH SCHOOL

Harpeth School teachers – Mr. W.P. Scales, Mrs. Scales, and Miss Edgmon

1st row: W.J. Marlin, Dick Jefferson, Oliver Pantall, Ellis Wallace, James Tomlin, Charles Watkins, Clyde Adams, Fred Lee Williams, Gerald Hood, Horace Edgmon, Howard Jackson, Henry (Buck) Tomlin, Hassell Campbell, Raymon Hicks; 2nd row: Clyde Pewitt, Fred Hood, Sara Addie Williams, Jessie Watkins, Fleming Jefferson, Fredrick Campbell, Alta Mai Williams, James Millard Williams, Leslie Watkins, Brown Jefferson, Jr., Richard McGee, Morris T. Hood, Reedy Edgmon, Homer Williams, Jr., Milton Tomlin; 3rd row: Lucille Jackson, Jean Pantall, Willie Hood, Katherine ___, ___, ___, ___ Anderson, Pauline Boatright, Margaret Lavender, Katherine Hood, Frank McGee, Inez Hood, Alene Jefferson, Willie Lee Edgmon; 4th row: Vashti Tomlin, Alma Tomlin, Mable Hood, Clarence Langley, Dalton Hood, Raymon Boatright, Elizabeth Jefferson, Christine Watkins, R.T. Wallace, Clayton Hood, Luster Tomlin, Lewis Edgmon, Edward Hicks; 5th row: Margaret Hood, Rachel McGee, Dorothy Tomlin, Lorene Jackson, Virginia McGee, Mary Poteete, Hazel Edgmon, Mary Lavender, Odell Stone, Lucy Watkins, Rosa Mai Hood, Virginia Buford, Mr. W.P. Scales, Mrs. Susie Mai Scales, Miss Ethel Edgmon.

BETHESDA

Harpeth School 1914-15. Teachers: Cyrus Dement and Miss Susie Mai Baugh

1st row: Howard Hood, Wallace Edgmon, Noble Heithcock, Walter Anderson, Filmore Hood, Horace Morton, Filmore Sowell, Robert Heithcock, Buford Jackson, Lewis Anderson, George Hood, Thomas Stoddard, Teddy Lavender, Murray Edgmon

2nd row: Teacher Cyrus Dement, Henry Hood, Gladys Tomlin, Effie Tomlin, Patty Jackson, Lena Wade Deason, Mary Thomas Tomlin, Bessie Mae Buford, Louise Tomlin, Maxie Tomlin, Grace Crafton, Virginia Buford, Mabel Wilhoite, Martha Crafton, Herman Tomlin

3rd row: Frank Williams, Jim Wilhoite, Mary Lois Morton, Gertrude Buford, Susie Mae Hood, Louise Buford, Allie Lavender, Rosa Dean Anderson, Eva McCall, James Anderson, Ethel Edgmon, Miss Susie Mai Baugh

4th row: Ben Wilhoite, Jimmy Davis, Eunice Pratt, Rachel Anderson, Hazel Wright, Mattie Alexander, Roberta Hood, Clarice Buford, Myrtle Tomlin, Nettie Hood, Elizabeth Jackson, Mollie Beach

5th row: Paul Hardeman, Jack Wells, Earl Morton, Gene Heithcock, Sam Davis, Charlie Deason, Leonard Edgmon, Veron Wright, Gilbert Edgmon, Carl Edgmon, Thomas Anderson, Rolfe Tomlin

Peytonsville School

Peytonsville School and W.J. Parkes, 1949

Peytonsville School, located on Gosey Hill Road near the intersection with Peytonsville Road, was under the tutelage of Professor Walter Parks and Miss Katie Lou Gatlin when a new concrete-block school was built in 1950. In 1961, the students were transferred to Bethesda, along with Miss Katie Lou Gatlin and Miss Elizabeth Houser.

Peytonsville School, 1951-1961, was a two-teacher school on Gosey Hill Road.

BETHESDA

Peytonsville School

Katie Lou Gatlin at Peytonsville School – Jerry Skinner, Paul Vaden, unknown, Michael Bruce, unknown back – Jane McGee, Tony Pratt, J.B. Robinson, unknown, Margaret Ann Williams, unknown, Ann Veach.

OLD HOMES AND SITES

HISTORIC WILLIAMSON COUNTY: OLD HOMES AND SITES

BY VIRGINIA BOWMAN

Home of Henry Reams – Mark Montgomery Andrews

The Andrews Place, one of the most interesting of all the fascinating old homes on Lewisburg Pike, is a two-story log structure built by Henry Reams. It is located nine miles south of Franklin and crowns a hill from whose crest and slopes yellow poplar trees were felled to build the sturdy walls in 1812. Henry Reams, born Christmas Day, 1786, married Sally North

(1795-1835), the daughter of Elisha and Rhoda North, in 1817, and lived here for some thirty years. They were the parents of nine children, with two sets of twins among that number.

Many years ago, on an adjoining rise Henry Reams gave the land for a church, but he was asked by Mr. John Cowles to swap the higher ground for a low-lying piece which he did. The church was then built on the low ground and was known as Prospect Methodist Church. It was first intended to be called Ream's Chapel, but with the passing of time, the name was changed to Cowles Chapel by which name it is known today.

John Cowles (1801-1882)

Mary Jane King Cowles (1811-1886)

After Henry Reams died in 1836, this place was bought by Mark Montgomery Andrews (1805-1890) whose forebears had come to Williamson County from Virginia when land across the mountains began to be opened. The first Mark Andrews to come here was born in Dinwiddie County, Virginia in 1740. He married Winfred Lyell (1738-1827), the daughter of Jonathan and Mary Dalton Lyell, and after his arrival in this county bought part of the large North Carolina grant to James Thackston from John Donelson in 1800 and settled near Bethesda. Those of his children who did not migrate here with him soon followed. Ephraim Andrews (1769-1837) was buying land in this county in 1804 from Robert Nelson and Thomas Cock; George Andrews (1765-1812) was buying property from Andrew Sprott in 1813. The eldest son, John Andrews (1764-1842), was a Revolutionary soldier who lived in Halifax County, Virginia, after the war then moved to Kentucky where he resided until 1804, he received a land grant for his service in the struggle for American Independence. In 1785, he married Rebecca Malone, the daughter of Daniel and Anne Chappell Malone. The names of Mark and John Andrews appear on the courthouse wall in Franklin with those men who served in the Revolution and are buried in Williamson County. However, family records suggest that Mark Andrews never actually saw service in the Continental Army but that his son John went as his alternate. In addition to these three sons, Mark Andrews mentioned several daughters in his will.

The Andrews men built substantial log houses near each other in the southeastern part of the county. One is preserved in a barn near the Ephraim Andrews cemetery just east of this home. The others burned long ago. The one remaining is an excellent example of pioneer architecture. It was built of poplar logs without knots or blemishes which are as sound today as when they were cut and trimmed in the early days. The front bottom log is forty-seven feet long running the entire length of the house. The old cabin has the usual dogtrot, but its great stone chimneys have been torn away. A scorched place over the huge fireplace is reminiscent of the blazing fire that once burned on the wide hearth. Since these families were well established so early it is clear they were of the excellent pioneer stock which contributed significantly to the building and growth of Williamson County.

For many years a huge grindstone was in use near the barn. The rock from which it was made was hauled by an ox-drawn sled from Pull Tight Hill near Cross Keys. A circle was drawn on the slab and holes were driven in. Hot water was poured on the pegs and when they expanded the outer stone cracked away. The round edges were then hand-dressed until smooth.

A colored blacksmith made the shaft and keys which still hold it in place. Over the years neighbors chipped away pieces of it; after their grindstones became lost or stolen during the war, so as to have something to sharpen knives and axes. Before this, it was forty-four inches in diameter and more than ten inches across the face. When on the frame it was difficult to turn because its size and weight made it unwieldy. It was preserved by descendants of Henry Reams and is on display at the Carter House in Franklin.

The place went out of the Andrews family in 1966. At the dispersal sale, many items of historic interest were sold. Fine antiques, boxes of rare books, and a number of pioneer tools—an adz, hand planes, broadaxes, and kettles identical to those on display in the Tennessee Museum which belonged to the state's first settlers—all passed under the hammer. Many interesting and valuable relics handed down from one generation to another in the family were preserved. One such item was an ancient walking cane that sheathed a sword whose blade is bright and sharp despite its great age.

For a while, the house stood empty with no fires on its great hearths, the wind, and rain seeking out new crevices in the thick walls. It seemed doomed to destruction but happily, it has been restored and now crowns its rise in renewed dignity. The large burying ground back of the house was reserved when the place was sold. It contains members of the Reams, North, Tennison, Parrish, and Andrews families.

[Editorial note: Since this was written in 1971, this historic landmark in the Harpeth community burned in the mid-1980s while under the ownership of Dr. Robert Oldham and his family.]

Moses Steele – Jimmie Dee Bennett Home

The Moses Steele Place

This home was built by Moses Steele in about 1825 and was one of the two brick houses in Bethesda in its early days. Located three-fourths of a mile north of Bethesda Road, it is an outstanding landmark in a community of fascinating old homes. Moses Steele was born December 14, 1802, in Bedford County, Virginia, the grandson of William Alexander Steele, Sr., who started with his mother and little sister from Ireland to America to escape religious persecution in the 1700s. The unfortunate young mother succumbed to illness and was buried at sea. When her canvas-shrouded body slipped into the water, the boy had to be forcibly restrained from jumping after her, so great was his grief at his mother's death and the terror of facing a new land among strangers without that beloved presence. Relatives reared the children but they were evidently separated as no certain trace of the child, Margaret Steele, has yet been found.

William Alexander Steele, Sr., married Elizabeth Helm in 1758; he served as a lieutenant in the Bedford County Virginia Militia in the Revolutionary War and died in 1808. His son, William Alexander, Jr., married Sarah Akers and, of their six children, two moved to

Williamson County. Moses Steele came first and with slave labor built his fine brick home. He then went back to Virginia where on October 30, 1827, he married Rachel Webber and, with her, returned to Williamson County to live. His sister, Catherine, who married Matthew Dabney Irvin, later settled just a few miles from him, and their brother, William, had a son to move here and marry Moses Steele's daughter.

Of Moses and Rachel Steele's five children, only two lived to maturity. One died in infancy, Sarah Ruth died as a girl, and the only son, William Alexander, fell dead as a child while riding on a wagon with his father's slaves on the way to the mill. Mary Elizabeth married her cousin, William Alexander Steele, in February of 1859, Rachel Ann married William Pillow Rucker, whose log home still stands on Jordan Road near Arno. William Rucker, his two brothers, Alonzo de Alvarado and John S., and their brother-in-law, Robert Archer Jordon, had all enlisted in Co. D, 20th Tennessee Regiment. Lt. A.D.A. Rucker was wounded at Shiloh, while Sgt. R. A. Jordon was wounded and captured at Fishing Creek and was again captured at Missionary Ridge. Captain William Rucker was elected Captain of the Webb Guards, later Co. D., when it was organized. When the army was reorganized at Corinth in 1862, he was not re-elected. However, loyal patriot that he was, William Rucker re-enlisted as a private in a cavalry unit and was killed in January of 1863 when Forrest attacked Ft. Donelson. He left his young wife with a little son, William, who was two years old the January his father was killed.

Jimmie Dee Bennett

Rachel Webber Steele died November 12, 1839, at the age of thirty-three. When Moses Steele died in 1875, he left the homeplace to his daughter, Rachel Rucker. Other property he willed to his other daughter, Mary Elizabeth. Mr. and Mrs. Moses Steele were buried near Bethesda in the cemetery of Benjamin Chapman, a Revolutionary soldier and kinsman of the Steele family.

This is a singularly beautiful house; time has not been able to efface its lines of elegance or remove the aura of charm still clinging about its walls. Inside and out it is a masterpiece of perfection. Its mantels are strikingly beautiful, the same in every room, and, with the staircase, are the result of painstaking handcraft. Since the second story has a door opening onto a porch, it would indicate that a two-story pillared veranda was originally at the front. The old home went out of the family years ago, but Moses Steele's descendants still recall with fondest memory happy days spent there in the past. It is owned today by Mr. and Mrs. Jimmie D. Bennett, Sr.

THE GORDON MCCORD HOUSE

The Gordon McCord House

This old home located east of Byrd Lane in the Bethesda community is unique with its great box bushes partially concealing the front porch. It was originally two log rooms built by Joseph Sprott but has changed with the years as the need arose. It was owned before it came into the McCord family by Ellis Jones whose sister, Martha Jones Sprott, lived with him. Since the McCords and Joneses were kin, this was the first place Mrs. James McCord visited after the birth of one of her daughters. As she went up the sidesteps with the infant in her arms, Mr. Jones met her with the question, "Cousin Tennie, what have you named the baby?" When she told him the baby had no name as yet, he smilingly replied, "Then you must name her Martha Ellis!" which was for his sister and himself, to which suggestion Mrs. McCord readily agreed.

James Allison McCord (1846-1911) married Mary Tennessee Lavender (1852-1940), who was the daughter of Anthony and Paralee Sprott Lavendar. James McCord was a Confederate soldier having served in Co. H., 32nd Tennessee Infantry, and had come to Bethesda from nearby Duplex. Among the nine children of James and Mary Tennessee McCord was a son, Gordon (1890-1965), who on March 5, 1919, married Mary Wallace Millard, the daughter of

Rev. Marshall Wallace Millard and Elvira Clayton Morton. The Rev. Millard was minister of the Bethesda Presbyterian Church for thirty-seven years, also preaching at the New Hope Church during this time in addition to his regular duties.

It is thought that Ellis Jones started the beautiful box bushes some sixty-five years ago. During the great blizzard of 1951, they were damaged but not killed as so many were elsewhere. One of the largest split down the center under the weight of ice and snow and now resembles two separate bushes. The place is in excellent repair and is still owned by Mrs. Gordon McCord who has five sons to share in her love for it.

James Allison McCord

Martha, Lora, Tennie, Talmadge, Lida, and Lera McCord

Front: William, Richard, Dale; Back: Mary, Gordon, Ernest, Rodney, April 19, 1942 (photo by Ellis Hatcher)

Richard, William, Rodney, Ernest, and Dale, April 19, 1942

Montrose

Montrose

Samuel Blythe Sprott, born in 1727, came to America from Scotland and was in Augusta County, Virginia, in 1747. That year he married Elizabeth Patton and moved on in search of a permanent place to settle. During the Revolution, he was a first lieutenant in Captain Bowman's company. Samuel Sprott died in 1795 and was buried in Union Grove Cemetery, Sandy Ridge Township in Union County, North Carolina. One of his descendants, Blythe Sprott, was born in North Carolina on December 29, 1792, the son of Andrew and Jane Sprott.

After emigrating to Williamson County, Blythe Sprott bought a farm and settled in the Bethesda community where he married Rachel Blythe (1794-1840) in 1811. He served in the War of 1812 and also in the Creek Indian War. Mr. and Mrs. Sprott built the house pictured here where they lived useful and prosperous lives.

One of their daughters, Mary Elizabeth (1832-1911) married Booker Preston Grigsby (1822-1919), the son of John and Sallie Turner Grigsby. He had come to Tennessee in a wagon when he was about thirty years old and was employed as overseer by Nathaniel Cheairs in Spring Hill. Booker P. and Mary Elizabeth Grigsby were each one of twelve children and twelve children were born to them. They live at this place inherited from her father at his death in 1868. The early Sprotts and Grigsbys are buried in a large family cemetery east of Byrd Lane at Bethesda.

Blythe Sprott

Mr. and Mrs. Ollie Turner Grigsby lived here after his parents died. It was Mrs. Ollie Grigsby who named the place Montrose for the beautiful roses she grew in such profusion. The house was originally two log rooms with a detached kitchen. Completely modernized, it is still in the family, owned today by Vivienne Watson and Cleo Grigsby.

OLD HOMES AND SITES

Ollie Grigsby

James Huff, Ollie Grigsby, Leonard Grigsby, and Glenn Grigsby

Booker Grigsby's 90th birthday at Montrose (home of Cleo Grigsby and Vivienne Grigsby Watson) 1. Lucille Bond, 2. Gladys Bond, Bob McCall (hat), Leonard Grigsby behind Sally McCall, John B. Bond, behind, Lawrence Bond, Robbie McCall, behind, Louise Bond, Lizzie McCall, behind, 3. Marvin Bond, 4. Cora Grigsby, Ella Scales, behind, 5. Ella Frances Grigsby, 6. Leo Grigsby, Ethel Grigsby, behind, 7. Charles Grigsby, Jr. (baby), C.F. Grigsby, Sr., Mr. Hughes, behind, Scales Grigsby, Aba Grigsby, behind, 8. Tom Lafayette Bond, Alma Grigsby, behind, 9. Cleo Grigsby, Leonard Grigsby, behind, Alice Grigsby, behind (10), 11. Vivienne Grigsby, Ida Grigsby, with child, Jessie Grigsby, Ollie Grigsby, Grandpa Booker Preston Grigsby, Suzie Lee Grigsby, with child, Elise Grigsby, behind, John Blythe Grigsby, behind, next to wife Suzie Grigsby (12). 13. Elizabeth Grigsby, Mary Kate Grigsby, behind, 15. Geraldine Grigsby, Blythe Grigsby, behind, 16. Frances Hatcher, John B. Grigsby, Jr., behind, 18. Kate Hatcher and Charlie Hatcher, behind, 17. Maggie Grigsby and Jim Grigsby, behind.

Matthew Dabney Irvin House

Matthew Dabney Irvin-Taylor House

Maxie Howlett, Dr. Howlett's daughter; Catherine, Alice, and Martha Irvin, daughters of Alex Irvin, visit their great grandfather's slave cabin.

Another of Bethesda's interesting old homes is that of Matthew Dabney Irvin. In 1838, he married Catherine Louise Steele (1816-1908) and had come to this county in 1847 from Campbell County, Virginia. Katherine Irvin made the long trip in a covered wagon sitting in a little straight ladderback chair, holding her baby. This chair, worn off to the first round by bumping her seven babies, is still in her family. The Irvins were not among complete strangers upon their arrival in Bethesda since her brother, Moses Steele, was there already as well as the Chapman kin.

The Irvins were Scots border clan Presbyterians who moved to Northern Ireland and from there to America to escape religious persecution. Two brothers, John and Matthew Dabney Irvin (1815-1879), came to Tennessee but the former went to West Tennessee while the latter settled in Williamson County. The Irvin house originally sat on a piece of land called Horton's Field back of the Tom Bond place. Soon after Mr. Irvin's arrival here, it was moved to its present location right on Bethesda Road where it is a familiar landmark in the community. Twenty yokes of oxen were required to move the house on logs across the rough fields. The old log smokehouse, kitchen, and slave cabin sitting in a row west of the house add much to its timeless charm.

The Irvins were all strong Presbyterians and, in her desire to promote that church in Bethesda, Catherine Irvin gave the land on which the Presbyterian Church was built in 1879. The manse was built on land given by Mrs. Irvin and her sister-in-law, Mrs. Mary Irvin Cox.

Mr. and Mrs. Irvin had seven children: Polly, Margaret, Elizabeth, Alice, Ida, William Dabney, and Richard Alexander. Both of the sons served in Co. D., 32nd Tennessee Infantry, along with their cousin, John Chapman. Lt. Richard Irvin died of pneumonia while in a Federal prison; in one of the battles John Chapman was struck while acting as color-bearer and, without missing a step, William Dabney caught the flag and bore it aloft into the swirling smoke and bursting shells. He was shot in the shoulder in the fighting near Marietta, Georgia, in 1864 and was captured. He was married and had grown children before the bullet ever worked out.

Richard A. Irvin, 1839-1864, Company D, 32nd Tennessee Infantry, CSA

William D. Irvin, 1841-1915, Company D, 32nd Tennessee Infantry, CSA

William Dabney (1841-1915) and Alice Alexander (1855-1944) Irvin had seven children: Alex, Shearer, Willie, Dena, Mary, Dabney, and Blanche. When the dispersal sale was held in the 1930s, wild turkey wing fans, candle molds, powder flasks, flax wheels, spinning wheels, and other pioneer necessities which had probably been crowded into the wagon with Catherine Irvin on the trip from Virginia were found. A pair of fine-blown vases and an ancient rolling pin were saved along with a few other treasures of a forgotten day. The house is owned today by Mr. and Mrs. Will Taylor and Mr. and Mrs. Walter Taylor and despite its age is better built than many modern homes.

BETHESDA

THE PLEASANT SCALES HOMEPLACE

Preston Scales – Charles Grigsby House

The old Scales house, high on the brow of the hill facing north toward Bethesda, is a familiar and beloved landmark in that closely-knit community. Pleasant Scales, the son of Samuel and Anne Wilson Scales was born October 1, 1839. His father died when he was two years old, and his mother later married Matthew Wilson who lived west of College Grove where he owned a fine old stone house in the Cove Section near Harpeth Lick.

On March 14, 1901, *The Review-Appeal* mentions in the news from Allisona "a very ancient lamp in regular use. It was purchased by Matthew Wilson forty-three years ago and was the first glass lamp brought to this section. His wife once fell down a long flight of stairs with the lamp in her hands and did not even break the chimney."

The Cove was often the scene of outrageous behavior by the Federal soldiers during the War Between the States. One day a Union soldier stopped at the Wilson house and asked for food. As he sat at the table eating, someone rushed in crying that the Yankees were about to kill Mr. Goodshire Wilson. Horrified, the family begged their uninvited guest to help them. He immediately left for this purpose, and his intervention prevented a tragedy that would have otherwise befallen them—a singular case of receiving a stranger and thereby entertaining an angel unawares.

Pleasant Scales enlisted in Co. D., 24th Tennessee Regiment where he served until the close of the war. In 1865, he became postmaster at Bethesda and was also a merchant there for fifty years. In 1876, he married Mary Ratcliffe, the daughter of Francis and Martha Reams Ratcliffe, whose beautiful home still stands on Lewisburg Pike. Gideon and Mary Ratcliffe had come to Williamson County from James City County, Virginia, and settled seven miles south of Franklin where he was long active in county affairs.

Mr. Scales bought the house pictured here and eighty acres from Moses Steele and his daughter, Mrs. Rucker, in 1874. It had been the home of William Pillow and Rachel Steele Rucker before he enlisted in the Confederate Army. After her husband's death at Fort Pillow in 1863, Mrs. Rucker and her little son William Steele Rucker went to live with her father where she continued to reside until her death in 1914, that place having been willed to her when her father died.

The Scales house was originally two log rooms with a dog trot between them. It was strongly built of poplar and cedar timbers strengthened after notching with long pegs. It was later weatherboarded and added to from time to time. One of the new rooms was always kept in readiness for the drummers who came to Mr. Scales's store once a month and for preachers who were holding meetings in Bethesda.

One room over the old dog trot was called the "lock room." It had one small window and only one door until another was cut through the log wall from the girls' room. Here in the "lock room" barrels of fall fruits, dried fruits, and flour were stored, the delightful fragrance of apples blending with the headier aroma of country hams when they were hung here for safekeeping around Thanksgiving and Christmas. The children loved the solitude of this room where they could play dolls, dress up in elegant clothes of a bygone day from the round top trunk, or just enjoy the nebulous dreams of childhood in peace and quiet. Here the older girls could read an occasional love story in safety, removed from the discomforting eye of a teasing brother should the tale prove sad enough for an occasional tear.

Charles F. and Ella Scales Grigsby

Many of the wide floorboards remain in the house; others were replaced with hardwood. Log cabins used for the smokehouse, laundry room, and cook's house were behind the dwelling. A detached kitchen was built over a cellar and continued in use until fairly recently.

When Mrs. Scales died in 1887, she left three small daughters—Ella, Marion, and Frank—whom Mr. Scales reared with the help of kind relatives. Another child, Annie, died before the mother. When Mr. Scales died in 1917, he was buried in the Ratcliffe cemetery with his wife and members of her family. The old house continued in the family occupied for thirty-eight years by Mr. and Mrs. Charlie Grigsby and their eight children. It is owned today by Mr. and Mrs. John H. Brittain.

BETHESDA

THE HOME OF WILLIAM ALEXANDER STEELE

W.A. Steele-Franklin Bond House

The land on which this old home stands was once part of both the Moses Steele and John Bond tracts. It was sold before the war to William Alexander Steele of Virginia by Tom Bond. William Alexander Steele was the son of William and Susan Moore Steele. William died in 1827 at the age of twenty-six, leaving a year-old son who, when he grew up, visited his father's brother, Moses Steele, in Bethesda and married his daughter, Mary Elizabeth, on October 15, 1850.

William Alexander Steele (1827-1874) was a Confederate soldier serving in the 4th Tennessee Cavalry under Starnes. Once during the war years when he slipped home for a visit, the Yankees learned of his presence in the neighborhood and came to his home in the dead of night looking for him. They banged on the north door shown in the picture of the house and demanded entrance. Mrs. Steele leaped from the bed and threw back the feather pad so her husband could slip between it and the straw tick.

She put the covers back in place and tossed her three little sons sleeping in another bed onto hers and hastily tucked them in. All the while the Yankees were pounding on the door and shouting threats. In her haste, she stepped into her husband's shoes but there was no time to stoop down and search for her slippers. Fortunately, her gown and wrapper hid them and, with a thudding heart, she opened the door, the candle in her hand leaping with the breath of air. The soldiers pushed roughly past her, glancing around the room with suspicious eyes. They went at once to the bed and felt all over it, moving the little boys about in their search, but they remained mute after their mother's swiftly whispered admonition to silence. She took them across the hall to the other room, then up the steps to the rooms above, moving carefully so the shoes would not show, her hand shielding the slender flame.

William A. and Mary E. Steele

Unable to find the object of their search, the Yankees left feeling that the wool had been pulled over their eyes but unable to prove it.

The William Cicero and Cora Steele Bond family

The two front rooms were the main part of the house in the early days. Mr. Steele added the rest just after the war. The ash floors are original as are the inside doors and the double front doors. The stair rail is the same one the Yankees slid their hands along as they went up those very steps. A beautiful Magnolia in the front yard was planted by Cora Steele, with the help of her sister, Ella. These were two of the eleven children of William Alexander and Mary Elizabeth Steele (1831-1911). The original old log kitchen is in the yard with its great stone fireplace and wide rock chimney.

Cora Steele (1866-1915) married William Cicero Bond (1862-1928) and at Mrs. Steele's death, he bought the place. Mr. and Mrs. Bond had three children—Lorene, Mary, and Howard, the latter inheriting the property after their parent's deaths. It continues to be the home of Mrs. Howard Bond, Mr. and Mrs. Franklin Bond, and their daughter, Jane, who make the fifth generation to live in this beautiful home.

William Cicero Bond

Lorene and Mary Bond, daughters of W.C. and Cora Steele Bond

William Howard Bond (1894-1966), WWI Veteran

THE JOHN PRESTON BOND PLACE

The land on which this house is located was originally part of the John Bond grant. It is a very old log building and, although it has been weatherboarded, it has retained the old stone chimneys and much of the original exterior. Its doors and walls are hand-hewn with strokes of the knife visible. In several of the rooms, the floors are the same wide boards of yellow and blue poplar put together when the house was first constructed. The one-bedroom floor is of beautiful curly maple cut from the place. The old kitchen at the back door and other outbuildings are log; these are still strong and serviceable though no longer used for their first purpose.

The house was built for John Preston and Jemima Chriesman (1838-1875) Bond. He was born March 12, 1812, the son of John and Elizabeth Preston Bond. At Mr. Bond's death in 1885, one of their sons, Thomas Lafayette, who married Cora Belle Grigsby, took over the running of the place. It is owned today by Mr. and Mrs. Marvin Bond.

The house is larger than it appears to be from the outside, having eleven rooms. These are furnished with a blend of modern and antique furniture. Recently an old spinning wheel

OLD HOMES AND SITES

and a cradle in which the slave mothers rocked their babies were rescued from the attic and carefully refinished. In modernizing the house, the best of its old features has always been retained whenever possible: therefore, it has gained much in comfort and lost nothing in charm.

John Preston Bond (1812-1885)    Jemima Chriesman Bond (1838-1875)    Thomas Lafayette Bond (1865-1932)

The John P. Bond Farm on Bethesda-Arno Road no longer stands due to neglect.

BLUE GRASS FARM

Cicero Bond House

Franklin was still in its infancy when the community of Bethesda, located in the southeast part of Williamson County, was settled. Its earliest inhabitants after the red man were sturdy pioneers from Virginia and North Carolina who took up grants of land for their service in the American Revolution or who bought property with an eye to making this their home. In this pleasant rolling land with its gentle hills and streams dotting the virgin meadows, log cabins soon began to appear after the early 1800s and saw a vast migration from the mother states. The Bonds, Steeles, Alexanders, Sprotts, Grigsbys, and others gave their new community a Bible name meaning House of Mercy. Churches and schools were soon constructed and today Bethesda has entwined the past into the present in a graceful and appealing fashion. Many of the old log homes remain but are covered with weatherboarding and further modernized for comfort and convenience. Only two houses were of brick in the early days, one built by Moses Steele which still stands and the other built by John Bond which unfortunately has been torn down.

John Bond was born in Ireland on June 11, 1760, and did not immediately find a place where he wished to settle upon his arrival in America. While sojourning in Ohio he met Elizabeth Bryant (1773-1847) whom he persuaded to run off and marry him. Her departure was so precipitant she took nothing from home but her Bible which is still in the hands of her descendants. Early in 1800, they arrived in Bethesda where Mr. Bond took up a thousand acres of land. This land grant is still in the family papers. They first lived in a log house while the big brick was under construction. Half a dozen or more of the pioneer cabins remained at the original site until fairly recently. Bricks for the new home were burned in a kiln near the old road which followed the creek.

John and Elizabeth Bond had eleven children and prospered until his death in 1848. Their son, Cicero, had taken over the management of the estate and was continuing in his father's wise and skillful farming operation when the War Between the States swept over all normal pursuits and, during the tumultuous Reconstruction days, he lost the major part of his property and his home. This was not uncommon throughout the South due to the exorbitant taxes levied and brutally collected by the occupation forces.

Bowed but unbroken, Cicero Bond moved to his remaining acres and built a two-story log home where he began that long, hard pullback to prosperity again. His coat and the little hand-turned sewing machine on which it was made still remain in the upstairs room. The material for the coat was made from wool sheared from sheep on the place, carded, and woven into linsey-woolsey by hand.

Expanded in acreage throughout the years, the place has remained continuously in the Bond family. J. W. Bond, Sr. and J. W. Bond, Jr., operated it together until the former's death in 1953. It was then owned and successfully operated by James Bond, Jr., a prominent dairy farmer, and registered livestock dealer, until his death in 1968. Today it is owned by the sons, James, Charles, and Danny, with Charles as the operator. His son is the fifth generation who has lived in the same house

Cicero Bond (1814-1886) and James W. Bond (1872-1952)

The old brick house John Bond built was torn down about 1955 and can be seen only when walking down memory lane—a fate shared by all too many of Williamson County's historic homes.

THE LABAN HARTLEY HOUSE

The Laban Hartley and Sam Anderson House at Cross Keys

Laban Hartley is still a legend in the Cross Keys community and even his home is unique in that it was one of the first in that neighborhood and is one of the very few old stone houses left in Williamson County. Located on Cross Keys Road east of Bethesda, it was built on land given to Mr. Hartley for his service in the Continental Army.

Laban Hartley was born in Snowhill, North Carolina, in 1742. He and his wife, Sarah Fagley (1771-1831) were the parents of six daughters and two sons whose many descendants represent the name in Franklin and outlying districts today. An enterprising Scots immigrant, Laban Hartley had his home constructed of yellow sandstone slabs three feet thick and so heavy it was all four men could do to lift them in place and so skillfully dressed that little mortar was needed to seal them. A Negro builder oversaw the work and, as was his custom, inscribed his name on one of the chimneys. The house was constructed high off the ground possibly for protection against prowling Indians and wild beasts. Tradition says seven years were required to finish it.

Laban Hartley had several occupations besides his farming activities. He and his sons quarried rocks and made them into millstones and grindstones. He had planted extensive orchards on a hill near the house and from their abundant crops enough brandy was made in vats in the basement to supply a tavern across the road and one in Maury County as well.

Since it was against the law to sell brandy to Negroes, those who craved the fiery brew crawled under the tavern at night, bored holes through the floor and barrel bottoms, and drank their fill. By plugging the holes they could return at their leisure; their ruse was not discovered until the barrels were found unexpectedly empty.

Before his death, Laban Hartley directed that one acre of land at Cross Keys be set aside as a family cemetery. In 1842, at the age of one hundred, with only a few strands of gray in his black hair. For some reason, he was not buried in the place designated. His grave is marked by a pyramid of stones in the Reynolds Cemetery at Flat Creek.

Laban Hartley's grave is in the Reynolds Cemetery on Flat Creek Road.

Unique chicken house at Cross Keys behind the Hartley-Anderson home

THE HOME OF DR. SAMUEL FLEMING AT HARPETH

Dr. Sam Fleming's home at Harpeth

Standing on the east porch of the old Mark Andrews place one looked directly toward the home of Dr. Samuel Fleming. Born December 7, 1821, he was the son of William Fleming and Mixey Thompson Fleming who lived at Sunnyside. He was well educated for the medical profession but would never actively practice after becoming disillusioned over the fraud he observed during his school years. However, he would dispense medicine to his neighbors when they became ill and were in need of his knowledge.

Dr. Fleming married Elizabeth Brooks who was a kinsman of President Adams. In its prime the house had a columned porch and, located in a wide lawn shaded with trees of primeval splendor, was a place of great beauty. Past its front ran a road meandering off to the hills, eastward where members of the Murrell family lived. Back of the house was an old cemetery destroyed so long ago that no one is sure of the inscriptions on the stones, although they were thought to have been Staggs—a name that often appears in old county records.

Samuel M. Fleming, Sr. (1861-1928), "The Millet King" of Franklin

Dr. Fleming died in 1875 leaving his wife with six young children to rear. One of these children was Samuel Milton Fleming, who was born in this house in 1861 and who, in later years, became a prominent grain dealer in Franklin and Nashville. He was fourteen when his father died and coupled with an ambitious nature was the desire to aid his widowed mother which prompted him to seek work at an early age. He began his career in a little country store near his home on Lewisburg Pike which was long a familiar landmark in the Harpeth community. At that time, it was owned by Tom Wallace who had married the oldest Fleming daughter, Mallie. When nothing more than a boy, Mr. Fleming would operate the cotton gin in the rear of the store all night. After Mr. Wallace lost a hand in an accident at the gin, he moved to town to serve as county court clerk. Mr. Fleming then took over the management of the store capably running it for some years.

In 1901, he married Miss Cynthia Cannon, the daughter of Newton and Jennie McEwen Cannon, representatives of two of the county's prominent pioneer families. Mr. and Mrs. Fleming lived in a large frame house near his old home for four and a half years when their two daughters were born. They then moved to Franklin where they built a home on Third Avenue destined to become a mecca to those who loved and revered Southern traditions. Here, for sixty years, Mrs. Fleming exemplified to the highest degree the finest attributes of her generation which reached from the days of Reconstruction to the Space Age.

Some years before his moving to Franklin, Mr. Fleming's business had expanded until it was necessary for him to transfer his offices to Nashville. He was a skillful and highly successful businessman with friends from every walk of life. He died after a short illness on May 7, 1928. His son inherited to a full degree his business talents along with Mrs. Fleming's sagacity and is a banker of international renown.

After standing vacant for many years, Dr. Fleming's old house has become a victim of time and the elements. No longer useful in our progressive age the little store joined the ranks of vanishing Americana in 1968. The site of Dr. Fleming's home is owned by Mr. and Mrs. H.W. Marlin, Jr. The store was located on the property of Mrs. H.W. Lavender and her heirs.

NOTABLE HOMES

"Historic homes are ornaments of the community that provide a sense of place and should not be taken for granted."

When William Cicero Bond died in 1928, his daughters Mary and Lorene took the smaller house and farm across the road so their brother Howard could have the homeplace for his family.

NOTABLE HOMES

The Thomas C. Bond Home and Farm is located on Bethesda-Arno Road and adjoins the J.W. Bond, Jr., Farm. Today, J.W. Bond's granddaughter makes her home here.

The home of J. Lawrence and Naoma Alexander Bond is on Bethesda Road. It is presently the home of their granddaughter, Lynne Laughmiller Davis.

The home of J.T. "Chub" Hargrove is located across the road from Cross Keys Baptist Church.

The home of Ace Wilson, located on Byrd Lane, is within sight of Bethesda Road. This home is one of the largest 19th century-era homes in Bethesda.

NOTABLE HOMES

Located just west of the crossroads on Bethesda Road and across the road from the Irvin-Taylor-King Farm, this house was used for high school classes in 1935 and 1936 while the new school was being built.

The Ebb Alexander House, located on Bethesda Road, is today known as the O.C. McMillan farm.

The Bluegrass Farm on Bethesda-Arno Road is the home of the Bond Brothers Dairy.

Stephens-Roberson-Woodside House on Ash Hill Road is a double-log house with a dog-trot.

Side view – Stephens-Roberson-Woodside House with limestone chimney

NOTABLE HOMES NO LONGER STANDING

"The destruction of a family home is a loss to the entire community."

The home of Henry Padgett was located on Lewisburg Pike at the intersection with Bethesda Road. Padgett operated a cotton gin behind his house. This site is presently the home of River Bend Nursery.

Lycurgus McCall, 1814-1877. The home of Lycurgus McCall, located on Cross Keys and Choctaw Road, was once known as McCall's Corner. Lycurgus was an educator and a magistrate who served the Cross Keys community.

John C. Petway, 1833-1910, Co. A 45th TN Inf. CSA. The home of John C. Petway, located at the corner of Bethesda-Arno Road and Cool Springs Road, was one of the substantial homes in the 12th civil district before it was destroyed by a tornado while owned by Logan Veach.

NOTABLE HOMES NO LONGER STANDING

Nelson Lavender, 1786-1864. The Nelson Lavender Home, located west of Byrd Lane, was one of the oldest log homes in the area. Sadly, it was torn down several years ago. Nelson was one of the founders of the Bethesda Methodist Church, and he is buried in that cemetery.

Sarah Crutcher and John Blythe Sprott. This is a drawing of the home of the John Blythe Sprott, William Dodson Hatcher, Alvin Blythe Alexander, and William Hatcher Alexander families. It burned in July of 1973.

Dick Waddey, Cicero, and Virginia Waddey Stanford. The Cicero Stanford Home stood near the Cool Springs Primitive Baptist Church on Cool Springs Road east of Bethesda. The Stanfords reared their nephew, Richard P. Waddey, who later inherited the farm.

In 1972, the James Waddey Cabin, built in 1820, was dismantled in Bethesda and moved to Memphis for the Mid-South Fair. The photo on the right shows the James Waddey Log House in Memphis today.

NOTABLE HOMES NO LONGER STANDING

The home of Marvin and Bessie Bond on Bethesda-Arno Road is no longer standing due to neglect. It was originally the home of John Preston Bond, son of John and Elizabeth Bryant Bond, who came to Bethesda in 1800.

The log home of William Lafayette McCall on Cross Keys Road was torn down many years ago.

WHO'S WHO IN WILLIAMSON COUNTY

Jane Bowman Owen

"Who's Who in Williamson County" was a series of articles written by Jane Bowman Owen for *The Review-Appeal* from 1935 until 1953. Mrs. Owen wrote nearly 900 articles which included interviews with people from across Williamson County. To add content and color, we have reprinted seventeen interviews with people from the Bethesda community in this series.

If one reads carefully, the reader may obtain a bit of history not found in any other source. Those interviewed not only tell their life story but add information about Bethesda unfamiliar to those living in the community today.

Rick Warwick, Editor

MATTIE SUE WARE ALEXANDER (MRS. C.E.), 1886-1959

Clarence E. and Mattie Sue Alexander

THE REVIEW-APPEAL, JANUARY 26, 1950

As Mrs. Clarence Alexander went about her ironing at her home on Lewisburg Avenue one cold morning recently, she began talking with a caller concerning the village of her birth – Bethesda – which to her way of thinking is the center of perfection.

"There are so many interesting people in that section of the county," she remarked. "It was a canebrake when the Indians lived there, and their flint stones can still be found in many places. Some of the best people on earth were its first settlers who cleared the land for farming and built homes of logs, many of which still stand. The old school building, erected over a hundred years ago, was torn away a few years back to make way for a modern store building being run by John William Beasley and his wife, the former Ellie Marshall McCord, who also have an apartment in the concrete structure.

"The original building, 42 feet long, had hand-hewn beams 16 inches square and put together with wooden pegs. The nails used were made by a blacksmith. It was in this building several generations were taught the three Rs by such teachers as Sim Wall, W.D. Irvin, W.W. Courtney, J.A. McCord, and John B. Gray, all of whom have been gathered to their fathers. Mr. German Marshall is one of those yet counted among the living. Early in life he quit the teaching profession and has for several years been serving the county as clerk and master.

John Black Gray, Bethesda's first public school teacher

German McEwen Marshall

Wirt Courtney, 1889-1961, U.S. Congressman

"In the old days, the children had to pay to go to school each paying ten cents per day. Mr. Booker Grigsby had five in school and said it cost him more for tuition than he made on the farm. The first free school was taught by Mr. J.B. Gray, father of Frank Gray, of Gray Drug Company.

"Just after the Civil War, the school was remodeled by Ben Waddey, son of the famous chairmaker, and John Hudson. It underwent other improvements in 1912 or '13. The children were not allowed to leave the grounds and at recess, they would go to the fence, call the merchants and they would bring chewing gum, candy, pencils, and tablets to them in exchange for their pennies. Pleas D. Scales was both merchant and postmaster for forty years.

"The old school was built on an acre of ground donated by Charlie Grigsby's great-grandfather, Andrew Sprott, who also gave two acres for the Methodist Church site. He was a large landowner. The several generations who attended the school represented the backbone of the community and their memory will ever be revered.

"It is a pleasure to think of those days and to visit the old landmarks – and they are many. In a number of instances, the land has remained in the family. Mrs. Alice Irvin, wife of W.D. Irvin, one of the first teachers and a Confederate veteran, lived in one of the first houses built in that section, and the place is now the property of her sons, Alex and Shearer Irvin, popular Franklin merchants.

"Another landmark is the Ollie Grigsby home, built of logs, and living with him are his daughters, Miss Cleo Grigsby and Mrs. Vivienne Watson, with her children. Still, another is the Pleas Scales place, home of his daughter, Mrs. Charlie Grigsby, which dates back also to the early days.

Alvin Blythe Alexander, 1882-1975, and Willie Hatcher Alexander, 1892-1977

William Dodson Hatcher, 1861-1911 and Annie Wilhoite Hatcher, 1867-1949

"Alvin Alexander and his wife, Willie Hatcher Alexander, live on the farm formerly belonging to his grandfather, which was later sold to W.D. Hatcher, Alvin's father-in-law. It is rich in historical facts if I could only recall them. Not far from them is the very old home of the late Thomas A. and Lucy Smithson Daniel, in which two of their daughters, Fannie and Nannie Mai Daniel live, and is the gathering place for all the other members of the family. Not only they but everyone else finds a welcome in this home where many family antiques are to be found, among them being the old loom used for weaving back in the days of slaves by Cousin Lucy's family. This house is also built of logs, as were the others, and later weatherboarded.

"The original Andrew Blythe place is now the home of his grandchildren, Julie, Addie, Jim, and Bill Eggleston, children of the late Ed and Anna Blythe Eggleston. The old seven-room log house has been replaced by a two-story frame. Down on the creek, running through the farm, the grandfather had a flour mill, which was destroyed by the Yankees during the Civil War.

"The J.W. Bond, with his son, James, Jr., and family live on the farm of his father, Cicero Bond, and this house is another landmark rich in ancient history, as well as now being the home of a well-known dairy herd.

"The Dr. Jesse Core place was later occupied by his son, Dr. J.B. Core, and his wife, Jimmy Sprott Core. After they died the property was purchased by the late T.R. Beasley, and it is here his wife and son, Thomas E. Beasley, live. Both doctors practiced for many years, and they brought more babies into the world than any other doctor in the county.

"The Jimmy Chriesman place is now the property of his daughters, Lula and Lizzie Chriesman, and on it live the Frank Williams family.

"My grandfather, W.M. Knott, moved to Bethesda from Bigbyville, in Maury County, and purchased a farm. It was here my parents, G.W. and Lizzie Knott Ware, also lived. After my grandfather's death, the place was bought by Joe Trice's father, Ewell Trice, and at his death, the son bought the property, tore away the old house, and built a modern two-story frame structure.

"My husband's parents, Ebb and Rachel Sprott Alexander owned a farm of 147 acres on which they raised a family of 10 children, all of whom are living except my husband, Clarence, who died in 1944, all living in this county except two, and were educated at Bethesda. After the death of his parents, Clarence bought the home place in 1940. We moved there from Murfreesboro Road with our family of five.

Ebb and Rachel Sprott Alexander

"Gordon McCord lives at the home of his parents, the late J.A. and Tennie McCord. It really dates back to the beginning and here a large family was reared who have proved a credit to their parents.

"The Will C. Bond place, where a son, Howard Bond, and his family reside, is another old home of note, being the original Steele homestead. On the same family tract live Howard's sisters, Mary and Lorene, but in a much more modern house.

"John Chrisman was the village blacksmith, doing a thriving business in the horse and buggy days. He was an artist when it came to making and mending any type of machinery used in his day. What he would think of this disappearance of shops and the existence of garages is only to be imagined.

"The house of Miss Minnie Sprott, who died recently and continues to be occupied by her nephew, Ebb Alexander, is filled with antiques from the front door to the back. The house, however, is not one of the antebellum homes.

"P.W. Scales and J.O. Grigsby were operators of general mercantile stores back when groceries, dry goods, harnesses, hardware, and feed were sold under one roof. Both stores burned in the same fire. The more up-to-date merchants, John W. Beasley and J.O. Grigsby, Jr., carry full lines but are arranged in a more attractive manner than were those of former days.

"Another old building is the Presbyterian manse, occupied for forty years by Rev. and Mrs. M.W. Millard, while he was pastor, later by Rev. and Mrs. W.L. Smith, and now by the present pastor, Rev. C.N. Ralston, and his wife. The Methodist parsonage has had many more occupants since this denomination has a different method of retaining pastors. The present occupants are Rev. and Mrs. C.O. Ruby.

"The village is justly proud of the large concrete high and elementary school building with its splendid corps of teachers. The building has been enlarged since it was first erected in about 1936 after the old one burned. The gymnasium is also a joy, and great pride is taken in the record the ball teams have made. Pupils go by school buses from all the surrounding neighborhoods to this highly recommended seat of learning. The lunch program is also greatly appreciated and gives the pupils a well-balanced diet under the supervision of Miss Jessie Bourne, home economics teacher, and her assistants, Mrs. Carrie Layne and Mrs. Grover Trice.

"The Home Demonstration Club has a new home. Mrs. Tom Beasley has given the members the use of a two-room house on her place, which they have been busy remodeling, and on Friday, February 3, will meet there for the first time. I expect to go out with Miss Crowley to enjoy a good lunch, one of the club's outstanding characteristics.

"Then there is the Bethesda Community Club, which meets the third Wednesday night of each month at the school, another wide-awake organization that has done much for the improvement of the community.

"I wouldn't have you think there are no later model homes at Bethesda. There are the J.W. Stowers, Seth Beasley, Mrs. J.O. Grigsby, Mrs. Ruth Reed, Charlie Hatcher, Lawrence

Leonard and Marvin Bond, H.A. McCall, Buddy Turner, and Will Giles homes. Most of the older homes, however, have been modernized and since electricity reached the village and all the countryside, many conveniences have lightened the home and farm work."

Finishing her ironing, clearing away all signs of her work, and laying aside her apron, Mrs. Alexander, a woman who can do more than one thing at a time and do them well, sat down and remarked, "After the death of my husband, I sold my farm at Bethesda to Artie McMillan, moved to Franklin, built two apartment houses and I live in one of them with my youngest son, Ross, a senior in Franklin High, where he is interested in athletics and girls. I have another son, Roy, in Sendai, Japan, a corporal in the United States Army. Nelson, another son, was stationed in Porta Rico [sic] during World War Two. My oldest son, Horace, lives in Wichita Falls, Texas, and my only daughter, Rachel, married James O'Neely, Jr., of College Grove. I am living my life over in my grandchildren. They have a way of making me forget some of the rough roads I've had to travel along life's way.

"I enjoy my home in Franklin and my connection with the work at the Methodist Church, but I find myself so often reliving those happy days at Bethesda where friendships are measured by acquaintances where every home is a house by the side of the road and each occupant is a friend to man."

FRANK M. ANDERSON, 1883-1955

THE REVIEW-APPEAL, JANUARY 11, 1951

One bright snappy morning last week Mr. Frank M. Anderson dropped by *The Review-Appeal* office to see that his subscription was in good standing. As is his custom he took time to comment on the weather, world conditions, happenings of the town and country.

It was not long before he was in a reminiscent mood and after settling back in his chair remarked, "It is amazing how time flies. It was 100 years ago last fall since my parents, Thomas P. and Mary Frances Cowles Anderson, were married. They had 13 children, every one of whom was born in odd years except my brother, Walter. John, father of Beaumont Anderson, was 28 years older than the youngest, Mary Thomas. Of this number five are living, Mrs. H.D. Jefferson, who was a twin, Mary Thomas, Walter, Chapman, and I. My father was 40 years old when he married, and my mother was only 16.

Thomas Page Anderson 1813-1884

Mary Frances Cowles Anderson 1832-1884

"Grandfather William Anderson bought an original grant of land from the owner which at that time, composed the greater part of what is now the tenth district. Of this land I own 200 acres, and my brother, Walter, 60. My father not only cultivated much of his 700 acres, but operated a sawmill, grist mill, and did carpentry. It took a lot of money to rear a family when our wants were few. No wonder families are limited to two or three children. Big families like ours are as extinct as the dodo bird.

Thomas Page Anderson-T.J. Moran house

"I was born nine years after the Civil War closed and most of the stories my grandmother and mother told me were about the war. They told of how the Yankees raided their homes, carrying away horses, meat, silver, and other possessions. I remember asking Mother if there would be any more wars and her answer was, 'Yes, son, the Bible tells us there will be wars, and rumors of wars as long the world stands.' I then asked if it were possible that I might have to fight, and her answer was in the affirmative. But I missed both the Spanish-American and World War One. The first was a voluntary service and I was not called for the next one.

"There was a schoolhouse on my father's farm, and it was there that all the Andersons received their early education. My brother, Chap, and I were among the first pupils to enter Wall and Mooney School when it opened in Franklin in the fall of 1889.

"My father had much ash, poplar, beech, and other timber on his farm. He sawed lumber at his mill which built many houses now standing. Among them is New Hope Church on Lewisburg Road, which is as erect as the day it was built nearly a century ago. It was with this congregation he served as an elder until his death. Walter and his son, Walter Bond Anderson, serve in that capacity today, and another son, Thomas, is an elder in a Nashville Presbyterian Church. On Sunday morning we were up as early as usual to be on hand for Sunday School and preaching. If there was no room for all of us in the carriage, we caught up horses and rode them. My mother prepared all her dinner on Saturday, and if we had company on Sunday they ate cold food along with the rest of us. There was always plenty to eat and to spare. No one ever thought of missing church and the Anderson pew was full from one end to the other for our parents had us with them to see that no shenanigans went on.

Mary Thomas Anderson (Mrs. Carrick North)

"Father's grist mill on the banks of the West Harpeth River was a great place for farmers to congregate. They brought corn and wheat in wagons or horseback and while they waited passed the time of day and if they got hungry they parched corn and ate it. This mill was the indirect cause of my father's death. In the spring of 1884, a freshet stopped up the race built for the water to run from the river to the mill. My father went down one morning about daylight to open it up. He fell up to his neck into the icy waters. By the time he reached the house, his clothes were frozen stiff, pneumonia developed and within a week his death occurred. Mother died before Christmas in the same year.

By this time, all the children had married and had homes of their own except Walter, Chapman, our little sister, Mary Thomas, and I. Our sister came to Franklin to make her home with an older sister, Mrs. Jefferson, and we boys went to live with our oldest brother, John. Chap ran the store, and we dealt in grain. Mary Thomas came out to keep house for us and to add cheer to the household. We had Vashti Early board with us while she taught at West Harpeth School. They became fast friends and later our sister married Carrick North and Vashti [married] his brother, Henry, sons of Dr. J.A. North.

"That was back in the horse and buggy days. My brother and I were great hands to break horses and on one occasion we became the owners of a balky animal that refused to move when overtaken by a stubborn spell. Chap said he would break him or else. He put some firecrackers in his pocket, hitched the animal to a cart, and started on his way. All went well for a while until the horse suddenly came to a standstill. After trying all the customary methods to get him to move, Chap pulled out a firecracker, lit it, and placed it under the horse's tail. When it went off so did the horse. A skyrocket could not have made better progress than they did going down that crooked lane. This worked so well my brother tried it again when his steed stopped in the middle of the river. This time when the fireworks began the animal overturned the cart and Chap almost drowned before he could get out of the water.

Chap Anderson

"In the ten years at West Harpeth, 1895 to 1905, many amusing incidents occurred which furnished much laughter then and even unto this day when we have an opportunity to visit together. When he married Miss Willie Eve, of Nashville, and established a home of his own we dissolved our partnership and he went to live on the Anderson farm which he, Mary Thomas and I owned together.

"I decided I wanted to try the West and went to Oklahoma. Most of the people with whom I came in contact were those who had done something fraudulent and were evading the law. I had not been used to that kind of associate so within six months I was back in Franklin where every man is my friend. Returning, I occupied a seat with a man who had never before seen a fence built of field stone. He thought they were wonderful. 'And to think,' he said, 'they last forever and don't cost a cent!' He had a different idea when I got through enumerating the probable cost. Just goes to prove we form opinions often without any knowledge of the subject under discussion.

"I bought Chap's and Mary Thomas' interests in the farm and am still running it, raising wheat, corn, tobacco, hogs, sheep, and cattle.

"For several years Chap and I were partners in the hardware and grocery business in the building now occupied by Bennett Hardware Company, and later with Bennett Hunter, we were in the same kind of business at what is Pointer's Corner. This we sold ten years later to Joe Trice and the late Fred Reynolds. I like farm life better than being in a store for the great outdoors appeals to me more. I get closer to nature, which is always fair in its dealings if treated right. It never fails to return an honest yield when conditions permit."

Mr. Anderson married Miss Annie Calvert, a Nashville businesswoman. Just two days before she was to retire from working in the Welfare Department, she fell and broke her hip. Her recovery has been most satisfactory and now goes all over the apartment in a wheelchair. They have an apartment in the old brick house in West End where the famous Campbell School was located many, many years ago. They are both members of the Franklin Presbyterian Church where his brother, Chapman, is a deacon and usher. His sisters, Mrs. Jefferson, and Mrs. North, with their families and the children of another sister, the late Mrs. Will Rucker, are also faithful members. Mrs. North, he says, seems more like a daughter to him than a sister, and this feeling must be mutual for she named her only child Frank Anderson North.

In speaking of his brother, Mr. Chap Anderson said, "He is one of the best businessmen I know, knows the value of a dollar and how to spend it. If given plenty of time he can give a good answer to any question. Maybe he won't answer it for several days, but when he does, it will be accurate and to the point. His farm is in better shape than it has been. On it is a big spring that has never been known to go dry in any kind of drought, and could not be pumped dry. When neighbors run short, they know they can get all the water they need at Frank's place. Brothers rarely come such as Frank, and to me, he has been a wonderful pal and counselor. Men such as he are valued far above rubies." A wonderful feeling for a man to have for his brother!

SAM F. ANDERSON, 1879-1944

THE REVIEW-APPEAL, DECEMBER 17, 1942

There is no one in the county who watches the happenings in both the Atlantic and Pacific Oceans any closer than Sam F. Anderson, a prominent farmer at Cross Keys, who has in former years traveled the seven seas while serving four years with the United States Navy and visited the countries now centers of the bloodiest contest ever known to mankind.

After enlisting in 1901, he made four extended voyages on the briny deep, the first taking him across the North Atlantic, at which time he visited the countries of England, France,

Spain, and Belgium, and went a short distance into German territory. He was a member of a training crew aboard the U.S.S. Dixie and came back to New York with a year's training completed.

On his second trip aboard the same vessel, he went to the French-owned island of Martinique, one of the Lesser Antilles southeast of the United States, an Atlantic paradise, carrying a load of provisions including clothing, food, medicines, etc.

The third voyage took them to South America, making the first stop at Montevideo, the capital of Uruguay, situated at the mouth of the Plata River.

The fourth, last, longest, and most adventurous voyage led across the Atlantic, visiting Spain, through the Strait of Gibraltar, to Algiers, and many other Mediterranean ports, through the Suez Canal, Red Sea, into the Indian Ocean, making calls at many interesting and important towns. They sighted Australia and the Solomons on their calls, winding toward Japan and China. In the Philippine Islands, they spent a month and six months on the island of Guam, where they were engaged in surveying. Returning to the Philippines they were transferred to the U.S.S. San Francisco retraced their route, docked at Norfolk, Va., and sent by rail to Philadelphia, Pa. His four years' enlistment having expired, he was paid off and given an honorable discharge.

Mr. Anderson looks forward to the day when his discharge and that of his son will hang on the walls of their home together, for Herman is now in Mission, Texas, where he graduated Sunday as a lieutenant in the Air Corps at Moore Field. He and Mrs. Anderson were present when the commission was given, having left Franklin on Monday previous. He says the thirteenth has no terrors for him for he received his discharge from the Navy on Friday, the thirteenth, and it was a Sunday, the thirteenth that his boy was commissioned. He also says Friday seems to be a lucky day, having made many of his successful deals on that day but did not choose it for his wedding.

Mr. Anderson was born within three miles of his present home, one of five children of Hartley and Elizabeth Rivers Anderson. He was left fatherless at the age of 10 but having a very capable and determined mother they did not develop one-sided as so many children do who are reared by one parent. He has two sisters. Sallie married Neil Skinner and lives at Thompson Station, and Martha Anne is the wife of Maynard Creswell, making their home in Franklin. A half-brother, Robert Anderson, is a farmer at Flat Creek.

He was reared on a farm and attended school in Harpeth Lick Cumberland Presbyterian Church, where his teacher was the late John Pinkerton, brother of Miss Nelle and Tom Pinkerton. His education was cut short by the death of his father for he had to make a farm hand most of the time and attended school between crops. He worked from early to late, plowing, hoeing, and grubbing, under the direction of his older brother, who was the "straw" boss with their mother ever keeping a vigilant eye on the situation, knowing that an experienced head was needed to keep things running smoothly. It was always his job to ride the old gray mare to mill, carrying the "turn" of corn or wheat, often jumping off to throw rocks at rabbits and so true was his aim that he frequently carried home one or two dangling from a string, and when he reached there made them ready for his mother to cook for supper. He also liked to hunt coons, possums, and squirrels with his neighborhood chums. He recalled one day he helped with killing hogs and late in the afternoon answered the call of the dog as he barked fast and furiously in a nearby wood. When he reached the scene, he found the dog standing excitedly over a hole by the side of an old log. He dug in and found a nest of six skunks. Not only was he looked upon with disfavor by the entire family but spent the time hating himself. The silver lining to the situation was in the fact he was not allowed to help anymore with the newly slaughtered meat.

Sam and Fannie Creswell Anderson

February 15, 1914, Mr. Anderson married Miss Fannie Creswell, daughter of William and Sarah Bullock Creswell, of Allisona, and they have two children. Annelle received her degree from State Teacher's College, Murfreesboro, and was the commercial teacher at Franklin High School before she went to Washington, D.C. where she secured a position with the F.B.I., and is pleased with her work. Herman attended Battle Ground Academy and Franklin High School and is now training to take his place with millions of others in defense of his country.

Except for the four years in the Navy and two years in St. Louis, Mo., where he carried a mail route, Mr. Anderson has made his home at Cross Keys. The house in which he lives was built by slaves before the Civil War and was four years in construction. It is of rock quarried on the place. To the original six rooms, three frame rooms have been added. In the basement besides having plenty of storage space is a shower where he can clean up before he joins the family after a hard day's work. He installed water several years ago, securing it from a spring on the hill above the house, and for three years they have enjoyed electricity, lightening the burdens of the home and farm.

Since his son entered the service Mr. Anderson has had with him Scott Reed, who has been more than his man "Friday." They milk ten cows and sell whole milk to Wilson &

Company, a cheese plant in Franklin. He runs a truck route and during the summer delivered daily around 4,500 pounds of milk, but less through winter months. He raises tobacco, corn, wheat, and pasture crops. His wife owns a steam pressure canner and sees that the family has plenty to eat throughout the year. He attributes his family's excellent health to their well-prepared, well-balanced meals.

Before he took unto himself a wife Mr. Anderson bought a Model T Ford and has never since been without an automobile and is not complaining that war conditions curtail its use, only too glad to do anything that will speed the close of the terrible conflict and return to his home, along with countless others, his soldier boy.

Mr. Anderson was for 22 years supervisor of road work in the county and many of the new roads and bridges were built during this period. He is a Democrat by inheritance and never misses going to the polls; is a member of the Masonic Lodge at Bethesda, and is on the board of trustees at Mt. Zion Methodist Church, where he and his wife have held their membership for many years. His son and daughter are members of Bethesda Methodist Church, all working toward the same goal.

Sam Anderson (far left) overseer of the road crew at Cross Keys. His son, Herman Anderson is in the back row.

Annelle Anderson

Herman P. Anderson, water fuel inventor

In looking back over his life Mr. Anderson says he and his wife have had many blessings, but the greatest joy of all is their son and daughter of whom they are justly proud. He feels that while his son will grace his country's uniform, the uniform will be graced by his wearing it, for a good son usually makes a good soldier.

WALTER ANDERSON, 1868-1958

Betty Bond and Walter Anderson

The Review-Appeal, December 12, 1940

When the state legislature convenes in January in the magnificent capitol overlooking the Cumberland River on one side and the wide-awake business section on the other, there will be men gathered from the ninety-five counties to pass and repeal laws which they deem advisable. Going for the first time as a representative in the lower house will be Walter Anderson, a dirt farmer, who was nominated in the August primary and elected without an opponent in the November general election, receiving each time a splendid vote from his friends over the county. He goes with the full confidence of the people he represents that the good of the county's affairs rests in honest hands.

    Mr. Anderson is a native of Williamson, born and reared on a grant of land that was taken up by his Scots-Irish grandfather, William Anderson, who came here when forests covered most of the land that is now under cultivation. Here his children were born and one of them, Thomas Page Anderson, married Mary Cowles and to them, 13 children were born, and Mr. Anderson falls along in the middle of the flock. Five of them still live and all stick pretty close to their native home. Chapman Anderson is Franklin's genial postmaster. Frank lives at the old homeplace, Mrs. H.D. Jefferson and Mrs. Carrick North also make their homes in Franklin, and Mr. Anderson lives seven miles south of town on the Lewisburg Road. The two-story frame house in which he lives was built in 1878 by his oldest brother, J.W. Anderson, father of Beaumont Anderson.

Longview, the Walter Anderson house on Lewisburg Pike

This house is located on top of a high hill 880 feet above sea level and bears the appropriate name of "Longview." From here can clearly be seen the WSM tower on the Nashville Highway and its revolving light flirts with the shadows by night. The home of Jimmie D. King, near Carter's Creek Road, is in full view, but a hill hides the home of Brown Kinnard, which is also on a high location. Cars can be seen going day and night on the Columbia Highway, their lights flashing down the road make an interesting sight on summer evenings. During the Civil War, the Confederates used this hill as a lookout.

Leading from the front gate is a winding road built up the steep hill and washing rains make it necessary to re-gravel often. It is a pull for either a horse or car to make the grade but the hospitality that greets a visitor more than repays for the energy expended in reaching the house. Electricity has recently been installed and running water has been enjoyed for a long time. At the north end of the house, a 4,000-gallon tank has been erected which catches all the water falling on the large roof and this constitutes the supply for the house.

Mr. Anderson says his brother was asked why he built a house on such a tall hill and his reply was, "I like fresh air." He certainly got what he was looking for, especially in the winter. Storms have often passed around the hill but only once was the house hit by one and fortunately, that did no great amount of damage.

Mr. Anderson raises grains and alfalfa for pasturage for his dairy cows. The milk is picked up at the gate by a truck and sold in Franklin. His barn and equipment meet all requirements and his cows are purebred Jerseys. He has always had a fondness for horses and rides over his farm daily a saddle mare which comes down through a direct line from his father's broodmare and they were known as "snow heel" stock due to having white heels.

He says the neighborhood has undergone many changes since he has lived on "the hill." There are only two representatives of old families in the locality that were there years ago., the Andersons and Mrs. Preston Scales, whose parents were John and Josephine Cowles Baugh, both pioneer stock. The old Lewisburg Road he has seen change from a mud puddle, that a horse could hardly travel in bad weather without miring up, to a macadamized oiled highway. The lighting system he has also seen revolutionized as well as the mode of traveling and farming.

For many years he has been road commissioner, for four years he was a member of the county court and also served on the high school board for a long time.

When a boy Mr. Anderson attended what was once known as Cowles School and one of his favorite teachers was the late J.A. McCord, who was familiar with every phase of imparting knowledge from A to Z. Later, he attended Campbell's Preparatory School. One of his favorite sports when he was growing up was hunting and he always brought home the game.

On one occasion his mother sent him to a country store for some groceries and there he saw for the first time false faces worn at Halloween. He took one back with him, put it on, and knocked at the door. When his small brother, Frank, answered the call and saw the terrible face, he gave one yell and landed in the family room with his arms about his father's neck. Mr. Anderson quickly disposed of the mask and hastened to join the others in wondering what could have frightened the little fellow. He never let the family know until long afterward what had caused the commotion. On another occasion, he caused much excitement when he tried to teach this same little brother some of the antics he saw a clown perform when he attended his first circus. After all his preparations the feat did not work out according to plans and Frank came off much the worse for wear.

He married Miss Bettie Bond, daughter of Cicero and Rachel Chrisman Bond, pioneer families of Bethesda, and of their eight children, six are living. Bess and Walter, Jr., better known as "Buddy," live at home and help run the farm. James [daughter] married Fred Kinnard, and they, with their family of three – Margaret, Anna McKay, and Walter Cannon Kinnard – are substantial citizens of Thompson Station. Mary Frances is an important member of the Roberts and McGavock force, Brownie married Mark Puryear and Tommy lives in Nashville, where he has business connections. He married Adalyn Weakley of Smyrna. They go home often but there are times when the fatted calf is specially made ready, Thanksgiving, Christmas, and Mother's Day. A day is also set aside each summer for a family reunion when his brothers and sisters and their families with Mrs. Anderson's brothers, George Bond of Nashville, and T.C. and Jim Bond, of Bethesda, with their families and other relatives, gather for a picnic dinner and a good time in general.

For thirty years, Mr. Anderson has been an elder in New Hope Presbyterian Church, was Sunday School superintendent for a long period, and now is a teacher of the Bible Class composed of both men and women. He never goes before them unprepared and spends a portion of each day reading the Bible and studying his lesson.

A man who fears God and keeps his commandments is a good one to send to Nashville to make laws under which his fellow citizens as well as himself must live.

Walter and Betty Bond Anderson, Carrick North and Mary Thomas North, Elizabeth Anderson Jefferson, and Frank Anderson

JAMES W. BOND, JR., 1906-1967

James and Leo Grigsby Bond

The Review-Appeal, May 27, 1952

James W. Bond, Jr., prominent farmer and stockman at Bethesda, in the twelfth district, says if you want business partners pick them while they are young. This he did and is training them in the right methods of agriculture and the livestock industry. These are his three sons: Jimmy, III, 15; Charley, 10; and Danny, 5. They operate under the name of James W. Bond, Jr. & Sons.

Each member of the firm has his bank account, issues checks, and keeps his personal records. At present about all the youngest does is deposit his share but keeps an eye on the business transactions as each member explains to him very carefully what it is all about. If he goes to Franklin or to the neighborhood store with his father, whom he thinks is overstaying his time, he will say, "Remember, Daddy, we've got those cows to milk when we get home. Let's go."

James and Leo Grigsby Bond and their three healthy sons live at Blue Grass Farm, consisting of 215 acres, part of an original grant of 840 acres purchased in 1809 for $2,040 by his great-great-grandfather, John Bond. The original deed, which bears the government seals, is still in the possession of the Bond family.

The present two-story frame house, of seven rooms, two halls, and two porches, has for its nucleus a log room of the original house. It was in this room James' grandfather Cicero Columbus Bond, and father J.W. Bond, were born and died. The latter, who passed away March 13 of this year., was the youngest of four children, all of whom lived to over 80 years of age except him, and he would have attained that mark had he lived until tomorrow. Not only was he born and died in this same room, but he spent a greater part of his life in it and never called any other place home. It was here in 1903 he carried his bride, Mary Steele Bond, and it was also here their children John, James W., Jr., and Mattie Elizabeth were born and reared.

John married a Pennsylvania Dutch girl and they, with their sons John and Robert, live in Lynbrook, New Jersey. The sister married John Glenn of College Grove and they, with their son John, Jr., 10, make their home in Clarksville, where John is the proprietor of Glenn's Pharmacy.

After completing his education at Bethesda High and Battle Ground Academy, James decided he wanted to follow in the footsteps of his father, who was an extensive raiser of registered Jersey cattle, beginning in 1887 and in 1947, his herd of 14 cows led the state in production.

James is 6 feet 2 inches tall and weighs 210 pounds but does not attribute his splendid physique to athletics played while in school but to early morning rising and steady work on the farm. His oldest son, not yet 16, is already 6 feet and James thinks he will be taller than he before long.

The mother died when James was 5 years old. His father took entire charge of the children, even the 3-year-old daughter. He did the cooking, canning, and housework and trained his children to not only be good students at school but splendid citizens as well. Taking the place of both parents he gave all his time to their care and raising livestock.

"Our father," James said, "always taught John and me to look after our sister. Each morning when she and I left in the old T-model Ford for school he repeated this admonition. One afternoon while en route home I ran over a calf whose feet came up through the floorboard. It took a lot of backing and going forward to get the car off the calf, which I finally did. In doing so I dragged it to the side of the road. We went on home scared to death for fear we had bought us a lame or worse still, a dead calf. We did not mention the incident at home and the next morning as we approached the scene of the accident, we were afraid to look. Much to our relief, the calf was gone and there were no signs of it having been dragged away. As far as we two were concerned the incident was a closed book, the last chapter of which we never read."

Another episode in which James figured prominently and did not reach his father's ears, took place while attending BGA in 1923. He and Robert Jennings, Jr., decided to race their old Fords to Columbia. Wallace Beasley was with James and fed the gas while Raymond Whitfield did the same for Robert. Nearly all the way they ran neck and neck, winding up in that same position. "Why we were not killed, I'll never know," he said. "And we saw to it that our parents and teachers did not hear of the race. Of course today, a stunt like this is impossible with such heavy traffic.

From the time James and Leo were students at Bethesda School, they were sweethearts. She attended State Teachers College, Murfreesboro, and taught school before they were married on June 13, 1936, after 13 years of earnest courtship.

They went to live with James' father who was a splendid cook, and with the training Leo had received from her mother, there is no wonder she is classed among Bethesda's best cooks. She did not give up her teaching and the greater part of the time has been a member of the faculty at Bethesda. This year she decided to stay home but was named a substitute teacher and has been busy much of the time at Flat Creek, Trinity, Peytonsville, Harpeth, and Bethesda. She has enjoyed this as it gives her time in between at home.

When the Thomas C. Bond farm of 505 acres was sold recently at auction, James bought 175 acres, which includes the residence of ten rooms, and half interest in 165 more acres. This gives him 555 acres for which to be responsible. He and his sons have a herd of registered Polled-Herefords, having at present more than 60, which he sells for breeding purposes, having recently shipped some to Indiana, Texas, and Florida. His registered Jersey cattle he also sells for breeders and at present milks 30 of his herd of 60. Claiming much of their attention of the father and sons is the flock of 108 Southdown sheep. In 1950 they showed some at the Tennessee State Sale, winning first place, and last year came second. This year they have an unusually large crop of lambs with which they have been most successful even if they did lose much sleep. The boys have OIC hogs, and each has his own Jersey calf. From the proceeds of these, they increase their bank accounts.

When Jimmy was small his father purchased a Polled-Hereford calf at a sale for which he paid $1,275. That was when a dollar went farther than it does today. The sum seemed fabulous to the young boy, so he asked his mother if his daddy was rich. When she answered in the negative Jimmy said, "Well, he must have more money than sense to pay that much for a bull calf."

Most of the land is in permanent pasture and as all the water on the farms originates within their bounds it keeps down the fear of disease contamination. The two older boys have saddle horses of their own, but for the present Danny rides behind his father as they make daily trips over the farms keeping a close eye on the herds and flocks. There is still the same danger as in Biblical times that thieves may break through and steal, or wild animals molest the young lambs. At any rate, the owners are always on the alert.

Jim Bond III    Charles Bond    Danny Bond

Another project on the Bond place is the flock of Plymouth Rock chickens for which Charley is responsible. He gathers the eggs, feeds the flock and when it comes time to select one for the table he decides upon the victim.

The Bonds tobacco allotment is six acres. This crop is cultivated with mules. When they have work requiring a tractor, they rent one. One of the essentials is a truck which they always keep busy. The tobacco is sold on the Franklin market and last year's crop was a splendid yield for which they received a good price.

The cream from the dairy herd is sold to the Nolensville Co-op Creamery and the skimmed milk is fed to the calves and hogs. The hogs are sold on the Nashville market. They watch the prices closely, buy feeders when the prices are low, fatten and sell them when they advance. Every corner has to be watched if a profit is to be made.

When the youngest son was born the parents decided to name him Daniel Steele, the first for Leo's grandfather, P.D. Scales, a merchant at Bethesda for 50 years, and the Steele for James' mother. The two brothers, Jimmy, who wears his father's name, and Charley, named for Leo's father, Charles F. Grigsby, went into conference. They finally confronted their parents with this statement: "The name is all right, but we are going to call him, Danny. If we have to go through life with a 'y' on the end of our names he can, too." And such he is called.

Danny has as his prized possessions a desk, a chest of drawers, and a safe, which his great-grandfather, for whom he was named, used for so many years. Another antique is a three-cornered cupboard, which has been in the Bond family for over a century and sat in the same corner in the kitchen for over 75 years. Then, from the Steele side of the house, they have a drop-leaf table and other valued pieces.

The Bonds are not only greatly interested in their home and farming activities but the community as well. James is past president of the Bethesda Community Club and for twelve years has been an elder in the Presbyterian Church. Leo is president of the Demonstration Club, a member of the Methodist Church and the Women's Society of Christian Service. Since she taught for 15 years in the Bethesda School, she feels she has had a hand in rearing the greater part of the younger generation. The two older boys are students at school and are eagerly awaiting the time when Danny can join them.

Bethesda Community Club, 1954-1955: 1st row: F. M. Houser, Mrs. Nannie Lou Hatcher Houser, J.W. Bond, Jr. (President), Leo Grigsby Bond, Lester Mosley, Gertrude Mosley, Mrs. R.R. Stevenson, Rev. Stevenson, Mrs. Walter Taylor. Standing: Herbert McCall, H.Y. Beeler, Leonard Bond, J.W. Bond, III, Nelson Jones, Mrs. Nelson Jones, Miss Cleo Grigsby, Dot Gillespie, Miss Frances Hatcher

The Bonds have a broad outlook on life and believe in working not alone for self, but for the betterment of the community. They never stand in the way of any improvement, which is for the advancement of the neighborhood, making it a better place in which to live. To know them is to admire their wholesome attitude toward each other and their community.

T.P. CRAFTON, 1873-1952

Addie Brown, T.P. Crafton, and Minnie Deason

The Review-Appeal, June 22, 1950

When Father's Day made its yearly advent Sunday in many instances the head of the house was made happy in being remembered by members of the family, either with gifts, words of appreciation, or in some other manner. Especially pleasing and gratifying was the dinner prepared by the good wife, who for the span of years has helped bear the burden of rearing the children, be they few or many.

Just at the edge of town on Carter's Creek Pike is a white cottage surrounded by trees and shrubs where lives T.P. Crafton, and with him is one of his 16 children, Inez Crafton, who sees that he has everything to make his last days happy and peaceful as it is in her power to provide.

Some of the children came, but some live as far away as Colorado and could not make the trip at this time. Anyway, at the request of the father, the yearly celebration is on Mother's Day, which is near the time of his birthday. This year, with the greater number of his children, 34 grandchildren, 7 great-grandchildren, and 2 great-great-grandchildren present, a basket dinner was spread on the lawn, and "a great time was had by all."

When Frances, next to the youngest started school at Thompson Station at the age of six the teacher, in trying to get that little scared look out of her eyes asked her about her home, playmates, etc., finally asking how many were in the family. The little girl brightened up and answered, "Pappy, Mammy, Leslie, Bob, John D., Fannie, Martha, Joe, Rosie, Buford, Ed Lee, Blythe, Inez, Mary, Ruth, Cora, me, and Alpha." There her conversation ended.

Mr. Crafton was born nearly 80 years ago in Bethesda, one of six children of John Thomas and Martha Johnson Crafton. His life has not been an easy one. Hard work on the farm kept him from securing any education and he has gone through life depending on others to do his reading and writing for him. But just try to beat him in a trade and you have another thought coming. Feeling the need for an education he made every sacrifice to keep his children in school as long as possible that they might at least secure a knowledge of the fundamentals.

As he sat in the living room of his home, one afternoon with his daughter, Inez, and a visitor, he said, "I began plowing at the age of 10, making a regular field hand from then on. Being the oldest of the family my father taught me to grub, transplant, chop corn, and do many other things before I could reach the plow handles. When I was 16, I went to work for an uncle on Flat Creek for $8 a month, board and washing. Every Saturday night I went home and at the end of the month took my wages to my parents.

"I was treated as one of the family at my uncle's and did everything his seven sons did. There was no such thing as an 8-hour workday back then. We were up each morning between 3:30 and 4 o'clock and worked until 9 or 10 o'clock at night. Many is the time we loaded hay in the field by moonlight, brought it in and put it in the loft by the same light. We were not allowed to use a lantern around hay for fear of a fire, but we used one to milk by, also feed hogs and other stock. I believe we did more work before sunup and after sundown than we did by daylight.

"Often after a hard day's work was over, we'd take our dogs, go fox hunting, and stay out until after midnight, but was up the minute my uncle gave the first call in the morning, had all the feeding and milking done by the time my aunt had breakfast on the table. We were strong and healthy and did not mind hard work, even when we followed the thrasher from before day until after dark and slept out in the open on the new straw.

"One day a mule threw me and broke my right knee, which laid me up for three months. My uncle and aunt took as good care of me as if it had been one of their sons who had been hurt. I have lived a long time and, in my way studied a lot of people. I find you reap just about what you sow, and I have tried to teach my children to do the same. Hard work does not hurt the body if a person lives right and takes care of himself.

"My grandparents at Bethesda were getting old and needed help so I went to live with them and made a crop. I had to help with the housework too, so did not get to put in as much time in the field. But first and last I seemed to make as much as well as knowing I was caring for two old people who were not able to help themselves.

"Just before my 20th birthday, I married Sallie Belle Tomlin, a neighbor girl at Bethesda. We went to keeping house in a one-room log house with a puncheon floor, paw-paw rafters, and covered with hand-hewn boards. The walls were seven logs high, and the chimney was built on the outside of the house of poplar logs lined with rock. It was so low I'd stand on the outside, lean over the chimney, and put the backlog on the fire. It was here my wife cooked on a skillet and boiled vegetables in an iron pot hanging from a crane. The first winter a heavy snow fell. When I awoke one morning, I felt something cold on my face and when I threw the cover back found it covered with a blanket of snow, which was a foot deep on the floor.

"After the birth of our third son, my wife died and if it had not been for such kind neighbors, I don't know how I could have managed. I'd take the children to the field, put them under the shade of a tree, and watch them as I plowed. Keeping one eye on them and one on the row in front of me was enough to make one cross-eyed. When the baby would begin to cry and the little fellows couldn't quiet him, I'd put him in front of me on a contraption I'd fixed on the plow handles, and he would go to sleep. Then I'd carry him back where the others would be asleep too and all would have a nice nap. This taught me to know a person can do if he half-way tries.

"Four years later I married Rosa Tennessee Tomlin, cousin of my first wife, who was the mother of the rest of my children and lived to see Alpha, the youngest, past her 9th birthday. All the older ones were married and had homes of their own and Inez had taken over the care of the younger ones. In 1936, at the age of 48, when my wife knew she was going to die, she called the children to her one by one and kissed them goodbye, and when it came time for Inez she said, "I'm leaving the children to you, honey. You'll have to be their mammy now, and I know you'll take good care of them." And she has, too. All are married now except her. She works as a nurse at Dr. Walter Pyle Hospital and takes care of me.

"Though all my children were born in Bethesda, I moved to Thompson Station several years before my wife died and rented the old Dave Crawford place where we lived for 13 years. My youngest children being girls did not keep me from having help on the farm for they went to the field with me and could do as much as the next one. They not only set tobacco slips, hoed and suckered them, but could hang the tobacco in the barn seven tiers deep to cure, then could take it down, strip, pack, and help take it to market. As soon as it was sold, I'd go to Joe Greer Nichols' store at Thompson Station to pay our grocery bill which would amount to several hundred dollars, for you know it takes a lot to feed growing children. Besides this, we always had a large garden and often I've known my wife to have as much as 900 cans of fruit and vegetables stored in the cellar. It took lots of sugar to can and feed the family, but Joe Greer never turned me down when I went to his store, and I appreciated it.

"Soon after I moved to the old Crawford place it was bought by Mr. Dudley Casey, and a better man I never knew. He lived at that time at the old Thomas Johnston place nearer town on the Columbia Highway. His heart is as big as he is, and that is saying a lot, for he is a mighty big man. Once he and his wife went to Florida on a trip, and he brought each of the children a gift, just something they didn't need but naturally wanted, such as beads, pretty purses, and other trinkets. Then when Christmas rolled around, he would bring all kinds of gimcracks to put in their stockings, and then in other packages would be things we needed, such as clothes, shoes, and food. For a long time, the little girls thought Mr. Casey was Santa Claus.

"After my wife's death, my health began to fail, and I saw I would never be able to do such hard work again as farming called for. I sold all my farming machinery, stock, crops, and other belongings. I took the money and bought this house of six rooms and two acres of land. I have enough room for a garden, a pasture, a cow, and two hogs. We raise Plymouth Rock chickens, which along with the two hogs we kill each year, furnish us with meat, also eggs, and we have some to sell. We are looking forward to soon having our own milk and butter from our young heifer."

As Mr. Crafton talked, he would often consult his daughter as to the accuracy of his statements. While Inez is busy at the hospital during the day he looks after the yard, hedge, flowers, chickens, and the four beehives, for he is most fond of honey and hot biscuits. He says only two weeks ago he bought the first flour in his life. He always stored his wheat at Morris Mill on the Duck River where it was ground and only used the last of it recently.

As Inez showed her visitor through her orderly arranged house, she was much pleased at the well-deserved praise she received, and when the kitchen was reached where the gleaming white electric stove, Frigidaire, water heater, sink, and shining pressure cooker, with other utensils, she said, "Now, wouldn't Mammy have enjoyed this?" Instead, she had to cook with wood, and often it was wet and green. But I never heard her raise her voice to speak a cross word and she always had patience with us. We never knew what it was not to obey her and

Daddy. They always had a hard time, and who wouldn't raising 16 younguns, but they were good and kind and tried to make life worthwhile for us. Now that Mammy is gone, I try to make up for all Daddy is missing in his old age."

Sunday was a happy day at the Craftons. Frances with her family live next door; Cora, her husband and son across the street; while Alpha and family reside on Columbia Avenue. Then Blythe and Buford live at Thompson Station; Ed Lee, Martha, and their families are a short distance from town on the Murfreesboro Road, and the others at Bethesda, Burwood, and Nashville, so it worked a hardship on none to come and wish their father a "Happy Father's Day." Cora, who married David Deason, a schoolmate at Thompson Station, lives in Colorado. There were present five generations and as they gathered around Mr. Crafton, who has led an uneventful, prosaic, useful life, also an honest, God-fearing one, was happy that thus far all has been well with him, and he can look the whole world in the eye for he has never harmed anyone and has ever tried to lend a helping hand.

FANNIE DANIEL AND NANNIE MAI DANIEL

Fannie Hardison, Hannah Evans, Nannie Mai Daniel (1889-1963), Lucy Smithson Daniel, Thomas A. Daniel, Tommie Lou Ware, and, Fannie Daniel (1880-1963)

The Review-Appeal, October 2, 1952

Living at Bethesda in a house erected about 150 years ago are Misses Fannie and Nannie Mai Daniel. The original part of the structure is of logs put together with wooden pegs. The rafters of cedar are also pegged together and numbered with Roman numerals.

Their parents T.A. and Lucy Smithson Daniel, married on November 29, 1877. In October of the following year, they bought this farm of 140 acres, and it was here their ten children were born and reared. As the family grew the house had to be enlarged to take care of them. It is located on a grassy knoll and to keep the rooms from being too high off the ground each one was built on a different level. As Miss Nannie Mai remarked, "We cannot change our minds without going up or down a step or two."

Lucy Smithson and Thomas A. Daniel

The house is a short distance off the first road built in that section of the county. When they see a car leaving the main road, they know they are soon to have company for this side road on which the home faces only goes a short distance past their house.

In the yard still stands the log smokehouse, probably built about the same time as the residence. In it is a salt trough hewn from a poplar log. It held on one occasion meat from 40 hogs and was not crowded then. Many people in the past years visited the place just to see this unusual smokehouse and its contents. A log cabin, the last of many composing the slave quarters, is also in the yard not so far from the residence and was used by the Daniel family as a servant house.

Fire destroyed the log barn which had a threshing floor where grain was trampled out by oxen. "The fire was the greatest excitement of my childhood," said Miss Nannie Mai. "A revenue officer was seeking law-breaking men thought to be hiding in the barn. Orders were given urging the men to come out, and when no one appeared the fire was started. I think I was more afraid of the 'revenuer', as they called him than I was of the terrible blaze."

Another barn was erected on this same spot. It was struck by lightning and also went up in flames along with farming implements, horses, mules, a supply of grain and hay, and the pet dog. When the present barn was built Mr. Daniel chose a new location.

The house has a long porch across the front. From one end to the other is a bed of blue hydrangeas, which bloom profusely from early spring to late autumn. Some of the blossoms are eight and ten inches in diameter.

Inside the house, the flooring of wide poplar shines from much polishing. Many pieces of priceless furniture, which have been in the family for years, add to the quaintness of the setting. A large spinning wheel, which has seen much service in bygone days; several dressers and tables of walnut and cherry, and a three-cornered cupboard put together with pegs are among the pieces. Then there is a Seth Thomas clock of the first model, which their father bought at a sale for 75 cents back in 1872. It was so old at that time the owners had ceased to use it. Mr. Daniel soon had it ticking away, and it ran for years without further care. Not realizing their value, he cut up three cannonball beds and a trundle bed. From part of the wood, he made a low table at which the smaller children ate. The other pieces were used for kindling. How priceless they would be today.

The house remains much as their parents left it except all but one of the large fireplaces have been closed up and gas has been installed for heat. An electric stove and Frigidaire along with running water have simplified the housework. On each side of the fireplace in their room is a window overlooking a lovely view. Under the windows, cubbies have been built into the wall where the sisters keep their Bibles, work baskets, sewing, and other articles in daily use. When the small doors are closed no one would suspect such conveniences are so close to the low rockers where the two ladies sit in their leisure hours. They do not then sit with folded hands for they are busy reading or sewing. Miss Fannie has made many beautiful quilts. Embroidered and crocheted pieces about the house bear testimony of her busy hands all down the years.

It was in this house the Daniel children enjoyed such a happy childhood. Of the ten, Charlie, Ross, Mary, and Felix have joined their parents in death. Bob, the only living brother, married Mary Hatcher and is a Franklin real estate dealer. Hannah, wife of Leon Evans, is a bookkeeper for Bennett Hardware company. Margaret is in charge of the Church of Christ Girls' Home in Nashville, and Tommie Lou is the wife of E.K. Ware, a farmer at Arno.

As there have been several sets of twins on the mother's side of the house, there was no great surprise to the parents, when they were blessed with twins, Mary and Margaret. Mary married Luther Alexander and when she died in 1929, leaving several children, Mary was taken by Granny Lucy and the aunts, Misses Fannie and Nannie Mai. Here she lived until she reached school age when she returned to her father's home. She continued to spend vacations with her aunts until she married Charles Bullington and now they return for weekends or when Charles can get away from his work to help them with odd jobs about the place. L.T., one of the sons, was taken to the Daniel home for several months when he was quite small and was suffering from whooping cough. In fact, all the Alexander children claim this as their second home.

Occupying a conspicuous place on the table in the sister's room is a picture of their nephew, First Lieutenant Donald Alexander, who was killed in the Normandy invasion while serving with the Air Corps during World War Two. Several letters were en route home at the time and were received after the news of his death reached his father. One letter was penned the night before the invasion. His father received a Bronze Medal presented posthumously for Donald's bravery above and beyond the call of duty.

All the nieces and nephews claim their Aunt Fannie is the one who made them mind, and Aunt Nannie Mai did the spoiling, made candy, and entertained them. But there is one nephew who is an ear, throat, and nose specialist in Nashville, and they go to him for any ailment. When he said on one occasion, "Now Aunt Fannie, I'm sorry but this is going to be painful and you will have to sit steady in the boat," and she replied, "That is alright, son, I trust you and I won't flinch." Being the soldier she is, she kept her word.

During the lifetime of their parents, as the Daniel children were growing up, Christmas was a great event in their lives. Mr. Daniel would take his daughter, Fannie, with him to do the shopping. She would be most particular to buy just what each one wanted, especially seeing that Nannie Mai had a Noah's ark each year, but would always return without a thing for herself, so unselfish was she.

Miss Fannie began her career as a cook when she had to stand on a box to reach the biscuit board and learn the art of sewing about the same time. The first dress she made was for Nannie Mai, sewed the sleeves in the wrong armhole and wondered why they looked so queer. Once when her mother was spending the day away from home, she made her twin sister's dresses from goods her mother had purchased for a quilt lining. She continues to make hers and her sister's dresses which are artistically designed and well fitting.

Miss Fannie claims Nannie Mai was the best child in the family while Bob was the most mischievous. One day a number of the children were prowling among their father's implements while he was at work on the barn. He became exasperated and told them to sit on a nearby log until he told them to get up. It was a hot morning, and led by Bob, they all sneaked away, except Nannie Mai. When the father completed his work, having forgotten all about the children, there he found the little girl, almost blistered, but obediently keeping her seat.

As a child, Nannie Mai was told there was gold buried under the house. She spent all her spare time digging for it and when she found a large flat rock she was sure the treasure was under it, but was unable to move the stone to satisfy her curiosity. Later, two colored men took up the quest and after digging out almost enough to make a basement, gave up in despair deciding it was only a hoax anyway.

After the others grew up and went to homes of their own, these two sisters stayed on with their parents. It was thirteen years after the death of their father before the mother, who had never been a strong person, followed. The remains were tenderly carried across the road to the family burying plot and laid to rest by the side of her husband under a large forest tree to await the resurrection. The days following would have been sad indeed but for the frequent visits of the brother, sisters, nieces, and nephews who hold these two in great reverence and have a strong attachment for the old homeplace.

Both the Daniel and Smithson families are of Scots-Irish descent. Mr. Daniel was born in Maury County, the son of Edward and Eliza Hardison Daniel, and his wife was a daughter of Charles and Mary Wilson Smithson, both of Williamson County. It was through her grandfather Smithson that Fannie Mai received her nickname. She was so chubby as a child, that her grandmother called her "Bunch." Her next younger sister, Tommie Lou, twisted it to "Punch," and such it has remained, sticking closer than her real name. She says, from a child, she has been accused of inheriting more of the Scots traits than any of the others. At the age of three, she lost a button off her dress. After seeking diligently for some time before it was found and having no pocket, she put it in her nose for safekeeping. This called for the family doctor, and much excitement prevailed among the children until Dr. Core succeeded in dislodging the offending obstacle.

Besides being the manager of the home, seeing that everything ran smoothly, Miss Fannie's sisters and brother claim she is one of the best business persons they know, and with the help of her sister, has made the farm pay when others about them have hardly broken even on bad crop years. She has continued to hold the reins and as one of her sisters remarked, "When sister Fannie speaks to this day, we all toe the mark. Even Bob steps when she says the word. She is always in the right and that is why we adore her."

Members of the Church of Christ and not being able to attend services every Sunday, they have their family worship at home after listening to a sermon over the radio. They are both devout Bible students and always try to follow the Divine injunction, "Whoso keepeth his mouth, and his tongue, keepeth his soul from trouble," and "He that followeth after righteousness and mercy, findeth life, righteousness and honor," for their "delight is in the law of the Lord, and in this law meditate day and night."

SAMUEL PERKINS EDGMON, 1871-1943

Samuel and Mary Jane Edgmon, parents of Samuel Perkins Edgmon

THE REVIEW-APPEAL, MARCH 21, 1940

Williamson County has in deed and word a man who 'lives in the house by the side of the road and is a friend to man," for out on the Lewisburg Road dwells Samuel Perkins Edgmon and his splendid wife, Mrs. Martha Jane ["Mattie"] Guffee Edgmon, who in every detail fill the desired attribution expressed by the author of the famous poem.

As he sat one evening last week by an open fire in his home he talked of other days as readily as if they happened the day previous. His 265 pounds of avoirdupois, well cared for by the 6 feet of height, fitted snugly into his spacious chair. The rain falling on the roof made music for the listeners who were well entertained for two hours by his reminiscences.

His parents, Sam and Martha Jane Guffee Edgmon, came at the close of the Civil War from Roane County in East Tennessee to this section. His father was a Confederate soldier and as most of the East Tennesseans fought on the side of the North he decided to move where those of his convictions were in the majority. The worthy couple settled near Triune, and it was there on March 21, 1871, Mr. Edgmon was born, next to the youngest of eight children, only one of whom was a girl. All of his life has been spent in this county except two years when he was very small and then he lived just over the line in Davidson at Brentwood. Over half of his life has been spent in his present abode.

As a boy, Mr. Edgmon lived with his parents on a farm near the Lewisburg Road and did all the tasks that usually befall boys. He not only learned to break horses but calves as well. He and his youngest brother were each given a calf by their father, and they broke them to harness and often hitched them to a wagon to haul wood for the family use.

On the farm of 150 acres, everything the family ate was raised and some to sell. In season Mr. Edgmon and his brothers followed the thresher from farm to farm, as was the custom in those days, eating and sleeping on the job. Some of the best rest of his life was received on freshly threshed wheat straw.

Mr. Edgmon was asked if he was a fisherman and his reply was, "I never caught but one fish in my life and that was on land. My mother sent me to Thompson Station for groceries, and while I was there a heavy rain fell, a regular gully-washer. The creek rose and I had to wait until it ran down. When it did, I found a catfish caught behind some debris. I took it home, my mother cooked it for me and I ate it before the others came in for dinner.

Home of C.K. McLemore

After his marriage at the age of 23, he bought the place of 40 acres where he now lives and spent much of his time in trading. For thirty-five years he ran a general mercantile store closing out last December. In all that time he never had an argument over a trade, nor was there ever a row by others in his store. He claims he has always had the best neighbors in the country and that people have much more good than bad in their makeup. This opinion is probably due to the fact that he has been a good neighbor, sees the best, and overlooks the frailties of humanity.

Mr. Edgmon was one of eight children, and his wife was one of a family of 12. They married 45 years ago in the home where C.K. McLemore lives with Dr. H.A. Laws officiating. They are both looking forward to celebrating their golden anniversary. They have four children, Mrs. George Cameron, who lives on the same road but nearer town; Mrs. Eaymond Pratt of Pikeville; Miss Ethel and Donald Edgmon, who make their home with their parents, the former a teacher in Harpeth School for the past 12 years and the son who works for the county highway department.

Since closing out his store, Mr. Edgmon keeps busy around the place milking, and raising hogs and chickens. He is cleaning out the store building now preparing for early hatchers. He used to be a great politician and hardly ever missed picking the winner but has voted only once in the past 15 years. He rarely leaves home now and has not been to Franklin in over a year. He likes for his neighbors and friends to drop by to discuss politics, war situations, trading, and any other interesting topic.

Mr. Edgmon has always owned six fox hounds and is a great lover of dogs in general. One day he swapped a man a case of laundry soap for a hound. He now has two fox dogs that really know how to hunt. They go out alone, chase game unaided, and bring home the spoil to lay at their master's feet. On recent occasions, they have brought in at different occasions two foxes, a groundhog, possums, and rabbits. His wife vouches for the truth of the statement.

Four years ago, Mr. Edgmon had a long illness at which time he was desperately ill for several weeks. His wife says his nurse was so pretty that he did not try to get well for fear he would lose her services.

A happy well-contented couple is these two. Mrs. Edgmon, with the expression of a Madonna, sat by quietly listening, smiling, and nodding her head when appealed to by her husband to verify a statement. In their home, they have electricity, water, radio, and other modern comforts. They both like to read, are home lovers, and have so many other tastes in common that it makes life together a genuine pleasure.

Mr. Edgmon says he had no trouble collecting before the World War but the years 1921 and '22 left him with several thousand dollars on the books that are still there. After that, he ran on a cash basis. He spent several days last week cleaning out the store burning his canceled checks, bills of lading, old statements, letters, and other papers that he had kept through the years. His ledgers he soaked in kerosene and set fire to them also for he said while he was at it he might as well make a clean job.

In bidding his guests goodbye at the close of a most pleasant evening despite the rain he said, My grandfather came to this country from Ireland. I guess I must have inherited something from him besides my complexion for I just don't worry but take things as they come. I am not a success as the world looks at it, but when I think of my wife, children, and home, I feel that I am not a failure.

MISS ADDIE EGGLESTON, 1894-1979

THE REVIEW-APPEAL, JANUARY 18, 1940

When the Williamson County Court met in regular quarterly session in April 1939, it was moved and passed that an elementary school supervisor be appointed to fill a long, much-needed service. Miss Addie Eggleston, of Bethesda, a very successful teacher of several years experience, was highly recommended by the school board, county superintendent, patrons of the schools wherein she had taught, and her principal at the time of the appointment, Charles Oliver, of the Bethesda High School. She received the unanimous vote of the court and entered at once upon her duties.

[During] the first month of her new work, Miss Eggleston visited each of the 63 elementary schools in the county and some of them twice where she found a pressing need for her services. She traveled more than 1,200 miles and burned up something over $40 worth of gas, to say nothing of other expenses. She worked and did all she could to smooth out knotty difficulties.

Most of her teaching has been in elementary schools and she knows their problems from A to Z. Her education forms a background for this type of work, and she has kept in mind from the first just how needs could best be met in improving school conditions. After completing her high school work at Bethesda, she entered State Teachers' College, Murfreesboro, where she received her B.S. degree. She spent some time at Peabody [College] and is still working on her Master's, majoring in school supervision. She is level-headed, practical, in sympathy with the profession she serves, and anxious to add her bit toward its success.

On her initial visits to the schools of the county, Miss Eggleston went heavily ladened with state bulletins and left one on each teacher's desk. This bulletin contained much valuable information of untold help to both old and new instructors. She realizes, as does everyone else, that education is based on intelligent reading, and without this art, no advancement can be made. The ways and means of reaching the desired end vary with different children, but it must be accomplished by the time the child reaches the third grade. The method used at the present time differs from that of decades ago. Just as the style of dress, mode of travel, ways of cooking, and manner of conducting public affairs have improved, so has the art of teaching. Fully realizing that there can be no advancement in other branches of learning until reading is mastered, Miss Eggleston has put forth every effort and endeavor to be of assistance to the teachers, not in a critical, but in a helpful way. She investigates to where parallel material can be obtained at the least expenditure and passes this information on to the teachers based on, she knows from experience, their limited means. She is in a position to help those most who carry their problems to her, for, capable as she is, she is no mind reader. She appreciates and courts confidence and is only happiest when she is of service. The teachers, she has found, are very receptive and this has made her work easier and more efficient.

Miss Eggleston insists that children naturally fall into the use of the spoken language, whether correct or otherwise, of the group with whom they associate. Care, patience, and eternal vigilance are necessary to instill the correct use of words which is best done while the mind is plastic and receptive.

Another phase of the work in which she is deeply interested is best methods of discipline, and teachers have been kind enough to say her suggestions have helped her greatly in solving their problems. She attends rural PTA meetings, hears their difficulties, and works with them in finding a solution.

Another project Miss Eggleston is endeavoring to promote is hot lunches. With NYA and WPA help, she hopes to put it over. She has 19 boys and girls in the elementary schools over 16 years of age who are receiving aid from NYA and are helping at school in many ways to earn their salaries and with their help, the lunches could be served if the food is forthcoming.

Another point being stressed is music and art. Through these outlets, the children can get more out of life than mere materialistic experience; can appreciate the beauty in nature and the philosophy of life rather than filling their minds with sordid ideas and sinking to their level. In no better way, she claims, can children find self-expression than that expressed in art. But in each of her projects, she harked back to "But reading is the principal thing – they must be able to read understandingly to appreciate or accomplish anything else. How can a child solve a problem in arithmetic if he can't read it intelligently?"

Miss Eggleston is well and favorably known over the county. Her father, the late E.E. Eggleston, was a prosperous farmer in the twelfth district and her mother, whose recent death was a great loss to the community, was Anna Blythe Eggleston. The union of the Eggleston and Blythe families formed as strong a combination as the county boasts. They reared eight fine boys and girls who are a great credit to the county and state. A sister, Julia Eggleston, is a member of the Bethesda High School faculty. Two of the boys live on the farm at the old home with their sisters, raise tobacco, grains, cows, hogs, and other commodities, sell milk, and are hustlers in general.

Edward Everett Eggleston House: Annie Blythe, Edmond Overton, Addie Core, Miss Lizzie Blythe, Edward Everett Eggleston, ca. 1925

They are all members of the Bethesda Presbyterian Church, working in the church and Sunday School, Miss Eggleston being a teacher in the junior department. They take active parts also in the wide-awake Bethesda Community Club, which meets once a month, and the ladies serve the best food ever at each meeting. It is one time when no man has to be persuaded to leave his own fireside to go to the school to attend these meetings. Not only is his mind improved but the inner self also. In the Bethesda PTA both sisters devote their time and energy in making it one of the strongest in the County Council.

In selecting a county school supervisor, the court made no mistake in choosing Miss Eggleston, who by disposition, talent, training, and adaptability possesses the prerequisites to make of the newly created office a great success and to meet the crying needs of the elementary teachers who find in her an answer to a long-felt necessity.

Miss Eggleston is surely living up to her motto, "He serves best who serves others."

HOWARD HOOD, SR., 1893-1974

THE REVIEW-APPEAL, AUGUST 14, 1941

And he digs from the earth all the wealth which it yields," the poet had in mind such men as Howard Hood, a prosperous, progressive farmer who lives on his farm in the Tenth District. Though he takes from the earth yet he is most careful to return the necessary chemicals so that next year's crop will be as abundant as the one just reaped. He claims that there are more thieves than one and he who takes from the earth without repaying it is worse than the fellow who runs his hand into another's pocket and takes away his cash.

Mr. Hood owns two tracts of land, one of 30 and the other of 90 acres, and besides cultivating these he has for the past several years cultivated the large farm of his neighbor, C.K. McLemore, working under the original contract, both satisfied with what the other does.

In cultivating tobacco and grains Mr. Hood uses a tractor for the greater part of the work. For his hillside crops, which it is hard to reach, he has four mules that never fail him in running out of oil or gasoline at the wrong time nor has to be taken to the shop for repair. On the other hand, they cannot accomplish as much in the same length of time and have to be rested in hot weather. He says both have their good points and drawbacks. For hauling he uses a large truck.

W.L. and Annie Howard Hood and family: Hattie, Tommy, Walter, Willie, Howard, Birdie

He was born within a half mile of where he now lives, one of seven children of Mrs. Annie Howard Hood and the late W.L. Hood, who started him on his long career as a thresher man. When he was only large enough to serve as water boy he would follow the crew from farm to farm only going home for the weekends for he liked to sleep in the new straw, listen to the men talk and eat the food prepared over an open fire by a colored cook. As he grew older, he made a regular hand and at the age of 15 he was put in charge of his father's outfit and from that time forward has not missed a year. For 23 years he threshed for the late Bob Hodge under one contract. He began spreading into territory farther from home and dropped his father's custom of feeding hands. When millet was raised abundantly in this section he often threshed as much as 40,000 bushels of wheat and millet in a season. Only last week he wound up a very successful season.

From a boy, he liked to hunt and often stayed out all night searching for coons and possums. The search often led him and his fellow hunters across streams that they had to wade and when they caught up with the dogs they could tell from the odor long before reaching them that the catch was black with a white stripe down the back. As he grew larger he led the fox hunters and the hills for miles around echoed the musical sound of his cow's horn blowing a call "to arms" and it has been told of him that when the chase was over the call he sent forth was really a refrain of "Home Sweet Home." One winter he fed 17 hounds, giving them all the bread they needed but letting them provide their own meat and water.

Hunting with him were men from far and near who liked the sport and always included Henry Matt Cotton and John Smith.

Mr. Hood's last venture in hunting is for birds, and men from Nashville like to come in season to join him, one of them being Sheffield Clark, Jr., son-in-law of Chapman Anderson. One of his nick names, "White Mule," was given to him by Ben D. Ewin, Sr. Back in the days when they hunted together, Mr. Ewin was sitting under the shade of a wheat stack awaiting the time for Mr. Hood to quit work. A blind white mule wandered by, pushed the stack over on Mr. Ewin, and continued on his way. Since then Mr. Ewin has never used any other name than "White Mule" when addressing his friend.

Another joke Mr. Hood tells on himself was on a dark night when ever so often he heard a hen give forth a squawk down about the barn. He armed himself with a pistol and flashlight to locate the thief whom he supposed was bagging his wife's chickens. He listened intently and when he was sure about where the thief was from the noise made by the hen he leveled the pistol, turned on the flashlight and there he was with his gun in his favorite milk cow's face. It was all he could do to keep his finger from pulling the trigger he was so astounded. He found the hen was in the trough where the cow was feeding and every time she was disturbed out came the squawk.

As a boy, Mr. Hood's teachers were Misses Mickie Thompson, Vashti Early, Susie Mai, and Sallie Baugh. His only whipping was given to him by Miss Vashti and that was for fighting and he says she made up for all the rest.

When he married, his only possessions were a horse and buggy and they were given to him by his father, but his wife is a good manager and they have taught their children to work. Howard Jr. is 18 and his mainstay on the farm; Reba will be a senior in Bethesda High this year, Dorothy Rose and James William attend Harpeth School, and baby Charles, 4, is the head of the family. Even the father who stands 6 feet 3 inches, weighs 190 pounds and, is 49 years of age, is putty in his hands. He says his idea of rearing a family is to give them a chance for an education and teach them the full meaning of "Do as you would be done by." Set them an example in this and he believes they will go right.

Mr. Hood is a Democrat, usually serving as clerk or receiver on election day at the Callie box; a member of the Mason Lodge at Bethesda, regular in attendance and

Howard Hood, Jr. and Frances Jefferson Hood

is now a senior deacon, member of the Farm Bureau and he and his family are members of New Hope Presbyterian Church. One of his accomplishments is playing the fiddle. He never had a lesson but his neighbors like nothing better than to hear him play all the old time tunes.

After deserting the buggy his first venture was a motorcycle which he bought from Tyler Rascoe. The next was a T-Model Ford, buying it secondhand from Fross Church and hired a Negro man to teach him how to operate it. They drove out to Felix Truett's place on the highway and as they went along the Negro explained the gears, stopping, starting, etc. When they drove into the lawn Mr. Hood took the wheel and he says if he missed a single tree he doesn't remember it. After an hour's lesson, the Negro drove him back to town and he started home alone. The car caught fire but he managed to put it out and reached his destination without further mishaps. From that time on he has owned cars of different makes and conditions but has always been able to make them run.

One of his neighbors said of him, "If Howard Hood tells you he will do anything, it is as good as done. If you are in trouble and go to him for help, if he has what you want, half, if not all of it, is yours. He is the friend who never walks by on the opposite side of the road when he sees trouble overtaking a fellowman. He goes about his business with a smile on his face, takes the changes and chances of life as a man should."

James William Hood

Charles Edward Hood

ALICE ALEXANDER IRVIN, 1855-1944

William D. and Alice Irvin

The Review-Appeal, December 2, 1937

Thanksgiving was a gala day in many homes but in none was it more thoroughly enjoyed than in that of Mrs. Alice Irvin of Bethesda, where the turkey, famous since the days of the Pilgrim Fathers, and a boiled ham, ante-dating the symbolic bird, graced her table with everything else heart – or rather appetite – could crave.

At the head of the table sat the head of the family – and she is the head, too. With her was her only sister, Mrs. Viola Johnson, and her children, Alex, Shearer, Dena, Willie, and Mary, with their families and a few close friends and relatives. She radiated sunshine as she watched those dear to her enjoy the fruits of her labor. For Mrs. Irvin has never yet taken her hand from the helm and turned the management of affairs to her children. She boiled the ham they had for dinner in the old-fashioned way – went into the back yard, had the large iron kettle placed on rocks, a fire built under it, and here cooked the ham until ready for the oven baking. And such a ham as it was! Everyone asked for a second and some for a third helping.

After dinner, the family gathered in her room where before an open fire, she sat in her usual comfortable chair near the window which looks out upon old Mount Pisgah, one of a chain of hills that extends for miles along the country in the Twelfth District. This hill in summer is a ball of green, hiding from view its ruggedness. Earlier in the fall it was a riot of colors when Mother Nature overturned her paint pot. But as she viewed it on Thanksgiving Day the trees stood in majestic grandeur with their bare arms extended heavenward as if thanking the Giver of all good gifts for past and present blessings. Here and there rose a cedar or spruce to break the bleakness of the hillside. Then, too, it adds to the beauty of this scene when snow covers the landscape.

The children talked of their childhood days, and she joined with them as they recalled incident after incident, some funny, others pathetic, while still others were of the days spent digging a living from the fields. When the time came to say goodbye, the guests reluctantly left but are looking forward to another day – only a year hence when they will again gather for just such another day and dinner.

Mrs. Irvin will celebrate her 83rd birthday in February and is far more active than her years would indicate. She was born in Lawrenceburg, a daughter of William and Antoinette Alexander, and of the six children, she and Mrs. Johnson are all that are left. At the age of seven, she came with her parents to live at Bethesda and all of her life has been devoted to the home and neighborhood activities of that section. She attended school at Mt. Carmel near Duplex under Profs. Sanford and Clay Mack and from here she went to Murfreesboro to receive her finishing touches.

Though only 10 years of age when the Civil War closed, she can tell today many interesting events of the time when word came that Grant had accepted Lee's proffered sword and the short-lived "States of the Confederacy" was a thing of the past and Confederate money was worse than useless.

From Bethesda had gone forth many sterling youths, among them William Dabney Irvin and his brother Richard. They were members of the 32nd Tennessee Regiment. Richard was killed at the Battle of Culp's Farm, near Marietta, Georgia, and that same day Billy was wounded in the left shoulder from the effects of which he suffered the rest of his life. After the war, he came back to Bethesda and not being strong enough to farm secured a position as a teacher of the local school.

One day he attended a Lodge dinner at Bethesda and saw a young girl come riding up, setting her white horse like a professional. She dismounted gracefully from a new red sidesaddle, turned the steed over to her brother, came laughing happily into the crowd of young people and was presented to the ex-Confederate soldier. He, though several years her senior, never let an opportunity pass to be with her and when she went for a ride on "Kit" he made it convenient to be near and going in the same direction and was the "Belle of Bethesda, "the name by which she was commonly known.

After their marriage, they lived for a year with his parents, Matthew Dabney Irvin, and Catherine Steele Irvin. They then moved to the place where she now resides and where their seven children were born, only two of whom, Blanche and Dabney, have followed their father into the "Land Beyond."

Home of William Dabney Irvin (1841-1915)

Mr. Irvin was a member of the Presbyterian Church and served the Bethesda congregation as elder for many years and was also a Sunday School teacher. His son, Alex, has followed in his footsteps in this, for a long time he has been an elder in the Presbyterian Church in Franklin. He often talked with his sons of the future and predicted many things especially in the political and financial world that would happen and true to his predictions, we are living today through some of the trials of which he spoke.

After Mr. Irvin's death his wife assumed the active management of the farm and is still "holding the reins" despite her 83 years. Until a few years ago she rode her horse over the farm and directed its activities, not asking or receiving advice from anyone. In fact, she made such a success as a farmer her advice is often sought by neighbors both white and colored. They find they rarely go wrong when her counsel is accepted.

The house in which Mrs. Irvin is spending the evening of a useful life was a log in its infancy but years ago was weatherboarded outside, ceiled, and papered on the inside, modernizing it but not destroying its comfort. In her room is a large fireplace, one of the original pleasures not altered, where logs are piled high and it is a pleasure to her to hear them crackle, see the flames leap high, and feel the warmth on a cold day. She has the reel and spinning wheel, which she used long ago but the loom on which she wove rag carpets she sold many years back. She was not allowed as a child to spend her time in idleness and remembers that at the age of seven, she made her father a pair of jean trousers. She knitted, sewed, and embroidered also. But the out-of-doors always had a greater fascination for her and even now she never does anything indoors if by any means she can accomplish it on the outside. She rarely leaves home and has not been to Franklin in several years, preferring to have her children come to her. Her six grandchildren are special pets, and she is looking forward eagerly to the time when her only great-grandchild, Pryor York Lillie, Jr., will be large enough to spend his summers with her.

Though Mrs. Irvin has led a very busy, useful life yet she has been one of the most attentive mothers and grandmothers, lavishing her love and attention upon them. To them, she is a jewel above price. Some of the things she has always endeavored to instill in them are the value of time, the success of perseverance, the pleasure of working, the worth of character, the power of kindness, the influence of example, the obligation of duty, the wisdom of economy, the virtues of patience and the improvement of talent.

W.D. Irvin sisters – Bett, Alice, and Ida

BROWN JEFFERSON, 1889-1984

Brown and Allein Elliott Jefferson

THE REVIEW-APPEAL, AUGUST 26, 1943

Brown Jefferson says it is not the possession of untold wealth that brings happiness – tho a little of this world's goods often helps – nor does poverty bring woe – although it is hard to continually combat the wolf at the door. There is a happy medium where a man, secure in the safety of his home, finds his family his greatest asset and most satisfactory pleasure. He was born February 9, 1889, next to the oldest in a family of six, son of the late Henry Dickinson Jefferson, who was judge of Williamson County, dying in office four months before completing his sixteenth year of service. His mother is Mrs. Elizabeth Anderson Jefferson, whose twin sister was Mrs. Willie Anderson Rucker.

   He was born at the family home on McLemore Lane, attended school at Harpeth when the building was on the same lot with Cowles' Chapel Methodist Church, his first teacher being his cousin, Miss Susie Mai Baugh, now Mrs. W. P. Scales. He says the house was small but there were plenty of pupils, some of them went in while others were going out and there was never a moment's let-up for the teacher.

For him the high spots of the day came when he and his cousin, Dr. R. S. Cowles, took their dinner pails, went down to the branch hard by, and ate their lunches away from the noise and as they munched away they built air castles, many of which he has lived to see crumble in dust at his feet. One of them has outlived a mere dream, as he always said he was going to live on a farm, for there alone he believed was true happiness. His cousin would often remark, "The farm is a mighty fine place on which to be, but I am going to be a doctor and keep people from suffering. You feed 'em and I'll cure 'em." Both boys have fulfilled these dreams for Brown has spent his life digging from the earth "all the wealth which it yields" while Bass Cowles is a doctor in Greenville, over in East Tennessee. He says one day in the midst of an air castle building he jumped up suddenly to make his speech more emphatic, lost his footing and into the water he went. His teacher sent him to her mother, who lived on a high hill just back of the school, to get dried out. His Aunt Josie did the job thoroughly, as she did everything else she undertook, but while the drying process was going on she had the small boy clothes in a clean dress belonging to a colored girl who worked for her. He never once thought of refusing to put on the garment and sat demurely by hoping and praying his Uncle John would not come in and see him.

He says the school was so close to the creek that when a heavy rain fell the water often came up into the building and then was when the fun began for they liked to paddle around and wiggle their bare feet in the mud. The school outgrew its building and another was erected some distance up the road toward Franklin on a two-acre tract purchased by the county from Dr. Cowles' father, Macon Cowles. This building later burned and the present one was erected, but he says they never had as much fun after they left the old school house which was purchased by Mr. Baugh, moved up the hill into his yard, and is now used for a storehouse.

Beaumont Anderson

Brown's father built a home on the Lewisburg Road where Robert Jordan now lives and when he was made judge in 1910 he moved his family to Franklin. Brown did not come with them for he elected to stay on the farm. He and another cousin, Beaumont Anderson, "kept batch" and ran the place. Neither liked the absence of home life so Brown married Allein Elliott, daughter of Mrs. Will Sowell, but reared by an aunt, Mrs. Fillmore Fleming. Soon afterward Beaumont and Minnie Claire Kittrell were married, and this brought to an end the bachelor quarters. Brown moved over to Allein's home with her aunt, and he says the job was an easy one for all he had was a trunk and farming equipment. He took over the management of the 125-acre farm and here their son, Fleming, was born. This firstborn, who later married Veral Harrell of Murfreesboro, is now with the Navy somewhere in the Pacific, entering service as a volunteer on last Christmas Eve, leaving his wife to keep the home fires burning at their home on Battlefield Drive.

The family moved to the old two-story frame house across the road from New Hope Presbyterian Church where they attended church and Sunday School and the family grew larger. It was here Elizabeth, now Mrs. Fred Hood; Brown, Jr., who with his wife and three-year-old son, Brown III, live on the same farm with him and is in Class 3, according to Army classification, and Frances, wife of Everett Harper were born.

H.D. Jefferson 1861-1926)

Frances Jefferson Hood

Fleming Jefferson, WWII

Desiring to have a home of their own where the growing family could enjoy more freedom, this industrious couple bought the old Fleming place near Cowles' Chapel where they both felt more at home. It was here two more children came to bless their lives, Dick, named for his grandfather and entered the Army Air Corps two days after his brother, Fleming, left for the Navy, getting his training at Madison Field, Wisconsin, while his wife and small son keep watch at home, and Allein, a nurse in an Army hospital in New Orleans, Louisiana, having received her training at Protestant Hospital, Nashville. Next in line came Frances, who now wears the name of Mrs. Howard Hood, Jr., putting in her appearance while the family lived at the Sam Fleming place.

For the first time in their lives, the family left the Lewisburg Road and went to the Sam Aaron farm near Thompson Station, where the children attended school. They found the neighbors as friendly as they had been on the Lewisburg Road, but at the end of the year they longed to return to former haunts and they "went back home" and when the next baby came to bless their home he was named for Brown's boyhood chum, Bass Cowles. He is now 19 and recently graduated with high honors from Naval Training Station, Great Lakes, Ill. The three youngest children, Virginia, Walter Lee, better known as "Buddy," and Margie, are at home with their parents who for the past ten years have lived on the Dr. J.W. Greer farm near the Columbia Highway.

Though the family has moved many times they have had very little sickness and of their twelve children and seven grandchildren only once has death crossed the threshold, and that was when Elliott, just younger than Bass, slipped away to be with the angels soon after he passed his first birthday. There has never been a broken bone or long spell of sickness in the family and the only accident is the one from which Brown is now recovering, received recently when a tractor overturned while he was riding it and left him with a back that pains him if he sits, stands, walks or lies down, and a foot that can carry little weight for the present and has caused him to lose more time from his farm work than he has since he was a barefoot boy.

Brown raises mostly small grains, corn, tobacco, and soybeans while his wife specializes in Rhode Island Red chickens which she uses on the family table, for all the children make it a habit to eat dinner at home on Sundays. When the weather permits they go out into the yard and have a picnic. Through the canning season, jars of all kinds of fruits and vegetables find their way to the larder for winter use. The children are all blondes with curly hair, and Frances, formerly at Jennette's Market, wears a fair sample of the Jefferson smile and Bass also worked before he entered the Navy.

When Brown was a very small boy he spent much time with his grandfather, Stillman Alva Jefferson, who lived to be over 90, and his grand father who was up in the 80's at the time of her death. They lived for 60 years in the house in Douglas community where his aunt, Miss Sue Jefferson, now resides. He says he could smell his grandmother's cooking long before he reached the house, and her red apples had a flavor that has never been equaled. Fried chicken, boiled ham, cake and everything else dear to the heart of a hungry boy seemed to be inexhaustible in this grandmother's pantry. His grandfather had cider in a demijohn in the cellar where it kept ice cold, and with this they ate ginger cakes. The house was always open to the grandchildren and never a "don't" was spoken. He promised himself then that if he ever had grandchildren he would try to be like these two people, and he has never forgotten this solemn vow.

His father was a surveyor and he made many trips over the county with him often carrying the chain, and on special occasions, he was allowed to carry the compass. He remembers helping survey the W. O. Carlisle place for the late Joe Parkes, also the place of J. A. Hamilton on the Lewisburg Road, and the Tom Tansil farm at Moore's Station.

Brown and his family are members of the Presbyterian Church, worshiping mostly at New Hope, where he was Sunday School superintendent for several years. He is also a Mason. He says small families miss the joys of the give-and-take system of large families, the self-denial, caring for younger or obeying older members, finding pleasure in each other's companionship and above all, the self reliance which is a great help in later years. Life after all is not what we get out of it, but what we put into it. He thinks Robert Louis Stevenson had the right idea when he said,

"To love playthings well as a child, to lead an adventurous youth, and to settle, when the time arrives, into a green and smiling age, is to be a good artist in life and deserve well of yourself and your neighbor."

HERBERT MCCALL, 1904-1984

The Herbert McCall family with niece, Frances Creswell.

THE REVIEW-APPEAL, SEPTEMBER 6, 1945

For one who has not much more than passed the halfway mark of the promised span of life of three score years and ten, to be a successful church worker, Sunday School teacher, schoolteacher, Boy Scout leader, Mason, Shriner, son, husband and father, and an active member of the Williamson County Court, Farm Bureau and Community Club is indeed a record of which anyone should be proud. This has been achieved by Herbert McCall, of Bethesda. Though the effort has prematurely added much gray to his once jet-black hair he in no way shows he has led a strenuous life. All this, and more, has he accomplished despite the fact he is an only child.

Mr. McCall's father, A.L. McCall, 70, makes his home with him. His mother, Alice Smithson McCall, responded nine years ago to the call all humanity must sooner or later answer. He has never moved in his life for the house in which he was born was also the birthplace of his grandfather, Charles Smithson, who willed it to his daughter, Alice, and at her death, it became the property of her only child and to the original 235 acreage the present owner has added 77 more.

Charles T. Smithson

Home of Herbert McCall on Comstock Road

The house was a double log structure in his grandfather's day and void of any conveniences. His parents remodeled, adding more rooms, weatherboarded the logs and now the seven-room, two-story frame house has running water and electricity, making possible such electrical conveniences as radio, Frigidaire, stove, washing machine, iron, and other smaller appliances. When times again reach normal, he expects to equip the bathroom that his parents provided in the remodeling process. A telephone keeps them in touch with their neighbors. Another endearing circumstance is that his two sons, Travis, 15, and Thomas, 12, were also born in the house that holds so many pleasant and sacred memories of four generations.

On the well-cultivated and watered farm are two tenants, housed in electrically equipped dwellings, who, raise 10 acres of tobacco, corn, and hay and milk 21 cows twice daily. The milk is picked up at the gate by a truck. On the pastures graze from 60 to 70 Hereford beef cattle. The corn raised is used to feed the stock, for cultivation is done with four good mules as well as a tractor and enough hogs are fattened to supply his and the tenants' families with meat and lard. The remainder of the acreage is in grass. The diary is equipped with running water and electricity though the milking is done by hand.

As a boy, Mr. McCall attended school at Bethesda and graduated from Battle Ground Academy in 1924, where he made a name as a splendid student, especially in Latin, and in his spare time wrote a Latin grammar which his teacher, the late Prof. Greer Peoples, insisted he have published, but he never did. His cousin, Luther McCall, said "Herbert and I both made enviable records under "Daddy" Peoples, he as a student and leader in literary activities and I as an athlete and leader in fighting when the teachers were not looking. I tell you, us McCalls were leaders!"

Soon after graduating Mr. McCall went to Atlanta, Ga., where for eight months he worked in a drug store for a cousin, John B. McCall, but never having been separated from his parents, he did not like the idea and returned to Bethesda. For ten years he taught at Ash Hill and saved practically all of the $65 he received monthly for he 'lived at home and boarded at the same place, all free of charge" as he expressed it.

It was while teaching at the one-room school he married a neighborhood girl, Mildred Creswell, daughter of E.S. and Willie Mai Culverson Creswell. Though they lived in the same community, Herbert attended school at Bethesda and Mildred at Cross Keys, yet they attended the same church and social affairs and from early childhood were sweethearts.

Lycurgus and Alice Smithson Herbert McCall

He carried his bride home to live with his parents and it is here, under the roof of his birth Mr. McCall says he hopes to end his days and from all present indications he will, and he further hopes his sons and their children will keep the family homestead intact, though he has learned by observation that it is impossible to control earthly matters after a person has passed to other scenes of action.

Mr. McCall farmed for several years after he left Ash Hill but when teachers became scarce in 1941, he was asked to take the school temporarily at Flat Creek School where he made such a splendid principal, that they would not let him resign. He has the upper four grades and his assistant, Miss Lola Glenn, the lower four, and he also has good basketball teams for boys and girls each year. Going to school in the family car with him is his younger son, Thomas, who is a bright member of the seventh grade. Travis will be a freshman at Battle Ground Academy, making his home in the dormitory, and will try to uphold the record made there by his father and one worthy of his younger brother's emulation when he becomes a

Dr. Travis McCall

student in this famous school of learning under headmaster Glen Eddington and his splendid corps of teachers.

Back in 1942, Dr. Don Peterson, of Franklin, a great lover of youth, visited Bethesda and sold the Community Club on the idea of the Boy Scout movement. With this enthusiastic body of workers as sponsor Troop 153, Boy Scouts was organized and with one accord, Mr. McCall was made Scoutmaster with a charter membership of 15 which has now grown to 26. Each year, he has taken the troop to Camp Boxwell near Kingston Springs, for a week's outing, engaging in swimming, boating, and other activities, as well as being taught the "tricks of the trade," such as pitching and caring for tents, cooking in the open, forest lore and much other worthwhile knowledge. The troop meets regularly on each Monday night at Bethesda School and matters not how pressing other duties may be the scoutmaster never fails to be present. This probably accounts for the never-failing interest shown by the wide-awake boys and even during vacation they keep up their meetings. Working with young people has become Mr. McCall's hobby and the Scout motto of "Be Prepared," has become his.

Representing the Twelfth District since 1930 in the Williamson County Court, Mr. McCall is always present, and it is the only days on which he is willing to have a substitute in his classroom, but realizing he cannot be in two places at the same time and unwilling to neglect the duty placed upon him by the voters of his district he is willing to forego the pleasure of meeting his classes on those days.

Serving as Senior Warden of Bethesda Masonic Lodge where he is a Shriner, he is also punctual in his attendance and loyal in his duties.

Mrs. McCall is also a great asset to the community as well as a splendid homebody. She is an enthusiastic chicken raiser preferring the Rhode Island Reds for her flock of around 150, using the hens for hatching but an electric brooder for raising the chicks in her well-equipped chicken house. Canning is one of her hobbies and her pantry shelves are always well filled. She is fortunate to have her parents and sister, Frances, living near her, while her other two sisters, Mrs. Mary Green, and Jessie Mai Creswell, live in Nashville. Her only brother, Murry S. Creswell, aviation metalsmith first class with the Navy for four years, recently was at home from transport duty in the Atlantic Theatre and after seventeen happy days with home folks and friends reported to Norfolk, Va.

Each Sunday morning at Bethesda Methodist Church is a regular family gathering for Mr. and Mrs. McCall, their sons, his father, her parents, and sister occupy pews, close together, and join in the worship. Mr. McCall is teacher of the Men's Bible Class, his wife a member of the "Willing Workers" and the sons are in the Young People's Class. They are all members and church workers, and the parents look forward to the day when the boys will take over responsibilities in the church activities.

During the war, the Bethesda Community Club ceased to function but now the gas is plentiful and other rationing will soon cease. The members hope to soon renew the work of the club for it was one of the neighborhood's main get-together projects and the suppers they served are among the never-to-be-forgotten events in the lives of those fortunate enough to partake of one of them. Mrs. McCall helped prepare the food and the other members of the family were there to eat it.

While the McCall family like to go to the towns 'round about them, they are always glad to get back home, for they are great lovers of the country and the vast outdoors. They agree with William Penn who once expressed it in these words:

The country life is to be preferred, for there, we see the works of God; but in cities, little else but the works of men; and the one makes a better subject for our contemplation than the other. The country is both the philosopher's garden and library, in which he reads and contemplates the power, wisdom, and goodness of God.

A. Lycurgus McCall 1876-1962 and Alice Smithson McCall 1879-1936

TENNIE LAVENDER MCCORD, 1851-1940

J.A. and Tennie McCord family: Martha, Lora, Gordon, and Talmadge on mules, Lula, Tennie Lavender McCord, and Lera

THE REVIEW-APPEAL, DATE UNKNOWN

At Bethesda in a house built over 140 years ago lives Mrs. Tennie Lavender McCord, wife of the late Professor J.A. McCord, who for 49 years was one of the county's most noted and best educators. Of their nine children, five of them are still living: Mrs. Edgar Hatcher, of

Thompson Station, Mrs. John Stephens of Hampshire, Mrs. John Brown Fly, who, like her father had made a success as a teacher and for several years has had charge of Split-Log School, Talmadge McCord of Nashville, and Gordon McCord, who with his wonderful wife, Mary Millard McCord, and five splendid sons, makes his home with his mother.

The front porch with its large square columns is shaded by four immense box trees whose ages are not determined. Originally the house was log, put together with wooden pegs, it was remodeled several years ago and weatherboarded. The roof of homemade boards had been replaced by one of more modern make.

In her room, before a bright log fire, this little woman of less than 90 pounds and with snow white hair sat one afternoon recently in her favorite rocker wearing a print dress, a spotless white apron, and a warm shoulder cape, entertained her visitors and was the life of the party.

On the mantel is a clock that for the past 65 years has not only counted the hours but the days of the month, the name of the weeks and the months of the year. Only once in all this time has it ever been to a jeweler's shop and then only received an oiling. It is a rare design and the tone as it tells the hour is a musical tinkle. It has tolled the final hours for the head of the family, four of their flock – two girls who passed away a few weeks apart, a grown son, and another, a younger mother who left behind three small sons.

This place where Mrs. McCord lives is part of a farm coming from her grandfather, Blythe Sprott, who came to this county from Virginia. He had 11 children and 75 grandchildren. He had gold and silver money hidden about the house and buried in the yard. After his death the children gathered around the table and a neighbor divided the treasures, piling an equal amount in front of each of the eleven heirs and they carried home their heritage in tin boxes.

Sprott-McCord Place in Bethesda

Her other grandfather, George Lavender, was born in Amherst County, Virginia, and both are buried near where she lives.

Her father, Anthony Lavender, died when she was a very small child, but she has vivid recollections of attending his funeral wearing an orange-colored dress and beaded shoes he had bought for her from Indian traders. He owned many slaves and these her mother disposed of to help support herself and 8 children.

Mrs. McCord remembers many incidences concerning the Civil War, especially when the

Yankees visited the family smokehouse and took all the meat of 40 hogs, much of their other food besides 7 head of horses and mules. They threatened to burn the house but were driven away by Confederates who arrived on the scene in the nick of time. She was always fond of pretty clothes and had managed to smuggle her greatly prized dresses from the house and concealed them under a box tree in the yard. She says in those lean years they secured soda by burning white corncobs, salt from the smokehouse floor, and used sweet potatoes for coffee.

James Allison McCord

While she as a girl was attending school at Duplex there came one day to enter as a student a tall, angular, barefooted boy, rather unkempt but with a very bright countenance – J.A. McCord. The pupils giggled, she was one of the leaders, but the teacher was quick to recognize in him a person of unusual ability and it was not long before he was leading the classes in algebra, rhetoric, astronomy, Physiology, and Latin. Though he had never before attended school he had studied at night when his only light was the fire. His days were spent working on the farm helping his widowed mother make a living for the family. To secure his first pair of shoes he killed a calf, tanned the hide, cut out, and made them himself. He walked barefooted to school through all kinds of weather, so determined he was to secure an education and allowed no obstacle to stop him.

In those days the school closing exercises were great events and Mr. McCord, boy though he was, wrote all the essays, speeches, and compositions used by the pupils. The girls were very much struck by his superior knowledge and studied to keep apace with him. The little blacked-headed Lavender lass thought more about her having good looks, pretty clothes, dancing, and having a good time than she did of lessons and the studious youth often helped her with algebra and other studies. After he began to teach, she was one of his favorite pupils.

At a party one night in playing a game of "snap" he chose her, but she refused to play because she thought the other boys were better dressed and answered their calls instead. They danced until day and as she was riding her horse home through the snow, the teacher rode along beside her and asked her to marry him. Her answer was that the matter was too serious to answer lightly and asked him to say no more about it until she had time to think it over. This she did and decided he was the diamond unpolished, that she loved him and several weeks later gave him her answer.

When she was 22 and he was 27, they were married and lived with his mother. She recalls that her wedding clothes were beautiful and that Mr. McCord paid $45 for his broadcloth suit for the occasion and that he wore it for a long time thereafter.

The years that followed were full of cares and rough sledding. She assumed the responsibility of the home and farm while her husband taught school all day and studied so into the night. She says through it all they were blessed with good health. In fact, for the past 50 years, she has had a doctor less than half a dozen times though she is 87 years old.

Mrs. McCord threads a needle without the aid of glasses and does the family mending. After the death of her husband in 1911 she and her son, Gordon, lived on at the home place. He later married and his family of boys have been her great pets.

To her 20 grandchildren and 4 great-grandchildren, she is known as "Ma McCord." They like nothing better than to go to her home and listen to the experiences of her girlhood. Thanksgiving and Christmas are special occasions when all the children and grandchildren are especially eager to be with this greatly loved little woman, who is always the center of attraction.

She has always kept her church affiliations with Mt. Carmel Cumberland Presbyterian Church where for years her husband was deacon and Sunday School superintendent.

Edgar and Lula McCord Hatcher family, Standing: Everette, James Ellis, Mack, Lawrence, Sara Lou, and Blythe Hatcher. J.A. and Tennie McCord children (not pictured): Lera Stephens, Lora Fly, Lula Hatcher, Gordon McCord, and Talmadge McCord

James and Tennie McCord family

ELLIE CLAYTON MORTON MILLARD, 1858-1941

Rev. M.W. and Mrs. Ellie Clayton Morton
Millard

The Review-Appeal, April 14, 1938

January 29, Mrs. M.W. Millard celebrated her 80th birthday in her cozy little home near Duplex, which she and her late husband built after he retired as minister of Bethesda and New Hope Presbyterian Churches in 1930. They had made their home since 1892 in the manse at Bethesda while he faithfully served these two flocks, teaching them by precept and example 'the way that leadeth to life eternal."

In this little village, they had become as much stabilized as the buildings and when they moved away it was as if the foundation of the village had been shaken. This picturesque couple with their kindly manner and sweet smiles were loved from the youngest to the oldest and their home was open to all who wished to enter.

At the rear of the house was a garden, which Brother Millard tended with the greatest care. It was here he planned the greater part of his sermons as he dug in the friendly earth and tenderly cared for the helpless little plants. Though a highly educated man he did not spurn the humble things of life. Not only was he a splendid English scholar, but he could also read Hebrew and Greek fluently and was highly respected as a theologian. People of all denominations admired him, and his love and sympathy were sought and freely given, especially in times of sickness and grief.

It was while attending Union Theological Seminary, then located at Hampden Sidney, Virginia, he met and married Miss Ellie Clayton Morton, of Prince Edward County, who was educated at Lynchburg Female Academy and was at the time teaching school nearby. She continued to teach until he graduated and was ordained. His first charge was at Mossy Creek, Tennessee. Being a native of this state, it was fitting that his first ministerial work should be on home soil. They went from there to Texas, and it was while stationed at Temple that the first of their eight children, John, was born. He chose to walk in the footsteps of his father and is now stationed at Greensboro, N.C. Another son, Ernest, died of pneumonia in Columbia, S.C., while attending a theological seminary. The death of this promising young man was a great blow to both parents.

While living at the manse at Bethesda, Rev. and Mrs. Millard celebrated their golden wedding, surrounded by five children, nineteen grandchildren, and a great-grandchild. It was a happy occasion, and the many useful gifts were only a slight token of the love and esteem in which they were held.

Life contained many joys and sorrows for this devoted couple which they always bore together. After his health failed, he gave over his responsibilities to a younger man, Rev. W.L. Smith, who has proven in every way his ability to fill the pulpits of both charges and other obligatory duties.

Rev. and Mrs. Millard moved to their newly erected home and there on the first day of 1937, he slipped quietly away to go on that long, long journey which knows no returning. Funeral services were in the Bethesda Presbyterian Church which he had served so long and faithfully and attended by an overflowing crowd of admiring friends, people to whom he had meant so much and his death had left them sorrowful.

Mrs. Millard has lived in this pleasant home. With her are her daughter, Mrs. Davis McCord, Mr. McCord, and their children. She still takes an active part in the church, Sunday School, and Woman's Auxiliary. She continues a close student of the Bible, which she has read through seventy times, some parts of it a hundred times and other sections eighty.

She has by no means lost interest in life. Last spring, she visited her son, John, in Greensboro, N.C., and in the autumn went to Virginia to visit both relatives of hers and her husband. Soon she contemplates going to Brunswick, Ga., to spend some time in the home of her daughter, Mrs. H.D. Cummins, and later to Memphis, where she will be with her son, Joe, Her other daughter, Mrs. Gordon McCord lives at Bethesda and she is often in her home.

Mrs. Millard's recollections of the Civil War are vivid. On one occasion she was sent by a Yankee to her kind-hearted mother for some wine saying he was sick and needed a stimulant. As she brought it to him, she saw the knowing wink that passed from one of the other, and shortly the entire group of soldiers feigned illness for a dose of the pleasing medicine.

Her father was mortally wounded at the Battle of Gettysburg and the lean years after the war were hard ones, but the healthy group of children managed to get a great deal of pleasure out of life as they struggled along. A very kind friend of her mother's put Mrs. Millard through college and she was thus able to help bear the family expenses when she began teaching.

Lives rich in good deeds, kind and wholesome advice, and devoted to the cause of the Master will live long in the memory of those with whom they came in contact.

Mrs. Millard said she had endeavored to shape her life in accordance with the clipping her mother kept pinned in her Bible:

> *"I expect to pass this way but once. If, therefore, there be any kindness I can show or any good thing I can do any fellow being, let me do it now, let me not defer or neglect it—for I shall not pass this way again."*

MARION GRIGSBY WARREN, 1913-1996

THE REVIEW-APPEAL, AUGUST 6, 1953

Among the popular Faculty members at Franklin Elementary School is Mrs. Marion Grigsby Warren, wife of Edward B. Warren, one of Franklin's most enterprising businessmen. For the past four years, she has been a first-grade teacher, giving freely of her time and talent, not only to her school duties but to any movement for the up-building of the town, county, and children's development.

In speaking of her childhood Marion remarked, "I am one of eight children of Charlie F.

and Ella Scales Grigsby, of Bethesda. I, third to the youngest, was born at the homeplace of my maternal grandparents, Pleasant D. and Mary Ratcliffe Scales. This home is located at the foot of Tollgate Hill. When I was five years old my parents moved to our present home located on the side of the high hill overlooking the village. Early in life, my father nicknamed me "Screwdriver" and Dr. Core, our family physician, dubbed me "Blue Hen's Chicken."

"I managed to outgrow these appellations but never the story my father tells on me. Soon after moving to the new home, I went through all the agonies of getting ready to attend my first wedding, that of Miss Susie Mai Baugh and W.P. Scales. I made ready for the occasion upstairs and as I started to make my descent to the first floor, I tripped on the first step and rolled to the bottom. My father heard the awful commotion and called out to know the cause. My reply was "My shoeses is slick." This remark has always lived with me. But I have ever held my own with my father because I have always had an answer for him.

"The two children, Harry and Kathryn, younger than I, were my problems. I shielded Kathryn from Harry's tormenting. He liked nothing better than mutilating our dolls or hiding them where they were difficult to locate. But our brother, Charles, Jr., even at that early age was something of a sleuth and would find them for us. This may have been the beginning of locating him in his present position with the FBI. For, like a bloodhound, he ever had his nose to the ground and was a boy able to solve any problem.

"At the age of six, I entered school at Bethesda and graduated at 15 as valedictorian of my class. "I never missed a day from the time I entered the first grade, two years of college, and eight years of teaching. It took a severe case of mumps to break this perfect attendance record.

"My elementary days passed without any great excitement but in my sophomore year of high school we had a thriller. One night we were putting on a play and just as the curtain was being drawn someone yelled, 'Fire.' The gas tank in a little shed near the school exploded and within minutes flames enveloped the building. Why, I do not know, I grabbed the sand table, used for making contour maps, and unaided carried it safely out of the building. The next day, try as I might, I could not so much as move the table an inch. I remember seeing a man walking up and down the aisle wringing his hands and repeating over and over, 'It's going to burn up.' Then I recollect someone caught him by the hand and led him to safety.

"In high school, I made a record at spelling, but arithmetic was my Waterloo. I was for several years a member of the 4-H Club, winning at the age of 12, second place in the county clothing contest. Miss Virginia Carson, Home Demonstration Agent, was my ideal and taught me many things, which have helped me so much in my afterlife.

"As my older sisters and brother, Charles, were teachers, I always declared I'd never teach. But Kathryn and I were doomed, and we followed in the footsteps of the others. After spending two years in college, where I worked my way through, I applied for a place in the county, but the board of education said there were too many Grigsbys teaching already and turned me down.

"I spent two years at home helping my mother who was boarding three teachers. Having three daughters of her own and the boarders going out with dates proved too much for my father. He never failed to ask them at breakfast what time they came home. One of the teachers, Evelyn Seay, solved the problem by naming the two large maple trees on each side of the walk "eleven" and "twelve." So, when the question was asked her, she'd reply, "I came in between eleven and twelve and got by with it. The others took it up and father was none the wiser.

"Always having an artistic turn, I planned parties for the neighborhood and surrounding communities, planning games, refreshments, decorations, painted napkins and paper table covers, and arranging flowers. I never wanted to be idle.

"After two years of staying at home, my sister, Leo, who married James Bond, Jr., was transferred from Flat Creek School to Bethesda and I was given the place she vacated. The first morning I started out in high glee driving the car for the first time and picking up 13 children along the way. Every place I stopped both mother and children were weeping and saying, "We want Miss Leo back." To myself, I said, "The Lord being my helper I'll live up to, or surpass, if possible, not only Leo's, but the teaching record made by any other member of the family." I'd grit my teeth each time the remark was made and on I'd drive. That first morning I led the group of 60 pupils, from the first through the eighth grade, in singing "Work for the Night is Coming" and I've been working every day since. Some of the pupils were older than I and trying to keep up with the reputation my sister had made I had no idle moments.

"I had some thrilling experiences at Flat Creek. I was trying to cross a swollen stream one day just after a heavy rain when my car stalled as the water came up over the seat. The children and I perched on the seat backs until Mrs. Trav Wallace came along, threw us a rope, which the boys securely tied to my car, and she pulled me out.

"The patrons worked with me in every undertaking from buying a piano to putting on a black-faced minstrel. At that time Sara Beasley was teaching with me and we conceived the idea of getting each child to contribute a rooster to add to the piano fund. I got a barrel, which was placed on the school porch and as the children came each morning the chickens were placed therein. One morning Sara was leading the devotional and I was standing back by the door with several of the larger boys. Just as we began to repeat the Lord's prayer and had finished the first sentence, Sara, from her vantage-point, saw a chicken fly out. Without raising her voice or her head she said, "O, Lord, Marion, catch the rooster." With one lunge

I was out the door and in the yard with several boys at my heels. That rooster did not have a ghost of a chance in escaping and just as the "Amen" to the prayer was being said we put him back into the barrel.

"After collecting enough roosters to finish paying for the piano, Superintendent F. J. Page gave us a day off to go to Nashville to select it. We did our selection in time to attend three shows, one of them being "Over the Rainbow." With our minstrel proceeds of $100 we started a school library. That night every seat was taken, also standing room, and those looking in from windows and doors paid full admission fee without being asked. This working together at Flat Creek sealed Sara's and my friendship, which has grown with the years and when we meet, we never cease to laugh with glee over our experiences.

"Another Flat Creek achievement of which I've always been most proud was that with Fannie Myrtle Smith. She had completed the eighth grade but had no way to go to Bethesda for her high school work. She would come to school each day and help me with my classes and in return I'd assist her with high school work. At the close of school, she went to Bethesda, passed the final examinations under Charles Oliver, and for the past ten years has been bookkeeper for Rose's Store and in all this time has only come up one cent short in her accounts. But I claim she taught me more in patience, perseverance, and overcoming obstacles than I ever did for her with her studies.

"The backing the people of the community gave me made it possible to leave feeling I have made good my vow to succeed, and I stayed four years – the length of time Leo stayed – and I left there with a lump in my throat.

"Leo was leaving Bethesda to begin her family of three sons, so I was given her place teaching the third and fourth graders. Here I again had a challenge in my sister's record, but I again matched her in four years of service and was sponsor of the junior class. During the summer I would return to Murfreesboro to continue my work on my B.S. degree at Middle Tennessee State College. I finally took a year out and graduated. I worked out part of my experiences in the cafeteria. I dried more hot silverware than I knew was in the world and prepared grapefruit galore each morning for breakfast. I was finally promoted to preside over the cash register. Even though I did not like arithmetic I never came up short.

"After receiving my degree, I went to Columbia to teach art in junior high at double my former salary. As fate would have it, I followed my brother, Charles, who resigned to accept a more lucrative place. While I was there, I went one summer to Penland, N.C. where I attended a handicraft school. Here I met people from 41 states, and the instruction I received has helped me in the art of teaching art.

"It was while in Columbia I broke my perfect attendance record when I had mumps. Seven of the twelve teachers were victims. One of them, Jane Napier, took me home with her at Napier Lake, and we mumped together in the same room.

"I was in Columbia when Pearl Harbor was bombed and so many of our boys soon left for duty. Eight of my Flat Creek boys made the supreme sacrifice."

"Again, I followed Charles. When he left Lockton School in Nashville, I went there to teach the third and fourth grades. While there, World War II closed and Edward Warren and I were married. We made our home here, but I finished out my term in Nashville. After the birth of our two precious daughters, Kay and Lyn, I began teaching the first grade at Franklin Elementary School. This was the first time I did not follow in the footsteps of a member of my family. While I was at school, my children were tenderly cared for by Miss Mary Andrews for the first two years, and the last two, by Mrs. George Cameron. They have been in good hands and these ladies took as much pains teaching and training as if they belonged to them. As Kay will enter school this fall, I hope to be transferred to the third or fourth grade to keep from coming in contact with her, making her less dependent upon me. Then, too, my college work was preparing me for the more advanced grades, though I asked for the beginners just to see if I could successfully teach them. And I believe I have.

'I am also of the opinion, 'Life begins at forty.' We've recently moved into our new home in West End, next door to Warren Funeral Home, where Ed is convenient to both his business and home. His influence over our daughters is wonderful and I'm so glad to have him near to assist in training them. During school days, they have had kindergarten training under Mrs. Copass, and dancing under Mrs. Thompson, both of which have been of great benefit."

Marion is a splendid manager. When friends are asked to eat at her table, they know a treat is in store. She and Edward are members of the Methodist Church where he is a steward, member of the choir, and Men's Club. She is past president of the Wesleyan Service Guild and is also a member of the Allied Arts Club and he of the Lion's Club. They love people and like outside contacts, but are always glad to be at home with their daughters.

To prove that Marion is a good manager when she was teaching for $55 per month, someone told her she was too extravagant with her salary. Her reply was, "I pay $35 per month on my car, $10 for upkeep and gas, $5 on my tuition debt, and that leaves me $5 for clothes, luxuries of life, and recreation. How can I have a bank account?"

When asked if she has a hobby, her reply was, "Yes, looking after my husband and daughters, cooking, sewing, teaching school, and answering the telephone."

One day she met Virginia Carson Jefferson on the street and her remark was, "I'd know those belonged to you and Ed. Their smiles and cheery greetings are just like those their parents have."

A wonderful teacher, friend, wife, mother and daughter is Marion Grigsby Warren.

RICHARD P. WADDEY, 1877-1962

THE REVIEW-APPEAL, FEBRUARY 6, 1941

Tillers of the soil probably get nearer to Mother Nature than those of any other calling. They watch closer her manifold wonders, how a small seed must be nurtured, tended carefully, studied diligently, and given every advantage in order that it may develop into the sturdy plant nature intended it to be. The same care is given fowls and animals under their supervision and for this reason boys reared on the farm, who are carefully trained to look for defects, try to correct them, and thereby raise better products, oftentimes grow up to make better fathers. This certainly has held true in the case of Richard P. Waddey, better known as plain Dick Waddey, a true dirt farmer in the twenty-first district.

He is a son of the late Tom and Polly Lowe Waddey, of Arno, where he and his brother, John, a bachelor, lived on adjoining farms. Their mother died when the baby, Dick, was two months old. The older brother was taken into the home of his grandparents, Gabriel and

Viney Lowe, and reared with the 2 sons and 7 daughters of that family, while the helpless little baby found a safe haven of rest in the arms of his aunt, Virginia Waddey Stanford, and her good spouse, Cicero Stanford, who were childless and welcomed the small bundle of humanity as a gift to them from heaven.

The father remarried and by the second union two girls were born and both are dead. At the death of his second wife, he again married and reared a family of six children, four of whom are still living, though badly scattered and rarely heard from.

Mr. Waddey was born November 29, 1874, and when he reached school age, he was reluctantly sent by his foster parents to the home of his father to enroll at Ash Hill as there was no school within walking distance of their home. He stayed seven weeks and each day the separation from his adored aunt and her husband became harder to bear like unto a millstone about his neck, and being a frail child from birth, he began to pine away and refused to be comforted.

In the school, and another member of the primer class, was an attractive girl, Maggie Stephens, who noticed his dejected air and tried to cheer him up, even to offering him choice tidbits from her lunch. Though he appreciated her kindness, yet it failed to compensate, and one weekend, he went home and refused to leave. Though his father and stepmother had been kindness itself, yet he could not endure the separation from his childhood haunts. The aunt and uncle were just as miserable over the situation and were only too happy to have him back. They entered him in Cool Springs School and took turns taking him back and forth, making the trip on horseback with the little fellow riding behind. On these trips, he learned more about life and its problems than he did from his books, for they were both true philosophers and never tired of explaining anything concerning life that puzzled the little fellow.

Later he went to Bethesda to such men as Enoch Chest, Joe Stephens, and other teachers of that day, famous both as instructors and disciplinarians. Mr. Stephens weighed close to 400 pounds and was too hefty to do much of the latter. He would neither tell his weight nor age and one day while in Franklin was tricked onto a pair of old scales by the pretense of a man claiming to be searching for a lost gold coin. All gradually left the scales and the weight secured. To say the air was blue when he found out what had been done to him is putting it mildly, schoolteacher or whatnot.

One of Mr. Waddey's feats as a boy was breaking calves to work to his slide. On one occasion he broke a pair to work well together under the yoke, but when it came to riding them, one was very docile, and the other never allowed any such familiarity. As Mr. Waddey was unhitching them one day Tom Walton, a neighbor and close companion, came by and asked to ride one of them. Mr. Waddey had already mounted the one accustomed to being ridden and readily gave his consent for his friend to mount the other. Mr. Walton found that the time elapsing between mounting and dismounting was exactly a split second.

Though Mr. Waddey weighed only 3 ½ pounds at birth and grew up to be rather a frail boy, yet he has developed into a strong middle-aged man, He contributes it mainly to the fact that he remained on the farm. He and his brother, John, are the only ones of the Waddey family who did, for the others were mainly mechanics or merchants. At the death of his foster parents, he found himself their sole heir. He still lives on this farm within two miles of his birthplace, known and respected by everyone in that locality, calling every man his friend, honest, kind-hearted, and generous never letting an opportunity pass to extend a helping hand.

Ira Waddey

July 30, 1896, he married Maggie Stephens, one of 14 children, all living, of John and Emily Giles Stephens, and the same little girl who tried so bravely at the age of six to console him when he grieved so over the separation from his foster parents. Their daughter, Emma Virginia, died in infancy; Lee married Hazel Hall of Lawrenceburg and lives in Cincinnati. Ira is a farmer at Rudderville. He married Kate Gant, a Mississippian by birth but grew up at Nolensville. They have two children, Richard Frank, who after graduating at Bethesda High School, has been engaged in farming with his father, and Kitty Margaret, one of Franklin High's most attractive and studious 1941 seniors, and both deem it a great treat to visit each week in the home of their grandparents five miles away.

Mr. Waddey raises tobacco, grains, hogs, and cattle, and Mrs. Waddey is very proud of her large flock of pure white Leghorn chickens, which is a paying proposition. Mr. Waddey began driving a T-model Ford many years ago and now has a large car of modern make. They have enjoyed trips to Cincinnati to visit Lee and his wife; to Bihalia, Miss., where they were guests in the home of her brother, A.N. Stephens; and to relatives in Wichita Falls and other cities in Texas.

Mr. Waddey's great-great-grandfather came to this county from Virginia and settled at Arno, making the trip in an oxcart, which held not only all his earthly possessions but his wife and two small children as well. He built a log house on a high hill which was many years later used for a school. John Waddey now owns this farm and R.P.'s joins it. This ancestor was a great hunter and trapper and must have been a successful one for he made enough money to pay for his farm of large acreage. His Grandfather Lowe, was a ginwright, and Grandfather Waddey, a chair and spinning wheel maker. In Mr. Waddey's home are four chairs made by his Grandfather [Benjamin Waddey] in 1866. His father was a member for three years of Starne's Regiment during the Civil War, enlisting at the age of 16, and escaped without a wound.

A good definition of Mr. Waddey is well summed up in the words of William Ellery Channing, "A friend is he who sets his heart upon us, is happy in us, and delights in us, does for us what we want, is willing and fully engaged to do all he can for us, on whom we can rely in all cases."

Richard Frank Waddey

Richard P. Waddey family (Ira C., Richard P., Maggie Stephens, and Lee S. Waddey)

LIFESTYLES OF THE PAST AND PRESENT IN BETHESDA

Interviews with Longtime Residents of Bethesda

A Project Associated with the

Tennessee 200 Bicentennial Celebration

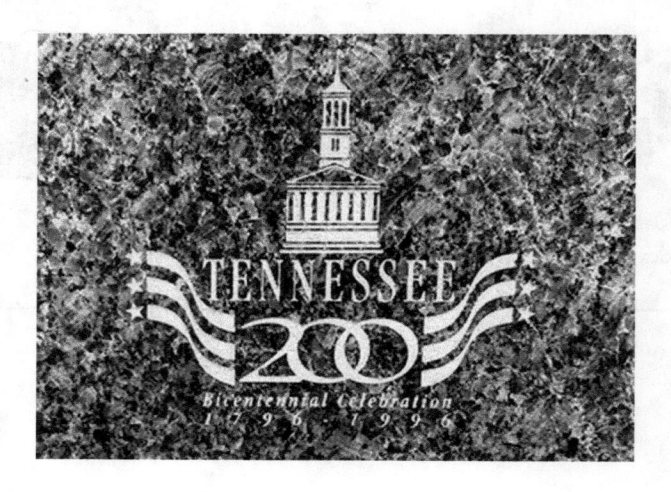

Prepared by Hugh Keedy and Jessie Bennett,

Co-directors of the Bethesda Museum

1997

INTRODUCTION

The interviews contained in this book were made during the first half of 1996 by Jessie Bennett and Hugh Keedy, co-directors of the Bethesda Museum. Part of the motivation for the interviews was to put into written form some of the reflections of those who lived in Bethesda in years past, reflections that otherwise would be gone forever with the passing of those interviewed. Since we began this project, we have had many people express their own regret at not having recorded–on tape or on paper–the recollections and stories of relatives and friends who have gone on. This collection of narratives is a small attempt to preserve some of the history and flavor of the Bethesda community, especially during the period from about 1910 to 1950. A second purpose for the book is as part of the Tennessee 200 Bicentennial celebration. A copy of the book text was included in the 100-year time capsule placed at Bethesda in July 1996.

Jessie Trice Bennett and Hugh Keedy

The material found here began with 14 taped interviews of selected persons in the community. Jessie has lived in the area all her life, is related to many of those interviewed, and had heard many of the stories before. She made the contacts and often jogged memories with "tell us about such and such that happened." Hugh is a retired college professor who felt comfortable with a tape recorder and computer. Both went to each interview.

INTRODUCTION

Following the 14 interviews is an article by Joyce Smith, a longtime local resident who has for many years written the Bethesda news column that is part of Community News, a weekly feature of the Sunday Review Appeal. Brief personal statements by Jessie and Hugh conclude the interviews. [A statement by William Thomas Byrd, Bethesda Museum Curator, was added with this publication.]

The tapes were transcribed into a word processor on a computer. The exact words of the one being interviewed were retained as much as possible, with only minor changes or omissions when there was a repetition or a change in mid-sentence. The one major deviation from that pattern was when Jessie or Hugh asked a question that was answered or responded to. In such cases, the beginning of some sentences reflects the essence of the question in the words of Jessie or Hugh and then merged into the response in the words of the one being interviewed. This method was chosen with the hope that a reader would prefer a more continuous conversational style rather than a series of questions and answers.

In some cases, the one being interviewed would mention things that related to some topic previously discussed or would return to that topic. Information about a specific topic was often collected and combined into a single narrative, rather than leaving it scattered. When this was done, there was still the effort to retain the exact words of the speaker as much as possible.

You will find words placed within brackets [ ]. Some are words that were not those of the one being interviewed but were placed there for clarity or additional information. In other places, italicized words are those of or about one of the interviewers.

Jessie Bennett and Hugh Keedy

Editor's note: The interviews were conducted by the Bethesda Museum in order to help preserve the family and cultural history of Bethesda in commemoration of the Tennessee 200 Bicentennial in 1996. When completed, they were added to a time capsule at the museum as part of the state-wide Bicentennial celebration and observance.

BILLY ALEXANDER, 1922-2008

Bill Alexander, Sr. with Jersey cow

Jessie: Just tell us something about your life as a little boy and later.

Well, I guess that would be pretty interesting, about my being born. Yes, I was born in Bethesda, at home. The story that I was told was that my daddy knew that I was fixing to come, and he went up to get Dr. Eggleston to come over. Dr. Eggleston was gone somewhere. He rode on over to Arno to Dr. Graham. Dr. Graham was gone. I may have told it wrong, because Dr. Core was probably the first one, he went to. He was gone. The word was out though, and when my daddy and the doctors all got there at the house about the same time,

I was already in the bed with my mama. Ha! I was already there with my mama, and we had three doctors. I was born in 1921 in the house that burned when lightning struck the house in 1973. [A new house was built on the same site.]

I started to school at seven years old in the building that was burned up here. My sister went to school in the old building down where the store is now. My first year was in the building that burned. I was there at the function or play of some kind that was going on the night it burned.

The Delco lighting system sitting right beside the school caught it afire. It burnt and I spent my eighth grade at school in the old Methodist church that was torn down [where the Masonic Lodge is now]. They had high school at that time in the white house on top of the hill up yonder, where Harry Grigsby did live. That was where the high school was while they were building the new school.

I grew up on the farm and we raised all we eat. I grew up through the thirties and it was a mega thing as far as money was concerned. But it was a happy time in my family. We worked hard and everybody had to do their share, but I never did go hungry. We always had plenty to eat. I did what I was supposed to and worked hard. My daddy rented a lot of land around Bethesda and with the mules and this and that and the other we farmed it. We never did go hungry through those thirties, but sometimes I think now they were better years than we have today. We didn't have the conveniences then we have now. We had to work hard, but we didn't have to have the money we have to have now.

Harry Grigsby

On the farm my mother kept chickens. She did all of the feeding and this and that and the other for the chickens, and they were her spending money. I've carried her eggs to the Bethesda store a lot of times to sell them and get sugar and other things we couldn't raise on the farm. The price of them was real cheap. I'd like to go out in the yard right now and get one of her chickens and eat it. They don't compare to what we have now; they were fed corn and were raised right there on the farm. The feed you feed them now makes a lot of difference.

We didn't have a dairy farm in the sense of what you would call a dairy farm today, but it is amazing the changes that have been made. Back in my early days we kept anywhere from eight to ten or fifteen cows and milked them. We sold some milk to the cheese plant and separated the cream from some. I remember doing that in the earlier days. I've got the old separator at home on my back porch. We used to separate the cream and feed the whey to the hogs.

We raised tobacco as the cash crop. The other crops we raised were mostly to feed the hogs and cows. Today you have to buy gasoline for your tractors; then you had to raise corn for your mules. You'd be surprised at how much corn it took to feed the mules through the year.

And this might be interesting – my daddy was a coon hunter. He loved to coon hunt. Him and Mr. Orr Chrisman did a lot of coon hunting together. He coon hunted all through the winter months caught possums, skunks, coons, and other wildlife. I still have some of the boards at home when he skinned them and hung their hides out to dry. Along in December every year a traveling man would come through buying hides. He would come back then in early spring and buy more hides. My daddy made quite a bit of spending money by selling those hides. The way I remember it, a possum hide would bring fifteen cents and a coon hide would bring a dollar and a skunk hide would bring fifteen cents. You could make quite a bit of money, which was scarce in those days, and it came in handy.

I had one sister. She went to school at Murfreesboro State Teachers College. After she finished she taught school for $55 a month up till she got married.

I've been living in Bethesda all my life, with the exception of the time I spent in the Navy during World War II. Other than that, I've been right here. I was in the Navy from 1942 to 1945. I served aboard two ships while I was in the Navy – in the South Pacific and also in the Atlantic. I came through the Panama Canal with an aircraft carrier and went into the Atlantic. Other than that, I've been right here.

I was in the Senior Citizens Center a while ago looking at the pictures of the graduates of the school. It brought back a lot of memories to me seeing the different ones that were there. They started [taking and] putting those pictures up the year after I graduated, so, my picture is not there. My year of graduation was 1940. I had a small class and there are not many left who graduated when I did. Most of them are dead – Billy Marlin – I can't remember other names right.

THE MILL

There was a mill that ground flour and corn. I believe it's in the book that my son wrote; I know part of it is. It was just the other side of my house on the creek. The property that the mill was on belonged to my granddaddy. He didn't own the mill; didn't have anything to do with it. He rented the land to the people. They used the building on it and they run the mill. After the mill quit running, Mr. Arthur Chrisman from this community, Mr. Orr Chrisman's brother, moved the mill across the road onto what is now Eugene McMillan's place. It stayed there until Hardy McMillan built a tobacco barn and tore the mill itself out. They used that old mill building for a tobacco barn for years.

The mill was run by steam, not a water wheel. They got the water out of that creek right there at my house to operate the mill with. I have one piece at home out of that old mill right now, sitting out back of the house. The mill was for wheat or corn or whatever needed to be ground. I was small but I remember it being in operation. An uncle of mine operated it some. I remember riding a horse with him, going around to different places.

RAISING TOBACCO

Tobacco raising has changed quite a bit. Today it is altogether different. Then, the people on the farm and the whole community, not just my family but the whole community, pretty well cleaned up new ground in the woods during the winter months. Working in those new grounds was quite different from working out in the open in the fields you work today. You had the roots and all that; you had to pick them up, you plowed them up, you cut them out. They cut the trees for wood and cut the brush off of it and piled the brush and logs. Then, along in the first part of March they had these brush piles, tremendous, big piles of them as long as this building and about ten feet wide. Then they set them afire and did what you call burning your plant beds. Burning the plant beds killed the weed seeds that were on them. In those days people didn't know anything about getting out in the open ground and raising tobacco. They thought you had to be in a new ground to do it. It did raise good tobacco.

You saved your own seed from the previous year. The seeds are small and come from the bloom on top of the plants. You normally clip the top of the tobacco plant off to make the leaves spread. But back in those days, you would pick out some of your best stalks of tobacco. You would let the blooms go on up and seed, and to keep your birds from getting those seeds, to save them, you would use a netting of some type and protect the seed and let it mature. You didn't cut those stalks of tobacco. It didn't take a lot of them; the average man would not need more than three or four spoonful of seed. You could buy seed, but most people saved their own.

There was no special preparation of the bed except to burn it off and get the ground broken up good. You would spread the seed around and then tromp it into the ground with your feet. I haven't heard of anybody tromping in a bed in years! After you got those seeds sowed, you just took your feet and walked on the bed.

If you didn't have money to buy canvas [to cover the beds] you used a domestic material to make your own canvases. The domestic material came in strips three feet wide, and you could buy it in bolts. Then you had to sew it together. That was always the women's job. The beds were nine feet wide, because the material to cover the beds came in three feet widths. I remember my mother; for a nine-foot tobacco bed she sewed three strips together. Still today, when you buy tobacco canvas, you find it nine feet wide.

Then you stretched the canvas over the tobacco bed to protect the young plants. If you didn't have the money to buy the domestic with, you used brush and laid the brush over the bed to protect the plants from the weather. That was done too.

There is a difference in the size of the beds. Now, most tobacco farmers sow about one teaspoon of seed to a hundred feet of bed. Their slips [young plants] grow up to be large stem slips because they have more room. Back then, you would use about five teaspoons of seed on a hundred feet of bed. From that you had a whole lot of slips. When you started setting them out you picked the best slips. Setting them by hand, you didn't have to have the large uniform slips like you have to have today with the tobacco setters. So, one bed would set out three or four acres of tobacco. When a rain would come you would pull off your largest slips. You would wait until next week when another rain came, and you would go back and pull your largest slips off again. Quite a bit of difference.

Now, your plants grew up and you went to setting your tobacco. Most of it was set in May. You pulled your slips [young plants] from the bed and you set them out. You waited for it to rain. Today, we wait for it to get dry; then you waited for it to rain. You plowed your rows with a bull tongue [plow] before you got ready to set and then waited for a rain. You would be in there barefooted. Everybody would pretty well pull off their shoes, the grown people and the children too. The young children would drop the plants fifteen inches or eighteen inches apart. The older people would come along with a peg [an object to make a hole in the ground] and put the plant in the ground by hand. I remember in my teen age years that if you would get a group of teenagers in there pegging that tobacco there would be a sort of a contest at who could go all the way across the field without straightening up. And who could get to the other end the quickest.

Of course, in those days the chemicals that you used were very scarce and they were expensive. So, the tobacco come up and got the worms and that type thing on it. You walked over the field and pulled worms off by hand and kept them off by walking through the field about once a week. There was spraying to some extent, but very seldom. Most people caught worms by hand because of the expense. I can remember going over that tobacco right now, catching those worms. We did get to using arsenic of lead in later years. Possibly though that is one reason that tobacco causes diseases now compared to what it caused back then, because of the chemicals that are put on it now.

There was also a big difference in the way it was cut. You had a tobacco knife that you started in the top of the plant and went nearly to the bottom with it, splitting the stalk. Then you cut it off and you left it split. In place of having the sawed sticks that came from the sawmills, you went to the woods, and you cut you some straight sticks. Most of them were sassafras. You had to hang that tobacco over those sticks. You hung it over that stick in place of spearing it on the stick like they do now. It was hard to handle because spearing it like they do now makes it stay on the stick easier. You had to have somebody there holding that stick while you put that tobacco over the stick, where it had been split. We carried the tobacco on the sticks from the field to the barn on a wagon, mostly. You have seen these tobacco wagons they use now, then it was something similar. You mostly just laid the sticks down on the wagon. Then, I can remember picking it up to hang it up in the barn and having it all slide down. You would have to straighten it all out.

I have the first spear at my house that I ever saw or remember. Mr. Orr Chrisman made it in his shop for my daddy out of an exhaust pipe of a Ford Model T.

Back in those days they used a lot of scaffolding out in the field. You would cut poles and put posts in the ground. Then it was cutting those poles with a crosscut saw and an ax, digging a hole by hand, and putting them in the ground, laying your bed poles down. You would build your bed and lay poles across it and hang that tobacco out in the field to let it cure for a couple of weeks. Rain would have some effect but not that bad, because the tobacco was hanging on those poles and didn't get any mud on it. It would just curve some but not that bad. That would cure it down to where it wouldn't take so much room. Tobacco barns were small, and a lot of people used the lofts and different places to hang the tobacco in their barns.

I can very well remember helping an uncle of mine, when I was 14 or 15 years old, building a scaffold. We hauled the tobacco in with a team of mules and a big slide and hung it on this scaffold. Just as we finished up, I was coming in with the last load. The mules got to acting up and I let them hang a post in that scaffold and tore the whole scaffold down. Ha! I didn't laugh at the time, and I remember his reaction mighty well!

We never had over two or three acres at any time. An acre did not yield near as much as it does today. Of course, you used no fertilizer. New ground grew a real thin tobacco in place of being a heavy, course tobacco. Fifteen hundred pounds, I know, would have been a big yield on an acre. Today, the yield might be from two thousand to three thousand pounds to an acre.

Hugh: Today we see few trees in Bethesda. Things must have been quite different then.

Yes, it was. New ground was one of the ways you cleaned the woods up, for your tobacco crop. Just about every family did it. Everybody in the whole country was doing the same thing. Right across from us here, that was called the "knolls." Why, I don't know. There were, I would say, 29 acres of beech trees there. That was pretty well all cleaned up to burn tobacco beds in. Right where William Marlin owns today, that whole side was in a beech woods. I can remember going in there and cutting, piling, and burning tobacco beds there. Finally, they were cleaned completely off, and tobacco was raised in that new ground.

MILLWOOD

Bethesda Methodist Sunday School Picnic in Millwood, 1912

Millwood [a wooded area close to the mill on Bethesda Road] brings up another thing I can tell you about my young days. My daddy raised a lot of hogs. Millwood belonged to Bett and Miss Alice Irvin who lived then where the Taylor house is now. At Millwood, the beech "masts" [a term then used to identify seeds from the hardwood trees] was good hog feed. My daddy would take some sows and turn them in there, and they would raise their pigs right out there in the woods eating those beech masts. They did a good job of raising a group of pigs; right there, just eating those masts. They make good hog feed. He would turn five or six sows over there in that Millwood and they would make their own living. After the pigs got up to pretty good size, he would go and take them home and feed them. This would be in the fall of the year.

THE FAMILY COWS

Several people in the community didn't have pastureland. Mr. Jefferson Dowell was one that comes to my mind. He lived right here next to the schoolhouse. His house has been burnt and a new one built back. He just had a small piece of ground and just about everybody had to have cows for their own milk. People that owned property like Millwoods would let people put cows on their land. I know Mr. Jim was one of them that did it; he wasn't the only one, but I don't remember the rest of them. You put a bell on your cows, you turn them loose in a place like that and then every afternoon you go over there and milk your cows and have your milk. That furnished pasture for the cows to run on. That has been a big change in the community. Everybody had heifer cows and they got their own milk and cream. You sold the surplus whether you had two cows or whether you had twenty. You sold your surplus that you didn't use yourself They had a milk truck that come through and picked it up in cans and carried it to the cheese plant, mostly to Lewisburg. They had other plants in Franklin, Murfreesboro, and Columbia.

You milked and put it in a milk can. Before they had such things as coolers, you put the morning's milk in cool water and it sat there all day, and then added your night's milk. Most of the time the milk truck would run every night. Over at my place now, I have a spring house. That spring house has a rock floor in it and crevices have been cut out of the rock that the water flows through. When I was growing up there on that farm the butter was put in buckets and was set in that cold water to keep it.

THE ICEHOUSE

I can remember they had an ice plant in Franklin. Every time there would be somebody passing to Franklin, you would have them buy a block of ice. It came in 100-pound blocks. Over at our place there was a place under the house that was dug out, a hole in the ground under the house. You hauled sawdust from the sawmill, and you took that block of ice, and you put it in the house, and covered it up with sawdust. Every meal when you wanted your iced tea or anything like that, you took an ice pick and a pan, and you went down there, and you picked off what you thought for that meal. I can remember going under that house right now with that ice pick, getting what ice we were going to have for dinner that day. Now, you didn't use it regularly because the trip to Franklin was a big one. You had to wait till you had an opportunity to be in Franklin and bring some ice home with you. A hundred pounds would last a long time, a week or longer if you covered it up well, even in the summertime.

I can't tell you very much about it, but up on the Paris Bennett place there was an ice house built up there. The people that owned the icehouse and neighbors around would dig ice in the wintertime. It was built out of sawdust in a hole in the ground. They put sawdust on the walls and on the top. It was built out of sawdust in a hole in the ground. They put sawdust on the walls and on the top of it and walled it in poles and posts stuck in the ground. That ice would keep till the middle of the summer after they dug the ice in the wintertime and put it in the icehouse.

GRANDMOTHER AND THE REFRIGERATOR

My grandmother – my mother's mother – was a widow for a long number of years and she lived in my home through my young days. When she came there to live, my daddy told her and my mother, "I will run the farm; you women run the house and we will get along good together." That was the way things went. He ran the farm, and the women ran the house. They said nothing about his farming; he said nothing about what went on at the house. Back in those days everybody kept horses and rode them around the place. Now you use pickup trucks. One spring morning my daddy and I saddled up our horses and went to the back side of the place to do some work. This was on up in 1936 or 1937. Here came a boy that lived on the place back there and told my daddy, "Mr. Allen, Miss Willie wants you to come to the house." So, we get on the horses and ride back to the house.

Clare D. Regen

As we go in there is a man there by the name of Clare Regen, and he was from Franklin. He was selling refrigerators that were called Kelvinators. They burned coal oil. Clare Regen was a salesman and he had been talking to my mother and my grandmother. My grandmother had offered to buy one and put it there for us to use. So, my daddy and me went in the house and they told him why they wanted him to come to the house; they wanted to know whether to buy that refrigerator or not. He was real interested in what he was doing on the back side of the place and his answer was, "I told you women a long time ago, if you all would run this house, I would run the farm. Come on, Billy, let's go to work." Haha. And they bought the Kelvinator. It was something that was unique at that time because there was no electricity in the country. We had our own ice and could make ice cream in it. The ice cream went in a tray just like you'd make it in your refrigerators today. At first it would be real icy, but they came up with a recipe where you used marshmallows and this, that, and the other in it and it made good ice cream. We'd been used to making ice cream by cranking.

COMMUNITY SPIRIT

That school was built by the community, mostly. That is another thing that changed, completely. The county furnished very little of the money that was spent on that school. The community pretty well did it all. Another thing that happened, the community wanted a gymnasium. And all of the community, not just one person but the whole community, went to cutting logs and carried them to the sawmill and had them sawed and built a gymnasium. Jessie, you should remember the old gymnasium.

Jessie: Yes, I played ball in it.

It's sitting right up yonder at Paris Bennett's right now. You'd recognize it. Paris tore it down and put it back up just about like it was. It's sitting there right now.

And, the community club, you had a strong community club. They met once a month and brought a covered dish supper, some of the best eatin' I ever remember. That was a big thing in the community and met once a month. [The club began in the late 30s and met up well into the 60s.] The men would come up to here and cut the school yard. The community kept it cut. I can remember very well going out in the yard and catching some of my mother's chickens, tying their legs together, walking up here to school with two chickens in each hand, and putting them in some coops. Everybody else did the same sort of thing. Mr. Tom Beasley, John Williams' daddy, would come to the school and catch those chickens and take them to Nashville and sell them. That's the way they bought things for the school. That's the type thing that the community did. It was called the Community Club.

I don't know where I would have been now if it hadn't been for this community. I built a house back and the community furnished part of the money, a pretty good part. And the neighbors also built the house back.

FIRST SCHOOL BUSES

Bethesda truck bus, 1925

I can very well remember the first school bus that was ever in Williamson County. I helped build the thing. At that time, the county required so many students [a specified number] to attend the high school to keep the high school. College Grove and Bethesda had a big rivalry between them. Some students lived between the schools at Bethesda, College Grove, Arno, and Rudderville. The men in the community, and women, too, probably, would get together and go see people at night to influence them to come to Bethesda school, so they would have enough students to keep their high school. Of course, the College Grove people did the same thing.

To make it enticing for those students to come to Bethesda, the Community Club bought a chassis for a two-ton truck. Mr. Charles Oliver was principal of the school and took a big interest in the community. He took those high school boys and built the bed on that truck. It was built out of plyboard and tin. The Community Club owned it and operated it and furnished the driver for it. They went into the communities that were outlying and picked up the students. The students had to pay something like two or two and a half dollars a month, to make expenses on the bus. They called that bus the Cracker Box. They wound up with two, and possibly three, buses and things operated that way for several years.

Charles Oliver

Bethesda's first automobile-modified bus, purchased from Franklin car dealer, Marshall Cook, a brother-in-law of Principal Charles Oliver.

One of the first school bus drivers that I recall was Franklin Bond, who started driving one of those buses before he finished high school. One of the first drivers – they had several – was named Jack Watson. He was Jim Ed Watson's father. Jack was also the janitor for the school and kept the furnace and everything running. I lived close by, and Jack would get me to come to the school and fire the furnaces and do some things. I'd come up early in the morning and I'd help Jack quite a bit. I'd rather do that than be in class.

I can remember very well, a school bus would come up the hill in the mornings, and I would be standing up there. When the driver went to shift gears, I would swing in on the back of it and ride the rest of the way to school. Haha!

MY OWN FAMILY

I met my wife while I was in the Navy, on a train going from St. Louis to California. She was going to California to visit relatives. She and I corresponded for a while, and we finally got married. She was from Kansas City and had never been on a farm before. Before we got married, I brought her here to the farm and told her what we were going to do. She was in agreement with it. We moved after we came back here from the Navy, into the little house that sits up there beside the road right now. We had no electricity in it. Our first two children were born while we lived there; we lived there seven years. We had three children; the third one was born after we moved.

I carried my grandchildren up there two years ago. That old cabin is about gone [it is unoccupied and in a grown up blackberry thicket], but I told them we lived there seven years and that the momma and daddy of two of them were born there. They were about the happiest seven years we have had. There were a lot of memories standing there with my grandchildren at that old cabin.

We cooked on a coal oil stove. There was a spring behind the house; we carried the water out of the spring with a bucket; we heated the water with a fire and a kettle out in the backyard. Therefore, I didn't have any electric bill to pay at the end of the month. The pressure was not on, then, to make money and keep the money flowing. They were happy years. We've been married 52 years when October comes. We've had a good life together. We've had some up and some downs, but who hasn't? We have had all different kinds of things happen, but Miss Eva and me have always stuck together.

Jessie: Tell us about your teeth.

I had my teeth pulled and got a new set of false teeth. They were good for about a year and then they said my mouth was changing, and this, that, and the other. I would go to him, and he would work on those teeth and three days later they would be hurting again. My daughter and son-in-law and two grandboys invited Miss Eva and me to go to Gulf Shores, Alabama, for a week on the beach. We left here in a van and drove down there. Ronnie Mack [McMurtry] pulled up close to the beach as soon as we got down there. Me and the two boys got out of the van and right on down to the beach we went. Miss Eva, Suzanne, and Ronnie Mack stayed back at the van; they weren't as fast as we were. And those teeth were hurting me terrible. I pulled them out of my mouth and handed them to one of the boys and I said, "Here boys, sail them out across that ocean just like you would a rock on Granddaddy's pond." Well, they grabbed them and sailed them! Well, they had been there before. Their daddy saw them throw something in the water, but he didn't know what they threw. And he yelled at them, "Boys, you know you're not supposed to throw that in the water." He went to pulling his belt off and the boys went to running toward him. I had to hurry up and get in between them to keep the boys from getting a whipping. Haha. And then they all got mad at me. "Here you are way down here, and you can't eat this, and you can't eat that. That dentist could have used the teeth and made you some more." Oh, they gave me a going over!

Well, that night come and time to eat. They told me they would let me pick out the place that we would eat. We drove around over the town there, and then walked around. I saw a place that looked like it would be nice to me, the most expensive place that I saw. It was a big, nice place. One of these kind that uses bought linen napkins. I went in and ordered a 16-ounce T-bone steak. Twenty-four dollars and something. Well, the rest of them ordered the same kind of steak. They didn't think I could eat that steak, but I did a good job of it. Got through and I put my chair back - they were all eating – and I said, "Whoo, I've got to go to the bathroom." I knew it was going to be a big bill 'cause that was a high-priced place that I had picked. In place of going to the bathroom, I went out and went back to the place we were staying and left the bill for my son-in law to pay. Hahahaha. Miss Eva got mad at me because I didn't pay my part of that trip.

But I'll have to tell you this to go with it. It hasn't been too long ago, just a year or two, when the telephone rang one night. It was my son-in-law. He said, "I just had to call you. I was thinking about you. Something happened and I just had to call you and tell you about it." I said, "Why, what happened, Ronnie Mack?" He said, "I am at the Depot, that restaurant down there, and some friends of mine came by here to eat and we were going to the boat show. I got up and went to the bathroom and when I got back, they were gone, and the bill was laying on the table. And I thought about you!"

Hugh: What words of wisdom would you have for people 100 years from now?

Treat thy neighbor as thyself.

FRANKLIN BOND, 1924-2007

Jessie: "Baney" was our school bus driver and still is, for how many years?
This will be 50 years. Half a century, so I ought to quit on them.

MY HOMEPLACE

I was actually born in Maury County. My mother went visiting and I happened to be born at her sister's house. My parents were living in Bethesda at the time in the old Steele place.

I still live in the old Steele home. Originally my great-great-granddaddy got this land as a land grant. It was really the Steele home then. They had so many children that they built a big home. It has been in the family ever since. It was put up for sale and my granddaddy bought it. I don't know what year they bought it, but the house was built before the Civil War. I have lived there all my life, 68 years. This is home to me.

With the home, I have 170 acres. At one time, we used to row crop, but it got to where you didn't make any money on it. So, we went into the cattle business. We have been in the cattle business ever since and have done very well. I don't row crop anymore – just fool with cattle.

When I was young, we raised most of our food. We milked cows for approximately 30 years. My mother got to where she couldn't milk, and my daddy got to where he couldn't get them up. We just finally quit and went to beef cattle. We had a good garden and raised corn and wheat. As the years go by, we have slacked off of things like that. We still have our own garden. We used to milk cows and sell milk and we had chickens and sold eggs.

William C. and Cora Steele Bond family

I went to school for twelve years at the Bethesda school. When I first started to school, we didn't have buses so most people either rode a pony or horse. I rode a pony for years, four or five, and finally got me a bicycle and then rode a bicycle back and forth to school until we started operating these buses in 1945. They didn't have buses then. When they finally decided to operate the PTA buses, Mr. Lane drove one of them and I drove as a substitute some.

I grew up here in Bethesda and stayed. After graduation from school, I started driving this school bus and have been on it ever since, except for the two years in the service. We married in 1951. I went into the service in 1952 and came out in 1954. I stayed six months in California for basic training and went to Alaska for 18 months, my wife and I liked Anchorage fine, but it wasn't modern like it is today. The weather was pretty cool. We have a daughter who was born there; she is Jane Bond Giles now.

I attended Bethesda Presbyterian church and used to go down there every morning to start a fire in the church. The only thing we had then was old wood stoves. I've been doing that off and on all my life. I have been in the church since I was 12 years old. I was accepted by Christ then, and when I was about 21, they elected me an officer in the church. I am an elder in the Bethesda Presbyterian Church and also write the minutes and keep a record of what happens in the church - keep a session book of it.

I remember Brother W. L. Smith, our preacher at the Presbyterian church in the early forties.

Jessie: I was about ten or twelve years old.

He had a little shocking thing that you would hold. Eight or ten people would each one hold that shocking machine, and it would shock us all the way around.

Jessie: He had a little wire and a little box; the electricity would go through each one. We thought it was exciting when it went through our hands.

Some people could take more than the rest of us. Jim Eggleston could take more than you could, Jessie.

Jessie: He carried around in his pocket a little miniature black dog and white dog that were mounted on small magnets. He used the magnets to make the dogs move and do tricks for the kids.

Hugh: I remember having a set of those myself as a kid; I haven't thought of them in years.

Jessie: He had a little trailer behind his rumble seat car, and he would go around the community to pick up everybody for Sunday school. He lived in Bethesda and was the full time [driver]. Back then they did visiting when anybody was sick. I remember him coming up to mamma's and sitting with the sick, or he would carry them to the doctor.

He had two churches, the Bethesda church and the New Hope church. They paid him a pretty good salary, we thought, at that time. I was trying to think what we did pay him; probably two or three thousand dollars a year each. That was a pretty good salary at that time. We furnished a house to live in Bethesda, right across from the old Dr. Core place. [It was torn down in about 1954 and a new preacher residence was built for the church on the same site.] Cliff McKay came here and said he would stay with us two or three years if we would tear the old house down and build a new modern house. He said in the long run it would help in getting a new preacher. But, from then on prices have risen and we have had only one preacher, Mr. Ralston, stay here for a while. At present to have a pastor live here like we used to would cost us about $30,000 a year, I guess.

WORKING IN THE BETHESDA STORE

As a boy, I didn't have too much responsibility. I helped cut the wood and get the wood in for the fireplaces and wood stove. I used to work at the grocery store at Bethesda. When I worked down there for four or five years for Mr. Ira Waddey I was general flunky for everything. That's where I got a little extra income. At that time people came in with orders. We just had to take the paper and fill out the order. We didn't have typewriters or adding machines and stuff like that. We added it on a piece of paper, how much groceries and stuff they bought.

They went to Nashville on Tuesday and Friday to get stock for the store. At that time stuff was rationed to the Bethesda store [during World War II]. I used to help unload the truck when it came in at night from Nashville. A lot of sugar was rationed, I very well remember at this time. People would come in and bust the sacks and take five pounds and carry it to the car. You never know where the sugar all went until you got ready to count up the groceries at night. A man or woman might say, "I got five or ten pounds of sugar." They would charge her for it. People were honest those days more than they are now.

We had gas pumps. Gas was 18 cents a gallon and was rationed. We had gas ration stamps. You might get five gallons for a stamp or ten gallons for a stamp. You had to purchase those stamps every month from the ration board in Franklin. Most farmers got most of the gas they wanted to operate with. Farmers didn't have many tractors in that day; most of them used horses or mules. Of course, tractors have taken over and they have done away with the mules. [The Ford 8N tractors were produced right after the war, and many are still in use.]

When stock came in from Nashville there were always eight or ten men there to help unload. They set things in the stockroom and then as they were needed it was put on the shelf. There were no bulk items then. We sold a lot of dairy, horse, and mule feed in hundred-pound sacks. At the time I was working in the store, people in the community didn't have refrigerators. Very few had electricity.

I used to go into Franklin and buy 2000 pounds of ice in 300-pound blocks and bring them back to Bethesda. People would come and get ice for their weekend. We kept it in what we called an icehouse, with sawdust in it to keep the ice from melting. It was right by the store and was well insulated.

BETHESDA SCHOOL

At school, we had what we called regular stalls to keep our ponies in. Each person had their own stall. We had to build a stall and have it ready for the pony to be left there. We would leave him all day and go get him and come home that afternoon. I never did take any feed for him; they just had to do without until we got back home. It was the same way with water. Some of them may have given their pony water, but there wasn't any running water down where the stables were.

For the water we got to drink, we used to go to a well out there that was pumped with a pump. The water would come through a metal pipe that had holes bored in it. The pipe was horizontal and about ten or twelve feet long. About 10 or 15 could drink at one time. Someone would pump and the pressure would push the water out. We used to make our own paper cups, too. They didn't have plastic cups then. The water that you didn't drink would go down into a concrete trough and out on the yard on the ground. We had plenty of water at that time. The pump was located on the west side of Bethesda school, as you went in the west door.

When the school burned the smaller children had to go to churches. We had to finish up at the Methodist church, where the lodge is now. We stayed in the Sunday school rooms until we got the new school building. The high school went down on the Bethesda Road, in a house across from Walter Taylor's. That was the school at one time until they got the new school building.

I remember when the school burned. I wasn't there. I was at home. It was caused by a Delco system that caught fire that night. There was a program at school the evening before. The school was heated at that time with a coal furnace. That had radiators in each room. Somebody would go up there each morning at four o'clock and start up a fire. The janitor would get it pretty warm. It wasn't like today. No air conditioning at all.

THE BETHESDA BUSES

There were two buses. One covered Flat Creek and one covered around Peytonsville. You had to pay to ride. I don't know how much but it was probably very little.

Jessie: I think I have heard a dollar a month.

They were made like a cracker box, a box built on a regular truck chassis. The county started operating their buses in 1945 and I started driving in 1946. I stayed with it until 1952, went to the army and stayed two years, and came back and started back driving. So, with my army time and my bus time I have 50 years at the end of this year.

At that time, we had very small buses, but now we have big All-American buses, all carrying 84 passengers. The old buses didn't haul but 36. The roads have been changed here. All roads used to be dirt; all are now highways. People have migrated and come in here, and it just takes bigger schools. I drove a route in Bethesda 47 years, and then left there and went to Oakview because I already had a route there. I've been down there two or three years.

On a typical driving day, I usually leave home at 6:45 a.m. and get back at 8:15. It takes about an hour and fifteen minutes to run my route. Then I am free 'til that afternoon until 2:30. I go back and carry students home and come back to my home. In between times, I do odd jobs on the farm. I drove for the Bethesda School Dragon team for a long time. When they closed the Bethesda high school down and went to Page, another driver and I rotated in taking field trips. I'm still driving field trips and basketball trips at night now. About the longest trip is to Carthage, Lawrenceburg, and Pulaski at the present time. I never did overnight trips.

BUS DISCIPLINE

Discipline problems are worse now than they used to be. Most mothers and fathers are working, and they don't discipline children like they did back in 1946 or 1956 or 1960. I can't remember many problems I've had. I got the name of being a mean driver and strict, but in the long run they appreciate it. My bus rules: I don't let them write or draw on the windows or let them eat on the bus. I try to make them sit down and stay in their seats. No scuffling or fighting at all is allowed on the bus. If they start, I put them on the front seat and make them ride for a week. I do my own discipline because I find it is better than carrying them to the principal. If a problem arises, I just stop the bus in the road and say, "Ok, you boys will have to come to the front seat and ride for a week." Most children don't like to ride on the front seat.

On the team's bus trips, I would have approximately 15 girls and 15 boys, the cheerleaders, and girls' coach, and the boys' coach. Most times the principal went with us as it was required at that time for the principal to go. We have been out many a night and come in at one o'clock with ice on the ground or snow on the ground. We often got caught out but we were very fortunate; we never had a wreck. On the way back most times we would stop, if we were going south, at Stan's restaurant over at Spring Hill

Jessie: That was a treat.

That was a treat for the children because they didn't get to go like they do now. They were very well-behaved on the trips. I had no problems with the boys and girls at all. [With the coaches and principal there, they had to be.] And they respected the driver, too. It is a little bit different today, but they don't give me any trouble today. Most times the girls' coach and the boys' coach at Page go along, and they make them behave.

What are the biggest changes you have seen at Bethesda?

As I remember, there are two or three big changes. The schools have really changed, gotten larger. Also, the roads have been really improved. The roads in the wintertime got awful bad around Bethesda. And there are a lot of new people moving into building new homes. Anywhere they can get the ground they will build.

Years ago I used to go up to your place [Hugh's]. I used to go to the Cross Keys store, open a gate there, go in and through a lot, down through a valley, across a creek down there, and around a pretty good size hill above your home, and on over into the hollow. Today the roads have been changed and you have a nice road in there. [It was paved in 1996.]

TOBACCO RAISING

G.W. Creswell at Cross Keys

I used to raise tobacco where you live, in front of your house, down in the bottom. I set tobacco there many times. That was the old Trice place. There was no pond there then. We were swapping work with Roy Creswell and Noble Chunn and Marvin Bond, and myself. We all swapped work. Each one had to have help to have the tobacco pulled and set. One man can't do it. I never did use the setting peg much; I came along when they had tobacco setters. At one time we had what was called a hand type, but we only used it about two or three years until we bought a regular tobacco setter. Two men would ride the setter and set one row at a time.

As I remember, we set on the left side of the Trice house, and we set on the right too, beside the road. On the left, across the little creek there was a little open territory of about a half-acre or an acre. [Where Jack Webster lives now.] Three months after we set it out, we had to cut it and put it in the barn. We used to hang tobacco in the barn there. There were at least four levels of poles to hang the tobacco on. We had spears and speared it on a stick – about five or six-foot sticks – and hung the sticks up on the cross poles after they had set in the field for about a week. There was a tobacco bed up there. Every farmer had his own tobacco bed. If we ran short of plants, we would share with each other to get each man's tobacco set. They used to burn the beds off each year, but they got to where they quit burning it and used chemicals to kill the weeds. They work the ground up after they put the chemical on, sow the seeds, and put a canvas over it to make it grow fast.

Hugh: that is really rocky soil there.

Well, it really produces. I can't understand how Creswell had his garden. He would really grow stuff, and nothing in it but sandrock. Little, bitty rock. Those rock in the ground, I think, will sweat and make moisture in the ground. You'll never get all the rocks out. The more you plow it the more they will come up.

Sum up what you would recommend as a philosophy of life.

Well, I've had a good life. Been good and healthy. I think it all lays at being a good Christian person working with people.

Jessie: You are one of two persons I have never heard say anything bad about a person, even though you may disagree at times.

I won't drive for too many more years.

Franklin, Margaret Vantrease, Jane Bond (Giles)

LEO GRIGSBY BOND, 1905-1997

CHILDHOOD IN BETHESDA

I was born in the old Sprott home down where Dwight Lynch lives now. My mother and father went there to live when they first married. It was what was called the old Blythe Sprott home and we lived there. I've heard my mother say I was just three months old when we moved from there to Bethesda. We lived in Bethesda in a house very much like the one I'm living in now. It was across the road from where the Watson's lived. The old home place was up on the hill where Charley and Carol live now, in back of the store. The home place is gone now.

At our home we had a water system where you run the water through a filter and then under the ground. It was rainwater. It was good soft water. It was really good to wash with. Then we had a spring, too. We had a bathroom, but we didn't have water in the bathroom. My mother wouldn't let us use the system water because she was afraid. She'd make us go to the spring and bring her water in the bucket and use it in the bathtub to take a bath. We didn't do that but once or twice a week. It was too much trouble.

My grandfather, P.D. Scales, my mother's father, ran the country store in Bethesda. In fact, he ran that store for fifty years. The reason for us moving there – my father stopped farming and went in business with my grandfather. He worked in the store, and he also was the assistant mail carrier from Bethesda. We had a post office at Bethesda then. He helped with carrying the mail and he also helped in the store.

Pleasant D. Scales 1839-1917 F. and S. 24th Tennessee Infantry CSA

Bethesda Post Office and P.D. Scales Store

When I was still living at home, we had three teachers that were boarding with us. They all came from town where they had grown up with bathrooms. It was quite different when they had to go outside. In the outhouse, you had to use the Sears Roebuck catalog. They had a lot of fun doing that. The last time I talked to one of them, Evins Seed, a minister's daughter, she said that was the happiest time in her life, those three years she taught at Bethesda. I don't know how my mother stood up under those boarders. They'd come in every night with a date. Every one of them had dates. One of the girls loved to eat sardines. They'd go to the kitchen and open sardines and eat them, even way up in the night. I don't know why my mother didn't run them off. I couldn't stand that. My mother kept boarders for several years. We enjoyed them. My mother died when she was 78 and my father was 81.

My brother, Charles, is the one that I took care of when he was just small. He always laughed and said I carried him around on my hip. I was holding him one day and I had him up on the foot of the bed. My mother was putting down the carpet on the floor and he kept jumping and carrying on. I dropped him on the floor, and he stuck a tack in his heel. He said that was the reason he was so foolish.

We had a good orchard down in the bottom. We had lots of apples. My mother would dry apples and can apples and make apple preserves. We had peaches also. We canned peaches and made peach preserves. My mother made the best watermelon rind pickles. When I married and went to live with my husband, they had peaches galore. I've never seen so many peach trees. We had to can every one of those peaches! I had a friend that would come and help me can I don't know how many hundreds of cans of peaches for Christmas presents. We'd can that many. I remember giving them to my brother Charles and his wife.

We had good gravel roads, but we didn't have too many bridges. For a long time, we had a footlog to go across the creek so you could go up to my house. I've heard my mother talk about her going across the footlog. One of the girls who was with her fell off into the creek and my mother jumped in and got her out. That was back when my mother was young.

We had a garage at Bethesda. Lester Mosley's father ran the garage. We had a broom factory. Mr. Henry Chrisman ran the broom factory, down on the creek close to where the storekeeper [John Buida] lives now. He had a little factory where he made brooms. It was actually a shop. Mr. Henry Chrisman's brother made the brooms in Memphis, and he was just working kinda under him, I believe.

CHURCHES DURING MY CHILDHOOD

Now, the Presbyterian church was on one side of our home, and the Methodist parsonage was over across the road on the other side of us. We went to church two Sundays at the Presbyterian church and two at the Methodist. I wish we still did that. In the church, the men and the women didn't sit together. The men sat on one side and the women sat on the other. They were in the same room in the sanctuary, but there was a rod down across the seats. The women sat on the left-hand side and the men were on the right-hand side. The men and women had Sunday school classes in different places too.

The choir was up in the corner. I remember my aunt, Miss Marion Scales, my mother's sister, played the organ. We sang so many of those old songs, "I Need Thee Every Hour," "Bless Be the Tie that Binds" and "Will There Be Any Stars in My Crown?" and all those old songs.

We had the catechism, and I think that would be a good thing if the catechism were taught now. They would learn more about the Bible. I know that later I taught catechism when we built a new church, and several of the girls I taught the catechism to said they were so glad I had made them learn it and said that had helped them more than anything. I remember getting the Bible storybook at church and memorizing the catechism, and I think it's really good. We had a minister not too long ago who was going to write another catechism. He borrowed two or three from me. I know the Presbyterians taught the catechism as much as Methodists, if not more. They taught what was called the Shorter catechism.

CHILDHOOD MEMORIES OF CHRISTMAS

We see a lot of deer here in our part of the country now, but the first deer that I remember ever seeing in Bethesda was on a Christmas eve. You know where I live now – there was a man that was living there, Will Sprott. There was a deer that came by on Christmas Eve and he shot it in the leg. They put it in their barn over there across from where the Cunninghams live [where Peter and Marilyn Hawkins lived before] all during Christmas. I remember us spending the day at our grandfather's and grandmother's; we always went there on the second day of Christmas and spent the day. We all went down to see the deer and all the children around went to see the deer. We had the best time going to see that deer. And, of course, the children thought that was one of Santa Claus's deer. It must have been because nobody knew where that deer came from. But it died.

At home at Christmas, we always hung our stockings up and had them filled. We had more fun just looking in the stockings on Christmas morning. We usually got a roll of candy and a roll of nuts. My daddy always got a box of oranges at Christmas time. Of course, we always had fruit and candy. We usually got a doll. I remember I got a little safe one Christmas. You know, my grandfather ran the store, so we got a good many toys.

One Christmas we went to my grandfather's house to spend Christmas Eve. They had a Christmas tree in the parlor. We decorated the tree with popcorn and little candles with little clips on them. You had to be awful careful because the candles might set things to fire. My aunt – she had taught school in Louisiana – used to bring lots of that Spanish moss, and she'd put some of that Spanish moss on the Christmas tree. The next morning, we all got up early. They had a fire in the fireplace and had candles on the Christmas tree. What hurt me so was the man and his wife that cooked for them, Linnie and Joe. Instead of letting them come in there in the living room where we were they looked through the window and watched us take our presents off the tree. That was a nice Christmas, but they didn't get to take part in it.

SCHOOL DAYS AT BETHESDA

I went to school there at the school building at Bethesda. I never went to school at a one-teacher school. Bethesda was a three-teacher school. We had the upper grades downstairs, and the smaller children went upstairs. There was a high school teacher who taught high school. Then there was a room on that side that was the fifth, sixth, seventh, and eighth grades. The seventh and eighth were taught together. Then upstairs there was the first, second, third, and fourth.

I never could understand why they let the little children go up the stairs. Some of them would hang out of the window, almost. But I remember so well that my husband's father, Mr. Jim Bond, when we first started to school, came and put planks across the windows. They were great big high windows and he put planks across so we wouldn't fall out the windows, which helped an awful lot.

My aunt, my mother's sister, was my first schoolteacher. She taught first, second, and third grade. She was one of the best teachers I ever went to. She was the mother of Shearer Irvin, who lives in Franklin right now. I used some of her ideas in teaching all through my teaching years. She was very modern in her teaching. Often times I would go home with her and spend the night. She lived up on the hill in the old home where Charlie and Carol live. I mean it wasn't the home they live in, but the old home that was up there. That's where she lived.

My aunt, my first-grade teacher upstairs, also taught some of the high school subjects downstairs. She taught English. I know there were so many of the older ones that said, "I did appreciate what she taught me in English because she was a good English teacher."

I'll have to tell you a story about Jessie's daddy. He was in the class and one day my aunt was teaching them adjectives. Maybe I shouldn't say all this, but she asked him what an adjective was and to give an illustration. He looked out the window and said, "Here comes a nigger with a red dress on." At least he knew what an adjective was.

Marvin "Mack" Clendenen

One teacher I went to, my seventh and eighth-grade teacher, would have spelling so that you stood up and spelled every day. If you stood up for a week without missing the words, why, she'd give you a nickel pencil. That was Miss Alice Paulette; she was a really good teacher. I'd put her up against any English teacher that I had when I was in college. She was just real good.

One of the nicest things I remember when I was going to school at Bethesda – we had a long porch on one of the rooms. Mr. Mack Clendenen – I imagine some of you may remember him over at College Grove where he was a teacher. We'd get in a line and run down the porch and jump into his arms. He'd jump us off the porch.

The teachers would get out and play with us. We had a good time like that. They'd play ball. They played softball and we had a goal, and we'd play pitching the goal, basketball, and things of that kind. We played a lot of different games. We played drop the handkerchief and "King, king can I go?" That's when two would run around and hit somebody's hand and then you'd go all the way around.

I remember when I was riding horseback and going to school, and the creeks would freeze over. One day my daddy had to go down to the creek and break the ice on the creek before the horse could go across. I was wet up to my knees. I had to stop and get dry before I got to school.

COLLEGE

I went through twelve years of school at Bethesda. Then I went to the normal school in Murfreesboro. Now it's MTSU [Middle Tennessee State University]. I went there, and my first year I had to take three subjects because Bethesda wasn't an accredited high school. I had to make at least a B on those in order to get my high school work accredited. Well, English and history were alright but when it came to that math, I had to take geometry three different times. If it hadn't been for a student teacher, I never would have made it. I finally passed geometry.

I had to take the state exam to get a teacher's certificate. You talk about something, when you take the state exam it covers every subject in grammar school. It took two days and you had to go to Nashville. Then, of course, I went back two years later and got a lifetime teaching certificate.

From then on, I was kind of stubborn, I guess. I decided I was going to take what classes I wanted to, rather than taking things that I didn't think would do me any special good. So, I've been to five or six different colleges. I probably have enough hours to get a B.S., but I just took what I wanted to.

I went to Peabody where I registered, and for six weeks I took three subjects. That cost me around a hundred dollars. I wish I had brought the papers [with me today that] I have from when I went there. Then I went to Trevecca College several different summers and took things that I really wanted to take. I took extension courses from the University of Tennessee. I took one under Nell Williams, who was our supervisor.

TEACHING CAREER

All together our family taught for 206 years. Then the second generation has taught 103 years the last counting I had. I taught 37 and the three years I was at Tennessee Tech made 40 years.

When I first started teaching, I was nineteen. I started teaching at Simmons Hill, five miles from Bethesda across Pull Tight Hill. I rode horseback every day. It was a pretty good road across Pull Tight. When I went over Pull Tight I'd have to wear a veil around my nose just to keep from freezing. We didn't have any holidays, but I'd spend the night over there at Simmons Hill with some of the families. We didn't have snow days. We went every day. We didn't miss a day. I finally started going to Simmons Hill in the buggy, and this Crafton girl that comes here to church now, Elbert Crafton, rode with me. I'd always pick up somebody and let them ride with me over there.

That was one of the best places I ever taught. They were the nicest people to me at Simmons Hill. That's where my grandfather came from. His mother was a Wilson, and the old Wilson home is still over there. His mother was a relative of [President] Woodrow Wilson. Their grandparents were some kind of parents to Woodrow Wilson. Woodrow Wilson's father was a Presbyterian minister and I've heard my father and mother tell about one of my ancestors going to Presbytery with Woodrow Wilson's father. He became intoxicated and they put him out of the Presbytery before they were done. But I think they made him go back into the Presbytery.

I taught over at Simmons Hill for five years. Of course, the people knew my background over there because I was related to the Wilsons. I always enjoyed teaching over there. I taught all the grades – it was a one-room school. I had thirteen pupils. We would have a devotional in the morning. We'd always sing and have the Bible reading and have a prayer. Then we'd start out with the beginners and the older children. I'd assign an older child maybe to help some of the beginners. We'd just help each other. That was the way we did things. If we were studying about peninsulas or islands, well, we'd go down to the creek and we'd make us an island and we'd make us a peninsula. We studied like that. We'd go outside when it was warm weather and have some of our lessons. They always enjoyed that.

We had a recitation bench. For the beginners, I'd put words on the board and let them pronounce the words that went with their book. Of course, they always had their book and tablets and pencils. They'd sit down in their seats and do the writing. A recitation bench was just a long bench that they all sat on. I'd stand up in front of them and maybe use the board in front and let them pronounce the words on the board. I'd talk to them and then let them come up and stand by me and read. Sometimes they stayed in their desks, and I let them read there.

Sometimes we'd have spelling bees. We'd divide up in the room and have two captains and then give out words. When you'd miss a word, you'd have to sit down. The side that could stand up the longest won.

The old ones, they'd be ready to be married when they were 19 or 20. I had two or three that ran off and got married while I was teaching there.

The school at Simmons Hill had a pot-bellied stove that sat in the middle of the room. The students or I fed it. They had plenty of wood. We had a great big pot and sometimes we cooked white beans on top of the stove, or we'd make soup.

When I went from teaching at Simmons Hill to Flat Creek, Flat Creek used coal a lot. That was how I punished one of the boys that was in school with me. One day when I had a new buggy and was going to school at Flat Creek, I picked up this boy. He had a great long old knife and he thought he'd use it. He cut the top of that buggy. He was too big and strong for me to use a whip on him. That's what I should have done. But I kept him in after school and talked to him. While I was keeping him in, he was using that knife to whittle off a piece of wood. I told him, "I'm gonna take my buggy whip and I'm gonna make you pick up every bit of that coal and put it in the coal bin." The next morning, he was there. And I stood out there over him with that buggy whip and I made him take every piece of that coal and throw it in the bin. From then on, he was a pretty good kind of fella. I taught his daughter here at Bethesda and she was unusually nice.

Flat Creek School

I'll tell you who else I taught that I enjoyed so much – the children from the Baptist Children's Home. That's who I loved to teach. The Baptist Children's home was out on the Nashville Highway, and I taught them when I was at Thompson Station. I had sixteen of them in my room at one time. And you talk about pitiful, those children had sad backgrounds. They could tell you the most pitiful stories. I just loved every one of them. If they'd see my husband coming to pick me up from school, they had to jump up and run out there and get in the car with him. I couldn't hold them. They were something else now, I tell you.

When the parents would come to see them, they'd tell me to be sure and not let them go off with any of the parents. They sometimes wouldn't pay any attention to them. They just didn't care. One of the funniest things two of them did was once when I went back to get somebody's coat and didn't see that all of them didn't get on the bus. That night when I got home, why, a lady down on the highway called me and said that she found two of my children in her house. Instead of getting on the bus, they slipped out and had run across and gone to this lady's house, slipped in, and got on the floor. She worked in the store at Thompson's Station, and she knew who they were. We had to call them at the Children's Home to come get those children. They'd try anything. Just to keep from coming to school, a whole bunch of them jumped off the bus one day when they got to school. The principal and some men ran those children until after dinner time until they caught them all.

MARRIED LIFE

James and Leo Bond

My husband and I started to school the same day. He and his brother sat together. Herbert McCall and his friend, Howard Hargrove, sat behind us. My aunt believed in mixing them up. She didn't put all the girls on one side. We sat two in a seat and so my husband and his brother sat in front of us. His brother was my boyfriend then. I think my first Valentine came from Herbert McCall, who was my other boyfriend. I still have the box of candy he gave out. Just a little green box of candy that he gave me for Valentine's Day.

After that, we were to have Epworth League on Sunday night, and I started going with my husband then. I remember the first date I ever had. It was at the Presbyterian church, and he came out and asked me for a date. I said, "Well, I'll have to go ask my Daddy." So, I went over and asked my Daddy if I could have a date. He said, "Well, I guess so." We went together for thirteen years until we married. We started out pretty young. We had to have a chaperone at first. On our first date, I think we went riding and went through Lover's Lane, which is Byrd Lane. That's where we went every Sunday night. He had a T-model Ford. The chaperone was a cousin of ours. I remember so well that she had never driven a car. But we put her off in the front and she drove the car; we sat on the back seat.

I'll tell you another place we went for entertainment. We had moonlight picnics, and we'd go up on the hill where my son Charley Bond lives. There's a cave up there, and back then people went in the cave. We'd go in the cave at night. I know my Daddy said, "Going in a cave in the night?" I said, "Well, good gracious, it's just as light in there." We'd take lanterns and all and go down in that cave. It's a wonder we hadn't gotten killed. Some people could go in that cave and come out down here at the Charlie Trice place. It went all the way under. Some of them had been through all the way clear down on the Duplex Road. That's what I've been told. I have some pictures made down in the cave. I should have brought them today. They don't go in the cave anymore. I think dead animals have been thrown in it.

We had good gravel roads, but we didn't have too many bridges. The cars would just ford the creeks we got stuck in the creek several times. One time my husband was taking me home and we went in a creek when it was too high. It just washed us on. We got out of the car and waded out. It washed his car on down the creek. We had to fasten the car on the footlog that night and come back the next morning. It ruined the motor and he had to do a lot of work on the car.

Cicero Bond, 1814-1886, and James W. Bond 1872-1952

We didn't have a honeymoon. James had a dairy, and he couldn't get off very much. We went over to Nolensville and got married at the parsonage over there. Brother Parker had been our preacher and he and Mrs. Parker, and Betty Ruth her daughter were our only attendants. I still hear from Betty Ruth. We married there at the parsonage and then we went on to – I can't ever remember the name of that place. We just spent one night and then came home the next day and started out cooking and working.

Before I got married, I was living at home. When we married, we went to the Bond's. We lived with my husband's father up there. We lived there with him for seventeen years. His wife died when his children were just real small, and he had lived there all by himself. So I lived there for seventeen years. That wasn't pleasant. I kept on teaching. I tell you don't ever live in a house with in-laws. He was sick and that was another main thing. We couldn't get him to stay in the hospital or a nursing home. He just cut up so until finally he got on dope; that was just worse and more of it.

After he died, we lived there until my husband died. My husband promised me if we ever had the house to ourselves, he'd have it reworked. And he did. He had it reworked from one end to the other. The house was in very good condition because Mr. Bond had kept it up. It was in good condition. Part of it was log. One of the rooms was log, and it had been added to. It was in real good condition and is now.

We didn't have electricity up there until '42, because the people that lived next to us wouldn't have poles come up on their place. So, we couldn't get electricity until '42. We had a terrible time. We used Aladdin lamps. We had a refrigerator. I guess it was the only one that you run by kerosene. You'd have to light it at night. We had a kerosene stove, and we had a kerosene refrigerator. We gave it to Mr. Roy. I think it's still down there in the garage if I'm not mistaken. It really ought to be in the museum. The refrigerator made ice at night. My mother had a kerosene stove and so did we. Like I said, it was 1942 before we got electricity.

We also had a shower. My husband put up a great big tank at the back of the house and fastened [piped] it down to a sink that we had in our kitchen. He fastened it on some way so that he could have a shower out on the back. The water was pumped up in there some way. I don't know how it got in, maybe he caught it off the top of the house. My husband would get up behind the house and take a shower. One day Mrs. Alamen came around the house. I don't know which ran the fastest. One went one way, and one went the other. She laughed about that as long as she lived. I kept telling them they needed to put a curtain around that shower, but they didn't think anybody would come up in that hollow.

We didn't have a bathroom until after we got electricity. We put in a bathroom. That's one of the first things we did, put us in a bathroom. One downstairs and one upstairs. There are two in that house now. I believe the outhouse was a two-holer. I kinda think it was, it was out there toward the barn. In the outhouse, you had to use the Sears Roebuck catalog. I don't know whether there's still one out there at the back or not. It seems to me I remember seeing one back behind the hen house. There was a hen house back there and my middle son raised chickens. He had charge of the chickens. I never did do any milking or anything at the barn. I didn't even raise chickens. My son did that.

I continued to teach, and I taught practically all that year. Then I stayed out a year or two before I went back. I had my three sons over five years, so I'd go back and teach. I taught in between. My mother kept our sons while I was teaching. They all married. They said, "We saw enough teaching with you." They didn't want to teach. My oldest one finished at the University of Tennessee. I never did get any of them to teach, but one year when I got one of them [to teach]. He taught one year, but he's the county agent now in Morristown. The other two finished at Austin Peay in Clarksville, both of them. They went in the dairy business.

My husband died while the youngest one was still in college. That's the reason he came back home. I think he wanted to be a veterinarian. That's really what we wanted him to do. He felt like he ought to come back home and help with the farm.

LATER LIFE

After my husband passed away, I left home and went to Tennessee Tech as a housemother there. That counted on my teacher retirement. I already had thirty-seven years teacher retirement. The three years I stayed at Tennessee Tech made me forty years of teacher retirement.

At Tennessee Tech I had to help the students. We had students that came in from, I think, eleven different countries. I would have to call them in and help them on their subjects. One of the Chinese girls got there the same time I did. I had to help her on English practically every night. They had to be in then by ten o'clock. We had some restrictions when I was there! They still needed restrictions, I tell you that.

When I was at the colleges, I took classes every day with the students. At Tennessee Tech I took public speaking, and I took Bible and different things. And then I went to Tusculum College, which was a Presbyterian college. I stayed five years there and went to school every day. If you didn't have too many students, they asked that you attend school. So, I went to school every day and enjoyed it. I took public speaking and Bible. We had a Bible teacher that lived there on the campus. She taught Bible and different classes, and I took Bible under her. It was interesting.

In all, I was in teaching 45 years, but I didn't get any teacher retirement off Tusculum. It was a Presbyterian school, but they had a Catholic president a good part of the time. He was the best one that they had. We had Catholic services every Saturday night there for several years. We'd go to the Catholic services, and I always enjoyed it. Most of the girls from Tusculum college were Catholics. They came from New York, New Jersey, Pennsylvania, Delaware, and Maryland. They came from all those states. The mothers would call me and say, "Take my daughter to confession on Saturday night." I'd have to go take them to confession and stay at work while they went to confession. I've taken them many nights to confession, but I didn't mind doing it.

At Tusculum my assistant was Catholic, and she had to go to confession. She grew up in Germany and lived there during the war. She could tell you more stories about the trouble they had. She believed in her drink. One time when I went back up for Christmas, she had gotten drunk, and they had fired her. They'd let her go. I had to take charge of both of the dormitories until they could get somebody to take her place. She came back to my dormitory after they fired her and said she had given the president a beautiful plant for Christmas. She told me, "I'm going up there to get my plant back. I'm not about to give them a plant and then they fire me." She didn't do a thing but go back up there and get that plant. She died in a nursing home about two or three years ago. The plant was in her room the last time I went out to see her. She still had that plant. She was the best-hearted person. She and my maid just made the dormitory for me.

Hugh: what is the greatest invention you have seen and what would you ask about things 100 years from now?

I'd say electricity has been the most important invention in my lifetime and then the plane has been quite important. We had the first television. My husband's older brother, who lived in New York, sent us the first television that they had in this community. But it would not work because we were down low in the hills, and we got very little use out of it. I wish we had kept it. I imagine my boys when they cleaned up after my mother and father passed away threw it away. I just hate it so much, because I know that television that he sent us was the first one here in Bethesda. But you could not get any reception from it, nothing to amount to anything, because we were so low down. Then we had one of the first radios that was run by batteries too. My mother used to enjoy that.

The question I would ask of people a hundred years from now is have they started building homes on other planets? Are the planets well populated now?

Jessie: What words of wisdom would you pass on?

I go and tell stories to the children in schools, and one thing I tell them is to always do your homework. For your homework, the first thing is get up in the morning and do things at home. Do what your mother had planned for you to do. Be sure you clean up your room and make up your bed and get things ready for the day. And then the second thing in homework is tell somebody something nice. Have something nice to say about somebody. The third thing in homework is something that you can do for somebody. Think of somebody that you can do something nice for: tell them they have on a pretty coat, tell your teacher she looks pretty today, and be good at school. So remember, always do unto others as you would have others do unto you. Remember the Golden Rule. That's one of the most important things.

I've had a very interesting and enjoyable life. I haven't stayed at home. So many said when my husband passed away, "Now, she's just running from trouble." I wasn't. That was the best thing that happened to me. I still hear from a good many of the girls now. I've been back to so many of their weddings. The preacher in Franklin now is the one that was at Wesley Foundation at Cookeville when I was at Tennessee Tech. He and I get together and talk. We put on several weddings and so on at the Wesley Foundation. I enjoyed working with them.

LOLA REED GLENN BOWERSOX
1918-2016

Jessie: I was telling a girl last night about you spanking me in the first grade. She said, "you mean Miss Lola spanked children? She wouldn't spank anybody." I said, "Well, she pulled her hands back and give us hot tea." Do you remember that?

Well, I don't remember hot tea. But one time I got sick, and my sister Alma went to teach one day for me. She said, "Now listen Lola, you go back, or they won't have a teacher. I'm not going. I wouldn't go back over there for nothing."

MY FIRST SCHOOL

The first year I taught I made $55 a month and paid twenty for rent and board. I went to a little place – a two-teacher school called Naomi. 'Course, it's not there now. It was down in the lower part of Williamson County. You go through part of Davidson and then you come back into Williamson. It was off to the right of Highway 100, about a mile or two miles off. The first district schools had what they called Highland Rim schools. They would start a month earlier than schools here.

When they assigned me that school, Daddy and Mother and Charlie and Ruth Reed carried me down there. I boarded with a man named Mr. Sullivan. Miss Redford, the woman that was the principal boarded there too. Mother had made me dress school clothes and I stayed five weeks before I came home. By then I had gained so that those dresses were bursting. They ate altogether different from what I had been used to eating. They had the whole grain flour–the bread was not bleached, and we had things out of the garden. I was so hungry for a piece of chocolate pie that I thought I would give anything for one. We didn't have any desserts. We had apples off of trees and things like that, but we didn't have a lot of sweet things.

Naomi School

I was so homesick I nearly died. I was teaching the first four grades in one room. She had five, six, seven and eight. One afternoon I was sweeping and Mr. Joe Pinkerton–he worked at Williamson County Bank–came by and was selling some kind of volunteer insurance, I think. And I was sweeping and crying. I was so homesick I thought I was going to die. And I said, "Mr. Joe, I want to go home with you. Take me to Franklin and I can get home from Franklin." He said, "No, Lola, I am not taking you. You went to school to teach school. If I take you home you will be through. You won't ever teach again. No, I'm not going to take you home." And he didn't take me. But I wanted him to.

Mr. Sullivan had a spring that had a basin chiseled out of limestone rock. Well, Miss Redford didn't think the water was pure enough, so she goes down with some Purex and pours it into that limestone basin. You know that stuff penetrated in and she messed that spring up for a week. Mr. Sullivan like to have had a fit. That was the spring for the school and the house too. There was no spring at the school. The kids had to bring the water in buckets from over at Mr. Blythe Trice's.

They poured it in a cooler-like thing; we did it the same way at Choctaw when I taught there. Sometimes kids that didn't have a cup would make paper cups by folding it like a hat, you know.

I was the janitor, too. We had to sweep our own rooms and then when it got cold, we had to see that we had our own kindling in. The county brought the coal and dumped it out – the same as later over at Choctaw. The boys would build a fire.

There was nothing to do and I wasn't concerned about plans for the next day. This lady who was the principal had taught for several years. She would sit up with a lamp and make plans and everything for the next day. When it got dark, I went straight to bed and went to sleep. Haha.

THE ITCH

One night I had already been asleep, Miss Redford called me and said, "Lola, get up and come here and look at me." She showed me all over her chest and said, "Have you ever seen anything that looks like this?" I said, "No." She said, "This is itching me to death." But I had seen little old boys at school with no shirts on, and bib overalls, doing all sorts of scratching. Well, I didn't know; I thought they were just nervous. Well, it wasn't long–two or three, maybe four days- after that I got to itching.

We stayed down there during this weekend and all, but right before we were to come home (the five weeks were up) my sister came after me. We were just going home for the weekend. Miss Redford's mother was dead and so she was going home with me. That was the first time I had been home, and she was going home with me. I had been itching the night before and told her, "I don't know what this is, but we are going to stop in Franklin. I'm going to see Dr. Walker." Dr. Walker and Dr. Nolen had their offices in that building beside where the Presbyterian church is. Dr. Walker asked what was my trouble. Of course, he didn't know Miss Redford since she was from Nashville. I said, "Well, there is something wrong. We are broken out with something and we are itching." The nurse came in there and we took our clothes off. When he went back out, he said, "Come here Dr. Nolen, I want you to help me diagnose what these girls have." Well, Dr. Nolen came in and they look at each other and just laughed. He said, "What do you say it is, Dr. Nolen?" And he said, "I say it's old itch!" We liked to have died.

We went on home and when we told her, Mother said, "Oh, my Lordy what will I do with you all!" Well, she fixed a couch and put us on the porch–it was August. And Miss Redford and I kept everything we touched separate. Mother wouldn't let us wash in anything. We didn't wash in any pan or anything they had. When we left, Mother, I am sure, boiled everything we had touched. But nobody got it in Mamma's house.

That was the awfulest itching I have ever felt. It was on my body. A lot of people, I always thought, got it on your hands between your fingers. But this was big old welts. I had seen those children at school, but I thought they were nervous. Haha! Is it a parasite or something that gets on your skin? I don't know.

MY NEXT SCHOOL

Fred J. Page

But then they transferred me. Mr. Page was the superintendent. I guess anybody who has told you about teaching school in Williamson County knows about Fred J. Page. Page School was named for him. I think he was superintendent for about forty years–a long, long time. Well, they transferred me from Naomi over to a school called Post Oak. A lumber camp came in – I guess it was almost like a virgin forest – and this lumber company had bought up a tract of land just to cut the lumber off. That school was already a two-teacher school, but the enrollment enlarged so they just put up kinda like little shanties. That was before the day of portables and mobile homes. The children of the men of that lumber camp came to that school, and they sent me over there.

The first time that Mr. Page came to visit that school, I didn't have sense enough to quit playing basketball with the boys on the outdoor court. We were chasing up and down–playing. Mr. Page didn't know I was out there. Mr. Blair was the principal. Both teachers were big, fat people, I mean. Miss Beulah, she hung off the side of the chair and Mr. Blair was nearly that big. I imagine I weighed 110 pounds then. I was skinny. Mr. Blair came out there and said, "Come on in here."

Post Oak School

Mr. Page wants to see you. He wanted to know where the other teacher was." I saw him go in, but I didn't have sense enough to stop and go in to see him. I knew who he was because he had been superintendent when I was a little girl in school, but he didn't know me. I didn't know you were supposed to go in and listen to him.

So, I taught in the first district at Naomi and Post Oak the first year, which was 1937-38. Neither room at Naomi had an attendance of over 35 or 40, but when I got over at Post Oak, Miss Beulah had like 50 or 60 in her room. He gave me the third and fourth grades, I believe. Miss Beulah and I taught in the same room. She was up on the stage. And talk about whether you spank anybody, one day I looked up there and she had put this little boy on that big fat lap and her hand looked like a ham of meat. That little boy's feet were kicking. Today there would be lawsuits. That's why we don't have any discipline in school; there's nobody correcting the kids. They just let them go. I think that little boy said a bad word and he got a whipping.

CHOCTAW SCHOOL

Then I went to Choctaw the next year.

Jessie said that she had Lola as her first-grade teacher at Choctaw.

Choctaw School

The school is right beside the road and is still standing, about two feet from the road. It was a public road that went up to Ed Biggers house. Robert Beech's daddy, Bob Beech, would come by the schoolhouse and he would be drunk. And I was scared of him as a bear and I would tell those kids, "Don't you all say a word when he goes by." It was a one-room school with eight grades.

THE SCHOOL CHRISTMAS TREE

Jessie, I guess you went with us to cut down that first Christmas tree. You know, when you look out at a pretty tree and it's standing out in a big open lot, it looks pretty. So, the whole bunch of us went – Ross Reed and Jake Hargrove, Junior Beard – we all saw this cedar tree and it was pretty. They said, "This is pretty, let's get it." And I bet you the trunk of it was that big around – I know when they cut that thing down, we couldn't carry it! They said, "Well, let's go and get Big Apple." That's what they called Mr. Blythe Trice. "Get Big Apple's cart and we'll pull it in." I said to go on and the rest of the kids and we just sat around and played on the hill. It was over in that lot close to Scott Reed's house.

Well, they brought the cart, and we broke Mr. Blythe's wheels off of his cart. We loaded that thing, and it broke. Well, we couldn't do it, so we decided to cut some of it off. You know how when you cut off a tree that big it makes a big hole. But they cut some off and we drug it on into Choctaw. Drug it in the door – it was so fat – we finally got it in the door. They had nailed crosspieces on the bottom. When they stood it up it the whole top bent at the ceiling. We had to drag it back out and they cut off some more. When we got through, it just had holes, but we went on and decorated that thing.

Jessie said she remembered that tree; it was the first year she went to school there.

That was the first time I ever tried to do a Christmas tree at school. A lot of what we put on it we made. We cut out strips of green and red paper and made a chain, and we did some icicles. We did have a few bought things, but we made a lot of things to put on it. But it was the worst-looking tree I ever saw. We went on and had a program.

At Christmas programs, the children would say little poems and sometimes we would do the Christmas story. We dressed some up like the wise men and like the shepherds, like churches used to do. They don't do it now. There were a lot of pretty little poems and things that kids would memorize and say. The parents would come. And they would sing a lot of little Christmas songs. In that old schoolhouse, there was a step-up that was the stage. But we couldn't get the Christmas tree on the stage. We put it down beside the stage and stood on the stage and tried to decorate it.

Gentry Trice at Choctaw

SCHOOL MEALS

Another thing the health department would get after us now. We cooked lunch on that potbellied stove. About that time the government started giving commodities. They would give us things like beans and cheese and canned tomatoes. I don't know if they gave us potatoes, or if we all had to bring a potato. I think the kids would bring a potato or two. Besides being the janitor, I was also the cook. Ha. There was an old sour taste to it but I never thought a thing about it hurting the kids.

Jessie: Well, it was good. We'd all eat it.

Well, we'd peel things and we'd put them on that big pot-bellied stove, and it would cook. I had a ladle and we all had bowls. I'm sure I didn't have scalding water to scald them when I got through. We would heat water to wash them, but I am sure I didn't scald them. I know they weren't sterile. We just made one dish. We either had beans, or we would have soup, more than anything else in the wintertime. It would be like a vegetable soup. We got beans in a burlap bag, and they lasted a good long time. And we had cheese. They gave us a good bit of cheese. I don't know how I sliced that cheese, but it would be in big quantities.

THE SCHOOLYARD

We didn't have any playground. The school property was a narrow little strip that came from Flat Creek Road and was right beside the road. There was also a little old coal house that they put coal in. The girls' toilet [an outhouse] was in one direction and the boys' in another. That space wasn't bigger than anything. When they played baseball, the outfield would have to get off of school property and over in Jack Trice's field.

Jessie: The girls played a lot on rocks nearby.

Yes, we played "billy goats" on the rocks all the time.

Jessie: As a matter of fact, that's what I got a spanking for – not coming back when you told us to. We were playing house.

We had a bell that you shook with your hand to call the students in.

I remember the old cooler that they had on a little shelf, back by the door. It had little braces under it and was green. The cooler had a spigot on it. The boys would bring water from Jimmie Lou's well, across the road at Blythe Trice's place, and pour it in the cooler. Then the kids would get the water from it in their cups. Mr. Blythe let me put my horse in his stable. I rode horseback.

I was raised on that hill where David Hargrove and Judy live. The way to the house now is not the way we got up there when we lived there. We went about middle way of the field and had to cross the creek, and we went around the hill in a buggy. Later, before Mother and Aaron sold that place, Mother built that bridge where you come straight in and go across to go down into the creek. That little red house on the right is where I was living. It was on my mother's and daddy's farm. Getting up that hill when it was bad was something else.

And fording that Rutherford Creek was something then, too. Seems like the creek doesn't flow like it used to. That one in Bethesda seemed like it used to be out a lot. The road used to go close to where the Presbyterian church is. When you got to the end of that swaggy like field of Franklin Bond's, before you get to where the bridge is, we turned directly and took a sharp left and crossed. You went down through the creek – that was called Bond's Creek. That creek was always up, it seemed like. Then you went on up on this side of the creek, and then we had to cross again when we got up to our house. It was a long time before they took the road out of that creek.

People that went to Comstock Road also had to cross Rutherford Creek to get over to their road. We didn't fool with Rutherford Creek. It was Bond's Creek that we had to cross. The Grigsbys had to cross Rutherford Creek to get up to where they lived. That's when they cut the road all the way around.

GYPSIES

Talking about that road where you go to school, gypsies used to come through the country. I don't know whether it would be fall or spring. There was a sawmill between where this road came up beside the Bond's field. They owned all the way from the corner up there to that first house that Luther Reed built. The Cartwrights live there now. There was a space between the road and the creek, and these gypsies would come along and set up camp. People would tell us that "the gypsies were still loose and were going to get us." We were scared to death. They would be boiling and cooking things over a fire and we would be scared to death. They did it year after year, and for a long time, I was scared of them. They would not stay but about two days. I don't know why they were set up there. I just know I was scared of them. Lois and Alexanie Trice [sisters of Jessie] would be going up the road with us. They were probably scared of them too.

The peddler that came through was not a gypsy. He would have things in his pack that he would show. He just came through and would stay one night. But I wasn't scared of him. I was scared of those that came in covered wagons and had stuff hanging out behind like chicken coops. They were pulled by horses. I don't believe I ever saw any mules. There would be four or five wagons, sometimes more. It seemed like an army to me because I was so scared. They would put down stakes and let the horses graze til they got ready to break camp. When we would come home from school and they would be gone, we would be tickled to death. We would go over there where they had had the campfire and all. I don't remember that they dressed so different from the way we did. I don't know where they were going or where they came from. They wouldn't stay long – two nights at the most. Most of the time they would be there when we would come in from school one afternoon and they would be there the next morning, but maybe the next night they would be gone.

MY OWN SCHOOL DAYS

I went to school at Bethesda, where the store is. That's where I started. If people had done me like my parents did to teachers, I would have had a fit. I was the oldest, and Mother and them thought I shouldn't go to school until the winter. I started school in March and was nearly eight years old when school started the next time. It was in the old schoolhouse.

They had the little ones upstairs, with a winding stair that went up. That Monday morning Mother carried me, and the teacher wasn't there. The boys had found some mice, little old baby mice, and I despise mice. I'm scared to death of them. They had found the mice in the trash can and had the girls running, chasing, and screaming. I started crying and wanted Mother to take me home. Mother hated to leave me there so bad, but the teacher came in and, of course, she made those boys quit chasing. I liked my teacher, Miss Mattie Alexander. I am sure she was Lester's [Mosley] teacher too. She boarded with Miss Cleo Grigsby and them. She was kin to Miss Cleo. Miss Cleo's mother was an Alexander.

BETHESDA CHURCHES

Back in the old days you didn't know if you were a Presbyterian or Methodist. Every Sunday we had our Sunday School at our own church. I think it was the first and third Sundays that the Presbyterians had preaching at their church and the second and fourth Sundays preaching was at the Methodist church. When the Sunday School was over, we would – if it was first and third Sunday – the congregation would all go up to the Presbyterian church and we would all have preaching together. And then when it was the second and fourth Sunday, the Presbyterians would come down to our church. Brother and Mrs. Miller, Marshall McCoy Beasley's grandfather, was minister here for thirty or forty years. His wife was always kind of late.

The Methodist church was where it is now. I don't know if the Presbyterian church has ever been anywhere but where it is now.

Jessie: No, the Presbyterian church building is over two hundred years old.

The Methodists have had two or three churches. They had a log church down where the Masonic Hall is. Mrs. Miller would come in. She would be late. She had long hair and she had a little comb. She would sit down, and she would straighten up her hair behind. It would be so cute.

Ha. And Brother Miller would pray the longest prayers. Oh. I would go to sleep and wake up and he would still be praying. Ha. Made Mother so mad. "Oh, stay awake!" She tried to make us stay awake. We didn't have preachers stay long at our church. Methodists back in the old days stayed about four years. You had to be a big church like McKendree in Nashville if you would get ministers like they did. We had student pastors most of the time. They would be Vanderbilt students and while they would be getting educated, they would be here.

The men went in on one side. We had two doors down at the old Methodist church the left-hand side was the ladies' side, and the right-hand side was the men's. And there was a rail that went all the way through. They had big columns in the old church; it was a pretty old church. The lodge was on the second floor. Around the back door, it was pretty. It had beautiful woodwork in it, but they burned up a lot of that good lumber and seats. I loved that old church. The chairs that you have in the museum [two pulpit chairs] came out of that church, but they are not the ones I remember first in that church. It seems that they had a little post that went up behind. It had a poplar floor in it, I am sure. I can see those wide planks in that floor.

DR. CORE

I was trying to think of what Dr. Core's name was. I knew it was J.B., but remembered it was [Jonathan] Blythe Core. His house was down where the Drurys live. He built on the part of the house that is there. He had a wing that came out and that was where his office and all was. I used to go in his office, and he had a little baby in a jar of something – a little child. It was preserved and it scared the daylights out of me. It set up on the top of his shelves. But I loved Dr. Core. He could make you feel better just to come around him, and smell – he smelled so clean.

Dr. J.B. Core

MY CHILDHOOD

My mother was born where I was born. That was my mother's father's place. I was the oldest of five children. I had two sisters. They were close together. I was about three years older than my next sister, and then Alma and Glyndon were just fifteen months apart. Mother and Daddy skipped four years before Leon was born. Then, when I was a freshman in college, my last brother was born. So, I was almost as much older than my young brother than my mother is older than me.

Daddy was a farmer. I would get up every morning and I loved the outdoors. I never did like to do housework. Ha! I would go to the barn with Daddy. We would get up at five o'clock every morning. The kids say to me now, "Why do you get up at five o'clock in the morning? Why don't you sleep?" Janice keeps saying, "I am going to get some blackout blinds." I say, "Janice, it is black pitch dark at five o'clock in the wintertime and I wake up. I don't want shades on my windows."

But we would go to the barn, and Alma, my next sister, would help Mother in the kitchen. Then my next sister tended to the chickens. She fed the chickens and gathered the eggs. All of us had to bring in wood in the afternoon after we got home from school. We had to have stovewood year-round. That had to be brought in all the time. But in the winter, we had another dose. We had to bring wood for the fireplace in the evening to heat the house. Alma, Thelma, and I slept in a bedroom with no fire and I still like to sleep in a room that is not warm. I think you sleep better. But that is what you are raised to be used to. I know we raised just about all the food we had. When people talk about the Depression, I didn't know there was a depression. We were so well off I didn't know. We had our own milk, we had Horton Park where there was a mill on the river. They would make a list of how much flour or wheat daddy brought and when he would go and get two or three hundred pounds of flour or meal, they would mark down on his records. I guess they kept it in a notebook.

With my daddy, we milked cows and would feed the pigs. We had horses we worked the farm with. We had to do all the feeding. Shucked the corn for the pigs. We always had to have a big bucket of shucked corn to feed those. I don't remember how many ears of corn you would feed each one of your horses.

We had a strange barn, a three-story. Underneath, the bottom was where the stalls and stables were. Then there was like a bridge over a little branch that ran down from the spring. Then you went into what would be like a hallway in the barn, on the middle level. That was where Daddy put his wagon and stuff. Then the cribs were off to the side. Daddy could back the wagons loaded with corn in and scoop it into the crib. Then they had the lofts with the hay. And it wasn't baled hay. It was put in there with a hay fork. They put it on wagons and would take it off the wagon. They fed hay with a pitchfork by throwing it down chutes to the animals. It went down the chute directly from the third floor to the animal stalls on the lower level. We had no more than eight or ten cows. Course, Daddy would milk more than I could, but as I got older, I could milk as fast as Daddy. When I started, I couldn't milk at all, and my sister Alma never learned to milk, and Thelma didn't either. Of course, they never went to the barn.

Sometimes we sold cream. For a long time, we used a separator where you let the milk set and the cream rises. Mr. Trav Wallace ran the store at Cross Keys. They tested your cream. and they gave you so much money by how much butterfat you had in your cream. You took your eggs there to sell and they had a light that you put your egg over to candle it. Bethesda had these too, but I don't know why we always went to Cross Keys with our cream. At the time we were living on the hill at David Hargrove's. It was called the "Old Giles Place" and the "Charlie Reed Place."

In later years we got the type of separator that had a handle to turn, but that thing was a pain in the neck to wash. Alma got to do that. Ha! You had to break that old thing down.

Ella and Trav Wallace

The white, long barn on Bethesda Road at one time was a chicken barn. The white house beside it was where Jean Gary's great-grandparents lived. My mother's mother died when she was a baby, and Miss Alice Irvin, Jean Sanders's grandmother, was so good to Mother. They were just close neighbors, so they made Mother's clothes for her.

FRUIT ON THE FARM

We had a real good peach orchard that had plums, pears, and apples. Mother would can and we would dry peaches. There was a certain kind you had to have to break off the seed cleanly to dry the best. We would pick blackberries. Back then you could buy sugar by a hundred pounds. We would get a hundred pounds of sugar and Mother would make jams and jellies and things out of blackberries and things that came in. We would get at least a tub full at blackberry time. We would empty our bucket into the tub. You can trip and spill your berries in the grass mighty easy! Daddy would carry a big tub. The whole family would go. Of course, the brothers weren't big enough. Mother, Daddy, Alma, Glyndon, and I.

Chiggers were around then, too. You scratched. Chiggers were a nuisance. My sister next to me, Alma, had fair skin. Chiggers nearly killed Alma. Some people's skin just can't take it. They didn't bother me like they did her. Glyndon was younger. I don't remember her being eaten up like Alma, but I can see the welts and all. Chiggers will eat you. Seems like Mother put something on our clothes and tied it around our ankles, but I can't think what. It was some kind of cloth and she had put it in something [probably coal oil] and she tied it around our britches legs. And sometimes in the barn you would get fleas. The pigs would sleep under the barn sometime and we always thought that's what made us get so pestered with them.

OUR "SPRING TONIC"

Have you ever heard of pouring coal oil on sugar?

Jessie: We heard of that the other day.

I'll tell you, back in those days in the spring of the year Mother would go down to Dr. Core's and he would give Mother enough calomel pills for each one of us. I think it was three. We would have to take those blooming things! We'd be fine. There would be nothing wrong with us. But, when we got through with the calomel and castor oil, we were so weak we couldn't walk! I said if I ever have a child, I'd never do that. That castor oil, I just couldn't stand that stuff, and that old calomel will make you... But I never did in my life give my kids a dose of castor oil. [That was a common spring tonic at one time.]

Hugh: In my mother's family everyone took a laxative every Friday night as a routine.

Daddy would always go out in the spring and would dig up sassafras roots. We would keep sassafras on the wood-burning stove. I just love sassafras tea.

CLEO GRIGSBY, 1905-2003

MY ANCESTORS AND HOMEPLACE

My great-grandparents came from Virginia, and they came in a covered wagon with ten children. My grandfather, Booker Preston Grigsby, was one of them and was about 15 years old. They left two in Virginia when they came. They came and it took them several weeks – I've forgotten how long they said it took them to come. They had to cut the roads through, and they camped. They had two of the children to die on the way over here. So, there were ten that got here. They settled around Spring Hill. The children married off and on.

My grandfather married Mary Elizabeth Sprott in 1830, I believe. Grant Sprott, who was murdered, owned the land where the house is today where I live. They came there to live after they married because she got the property and it was just, you might say, one room with the upstairs.

There wasn't much upstairs. It wasn't sealed, just one room and a hall. The kitchen was on the outside and we had to go down steps. The building was separate, out in the yard. There wasn't even a dog trot between them. They had 12 children born in that house. They finally enlarged it some and built some more rooms. I remember the kitchen being out there, but we never did use the kitchen after I was born. It was a place where they did a whole lot of their washing and things like that.

My father was born in the same house that I am living in now. My mother was born a little ways from it, over on the Lewisburg Pike. They were born in 1868 and 1870. My father married and they were there in 1898 but moved in with my granny and grandpaw and lived with them until they died. My granny died in 1911 and my grandfather died in 1919. Granny was a cripple and got up one night and fell and broke her hip, I guess it just gave way on her. She was bedfast for several years, and I waited on her a whole lot. I was about six years old, I guess. I waited on her until she died. I have been living in that same home for 91 years.

Booker Preston Grigsby and Mary Elizabeth Sprott Grigsby

CHILDHOOD MEMORIES OF HOMELIFE

My granny was present when I was born, and Dr. Core was up. I was born on a Saturday and of course my granny helped with it. I don't remember what time. I don't know if they told me that or not. Ha! We were on the farm. My granddaddy and father both worked the farm. They had mostly corn and hay and tobacco as I remember. They always had cattle and hogs. I know they didn't have sheep. They never did have too many cattle, but they did have a good many hogs. We always saved the dishwater and stuff like that for the slop for the hogs. We didn't raise any cotton on the place at home, but they did raise it on the Alexander place. I remember them raising it and picking the cotton. We didn't have much income. We just had living expenses.

We generally bought the cloth for our clothes and my aunt would make most of our clothes. She did it by hand. My mamma didn't have time to sew much, and my aunt made most of our clothes. We got our material from the grocery store. They kept everything, dry goods, and everything. I remember, even after I began piecing quilts, I would be able to go down to the store and buy material for the lining and things like that. I remember another thing we don't do today. Every year they would come around buying rags. We always saved all the rags. I wonder why they don't recycle rags today.

On washday, we always went out in the yard. We had an old big tub and a big old iron kettle out in the yard that they heated the water in. If the clothes needed boiling, they put them over in there and boiled them. They made their own soap. We had what we called an ash hopper out in the yard. All the heat in the house was from a fireplace. The ashes that came from the fireplaces were always put in the ash hopper in the yard. They kept a bucket underneath it and when it rained the lye from the ashes would drain in the bucket. That was used to make the lye soap. They made their own lye soap and they washed with the lye soap.

They made their own hominy [also using the lye from ashes]. We always had a pot of hominy. I remember them making hominy and I have helped some with it too. It was generally cooked on the open fireplace, and it took a heap of heat to do it. Then we had the old Dutch oven [also called a reflector oven] that we could set before the fireplace and warm the food a little bit. Also. we covered potatoes and eggs in the ashes of the fire and cooked them there. A lot of cooking was done in the fireplace. After they built the kitchen onto the house, they always had a swinging arm above the fire to hold pots over it. That's where we cooked a whole lot, on those pots. At first in the new kitchen, there was only a fireplace, but then they got a stove.

Most of our bread was biscuits. When we killed hogs, they made their own lard. I remember Pappy having to carry the corn down to the mill. He would carry it down to the Willhoit's mill up close to where Horton Park is today, or the Hardison's mill, down at Rabbit Hill. He would take time about to carry his wheat and the corn. When he would bring them back, we would pour them into big barrels. We had in our kitchen two big old wood barrels. When he brought the flour and cornmeal back, he would pour one of them in one barrel and the other in the other one. We made a whole lot of crackling cornbread.

The only way we had to take a bath was to heat the water in the kitchen. We would all take turns going to the kitchen and getting in a big tub of water to take a bath, maybe once a week. I don't remember if we used the same water. I washed in a pan of water more than I did take a bath. I always washed my hair in lye soap. It seems like I miss it today. I think it was one of the best things you could wash your hair in.

At night while I was a child, we played dominos and checkers a whole lot. We would get down on the floor to play marbles. It was on the bare floor a lot, but sometimes we had a woven rug that I guess Granny made, on the floor. Finally, we got a carpet, a straw carpet.

At Christmas time we didn't get too many toys. Pappy would buy a half crate of oranges. That was the only fruit we ever had during the year, except what we raised. We got an orange and mostly candy at Christmas time. Our tree was a cedar and we decorated it with popcorn and paper things that we made.

Our beds had a straw mattress and a feather comfort. We did not have rooms for everybody. During thrashing time, we always had people to come around and thrash the wheat. They would stay at night We had to make room for them to sleep and eat.

All the traveling was done mostly in buggies and wagons. We used to go once a year hickory hunting. We went way down the road to the hickory trees. We picked up walnuts and sold walnuts a whole lot. We always picked enough blackberries to make what we wanted to cook with, and then we would sell them. We sold them to neighbors. I have picked a whole lot of blackberries for a dime a gallon. Finally, they gave us twenty-five cents a gallon for them, and we bought our first ice cream freezer with the money we saved. We had one old person, Minnie Sprott, who couldn't get out and didn't have any children to pick for her.

SCHOOL AT BETHESDA

I went to school down where the store is. At that time there was just a lower room and an upstairs. The little children had to go up the stairs to get to their room. At that time, they just had two teachers. They added an extra room when I was in the fifth grade. I think I mostly carried my lunch wrapped in paper. Some carried lunches in little flannel bags or tin buckets. We carried it in tin buckets a whole lot. We took meat and biscuits because that was what we had to eat. We never did carry chitterlings to school, I don't think. I went through the twelfth grade there and graduated in 1923. Then I took the teacher's examination and passed. I never married.

MY START IN TEACHING

They gave me a school to teach, at Trinity, in the first four grades. I taught there four years and then went to Rudderville, where Page High School is now, and taught there eight years. Then I came to Bethesda. During that time, in the summer, I would teach. For five summers I taught down in the first district for a month. They were raising cotton, and they opened the school in July but closed it in August so they could pick. The teacher that was supposed to be teaching there was in school and could not open that school. I went for five years down there and taught one month, July before they opened the school in this district. I went to school at

Murfreesboro during the summers. Every six years we would have to go there to renew our teaching certificate. I had to use several summers to take credits to finish high school to be accredited because the school down here was not accredited. I had to take extra work, some of the same things I had in high school. It took several summers to do that.

Then I kept going in the summer and finally got my BS. I kept going and got my masters later.

When I was teaching, we only made $50 a month. I had to board and pay $20 of that to board. I had to be carried to the school at Trinity in a horse and buggy on Sunday afternoon and my brother would come and get me on Friday afternoon. When I went to Rudderville, I still boarded two years, but I sort of saved up a little money. I don't know how I did it. We, my brother helped me, bought a car and I drove back and forth.

Trinity School

MY CARS

The first car we had at home was sort of a little van, closed up. It was a Ford, I think. The one I got to go to school with I bought in 1930. It was a '30 Ford that I bought. I guess I used that Ford for 15 or 16 years and then I bought a Pontiac and used it for about 15 or 16 years. And then bought a Dodge and used a Dodge for 15 or 16 years. Then I bought the one I've got now. I've been using it from 1976.

MORE ABOUT OUR FOODS

I don't remember when the new kitchen was built. When I was telling about cooking on the fireplace, it would have been about 1906 or 1907. They finally got a range in the kitchen, and it had the four cooking eyes, a water reservoir on the side, and a warming oven up above. We still kept those pots hanging in the fireplace to use from time to time.

We always had a right big garden, and we saved everything we could to can. We would can everything that could be canned. We had the old blue canning jars that we used mostly. People thought the blue ones kept things better than the white ones. I don't know about that. The tops were zinc tops. Then, pappy would go out and dig a hole in the ground and put hay in it. We heeled our Irish potatoes and turnips and sweet potatoes and kept them like that. Our meat, we always had plenty of meat hanging in the smokehouse. We had our own chickens. We had eggs when we wanted them. We had our own milk; we had cows. We never did raise dairy cows too much. We just had a few beef cattle. We always had to milk. I was brought up milking. That was one of my jobs, go to the barn and help milk, morning and evening.

We always made sauerkraut in big kegs. I have seen my daddy get out and chop those cabbages and beat them down and salt them. I can see him carrying stone crocks filled with kraut. We made pickles the same way, in crocks. We had a cider mill and made cider. I think a few times we made wine, using blackberries and elderberries and things like that. We dried apples and peaches. We had our own orchard, and we had a cherry tree and always made preserves. We dried our food by peeling it and slicing it as thin as we could. We laid them on a flour sack up on top of the houses – on tin roofs – and dried them. We put them on the tin roof to get the heat from underneath and the sun above. We would always have to watch and bring them in at night. If it began to rain, we would have to bring them in. We tried to cover them with cheesecloth or something like that to keep the flies off.

We had a spring that we used for a while, but as long as I remember we had a dug well – a big well with plenty of water. We also had a dug-out cellar that we could keep food in, right near the well house. You would have to go down in the cellar to keep our food. Occasionally we would have to carry it to the spring if the weather got too hot. We would carry it down and set the things in the spring. I don't remember a milk ditch; we just tried to make things heavy enough so they wouldn't float away. We didn't have to buy too much from the store because we had our own meal and flour. We bought a little sugar. Things were right cheap in the store. I don't think we ever paid over ten cents for a loaf of bread if we had to buy any. Eggs were cheap but we didn't have to buy eggs. If we sold eggs – sometimes we sent eggs to sell – you couldn't get over 25 cents a dozen if you got that.

My daddy would buy us a keg of salty fish and we would bring them home. We always, the night before we were going to cook it for breakfast the next day, took it to the spring to soak the salt out of the catfish. One night I remember some varmint got it all and we didn't have the catfish the next morning. That was the only time I remember anything getting it.

BETHESDA

The store was where it is today. We had two stores there next to the school. My uncle ran one of them and Leo's granddaddy ran the other one. One of them had the post office in it. While we were at school, we used to walk the fence. They had a plank across from post to post, and we used to walk the fence over to the store to get things. I remember the flagpole was there and I've seen the boys get out of the windows upstairs and climb out and hit it. I don't see why some of them didn't get killed or why some of those children didn't fall going down those steps.

Bethesda Methodist Sunday School picnic in Millwood, 1912

We had a sawmill and a broom factory. We always had a 4-H Club in the school, and we had community clubs to go to. Our church group always had a youth group that met. We always had the church picnic over in the Millwoods. The men folks would put up swings and we had a big picnic over there every year. They would play games; they always played ball. When we were children, we played anty-over and puss-in-boots and I don't know what all. We played a heap of marbles.

We just had two churches, the Methodists and the Presbyterian. We would alternate the sermons. We had Sunday schools at both churches but then on the first and third Sundays we would have preaching at the Presbyterian church and on the second and fourth there would be preaching at the Methodist church. The Presbyterian church was where it is today, and the Methodist church was down where the lodge is today.

FUNNY THINGS WHILE TEACHING AT BETHESDA

I remember all the boys walking off one day. They all walked off and stayed all day. They came in that evening all bringing switches. Haha! I remember whipping a boy because he came in with polecat smell on him. Ha! We had to get out and burn cedar around him before he could come in. To get rid of polecat smell you take cedar brushes and burn around. When we got through with burning the cedar brush, I wore him out with what was left. [Jessie helped with the details of the polecat incident.]

One day someone went by and called the school names. They all chased him down and ducked him; that was Mr. John Trice that they ducked. When anyone went by the school and called it names the boys would chase them and duck them. We had some good times.

Hugh: What is the greatest invention?

I guess electricity. It has been the biggest help in my lifetime. It was a long time before we got it, in the forties. We just used old lamps and candles. I don't see how we went through school as much as we did and have any eyes left. When we first got electricity, I think the Frigidaire was the first thing we bought. Maybe we bought a radio, but we didn't have too many electric things. Our first radio was one that we put over our ears to hear.

I remember the first radio I listened to. I had to stop one night because of the creek; I couldn't get home from Rudderville. I spent the night with Tom C. Bond and Irene. They had a radio and I enjoyed listening to that.

I wish I knew something about the computer but I'm too old to learn it. It must be a wonderful invention for those who are working with it. I don't see how they do without it now.

AGNES HARGROVE, 1905-2005

MY EARLY LIFE IN DETROIT

I was born in Marshall County and raised there. I met my husband in Detroit. He was from Williamson County. I had an aunt, Uncle Raymond's wife, who was on vacation out here. She was 19 years old and had a 19-month-old little boy and twin girls. Some of the family had brought her down and when she had to go back to Michigan, they insisted that I go with her to help her with the babies. I went and I stayed. That's how I got to Detroit. I got a job and worked up there for a year in S.S. Kresge, which now is K-Mart. I enjoyed the work. It was in a Jewish community. Nothing but Jewish people, and they were all just as nice as they could be. I went up in 1937, married in 1938, and stayed in Detroit for ten years.

We had to leave Detroit on account of my health. I couldn't stand Michigan. I was kind of dreading coming back because I didn't know anybody. We had gone to Detroit and stayed ten years, so when we came back, I only knew my husband's people and a few people right around there. So, much of what I know is what has been told me. One thing – I had always heard that Little Texas was rough and Cross Keys was rough and [men] drank a lot and gambled a lot. Well, back in those days they did it everywhere, to some extent.

We came back and stayed six months over at Eagleville. We ran a store for Mr. Crosslin over there. He had a new subdivision built. We got a house that wasn't even finished and lived there six months. We came back to Eagleville in July, and in January we moved up here and rented from Miss Fannie Anderson for ten years. Then we rented on Pull Tight Road for two years and then we bought this, the old Irvin house. [Jean Sander's interview includes more about this.]

My son had two Guernsey cows that he milked and sold cream when he was just nine or ten years old. That's how he got his start, milking and a little runt pig in a tobacco box that T.R. Clendenen gave him. He had nice brood sows and had three litters of pigs, so he got his start to buy his first car when he was a kid.

Then when my grandkids came along and started to school, I was Grandma Hargrove and I'm still Grandma Hargrove to Hickman and Ronny and Josey Spears and Kenny Daniel and all them boys who used to come and play with our kids. All the schoolboys and little girls would come, and play. They still come and eat with us occasionally and bring their babies when they have a baby and all that. I've got some of the baby pictures hanging around now of the kids to who we are still Grandma Hargrove and Pappy.

THE CROSS KEYS STORE

I believe it was a Turner that built the log store, the first one. I think Joe Trice got it, and then Trav and Bud McCall bought from him. Then T.R. Clendenen bought from him.

I don't know when the store was built but I know it started out with a log store down back of James Trice's yard, toward Bethesda a little bit. The old rocks were still there and there was an old dug well here. That was the first store. I think an old Mr. Turner had that store – maybe John Turner.

Jessie: Harry Grigsby and John Williams had the store there in the thirties, but that was later.

Wilton Johnson was running it, and we took over from Fulton, well actually Joe Trice.

Fulton just run the store. We started in 1947 and went for 10 years. We sold out to William Marlin, and they sold out to Hugh Hawkins, I think, and then he sold to Robert A. Flippen. Later Robert A. had the store torn down and built a new one. He was in the old store at first. There was a big water tank right at the back door.

Jessie: There were old logs out on the front porch that we all used to sit on.

Robert A. must have built his store before the other one was torn down, because he would have had his stock to move.

Joe Trice

Jessie: It was in the late '50s.

We came in 1947 and bought the store. It was run down. There wasn't anything in there, much. Very little was there when we bought it because they were going to get rid of it and they let the stock run down. I had never clerked in a country store; neither of us knew a thing about it. We had a lot of learning to do. I did some crazy things. I think Jessie's mother could tell you a lot about our running the store.

This was a big two-story building where the two pine trees are at James Trice's house now. It was in the road, almost. It had an upstairs to it, and that's where we kept the stock. As we needed it, we would bring it down. We found a lot of old shirts with what years and years ago they called celluloid collars. I think you buttoned it in back and then you snapped it on. We found a bunch of them. We found a lot of bills from whoever had run the store in years before, up in the logs upstairs. There were bills where they had took eggs to Nashville. Back then you hauled them on a wagon. And they would sell meat or hams for ten cents a pound, eggs for a nickel a dozen, and such as that.

The Lewisburg paper not long ago had a whole section of 50th anniversaries, people who had been married 50 years. One of my cousins was one of them, and he had in his write-up that they walked about three miles to what they called a rolling store. It traveled the roads in what was either a converted school bus or a big old truck. They carried their eggs in buckets or something to sell them, but they got turned down. He said, " I've been feeding them to the hogs; I can't take them to Nashville. They are flooded with eggs at two cents a dozen." They needed to sell them to get a 15-cents-a-pound of coffee, maybe. And the prices have changed since we had the store, ha, and they'll change before somebody else gets in there, I guess.

We were general merchandise. We had over-the-counter drugs: aspirin tablets, BCs, tonics, and all that. Clothing, all kinds of dry goods, shoes, ammunition. Mr. Joe Trice couldn't handle dynamite in Franklin, but we could out here in the country. So, through him we furnished the electrical company the dynamite. We didn't keep the caps there, so there wasn't any danger. He wanted us to, but no, I didn't want that.

We had stamps and of course paper and envelopes. A lot of the schoolgirls – I won't call their names – had their boyfriends. One of them lived in Florida and her daddy and mother didn't want her corresponding with him. But she'd leave her letter there and I'd stamp it and put it in the mail for her. There were just so many things like that.

We had a community of good honest people. Jessie can tell you we had good honest people as far as paying their debts is concerned. I don't know otherwise. I know one man, when we went out of the store owed us $1.83. He wasn't a big spender. He bought what he had to have, and he didn't let it run over too long.

Now, we carried so many people a year, many people. Take Uncle Will; he had sheep, goats, cattle, tobacco, and hogs and was always selling livestock. He would run his bill for the whole year. He didn't want to see a ticket on that livestock – nothing. He would haul cottonseed to the mill and get cottonseed hulls to feed his cows. Sometimes Lee, his son, would go with him to help load his stuff. They would go at night and get in line to get the hulls in Nashville. When the end of the year come we had a settlement. We kept up with everything and there was never any complaint. We'd give him all the bills at that time, but I don't think he could read anyway.

One time a man owed us four hundred and something dollars, and it come out in some odd cents. He came back and said, "I believe you made a mistake, Miss Agnes." We kept little tickets, you know, so I said, "Well, let me go over it." I took them to the kitchen down at the house and set down where I wouldn't hear all the talking and noise at the store. I went over it once and it came out fine. I went over it twice, and the third time I had made a three-cent mistake in that. He thought I had made like a couple of hundred dollars. But he didn't get ill about it because somebody had just missed figures. The tickets – you'd get one and I'd keep one. That's the way that was.

We had a few drifters, just a few. One time a man lived in the neighborhood, but he didn't belong in our neighborhood, let's put it that way. This was a close-knit neighborhood. He wanted some gas and cigarettes, and when I went out to pump his gas, I saw that the car was full of clothes in the back – boots and everything. I guess he thought I saw that. He wasn't sharp or he wouldn't have said a word, but he said, "I'm taking a bunch of my clothes to the cleaners." I said to myself, "Yeah, you're taking me to the cleaners, I guess." He was headed to Detroit, right then. He didn't pay for the gas or for what he already owed. We had a few like that but they didn't belong in the community.

People would come at night and sit around and say, "You should get this, you should get this, and you should get this." So, I decided on two of these [suggestions] at one time. One of them you may not remember, a tonic called Wampole. All older people used to take Wampole. It was a spring tonic and they just had to have it. It might have had a little kick to it, I don't know. Somebody was wanting us to stock Wampole. Owen Farrar took it, and I remember a lot of the customers – Lee Crafton and Uncle Modee Crafton, Mr. Will, and a lot of the older people took that. And at the same time another farmer said, "Well, I know what I need and use a lot. You need to get some twisted clevises." I was raised on a farm, and I kinda knew what they look like. But I wouldn't know what they were for – something about harnesses or hitching up a plow. I always had to write the orders out for Johnny, who went to Nashville a couple of times a week, and sometimes more often than that if he had livestock to haul. He got to C. B. Ragland, and he was reading the order off I had down "twisted Wampole." He said he didn't bring me back either one. That was one bad mistake I made.

I could keep you here all day and tell you those funny things as well as about the business end. Another time I had down "rat tail comb" on an order. You remember when you get a permanent, they used a comb that had this little, long end, to twist your curl with, I guess. I never had but two permanents in my life, so I wouldn't know that I knew what you used it for.

When he was giving the order out and he come to that rat tail comb, he didn't call it off. He came back and I said, "Where is my comb – everybody is wanting a rat tail comb?" He said, "I was afraid to ask for it." Ha! There were a lot more things than that, but those two things I will never forget.

Everybody helped us in telling us what would sell. So, we ended up being a general merchandise store, from farm equipment to house furnishings. We bought C. B. Ryan and so many different ones their furniture when they got married. We had cosmetics, we had men's clothing, shoes, piece goods, and all the sewing needs. The schoolgirls would stop when they had a sewing project, you know. I remember May Alice Giles was the very best one to wait on because she let me suggest her sewing projects at school in home ec [economics].

We had feed, fencing wire, you name it. We had two old gas pumps. They were electric, but before that you pumped it. [Hand pumped the amount of gas into a glass container at the top of the pump and then drained it into the car's tank.] I think one of those old pumps is still around there maybe. We had gas and oil. There never was but one man that asked me to put his oil in; they were all real nice. One man parked completely across the road and wanted me to check his oil. It was so thick it looked like mashed-up coal; it was so thick it wouldn't run. I said, "You need a quart." He needed five quarts or whatever it took for a change.

The candy was kept in a big glass case, and on top of it we had open boxes. I never did see but one child take candy. This child – I won't call any names – didn't have to take it. She could have bought all the candy she wanted. I knew what kind she wanted; she wanted Hershey bars. They were very thin. But, instead of her telling me what she wanted, she wanted to get the sack and get them off of the top herself. They were just this thin, but I watched her one day and she had them about that thick when she put them in her little nickel sack. Instead of getting one she had a stack of five. I just walked around real kind and said, "do you want to pay me for all that candy." She handed me back four of the bars. I think I did her a favor by calling her hand, and I never did think I was being mean to her at all. After she moved to town I thought about Roses and a lot of those dime stores that might get into trouble if I hadn't talked to her.

We burned a big pot-bellied stove with coal, a big, tall thing. We never wanted for home-cooked food. You remember, Jessie, how I used to cook it. I bought a flat-bottom iron kettle. I would put my meat in the bottom, my green beans on top of that, and let that cook a while. Then, my squash, my okra, my onions, whatever I wanted on top of that. Then I would have a good supper. One pot. It was really good!

We didn't play cards at the store, but they did at Bethesda all the time. It wouldn't always go right down there. I didn't want anything that would be a problem. You know you can get pretty wrapped up in a card game. Then I didn't want to have to walk around them either.

The shelves went nearly to the ceiling. We didn't have ladders that rolled like in some places. You could take something and reach up or you could just climb up there on a box or crate. A lot of the little things that happened in the store I will never forget. One little feller kept eating grapes one night 'til I thought he was going to be sick. Everybody was around the heater, and he was in back. His daddy or momma finally noticed him and said, "Where are you getting them grapes?" He said, "Well, Agnes has got plenty of them!" Lot of kids were funny. We got grapes and bananas in Nashville. Oranges, apples. Never will forget another thing. Two ladies – old maids – from Bethesda came. They bought their flour from us and their winter galoshes [overshoes]. It was close to Christmas time. Miss Loreen Bond went back – we kept the fruit and all the furthest away from the heaters – and got some fruit and stuck it up to Mary Bond's nose, said "Don't that smell good?" and laid it back down.

We had a box full of all kinds of ice cream. Then the big ice storm in January 1951 made our lights go off for 14 days. We had to dump all the ice cream on the garbage heap across the road. If we could have put the box out on the porch it would have been all right, but we didn't do that.

The school bus sometimes let off a bunch of kids at the store. They picked up a bunch in the morning and let them off at the store a lot of times while they went on up to Pull Tight and turned around. They could get a cold drink, a nickel cold drink back then, a nickel popsicle, or a nickel little cup of cream. We always enjoyed the kids, and occasionally I have one tell me something I did back then. Not long ago, Joe Farrar did something for me, and I was thanking him for it. He said, "I can never do enough to pay you for what you did for me when I was growing up." He said every time that I gave my boy David a clean handkerchief in the morning and his mother could not find one for him, I would give Joe one too. And, if Mike Trice's shoes were untied, I tied his shoes. I polished shoes. I furnished Kleenex. I helped with the lessons while waiting to be picked up. Lot of times I would help Mike. I wiped noses and furnished paper some too. But I enjoyed every bit of it and they haven't forgotten it either.

There have been a thousand little different things that have happened. I got blamed for a few things when it wasn't my fault. One time a man came, and his wife was home with a little baby; they had a bunch of children. He had a little tiny toddler with him, a little girl. It was cold weather, and the little girl didn't have enough clothes on for that. He would go out the front door occasionally to the front porch. Then he would come back in and leave the little girl out there. I knew it was too cold for that little girl and I went and got her. He gave me a good cursing for making her cry. Well, I brought her in, and she was afraid of me. Just little things like that.

Our hours of operation were unpredictable. People started calling us if they had a calf or something go off. One of Shiney's uncles would come ahead of time and say he was going to have a calf about so and so to take to Nashville. He'd want a stand of lard – that's fifty pounds – and he'd want to get that lard now, when that calf was two weeks old, and not pay until we sold it at four or five months old. And he would want that lard with no interest paid on the price. They would get us up anywhere from four-thirty or five o'clock. Shiney would take the truck and go to loading up livestock. Here one thing, and something else another place. I would have to get up and do at the house what I could get done, and then get ready and come on up to the store and open up. If it was summertime, I didn't have to build a fire, and that made it a lot easier.

Sam Anderson, road foreman, working the road at Cross Keys. Son Herman on back row sitting on the hood of the truck.

I had regulars that come every day and sat all day. Herman Anderson was one. Herman was working on a project he had from Oak Ridge. He knocked the lights out in this whole community, even up on that hill back of where Shela Bennett lives. They said if he could just bridle that and get it together like he was trying to do, he could furnish Williamson County with electricity. He wouldn't tell you nothing. He would come up there and sit. They didn't bother anybody. Herman would come up the road when I would be sweeping the front porch. He would come in and set on a keg and bend over; you couldn't see what was in his hand. He would sit there, and he might not go home for lunch. He would sit there all day. That kinda got on your nerves a little bit. Herman was smart as he could be, a really intelligent person, but he couldn't finish a project, you might say. He didn't talk much but he was nice-mannered and smart as he could be. [Note: Herman attended Bethesda Community Days on August 27, 1996, and was still working on inventions.] We tried to close maybe at nine. Roy Creswell was the last one out the door at night.

Few had televisions back then. T.R. Clendenen had one, Scott Reed had one, and we did. Some of them would want to go down there and watch the wrasslin'. I didn't care for that fake wrasslin' in the first place. Then, we'd get to bed maybe at ten o'clock. It wouldn't be maybe an hour 'til somebody would be hollering, and they would need ten or fifteen or twenty dollars. We had it at the house at that time. They would be out and need a cab fare or something. One night it was one o'clock in the morning and it was the judge out of Franklin and some friends.

One of the women fell off the back porch when she started out. I could tell you a lot; if I was educated, I would write a book!

G.W. Creswell, Irma, Roy, Bessie, Ruth, and Bill, 1914 at Cross Keys

THE BURGLARS

We were lucky. We were broken into only one time. We slept in the room toward the store. They went under the floor and sawed a hole with a keyhole saw. It wasn't a very large hole. The thing was, they sawed in under the stair step and then had to make a second hole. The store was above ground at the back enough so kids could crawl under there. They sawed under there; sawed two holes. The front door didn't lock; there weren't too many locks on places. You barred doors any way you could. We had like a buggy axle. There was an iron latch thing on both sides of the door, and you just put that axle through there. Well, we never did see that anymore. They took it and threw it somewhere. Everybody was looking for it. You know how people used to walk through the woods and through the fields, up and down the roads. Everybody walked. But they broke in and the only thing they did was drink a bunch of cold drinks, eat off of a whole stick of baloney, and wrap up, I reckon, in some yard goods. I don't think they even took cigarettes.

LUNCH AT THE STORE

A lot of people ate lunch at the store. I think of Mr. Leslie Stevens., who ran a mill that ground corn for cattle and other things. He and his oldest son, Gene, worked all through the country up here; they went miles and miles. When they would come in the store, Mr. Leslie's eyebrows and his face would just be that thick in dust. I think that was not healthy. Gene, you know, didn't live long and Mr. Leslie did not live to be an old man. But they worked at that. They would come in and eat. But they would have to get their eyes and mouth clean enough to eat. And their eyes were usually just as red as could be. Anyway, they usually ate Viennas [sausage] and crackers.

I got to where I could cut a pound of baloney without laying it on the scales. It wouldn't be a fraction of an ounce different. Then, some wanted a baloney sandwich with cheese on it. I cut baloney until I didn't want to see it or smell it. Then, sardines – a lot of them liked sardines and a coke. Owen Farrar always ate sardines.

Jessie: I can see them under the old tree.

Crackers were in two-pound boxes at that time, but I can remember when they came in bulk. One time Grover Trice [Jessie's father] was in there, and Shiney was off hauling hay. I had David, my small son, and he got the crackers out. We had been having them in squares of four and these were single crackers. Grover told David he didn't want those old stale crackers – somebody else's crackers. It kind of made me mad. They were single and he thought somebody else had left them I guess. Years ago, crackers were in barrels, but we didn't have them.

Most everything was in kind of bulk. You took your own containers to get so many things. For vinegar, you had to take your vinegar jug. When I was about six years old and my brother seven, we had to walk about two miles to the store. My mamma was home with three little ones. Cecil made me carry that jug all the way because I couldn't say vinegar, and he was going to make me ask for vinegar.

Those nickel sticks of peanut butter and big old nickel sticks of candy were ten or twelve inches long – nickel sticks of candy. I had an uncle who came out one time when we all had whoopin' cough. He wanted to take us to the store and my mother didn't want us out, but anyway, he insisted. He walked with us to the store and got us all a big stick of that candy and we just about eat that stick before we got home. But it cured our whooping cough! It sure did.

We were all so sick with that candy. We got over that whooping cough. I think he knew what he was doing!

THE LOCAL BANKERS

Another thing, too. We were bankers. Jessie Bennett knows that. Charles wouldn't have married her if we hadn't let him have the money to get married. Haha! He wasn't the only one. I could start naming them, but they always paid us back. Not a one of us beat us as far out of borrowed money, not a dime. Way later, one of them got mad one time. He was a dancer. He and his daddy and his brother all liked dancing. He'd come by one Saturday afternoon with tie waving and white shirt, all slicked up, and wanted ten dollars. Well, he didn't stop back by to repay. We let a few weeks pass and when I was sending out some bills, I sent him one. I didn't send out bills for a long time, and then I got to sending out some bills. We got all kinds of answers back from them. He came in when he got that bill. He came in that front door and back to where the register was, plopped that ten-dollar bill down and turned around and never said boo to me or nothing. I had sent that bill and his wife got it; he didn't want his wife and Miss Lizzie, his momma-in-law, to know about it. I had a few that borrowed money to go to Kroger's and trade.

THE COMMUNITY FUND

Another thing while I was in the store. We kept the flower fund, for when somebody in the community passed away. Everybody was good about that. I kept it up for the whole ten years. I had a notebook that I still have in the cedar chest. When somebody in the community passed away you put down who it was and dated it. Anybody that came in who knew him, or didn't even know him, would give a quarter or fifty cents. Usually, it was a ten-dollar wreath back then. It would be about $35 or $40 for the same thing now. I took care of that fund. Sometime there would be money over, sometime there wouldn't be enough. But it would always balance out, until toward the last. The community seemed like it was thinning out; some of the older ones were passing away and these young ones didn't have the money.

A STUPID PRANK

We had a few pranks pulled on us. Mr. Fleming Williams, who was later our sheriff, was our gasoline man at one time. It was kind of a stupid thing to do, to tell you the truth. You wouldn't do it now. Here comes this man in with his collar turned up and black glasses and cap down over his head. He came back and sat down on the old bench by the heater and looked around a little bit but didn't look up. He sat there and sat there. Grover Trice got up and went back to get close to the front door. Others got up and went real close to the front door where they could get out. He sat there with that big old coat on. He had to finally let us know who he was. That was so stupid to do, because he could have got shot. Some of them kind of gave him a little rough talk about it, and, said he should not have done that.

Well, I was where I could put my hand on my gun. He wasn't going to rob us. I had a pistol behind the counter. When I would go down to Miss Fannie Anderson's to spend the night with her sometime, she would be alone. Shiney would tell me to stay at home and let Miss Fannie come with me, but I wasn't afraid. Anyway, I would push that gun and my money bag in that milk bucket, and I'd go to the barn to milk, down across there. If anybody had seen me, I was going to milk. I never was really afraid while I stayed there.

Sheriff Fleming Williams

THE NIGHT PROWLER

One night, somebody was out at the road. David was at home that night. He was just a kid, but he was big enough to have a rifle. He had his rifle laying under his bed, and he heard this man hollering "ho, ho" real loud. It was a moonlight night, and I could tell he had on striped overalls like convicts wore back then. I went from the kitchen to David's room. He had already heard him, and I said, "Now don't you get out of the bed, you lay right there." I said that I was going to look through the curtains and would not let him come on the porch or get in the door unless he tells who it is. He stood there and hollered a while and went on down the road. Several of these things happened but I wasn't too afraid.

PULL TIGHT HILL ROAD

Pull Tight Hill Road was where it is now when we came. It used to go by the church up there and come out over on the Allisona Road, just about. That's where it should have always been. Mr. Sam Anderson, I think, was foreman over the roads when they built Pull Tight where it is now. It was dangerous even in horse and buggy days; it really was a dangerous road. It never should have been put around that hill. And they have signs now: *Travel at your Own Risk*, and *One Lane*. [They were put up after several cars got stuck and one went over the side of the hill following a winter storm in early 1996] When you are coming toward Bethesda you are on the outside of the road. This couple that walks for their health up and down walk that because there is not much traffic. They said that back under that blacktop they put on there, that's all gone. The safe side is too bad for me; I don't want to go over it. I hope that someday they get a road through where it should be.

Sam F. Anderson

There weren't many phones back then. Very few phones. The store had a phone and Miss Fannie had one. All the traders would stop at the store: Horace Johns, David Ivy, Mr. Charles Rigsby, Jimmie Robertson, Bean Stephens, Mr. Quirk from Columbia, a whole bunch of traders. They would all stop at the store. I'll brag on myself a little now. They would say, "Come out here, Miss Agnes, and see what you think these shoats will weigh." I would say, "Well, they look like they ought to weigh about 15 pounds apiece." Well, that's what they averaged out. One time there was a cow on the road, Mr. Trav's cow. I called him and said I believed he had a cow on the road, a calf like. I described it, "It's a Hereford, white." He said, "What size is it." He knew the sizes of his – he was in the cattle business next door and across the road. I said, "Well, it will weigh 450 pounds." It weighed 455.

Another thing I had to do was a lot of hay hauling back then. There were a lot of dairymen around here. You [Jessie] remember Earl Harris and a lot of dairymen. That is about a thing of the past if it wasn't for the Bonds. Anyway, my husband did a lot of hay hauling from Indiana and Ohio and different places. I had to figure that hay, and you've got to get it down to the pounds when you are hauling. It was baled then, not rolls like today. I learned how to figure that out. If

Hawkins Giles milking a Jersey cow

it was $20 a ton, I learned how to figure the price per pound. They hauled a lot of logs. The sawmill was somewhere down here around Bethesda, at Jimmy D. Bennett's, back in there. In school, we didn't have to figure board feet of lumber and all that from the size of a tree and the length of it. I learned that. Mr. Hugh Hawkins helped me to learn to figure out a corn crib of corn and how many barrels were in that crib. I had a lot of help. I had to! Once I could get it going it was all right. I had to do all of that.

It was a general store. We had sheep bells, cowbells, and cooking vessels. A girl was in the store – a lady from out at Beech who was visiting some relatives around here, from Michigan. I had cooking vessels and she said she worked at the plant where that was made. We had just about anything you could think of. If people asked for it we got it. We had shelves all the way except at the back and front. Then we had counters about so high. Mr. Ed Biggers made us something like a stairstep to put the glassware on. It was a long one – that store was a long, long store. It was a three-step. That's where I kept table lamps and glassware – it wasn't plastic back then, no plastic.

ROADS IN THE FORTIES

The road was so dusty it kept me dusting all the time. Some people from Franklin, a Houghland man, and his son, came out and ate lunch in the store one day. I was dusting when they came in and apologized about everything looking so dusty and all. I told them how long we had been working to try to get a road. We rode at night, talking to people, but they didn't want to give up a little land. Not all of them. When you build a road in certain spots you've got a surplus and in certain spots you need dirt. That is how come the pond down here in our front lot. They needed dirt for this road. Anyway, that man took a little piece of paper out of his pocket and wrote a lot of stuff down. If he ever did anything to help, I didn't know it, but maybe he did.

We finally got a road. When we moved here the only way they told us was when we were going up and down the road to watch for a certain cedar tree. That's where we turned in, or we would have passed it. This road, the sides of it, was just like a woods. And rough! You could follow the road, but it was almost like going through the woods. We gave all the road in front of our house. One morning the road crew was going to have to quit work if they couldn't get dirt. They had gone just as far as they could. Shiney told them to go in the lot and get all the dirt, just so you leave my front doorstep. I said, "I want a little more than that left."

Then there was quite a bit of woods around. There were some fields on the sides, but the fence rows were like from here to the door wide. People traveled through the woods the nearest way was how you went because everybody, nearly, walked back then. There weren't too many cars. There was Miss Fannie, she didn't drive or have a car. Sam Reed didn't have a car. I guess Chub Hargrove did. People used to go to Franklin from here in buggies. That was not long before we came here.

DOCTORS

Another thing, if anybody needed a doctor they always came to the store and called. One time I called Dr. Ellis at Chapel Hill. He had just like a mail route through here. He would stop at these older people. He'd stop over at Jimmie Lou Trice's. He stopped at every house nearly, because a lot of them were old people. He made them feel good. He was pouring dope or something to them, I reckon. Anyway, one time I called him for a man who lived off of Comstock Road. Dr. Ellis asked if I was going to pay. I said, "No, sir, I'm not going to pay!" I couldn't have started that. No way.

One time I was trying to call to get an ambulance or a doctor or whatever I could get. This schoolteacher's wife down on Critz Lane wouldn't give up the phone [it was a party line shared by several users]. She asked me twice, but one time she asked me when I was calling for a doctor, do you need a doctor or "Do you just want to talk to him?" I said, "There is a man dying. I guess I need a doctor." That was Mr. Green.

Doctors charged probably five dollars for a visit in those days.

HOME LIFE

I sewed and made all of David's clothes until he was nine years old. I had a brooder and raised fifty fryers and kept a fair house. I would be hanging clothes out at one o'clock in the morning several times. We were supposed to have Sunday off but when Sunday morning came somebody would need something. I would have to go up there. It may be a pound of coffee or a box of crackers or just one item. By that time another would come in, and by that time another come in to use the phone. 'I would be standing there with my loaf of bread in my hands wanting to get out the back door, them on the phone. There were two men in the community who called their folks every Sunday morning and talked and talked and talked. I guess I was kinda mean about some of it but never had a problem so far as ill feelings.

The neighborhood always helped each other in canning beef or killing chickens. We butchered our own hogs and later on made sausage and all that. Me and Miss Fannie worked a lot in that together. She taught me a lot.

We did a lot of quilting. Neighbors come in to help quilt or if your house needed papering. Elsie papered every year nearly. Miss Fannie would buy the paper and have the house papered. One day they tried to match that paper. They finally thought they had it. I went down there and looked at the front hall, and it was all out of shape. It was pretty though.

The kitchen had paper on it for years and years and years. Dated way, way back. We took all that off and pulled hundreds of tacks out. Hundreds! It was hard to get them out of that wood; they had good wood back then. Once Doc Crafton was painting. He said he was paying for the paint and got good paint. He come up to the store and popped another gallon up there; it had done gone in the wall because he didn't use any primer. It was gone; you couldn't tell there was anything on it. I forget now what he did. Got some primer, I guess.

There was a lot of enjoyment to it and there were a lot of headaches to it.

ANNIE LOU REED MCCORD
1896-1998

Now, I don't know anything.

Jessie: Well, tell us about how you met that wonderful husband of yours.

Well, I just don't remember nothing worth telling, only he courted me for two years to get up courage enough to ask my daddy for me. I have lived where I live now ever since I have been married. I have had hard work and clean living.

CHILDHOOD MEMORIES

When I was a little girl, I went to school at Bethesda. Walked two miles. In my lunch box I had sausage and biscuits and fried peach pies. We had one lunch box and my oldest brother Henry handed out everyone's lunch. And he just wanted biscuits and molasses. He took his finger and made a little hole in the biscuit and poured it full of molasses. He carried the molasses in a jar.

I was nine years old when I stood up in a chair and learned to make biscuits. It took a big wad of dough to bake three pans of biscuits for nine children. I made all the biscuits myself. We put homemade butter on our biscuits, churned in an old dasher cedar churn. With the milk that was left from the churn we made buttermilk. There was a big pitcher of buttermilk on the table all the time, and sweet milk too, and coffee for my daddy. It was cold enough in the kitchen to keep things cold. The wind would come up between the cracks. They didn't have no rugs on the floors.

My mother and daddy washed by taking the clothes down to the creek. They had a big pot down there and they washed the clothes on a rub board. They put them in the pot and boiled them with homemade lye soap. We carried the wet clothes to the house. In the yard, we had a big wire clothesline and we hung them on that clothesline until they got dry, or they froze dry. We had to wait until another day to iron because they didn't all get dry. We didn't have electricity, so we used big old steel hand irons. We built up a fire out in the yard and got them hot and sat out there and ironed the clothes in the sunshine.

Annie Lou, Napoleon holding Floyd, Fannie holding Willie Alice, standing: Buford, Henry, and Charlie Reed

After a hard day of work, a typical evening at our house was for Henry, my brother, to pick the banjo and my father would play the fiddle and I would play the piano. And we just had music! We didn't dance, no. We never did dance. I played the piano by ear mostly. I took music for a little bit from Miss Powell over about Triune. And Jimmy Lou Trice took music over there at the same time. I have no idea what a music lesson cost then. My daddy wasn't able to have many lessons because with nine children he didn't have much money. But we had a lot of fun and we had plenty to eat – and good eats. We raised everything we ate. We had a big orchard, made cider and we barreled it up for vinegar. We had a little – what they called a Speck stove [brand name for a step-type stove]. It had two caps down here and two caps up here.

We didn't have no bathroom. The boys all went to the creek and the girls brought in a big wash tub at night and got back in the back room – in the kitchen – after everybody else was out and locked the doors. I had two sisters. Six brothers and two sisters. I had my 100th birthday in December – the 30th of December. I was born in 1895 and we married December 26, nineteen and fifteen.

MARRIED LIFE

We got married sitting in a horse and buggy down at New Hope Church and then we drove on to Franklin to my Aunt Win Reed's and had a wedding dinner. We come back home that night and that was my honeymoon. Charlie and Fannie [Trice] married the same day Walker and I did. We came back to my husband's home, which is here, but not in this house. I have lived here since I was married. We lived together 60 years, happy years.

I said all the time that I wouldn't live in the house with no other woman when I was a growing up. And I never lived nowhere else. I lived 19 years in the house with Mrs. McCord. She was Jimmy Walker's girl from Virginia. They came down from Virginia.

My husband for his hobbies mowed the yard and chopped the garden, and he pieced quilts and crocheted. He also caned chair bottoms [one was for Jessie] after he retired from being a carpenter. When he was a little boy his mother, Mrs. McCord, set him out in the yard and give him a bucket full of old nails and he drove them everyone in the ground, pulled them out and drove them back again 'til he fell asleep. And then she would take him and put him to bed. And she said he was a natural-born carpenter. He loved to drive nails.

He helped to build Camp Breckenridge up in Kentucky during the war. He worked up there for three months. The last house he built in the Bethesda area was up here on Flat Creek Road – that pink brick house. And he built Johnny Hatcher's house, and he built barns for everybody. And he built the smokestack at Bethesda school when it was up on the hill, where you [Jessie] went to school.

My husband was a magistrate for five weddings. The first one he had here at the place was a double one. Another one that he married – they come in here and we were gone to prayer meeting and his mother told him – they wanted to know where he was. One of them was Lillian Burkhart and Robert Biggers. And we come back from prayer meeting, turned in our road up yonder and somebody flashed their lights. I said, " I'm not going – we better not go in there. Somebody is down there drunk." And he said, "Well, I'm not going to let nobody run me out of my home and we're going on." And they come on and about that time Robert got out and came to the buggy and told him what he wanted. He said all right, I'll get out and go see. He struck a match and looked at Lillian and said, "I believe she'll pass." And he married them right up our lane up there – he married that couple, and they wanted it to be a secret. She was teaching school and was boarding at Miss Carrie Trice's, in the old rock house [the old Laban Hartley house]. He married six couples while he was a magistrate. We didn't marry anyone in the house. He would have to go out to the buggy.

At Christmas – we always had a Christmas tree – and he would help me roll [wrap] the gifts and everything. He wouldn't waste the paper to roll mine. It was a box of chocolate-covered cherries tied with a twine of string. He didn't wrap mine. He just thought it was wasting money. When I was a little girl, before I was married, we hung our stockings up and I'd get a pretty doll in it. I also got three or four pieces of sugar candy in my stocking. We didn't get much. We did get raisins-on-a-stem [not in a box]. My momma always got a present on the table. They say that's what Santa Claus left for momma – a whole hoop of cheese. They cut the cheese with an old sharp butcher knife, sharpened on a grindstone with somebody turning the grindstone and my daddy holding the butcher knife.

HOG KILLING AND RELATED MATTERS

They had to have sharp knives when they killed hogs. When they killed hogs, they built a big fire around what they called a scalding tub down at the creek. They filled it full of water and when it got boiling hot, they'd have one of the hogs already killed. They'd put him in there and get all that hair off of him.

Well, Elizabeth and Dorothy went out here in the lot one time and we had six to eight shoats, and they decided they wanted some fresh meat. They went out there and caught that pig and drug him – a great big hog – in the yard and I stuck him with a butcher knife. And they put him in the wash pot and got him clean. He was really clean, but they didn't think clean enough and they come to the house and got razor blades and just about cut all the hair off of him. They hung him up and I took the butcher knife and done the rest. I got the chittlins [chitterlings] out. That's all I know about 'em and I don't want to know no more. I can't bear the smell of them, but they cooked them at my mother's – rolled them in batter and fried them and they were the best looking things you ever looked at. But I took one bite, and I couldn't swallow it. And I never have took another one. No!

The water down there runs over a rock bottom in our creek, and we stood there with our overshoes on and ripped them hogs open and they just went on down the creek, the insides you know. And we washed them [chitterlings] and put them in a tub of water and set them in the smokehouse and they froze over, and I broke it and got them out and put them in a two-gallon bucket. My husband got on what they called the Interurban that run from Franklin to Nashville where my brother lived, and he loved chittlins. He carried him that two-gallon bucket full of chittlins to Nashville on the Interurban.

There was a lady came down from up in Wisconsin, and she said she never heard of a chittlin. Said, "What is a chittlin?"

We didn't have no balloons then, but we all had our bladder [from the hogs] and we hung it over the fireplace. And Christmas morning we popped them bladders.

Jessie: I remember that but hadn't thought of that in years. You would hang them up on the wall and when they dried, they would pop. We all fought over them.

We put some popcorn in them before we blowed them up so they would rattle.

We salted the meat down. We would lay it out on the roof at night and then we would salt it in a big box and let it lay for so many weeks and get it up then and hang it up and build a fire under it with hickory wood and smoke it. We hung it up in the smokehouse. We would go to the smokehouse and get a big ham and cut it when anybody comes to spend the day. We'd have ham.

One time my grandmother was there, and Mrs. Alexander and Dr. Blythe Core was all going to be there for dinner, and you know what was going to be on the menu. I couldn't get it in the skillet right. It wouldn't fit in the big old iron skillet. And I just took the butcher knife and cut it up in strips and laid it in there and when it got done there were little strips about like my finger. And, my father said to me, "Sissy, what happened to your meat?" And I didn't like for him to reprove me, you know, in front of guests. So, I said, "Well, I cut it to fit the skillet."

Oh, did we make sausage! We would cook a sack of sausage when we boiled a ham. When it got done, we lifted the sausage sack out and just left it stay in there 'til it got cold and we'd take that cloth off of it – made out of brown domestic. The sacks were great, long sacks – and it was the best meatloaf you ever had. Slice down through it. You would leave it in the sack 'til you take out the ham and take out the sausage and leave it 'til it gets cold.

Late in the fall my daddy would have to kill a shoat [for meat], and he killed goats, too. He had goats. We trimmed the meat all around to get all the fat off of it and that would make your lard. You chopped up the fat in pieces and put them in a pot and stand there and stir it and stir it and stir it until it got to be cracklins. And then you lifted them cracklins out and strain it into the lard stand [a large metal can] that we had setting there. Oh, them cracklins makes cracklin bread! They said you would sing, "Get out the skillet and hang on the lid, the white folks gonna have shortnin' bread." Shortnin' bread was like cracklin bread. It was s-o-o-o good!

We milked cows and sold milk. We put it in cans and cooled it down here at the well. There are six wells here on this place. And there were slaves here.

SOME FAMILY STORIES

Elizabeth Crunk went with her aunt to visit with the neighbors over here where your boy lives now. We had read storybooks to her. We had an old story about the king, and he said, "Fe-fi-fo fum. I smell the blood of an Englishman." And she got it mixed up and when she got over there with her aunt, she jumped up in a rocking chair like she had never seen a rocking chair before and got to rock, rock, rock and saying "Ke-ki-ko-kum." She yelled that as loud as she could. Ira brought her home and said, "I don't intend to take that young 'un nowhere else, never. Never again."

When we were at home the boys would get out and play ball. The girls got out and played marbles and hopscotch. We jumped ropes. One would hold one end and the other girl would hold the other and one a jumping. Sometimes they would holler "Pepper" and they would get it that much hotter – that much faster. And the boys would set down and play marbles and mumble peg – they drove a peg in the ground, and you had to get down and pull it out with your teeth.

One time Minnie and Joe Will Hazelwood went off to town and left all them children there – ten children. Annie Lee was a baby at that time. They were a playing hiding and seek and they run by the churn and they just stood her up in the churn and they went on to play hide and seek. And they couldn't find her. When they found her, there the little one was setting in the old cedar churn.

Elizabeth McCord Crunk

And one day Elizabeth and Dorothy got into a fight. Elizabeth hit Dorothy and Dorothy cried. I said, "You go over there and tell your little sister you are sorry." She went over there, and she said, "I'm sorry ... but I ain't." She used to ride the harrows here with three mules hitched to the harrow for our daddy to sow seed. She worked out with him. That's why she likes to work out now.

Well, one time I was setting out on the back porch. I had washed my hair, and I was setting on the couch letting it dry. It had blowed up like a balloon, and Jessie [Bennett] come to the back door to get Mr. Walker to bottom a chair. And she saw me, and it scared her to death. She just fell back out the door. Yes, he liked to joke.

Jessie told a story about Mr. Walker. He fixed a chair for her but when she came to get it he told her it was in too bad shape to fix. He had a piece of cardboard over it, but when she picked it up, she found that he had fooled her. She still has the chair.

THE PACK PEDDLER

And one thing I do remember that I doubt if anybody else does – there was a pack peddler that come through the country. They'd stop over at the store and ask where they could spend the night. He was a walkin.' He came over there and Pappy let him stay all night. He wouldn't turn nobody away. And, then next morning he'd open up his pack and the first thing he would do would be give my mother what we called a bedspread – a counterpane – and it was blue and was real pretty. And he had beads – that's one thing I wanted, a string of beads – and they were right there. You didn't have to order them. A pack peddler is a peddler – he's a Jew from the old country – and he came over here to send back to get his wife in years to come. He just had everything in that pack. He unrolled it – it was wrapped in what looked like black oilcloth. It had men's razors that had handles on them. They wasn't any old little safety razors. They had a handle and you opened it up. And he had mirrors in there and he had needles and thread and thimbles and French harps for the boys and pocketknives for the boys and just everything you wanted. I don't remember what anything cost – I didn't know how to count money at that time. That was the only pack peddler I ever did see. He strapped the pack on his back that he pulled up pretty good. The second time he came in a little wagon and drove a little mule and he walked behind. Martin Tohrner here in Franklin for years bought scrap iron and everything, and he was a Jew.

CHURCH

We went to church in a horse and buggy. And I was playing the organ one night and I got up to play the organ for the last song of the revival, and my ankle turned, and I fell sprawling in Mr. Billy Hargrove's lap. He always set on the front seat with a big palm leaf fan – it was hot in that church. On Sunday evenings we visited the shut-ins – the old folks that was older than we were.

I went to revivals – Presbyterians don't have revivals, do they? They had revivals as long as I can remember. When they held revivals outside, they called them camp meetings, but we never did have that – we just had them in the church. When I was young the men and women did not sit together at church. They had two doors, and the women would sit on one side and the men on the other.

We had fellowship dinners and homecomings and everything like that. When I was married, we would always keep the preachers. And we had a woman preacher Jane Derryberry. Dale McCord – we kept Dale after he got out of school. He was going to make a preacher and he didn't have no way to go nowhere, and we'd keep him here in our home. And he couldn't preach much. We had a nice time together.

POLITICS

I don't know nothing about politics because I don't believe in them.

FUNERALS, WAKES, AND THE SICK

There were no funeral homes when I was a little girl. They had the funerals at home. I was setting up one night up on the hill up here and this girl – Mr. Biggers girl – had cancer and she died. We didn't have no telephones and Walker was coming after me next morning at four o'clock and she died about midnight. They had to go to Doug Davidson's to call the undertaker. He come in and he looked at me a minute and he said, "Get that kerosene lamp over there and stand at the head of the bed while I embalm her." And I saw him, what he done – start there and clip, clip, clip. Makes you shiver! They brought the casket that night and got her through with and I had to stay the rest of the night. Back then when someone died, they had the funeral there at home. They set up with her the night before. They didn't take children to funerals. They brought Mrs. McCord back here that night.

At a wake, they sat up with them. I hope nobody woke up. I heard them tell a story about somebody that had rheumatism and raised up in the casket. Some of them started out the windows and everywhere.

I was setting up with a lady that was sick one night – I went around and set up with everybody. I took a nurses' course one time for six weeks. And I was setting up with Mrs. Lulu Robinson and her husband had gone off to take a nap. I had to drop the medicine 15 drops. When I got back to the bed to give it to her, she had took a double white blanket and put her head under it. I throwed that white medicine into the fire, afraid that she'd smother to death before I could get her out. It was no laughing matter.

One night we got her up – Miss Irene was setting up with me that night – to rest her back before putting her to bed for the night. There was a big old iron poking stick [fireplace poker] in the corner and she said, "Miss Annie Lou, will you change corners with me?" She was setting over in the other corner. I said I would be glad to but I picked up the poking stick when I started. She was going to get that after me.

BEING A GOOD NEIGHBOR

I walked from here to where Roy Cooper lives and picked strawberries. The Robertsons lived there then. I picked them a gallon and me a gallon, and them a gallon and me a gallon. And I'd walk back home and tote my strawberries. You know how far that is. I walked all over this country. I didn't let nobody move in and live a year in this country but what I didn't visit them. Josephine Ketchum, my neighbor for 30 years I reckon – the first head of cabbage I had one time I cut it half in two and sent her a half a head to make slaw, and I had a half a head. She was talking about it Sunday evening when she was over here. She spent the afternoon with me Sunday and she was talking about how long we had been living neighbors together, about 30 years. She was the first one to get to me when Walker died. You know, he fell dead up the lane – right up the lane there.

MY 100TH BIRTHDAY

I don't remember my 100th birthday party too well. [*A tongue-in-cheek remark.*] I tried to remember everything, but I couldn't remember all of it. And, when Hap and Annie Lee Neal come to wish me a happy birthday, Hap looked down at Annie Lee and said, "Annie Lee, she don't have as many wrinkles as I do."

Jessie: what would be your philosophy of life to someone 100 years from now?

I don't have no words for them if they ain't got no better – I don't know. Work hard and clean life. I hope the ones that take the time capsule out have the strength not to read it. Who would want to read all of this mess.

Jessie: wouldn't you like to hear something that happened 100 years ago?

Yeah! If you put this in a book, you'll be ashamed of it, and I will too! I'll be ashamed to hear it, I sure would.

BESSIE TAYLOR MOSLEY, 1905-2004

    I was born right here, not in this house, but in a' old log cabin that was here. I've been in this house as long as I have lived. In fact, we tore the old log cabin down to build this house. I was born in 1905 and you, like a lot of other people, probably won't believe me, but the road came right down the creek here. All the way down the creek. I know there's people that have argued with me. They're wrong. I know. I was born here. When the creek went up, you didn't get out. If you died, you waited until the creek went down. The road followed the creek to down yonder – you know where this last road turns at bottom of this field down here. The road followed right around down into the creek. There was a little spot of sand down there, but it didn't amount to nothing – about the size of that bed as you come over it. You got out of the creek up yonder just before you get up to Ellie Marshall's place, about halfway between where we go out on the road and where her garden is. Finally, the county got that road over there [Bethesda-Duplex Road]. The people that owned the land didn't want to give the land for the road, but they finally got it.

It was about 1919 or 1920 when they opened up that road and they left us sitting back here. I'm still here. But they never would let us have a road across there. We had a terrible time getting it, now after Charles [Giles] come up here he was able to get out and start pushing – and we liked to never got a road through here. They had to keep Squeaky [Clifford Grigsby] drunk for a month. Haha. We finally got the road and proud of it.

We got out through the creek bed. From right here we went up the creek until we got up to the road. We rode in a homemade slide. It was two logs, about eight or nine inches in diameter. They would go out about seven or eight feet – however long you want to. But you've got to have them with a crook in them, where they turn up. Then they hack off the bottom of them and make them sort of straight instead of round. And you would hook an old mule to them or old horse - something – and here you go. Now ya'll won't believe this, but I have seen that creek up halfway to this house here. That's right.

CHILDHOOD DAYS

I had two sisters, that's all. No boys. My daddy was a hard worker, I don't think there was anybody that worked any harder. I was the middle child. My older sister died, and on her 19th birthday is when she was buried. The second day of December. We never did know what happened to her. She married, was married about two and half years, a little longer than that.

And she got sick, and they thought she was going to recover, and my mother went and stayed with her from in the fall until the coming May and she just got worse and worse. She was down in bed, and they brought her home. Dr. Core brought her home himself. They put her to bed, and she never did get up anymore. We'd take her up and sit her up for a few minutes at a time. We never did know what was wrong. We had all kinds of doctors come and look at her. She left a 21-month-old baby that my daddy and mother raised. But we made it. My sister that died was Bertha. The other one was Mary Sue; she died in '87. She married Emmett Jennette, and they lived in Spring Hill. Then moved to Nashville and he died in Nashville.

I had a hard time back then, getting by I'll tell ya. We raised every single thing we had to eat. Fattened the hogs and killed the hogs. We got up at three o'clock in the morning and started, and I was my Daddy's boy. Now I worked in the field from the time I was six years old, and I done it all.

You should have seen me grinding sorghum cane to make them molasses! You raised sorghum like corn, you know, only planted thicker. And then you take all the fodder off of it and cut it down and then you had to cut the seeds off of it. It would be chicken feed when you get the seeds off. Of course, you haul it [the sorghum stalks] to the old mill. It was right up the road here. The mill had two [horizontal] wheels – I don't know what you call them. One wheel had a great long pole on it and you hitched the mules to that pole, and they'd go around and around turning one of the wheels against the other. You had to sit and poke canes in there all the time, between the wheels. Juice would come out. There was a pipe for the juice to come through, and it had to come under our road. The sorghum pan was setting over on the other side of the road, right against the fence. When the juice got there it come out in a big tub we had there. Then you lifted that up onto a big tub that's on a stand way up so high. Then when you got it cooked off up at the upper end, it run off, and into a great big ol' thing, a pan about the size of a box like you were gonna put a coffin in or something. Of course, it was made better. That box was in little things [compartments] about so wide and you had little sticks to push the syrup along. There were little "windows" and you'd push it and it would come through. There was a fire under the pan, which was sitting on sand rock, and as you pushed the syrup along, it would be cooking all the time. We made sorghum every fall and my daddy made it for the public.

Daddy had a wagon and he hauled phosphate. It was about the time I started to school, about 1911 or 1912. He hauled it somewhere. I don't know where they ground it up at and I don't know where he got it at. I just know he hauled phosphate. Bought a brand-new wagon to have to haul it in. They used to haul something from Clovercroft, too.

Mr. Joe Harmon, Elise Thompson's daddy, lived down here, you know where Ellie [Beasley] lives. He had a corn wagon, like my daddy, and he'd come up this road and they went together. Mr. Joe come up there when, oh, it would be so cold and frost stickin' up. He'd have both hands sticking in his pockets and dancing around to keep warm and he'd be singing saying, "The creeks all muddy and the cake's all dough. Never mind the weather so the wind don't blow."

Charles Giles bought my daddy's place after he died. It was right around the corner there. So, we lived here 'til I was eleven years old. Now, he'd come back home after he was married about five or six years and lived somewhere else. But he come back here in this old log house here – nobody lived in it – to take care of his mother and daddy because they had gotten old and couldn't do. They lived up there in the old log cabin; that's where my daddy was born, up there in that old log cabin. That cabin is now down there in the back of that nursing home,

Franklin Manor on Columbia Avenue. Ms. Laura Loftin owned it and bought it and put that down there. Lewis [Mosley] told me not long ago that they were letting it go bad on top, letting the roof get bad. I wish they wouldn't do that.

After he moved, we moved up there. The old place was just like Charles got it. It was growed up and that's where we made them molasses. We'd sell them for a dime a gallon. Oh, we made money. We grew some of the cane ourselves, but people would bring stuff in. Cleo [Grigsby] knows something about that. Ms. Dolly use to bring sorghum over here, and the Irvins, and a lot of people around here would bring the cane here. He didn't charge for them using the mill. We made it and ground the cane, and he cooked the molasses. They just brought it to the mill, and then he took, I don't know, a fourth or third of the molasses. They used to have a big barrel full and take it to town somewhere and sell it, I don't know where. He'd have some upstairs to sell and if anybody wanted a gallon and they'd come and get it for ten cents a gallon. Boy, we were making money.

People wouldn't believe it now, but we paid for that old place. Course, it was three others besides my daddy that had a share in it after he died, and he had to buy them out. Now we paid for that place a sellin' tobacco for two and three and a half cents a pound. A lot of times the lugs [tobacco scraps and ends] would go for a penny. We dug and cleaned up a little bit every fall, getting ready for the next spring. The place cost, I think, $1,200 when we bought it. It was fifty-two acres, and I've still got seven of it.

HARD WORK

We had a good life, it was hard work. Nobody had better parents than I did, and I mean they were top notch. We went to church over at Ash Hill, we walked or went in the wagon, one or the other, about three miles across there. We had a great big old tobacco barn, it had seven tiers. I went to the top – I'm the one that pulled it up to the top! We'd throw that hay. We didn't have balers; we pitched it on a wagon with a pitchfork. Throwed it in the barn loft and somebody was up there to drag it back and pack it back.

We got up at three o'clock in the morning, and we went to bed as soon as dark comes. Nobody had to tell us to go to bed. My mother never was a healthy lady. She was always sickly like, but she always had dinner cooked for us. Sounds crazy but we always ate all the meat except the hog jowls. My daddy would take it to the store and sell them and he always stood there and bought it in coffee and sugar. We'd get my mother a big can of coffee and he got sugar for the rest of us. We'd have a great big old… we called them dumplins then… you made a piece of dough like this and put your fruit in there and a little sugar and you'd fill the pan up with that and we'd put butter and sugar all over the top of it and we'd put a little water on it and put it in the stove and bake it. Now, that was a pan of dumplins, a pan about this big around. We had two of them. It sure was good. We'd eat one for dinner and one for supper. You had to eat when you worked like that.

To get our flour we raised a little wheat and carried the wheat to the Duck River and carried a lot of corn down there for meal. My daddy in the loft upstairs had wires hang down here and poles across it. He'd take 100 pounds of flour up there and lay it across there where nothing can't get to it, you know. When we needed it, he'd bring a sack down and empty it. Didn't have these fancy flour bins; had barrels then. We had a barrel of meal and a barrel of flour.

This house [the one she lived in as a child] was originally a log house. This one up here was built in 1876. My daddy was four years old when that house was built. There was another old house that stood there, and they built this house, and my daddy was exactly four years old.

LOG STOOLS

In building this house, they had ends of logs that they cut off, just right for a good stool to sit on. My daddy and my uncle got them stools and made them, and that's what they put over behind the table to eat on. That was in eighteen and seventy-six. My daughter has got my daddy's old stool in her house right now. They gave it to her son David – he'll be 25 in August – and he was raised sitting on that stool, too. And she's still got it and wouldn't take nothing for it. It was slick; it didn't have a back and was just like it was cut off

SCHOOL AT BETHESDA

I went to school at Bethesda High School, it was right up here almost in the place where the store is now. The class I was in was 1924, and it was the last year they had a twelfth grade. There was just three of us in the class last year. Some of them would move away and some of them would go to town. James Bond, you know, went to BGA. He moved on. I don't know; I reckon I was about 14 and maybe Cleo was – she wasn't that old. We was 14 or 15 years old and Cleo Grigsby and myself made fires.

In the school, there were two rooms downstairs and one upstairs. The music room was on the end of the front porch. It was piano music, and just the ones who could afford it – that wasn't too many – took lessons in the room.

They had four little heaters. There was a little music room and then there was three school rooms. We had to make fires in them things; the boys wouldn't do it. We walked down on a cold morning; it was cold. Cleo and I, we got up – she got up early, too – and we was always there on time and we started to making fires. Well, that suited them so good they paid us fifty cents a month for making them fires. Boy, we was rich! Some of the mean boys – you know there was always a trash can there to catch the paper we'd keep full to start fires with – those stinking things got to where they'd go around collecting in the evening and emptying that in the fire to burn it up so we wouldn't have anything to start fires with. We'd take those papers, and we'd pick up chips and everything else. I bet we had the cleanest yard of chips of anybody, but I guess we enjoyed it.

My subjects at school were spelling, English, and we had some kind of math every year. And geography. We had a reader book. After we got on up we had some science. And, then we had Latin. We had Latin the first year and then we had Caesar the next. And then we were supposed to have Cicero, but some way or another we didn't like Cicero and we got another subject. We had history books that thick—if the kids now have everything in them clear back like we had them they would be this thick. There is no way they can teach everything that has happened.

When I went to school we had desks, two pupils to the desk. Below there as a place to keep your books in, you know. Of course, you had to write on the desk in front of you. When we got ready for class, there was a long bench that come about two-thirds of the way across the building, to sit on. You would have the class go back and the next class would come up. You had a blackboard all across up there for when you didn't understand anything, why, put it up there. Tried to get it through to us. Had tests – would write the questions up there. I wasn't bad in math myself, not meaning to brag about it, but once in a while I'd get hung up, you know. And you go to the teacher and ask him. He'd say, "Go back and ask Cleo, she's got more time." Now Cleo Grigsby taught me more math, I think, than I learned, after I got up higher. Mr. Reed was my teacher then. Let's see, I had Mr. Coleman, Mr. Wingo, and two years had Mr. Reed in high school.

They didn't teach penmanship in those days. When you were in the first grade, they would teach you a little – the sounds of the letters. We had inkwells. We didn't use them but they was there. Ha. We wrote on paper. We didn't have to use the old slates. My sister did, what little she got to go to school. We had an old slate at home, but I reckon we finally broke it up. We have thrown away things you all would have a fit over. Could have filled a gully full. You all couldn't imagine. Cleo and me was laughing about it one day; she said "Bessie, we've thrown away stuff like that." I said, "we've both thrown away stuff like that."

MORE ABOUT THE CREEK

I was going to tell you about the creek; oh, it froze. There used to be ice about that thick [four or five inches] on it. The kids used to cut it out and bring it out and bury it in the sawdust out here and have tea way on up in the summer. And they skated, oh, they skated up and down there.

Anyway, when I was going to school it would freeze over up yonder. There were slick rocks across there and it would freeze on them rocks. That was my crossing place to get to school. When I went to school back then, we didn't just have two or three books – we had seven and eight. And every night of my life every one of them books had to come home, if not they had to know the reason why. They had to come home, and I had to use them. But anyway, they would be so slick I couldn't walk across there. I'd throw my books out that-a-way. We had little sacks that had one little hole where you stuck your books in – half one way and half the other – and threw them on your shoulder. A lot of book satchels were made just out of plain bed ticking or some kind of domestic that men made their work shirts out of – real slick stuff. Something like a twill. I would throw one end of them books out there and ease and pull myself and help get myself across there.

When the creek was up, we had to walk through these fields out here and crawl over a wire fence, go around about where Mr. Britain lived and down where that bridge is crossing the creek [on Bethesda Road] now. There used to be a wooden foot-log, we walked across there, and we walked across that on up to the school building there where the store is now.

TEACHING AT ASH HILL

I was out of school one year and carried cream from up here to the Cross Keys store to have it tested and sell it. Carry the cream in a bucket up there to the store, and it was tested and then sent on the Nashville. Miss Lizzy Hargrove and them was testing. Trav Wallace was running the store then. But anyway, I was out of school a year and carrying a bucket of that up there. Mr. Wallace McCall was one of the school commissioners. He passed me and he stopped and got to talking to me and wanted to know how about me teaching school at Ash Hill. They needed a teacher. I said, "Well never did nothing about that, no, I didn't want that at all." He just kept on, kept on, and said, "Why don't you try it." I said, "I don't teach school, I don't have no certificate or anything." Well, the teachers' exam was coming up – I believe the last of July, before school started in August – and he wanted me to take it. He kept after me until I did. I went and took the board state exam for teachers, and I ended up over there at Ash Hill about 33 kids and all eight grades. All eight, every one of them.

I went to school when I was teaching by a horse that I had to ride. I didn't have a dress to wear, didn't have a saddle I could use – went to Franklin and borrowed fifty dollars at the bank. Mr. Shearer Irvin went on a note for me to have fifty dollars to buy me a pair of shoes and thread and material to make three dresses and to buy that saddle. It just took two months to pay it off. After the war started teachers got sort of scarce. They come after me – Mr. Charlie Grigsby – and begged me to go back to Ash Hill and teach. Well, I didn't want to, but he kept begging me 'til I said, "Well, all right. Gonna' get ninety dollars a month then instead of sixty."

It was a one-room school. Roy Smithson up here, he was one of my kids that started school with me then, in 1925. There are one or two of them around, but not too many. I just taught one year. I didn't like it a bit. And I married, too, like an idiot. Married a man that had four kids and that took a lot of time washing and ironing, with nothing else but cooking.

THE T-MODEL CAR

We had a T-model during the 30s for one year and then it broke down. It was old and we could not ever find the parts to fix it. It set right under the tree out there and everything about it that could rot was rotted off. It was a little run-about, I think they called it back then. It just had a short back, you know. But after he got this, he cut it off back there and he put a wooden bed on it about so long, and that's where he hauled extra tires and whatever he had to have. If I could think of that man's name, where he bought it … . Miss Nannie Daniels used to ride when we was going to Dr. Eggleston to work. She'd ride about as far as she could. And we had a flat tire coming home one evening. We had stuff piled up knee high and Miss Nannie would get this pole under there and sit on it for me to get the wheel off. We had a lot of fun!

Shearer Irvin, Sr.

One little boy, Ethel Holly's, started school with me over there. He lived right on the side of the road, and I'd pick him up every morning and go on to school and bring him back. One evening I was thinking about something else, and I got way up the road there and Jim said, "Miss Bessie, wasn't I supposed to get off back there?" So, I had to take him back.

TOLLGATES

They used to have tollgates on the road, and they couldn't get by until they paid. There was a little house there for the toll keeper to live in. They would take the rope loose. I think it was a nickel for a horseback to go through one. It was a dime for a buggy, but you could go there and back. There was one over here where the Harrises live, at the top of that hill right there where they live, and there was another one down yonder where you turn in to go to

James Hood's, the old Hood place, on Lewisburg Pike. I know there was one somewhere over towards College Grove, but I don't know where. I didn't get that far away from home.

TRIPS TO FRANKLIN

I didn't ever go to see Franklin until I was twelve and a half years old. I had to go then to get glasses. I couldn't see to read my schoolbooks – had to have them glasses. On my first trip I walked and walked and looked until I blistered both heels. We went to Franklin in a little old buggy. My daddy carried me – there was just room for two to sit in the buggy. But I got there and back.

When my daddy had to go to town or anywhere, he had to go in a wagon. He always buys some cheese and crackers for his dinner, and he'd be gone all day to go over there and back in a wagon. He always bought us a little sack of cheese and crackers when he come back. We were always glad to see him coming back.

Herbert McCall's granddaddy lived over here on the road. He was my mother's uncle. [Mr. Herbert's daddy was Curd McCall; his granddaddy was Alice's Giles daddy, Travis' McCall's great-granddaddy, Susan Fisher's great-great-granddaddy and Jessie Bennett's great-great-granddaddy.]

Herbert's wife, Aunt Matt, and Mary Tom would walk through these cedars here going to the store. Aunt Matt was just as country as she could be – she still wore that old apron. She come back down this creek – she didn't talk just as plain and she said, "You kids, go on and git some cheese crackers." She would have her apron full of cheese and crackers. She would fill us kids up with that cheese and crackers.

Herbert McCall

SEWING AND CLOTHES

We used to have one of the old looms up there like you made cloth with – wove your cloth – and made your clothes and bedspreads and things. Somebody set it up there in the loft and let it rot down. But I've seen my mother take them old – what did you call them – cards, and get that wool or cotton in it in little rolls. And then they had this little wheel in a spinning wheel that they hooked this thing on, and they pulled it out this way and it made the thread. And then they put it on a spinning wheel.

We made our own quilts. Just about all the clothes we had was made out of the cheapest calico you could get. We got the calico at the store; we had two stores up here, now. There was an oak this way a little bit, out in front of where the store is over towards Dury's place [the old

Core place]. The Scales owned one, this one this way, and Mr. Jim Grigsby owned that one over on that side. They were there before I was born.

FIRES IN BETHESDA

And then nineteen and twenty-eight, both them stores and ... my husband had a garage right across the street in front of them stores. And he had a grist mill in there – worked on cars, done work on them, and ground meal in there, and he sharpened tools. He had an emery – he sharpened plow points and things. Well, one night – we lived in an old log house across the road right over here [on Bethesda-Duplex Road next to the creek] in an old house that burned down [later]. That's where we were living. It woke me up, the awfullest light in my face and I raised up. I commenced to shaking my husband and said, "something's afire." And it was them stores, both of them and the garage. All of them burned at one time there. Yes, sir!

And, of course, he jumped up and took out and I had to wait until the kids got dressed. Went up there and it had done got so big then I had to go around up preacher Millard's place and come around to the back of the shop and come down. And I walked in that thing, and he was standing there in that shop, it a burning, taking the belts off of the motor that he used to sharpen his tools with, and everything. And that thing, it was heavy! But neither one of us said a word. He took that off to where it could be moved. I walked up and took ahold of the thing – it was setting on some kind of rods, I don't know what you would call them. But, anyway, I took ahold of the two on this side and he got on the other side, and we carried that thing out of that building clear across the road over next to the fence that went over to the schoolhouse. And, I said "This is as far as I can go." He said, "Well, let's set it down. There's no need of carrying it any further anyway." Anyway, that motor that we carried out of there – the two of us – it took five men to load it to bring it down to the house. That shows you what being scared to death will do! They thought the fire started for a cigar that somebody was smoking and throwed down.

Dr. Core was standing on the other side. He said afterward that somebody said, "Well, there's a woman over there!" He [Dr. Core] said "Yeh, that's got to be his wife. Nobody else would be over there."

That grist mill kept us in meal to make bread and chicken feed, you know. And, you know, I would give anything if I just had five pounds of meal like he used to make in this thing. This mill was run by a motor [instead of a water wheel]. It was just a hopper like; you throwed the corn over in it and it would shake it around and it would come out down here meal. And there was a sifter there that kept the bran [chaff] out of it. But it sure was fine meal! The meal you buy now has got so much flour in it I don't like it, but I have to use it for my cornsticks.

After the garage burned my husband worked in the yard down here for the rest of that year. Then we moved right up the road there. Then he just worked on cars. While we were living there, we started this house and built it. Daddy gave me four acres of land here to put the house on. Mr. Charlie Reed helped my husband and me to build this house. And my daddy helped; he done a lot of carpentry work. But there's a lot of nails in this old house that I drove in there. Ha! I know me and Henry's daddy put all that weatherboarding on that side there. We moved here in May of thirty-two. That [construction] was done in twenty-nine and thirty. We moved here the last of May and Mildred was born on the 20th of June. She is my only child.

I don't know if it was that year or the next, but Dr. Core's barn down there – he had a great big barn down there back of where the store is now. Well, it caught fire and burned. I had to set up all night with that. Well, another year Mr. Jim had a great big old barn set back up the other side of this old house over here. And there was an old mare in it and it was full of hay. And one night that woke me up with light coming in, and that thing burned. We had fire all around us. Don Walter, Dr. Core's grandson, lived with Dr. Core, and he had a little chicken house there. He raised chickens and sold eggs and fryers. And that fire from them stores burned his house and got fire and burned the house up – with all them chickens there. That was a shame. I don't reckon anybody had any insurance. I know we didn't have any.

90TH BIRTHDAY

My 90th birthday party – I didn't want to have that, but they kept a beggin' and a complainin' til I finally give up. Oh, they had cakes galore and big ninety on it and invited everybody could think of. But there was a lot – Franklin had the Christmas parade at the same time, and they didn't have as many as they thought they would. But it was nice and had all sorts of treats there. Anybody wanted to eat, drink .... Very nice. Albert Hartley and Sis came by from the parade when it was just about over. And Roy Smithson and his people was in Alabama, and Otis and Marie and them was in Texas that weekend.

Well, we come home. My daughter and her husband brought me on home, and I was tired. We'd had a big day, you know – it had been all day long. I come home and I got out of them duds and I set reared back. Well, here I was going to rest 'til bedtime. That stinker up here [Jessie Bennett] called down here and said, "Are you ready to go?" I said, "Go where?" Over to Spring Hill. I said, "I don't think I'd go, I'm awful tired." Well, I hung up. Directly, Charles [Bennett] called back again and said, "I'll be down there after you in just a little while, now." I said, "Give me fifteen minutes, Charles." So, I got up and grabbed me some clothes and here we go over to Spring Hill. They had music over there – they just got one room there. Anyway, they had just a regular band - banjo, guitar, fiddle, and all this stuff. Good music to dance by. Haha! So, I got out there with Charles and we cut a rug for one piece. I was so tired I couldn't hold out long cause I'm short of breath anyway. It was hard, I'll tell you.

Jessie: What do you contribute to living a long and happy life, Miss Bessie?

Hard work! Hard work and good living. I reckon I never – ever time I've been to a doctor after I began to get in bad shape, why [he would say] "Did you ever smoke?" I said no, I never smoked or drank either.

No sir, I never did smoke the first thing. Well, I smoked a cross vine one time. That was an old vine you cut out here. I think I smoked a roll or two out of rabbit tobacco. There used to be an old vine up there on the fence the other side of the Presbyterian church. It had cross vine on it and I guess all of us that was big enough smoked it some. I don't call that smoking. We didn't inhale it or anything. We just puffed it out.

I never did make things to smoke out of coffee grounds, but I'll tell you what we did do when I was a kid. I can remember some of them taking something and pulling the soot out of the chimney of the fireplace, and put a little sugar in it, and put it in something, and get them a little [elm] stick and chigger it up [fray the end by chewing on it] and make them a brush [to pick the mixture up with]. And they dipped snuff to beat the band! Haha! Yeah, I've seen kids do it!

Jessie later recalled her grandmother using snuff by dipping the end of a small stick into snuff and then chewing on the stick. Obviously, those kids had seen someone do that. Some users put a little pinch of snuff inside their lower lip instead.

LESTER MOSLEY, 1919-2007

Gertrude and Lester Mosley

EARLY DAYS

I don't remember much about my young life anyway. I was born in Illinois and came down here when I was about seven years old. It was about 1923 or 1924. We came down in a Model T Ford. It took us about six or seven days. I don't remember but one thing on the way down – the old cobblestone roads we came over. They didn't have highways back then. It was wintertime and it was cold. We stayed in homes sometimes and motels some, I guess. I know it was so cold that we had to take a lantern and light it and put in under a blanket for us kids. I had three sisters older than I was. I still have some pictures taken on the road while we were coming down.

We came to a house that is just west of where the Lodge is now – a two-story frame house. It belonged to Mr. Jim Grigsby, who owned everything from where he lived on west for a way. There were two big rooms and then the house started branching off, with the kitchen off from the rest. Outside, there were several large pecan trees. [Note: The last one was blown over in a storm in about 1993.] The spring house where we got our water is still standing. We had a trough in there that you set your milk and butter and stuff in.

My mother died then in 1925 in the house we moved to. She was sick a lot, but we had an old country doctor, Dr. Core, that lived where the Ralph Drury house is now. I know that my daddy would send me, and me only eight years old, probably, to get him. I was scared to death, and they said they could hear me running on the road. With my old big shoes on you could hear me running for a mile. I'd go get the doctor to come down for my mother. I never heard my daddy say how he paid the doctor.

Dr. Core's home in Bethesda showing log house where newlyweds Gertrude and Lester lived.

All I remember was that before she died, my mother made a lot of light bread. We drank a lot of milk and ate a lot of light bread. I guess that was our main source of food. We were raised up poor, as the old saying goes. Later on, we had a cow or two and churned our own butter. I don't remember exactly whether we had the old wooden churn, the dasher kind you raised up and down, or the small churn on a glass jar. As a kid, we always liked to see something moving.

After my mother died, my daddy remarried a couple of years after my mother died. My stepmother is Bessie Taylor Mosley. We lived in the house that she lives in now. Mr. Tom Beasley furnished the wood, and he furnished the money, I am sure. And he had to pay him so much a month. She was a schoolteacher, so I guess she has already told you about riding a horse to Ash Hill school over there.

We grew up poor. I remember at Christmas time – that's when we lived down there on the creek - my daddy would come up here to the store and he would buy 50 pounds of pinto beans and 50 pounds of white beans. Sometimes, he would buy a keg of fish – little salty fish that come in barrels. I don't remember a Christmas back before my mother died, but later on, like I said, all we got was food. My stepmother used to bake a lot of cakes and candy, and that was good enough for me. But as far as a lot of Christmas trees and presents and things, I don't think we had nothing like that.

I remember going to church with my mother down here where the Lodge Hall is now. There used to be a big two-story church building there. It was a Methodist church, and the lodge hall was up over top of it. We were right next door to it then. I remember going with my mother, and when we were able to have shoes, you know, they would cram a pair of shoes on your feet. You would have to pull them off while you were in church and then you couldn't get them back on. I remember that part of it. Let's see, I joined the church in about 1926, I believe. Of course, we had Epworth League, and we were up there for that. Epworth League, they called it back then, like MYF [Methodist Youth Fellowship] is today.

I went to my first school right there where the store is now. I guess the first eight grades were upstairs and the high school was downstairs – they had all 12 grades. I didn't have far to go to school, and we walked to school. I don't remember what we had for lunches, but it probably was not much.

I was in the first class to finish in the new building, in 1936. You see, the school burned, and I finished school down there right across from Ruth Taylor's – in that building there. The high school used that building. The grammar school went to the Methodist church, and I think some went to the Presbyterian church. But they got a new school completed enough that we graduated on the stage in 1936 in the new building. We were the first class to graduate.

MY FATHER AND HIS WORK

My father, Henry Mosley, was a farm worker, a laborer, in Illinois. Then, when he came down here, he opened up a garage and was a mechanic. The garage was on the northwest corner at the intersection of the roads at Bethesda, across from the school at that time. He was a mechanic and had a grist mill where he ground corn. I don't know how he made the transition from farm worker to a mechanic. When you had your own machinery and it broke down, you fixed it and got experience through trial and error, I suppose.

I don't know how quick after we got here that he built the garage. Of course, after that, it burned at the same time the two stores did. Then, he built another garage near the southeast corner. That is the building with the tin roof on it that stands close to the back of where the store is now. Mr. Ross Gary built that for him.

THE GRIST MILL

He had a grist mill in it and when I got about 10 or 12, I started running the grist mill on Saturdays, when I wasn't in school. A grist mill was the only way people had of getting meal back then. You didn't buy it from the store. You harvested your corn out of the field and when it got dry enough to grind, you brought it down there. They'd bring two or three bushel sacks and we'd take our toll out – I think it was every seventh pound – for our work. With our share we'd grind it up and sell it or grind it up for chicken feed. That was one way we could get some cash. And a lot of people would bring wheat down there and we'd make flour. Of course, we'd make the all-bran flour.

We had several different engines to run the mill. Over in the place that burned we had a great big old gas engine with big side wheels on it. I know I wasn't big enough to start it because you had to turn it backwards, stand up on the wheel, and get it over to get it going. After we moved to the new garage we had an old truck, I believe a Mack truck. Right in the middle where the drive shaft was, we put a pulley and disconnected the drive shaft, and run a belt from the pulley to the mill.

The mill itself was not very big, maybe as big as a table. There was a big hopper above into which you poured the corn. The corn trickled down between two big rocks that turned to grind the corn. You adjusted them for fine or course meal. When it came out into a sifter that would shake and shake the husks out in one place and your meal out in another. The rocks looked like flint rocks. They were round and had curved grooves in them all the way around. I've since seen them laying around – I wish we had one now – where people had thrown them out. Over time, the grooves would wear out and you would hire somebody to come with a little old pecking hammer. It would take him days to sit there and peck new grooves out. You had to know just exactly how to do it, I suppose. You adjusted the two stones where they would come together, to where a grain of corn would just come through and be crushed. The stones had a common axle, and one stone would be turned past the other one, which stood still.

I know that people would run out of meal in the fall of the year before the corn got good and dry. They'd bring it down there and you'd put it in and try to grind it, and it would come out in little "worms" rather than meal. They had a hard time back then, I'll tell you.

GERTRUDE

How did I meet Gertrude? When I was going to school, I didn't have a car. I guess it was along in the junior or sophomore class. Some of the classes would have a weenie roast or something like that. Some of the classes were having a weenie roast and had it up at Jessie's mother's house. I don't know why. Maybe they asked her. I didn't have a girlfriend – I was too bashful to even look at one. But some of the boys brought some girls from over at Arno. Thomas Ham, Woody Junior Smithson, and some of them were invited I suppose. Anyway, I was supposed to go, so a friend of mine, Thomas Ham, picked me up. His daddy had a car, an old '28 Chevrolet I believe. They were supposed to leave the cars down by the store and everybody walk up there. We didn't have girlfriends, so we didn't care much, but at the weenie roast we were playing a game called pick up sticks. Lay a stick out in the middle and line up on both sides – choose sides. Each person had a number, and when someone would call out a number the two people with that number would see who could run and grab the stick and run back. Anyway, that's where I saw Gertrude. I tried my best to catch her, but I never did. I got lucky enough to have the right number, but I couldn't catch her – she was too fast.

I kinda had my eye on her, and then after it was over with, Thomas Ham and I, instead of walking with the whole crowd, came on fast and got his car. We were going back and pick them up and get us a girlfriend. But that didn't work out either. They wouldn't ride with us. I didn't see her for I don't know how long after that. Then, one night at College Grove we were playing basketball. I was on Bethesda's team and Bethesda and College Grove were always big rivals. It must have been a tournament, because I had already played and was standing around one of the two big pot-bellied stoves in the gym, one on each side. A friend of mine, Vernon Overton, was dating Gertrude's sister at the time. I was standing over by the stove talking when he said, "Come over here, I want you to meet somebody." So, he introduced me to Gertrude.

And from there on, things got better. But, oh, it went for a long time – I would have to wait for a special occasion. I know Harry Grigsby carried us, a whole bunch of kids, to Shelby Park one time for an outing. He invited me to go along with him and I invited Gertrude to go. During our courting days I didn't have an automobile. I would have to get somebody that was going that way, and I would ride over to see her. Then I would walk back four miles. Finally, I'd get my dad's Model T. Back then, that was the only transportation we had, and I'd go over there in it. I know one night it was so cold it froze up and I couldn't get it started and had to walk back home in the cold. We went together about five years before we got married.

And the creek... when I was courting the creek would get up. Of course, I was courting pretty heavy then and just had to go, you know. And the creek would be so high you couldn't hardly ford it. Whenever the water gets up over the exhaust pipe it drowns out. Well, you see on them old Model Ts right up next to the manifold there was a big nut. Take that off – disconnect that tail pipe. Of course, you had a terrible racket but until water got up that high and you didn't get stuck in a sandbar you can go out of there. So, you can go up the creek with water waist deep. Sometimes a sandbar could wash down, and you might get hung up in there, but we were pretty lucky.

Gertrude wouldn't be in there with me. I'd just be going over to see her. I don't guess we ever went anywhere together in the old Model T. After a while if we did want to go somewhere, her daddy used to loan us his car – to go to church in it, or go to a movie, or something or other like that.

MARRIED DAYS

I don't know how much my daddy paid for rent, but I do know that later we paid $25 for rent when we got married. I don't know when, but we moved out of that first house and built down there where Bessie Mosley lives now. Charlie Reed built that house. That's where I was living when I got married. The Dr. Core house up here had a big building, and then it had a string of little houses off from it and went into his office. Mr. Waddey was also living there at the time we got married, and we rented three rooms – it was the old Dr. Core office – and that was our first place to live. You would walk from his office – it was all closed in and there was a bedroom between, but you went on into the big house then. They finally tore down the office part and left the dog trot for a while, but then they tore it all down. We didn't live there but about three months. Mr. Tom Beasley owned the place, and he was in Springfield at the time. He moved back and the Waddeys had to move out and we had to move out. So, we moved down where Ellie Marshall Beasley lives now. That was the old Methodist parsonage at the church.

We moved in that and stayed there about three months, and I don't know what happened there, but we had to move out of it. Next, we moved upstairs in the old school building that was there at that time. There was a store down underneath, of course, and there wasn't anybody using the upstairs, so we moved up there. That was in 1941. After the new school was built in 1936, they had turned the old school into a store on the first floor. We had long outside steps going up the back, and I had to carry buckets of water for my wife to wash with. After a few times of that I went and got a washing machine; that was our first washing machine. We moved three times the first year we were married, and then I had to go to the service.

We didn't have water, so we didn't have a bathroom. Well, when Mr. Tom Beasley lived there, he lived upstairs and ran the store downstairs. He had a bunch of kids. So, out at the back of that store he built a porch level with the upper story and then he built him a john out there, on this porch. It was a big square thing, I guess four feet square, and he walled it up with plank on all four sides up there. That was his john; they didn't have a bath, just this john. Everybody thought that that was pretty neat, having a john upstairs. Below, the john extended all the way to the ground.

I went into the service in October 1942. I went to Richmond, Virginia, and stayed there about six months, and then went overseas to England. I was with the aviation engineers. We weren't the air force but were connected because we built air bases for the planes. We stayed there about three years and then went to Germany before I came home. I was gone nearly four years altogether.

I got out of service in January 1946, and my brother-in-law owned the old house over where George Ryan lives now. It was a big two-story house. Mr. Bud Walker lived there, and we moved in and had just one big room and then a little room off to the side of the kitchen. We lived there until we built the house where we live now. I cut all of the framework out of beech wood from the Taylor farm, which was full of beech trees. My brother-in-law, John Edward Crafton, had a sawmill and sawed it. A fellow by the name of Jimmy Smith, a carpenter who had always worked for someone else and had never gone out on his own, built the house. It was the first one he ever built on his own. I was drilling wells at that time. I would work all week and come in on Friday night, and it would take just about everything I made to pay him for that week's work. And I believe – wish I had kept better records – somewhere around $7,000 is what that house cost me.

WELL DIGGING

Before I went to the service, I had done a little bit of everything. After I got out of school I worked in the store at Cross Keys for Harry Grigsby and Mr. Webb, his brother-in-law. They owned the store up there. And then my dad, being a mechanic, had some fellow talk him into the notion of buying a well machine for drilling wells. He said that anyone who drilled wells needed to be a mechanic. So, he bought that thing. After he bought it, he had somebody else running it for him for about a year or two. That didn't pan out too good with the other fellow, so I told him, "Shoot," I believe I can run that thing." So, we did. I took over then and so I run a well machine then, me and my dad, until I went to the service. While I was in service, then, my dad and my uncle run the well machine and when I come back, I went and bought me another one. And so, I drilled wells then until 1950, I guess. I bought a new factory-made machine – most all old well drilling machines were homemade. I went to work at the Nashville Bridge Company, and I had another guy running it for me.

Jessie said she remembered him digging wells all around when she was little.

I went to work at Nashville Bridge in 1950 and stayed there until 1985. I was a crane operator – they called it a whirly crane operator. Most people think of a crane operator of an overhead crane.

To run the well-digging machine I had a Chevrolet engine motor on the old machine. On the new machine, it had a power unit. We had a tower that was mounted on a truck. It rested on the cab of the truck, and we raised it up when we got to where we were going. The towers were not quite as tall as they are now. I guess they weren't over 25 feet, or something like that. Basically, they were the same design as now. Of course, when they designed them back then they did their own thing, just about. Still, it was just a churn-type drill – a hammer drill, they call it – and cable. Of course, you had to have some spring on that cable, so they used a Manila rope about 25 or 30 feet from the drill. You spliced the end of the steel cable – that's what gave it the spring. Back during the war, you couldn't get Manila rope anymore. So, my dad rigged up a set of springs across the top, out of old car springs – you know, the coil type – to give it that shock. It made a terrible racket, but it worked. The new machines now have a bunch of discs at the top of the derrick where the pulley is.

The drill will turn itself most of the time because it is like a chisel. When it hits here and makes a groove, well, if it hits off just a little bit it's going to spin it. You didn't have to turn it except in mud when you first started. A lot of times we didn't have much luck. Down at my place, I drilled 14 wells and still never did get enough water to run an electric pump. The old saying is, "a shoemaker's wife goes barefooted." A well digger's wife goes without water.

THE CROSS KEYS STORE

The Cross Keys store, where I worked for a while, was just a long building and they had just about anything you wanted. My main job, I guess, was I went around over the country and picked up cattle and calves and hogs and carried them to Nashville. They usually went about two days a week. Instead of having all the groceries brought to them, well, you had to go to Nashville and pick them up. Course, these farmers didn't have no way of taking their produce off – cattle and eggs and all that kind of stuff. So we'd pick them up. They had about a ton-and-a-half truck – big sides on it to carry the cattle. You'd have to wash it out before you would pick up the groceries and stuff and bring them back.

Inside the store, there was one long room. They had a walkway right down the middle. They had counters on each side, the whole way. Part was closed in for candy and stuff like that and then on down further if you had overalls and shirts and dry goods and stuff like that, they would have them stacked up on a counter, down further. I don't remember about women's cloth much – I don't believe we had any at that time. And then the hardware – they had hardware of all kinds. Horseshoes came in kegs. Bales of stuff would be lined up in front of the counter. Then on one side they would have all of the canned goods, you know, that you could buy. Shelves went all the way to the ceiling. I guess the lighter cracker boxes and stuff like that would be on the shelves higher up. We had a little step stool to get the top items. Some of the older stores, if you go to some of these old towns, had a ladder that ran on a track from one end of the store to the other. [There is still one at Burwood]

They had a big pot belly stove setting out there in the middle that we heated with. Back at the back mostly was where people would bring in a dozen eggs or ten dozen eggs and we would put them into regular egg crates.

Jessie remembered as a kid taking one or two eggs to the store if her mother would let them.

They candled the eggs that were brought in. They had a box about so big that had a light in it to tell whether an egg was bad or not. Outside they had a building where they put chickens 'til we got ready to carry them off. We'd catch them and put them in coops and carry them to Nashville.

While I was working in the store for Harry – we had a little pickup truck – I'd go around like over here to Ash Hill and around. I would stop at people's houses, and they would say they needed coffee, or I need this or that. Then, I would go back to the store and the next week I'd bring it back. That was kind of an offset from the rolling store.

CROSS KEYS

In Cross Keys there was the store and a blacksmith shop right across the road from us. T.R. Clendenen built him a little shack on the other side of the road there. He had a portable grinder at that time, on a truck. If a farmer wanted some feed ground, they would go grind feed.

Then there was Crosslin's portable store. It was just a truck that had all the groceries that you wanted in it. It would just ride the road every day. You didn't have to call them. They called it a rolling store. You would just go out in the road and stop it. You would go in and most of the time they would have everything you wanted as far as food is concerned. I don't know if they carried milk or not. That was a big thing here in the country for a long time. A fellow by the name of Crosslin lived up here at Eagleville ran it. The people at Crosslin Lumber in Eagleville today are some of the same people. It was just a big truck like you would call a van truck now.

WORKING WITH TVA

While working at the store I was getting a dollar a day and my board, what you could eat, you know. Harry and I batched – we lived upstairs in the store. That's where I was working, but then I went to work for TVA while I was there – it must have been around 1938. When TVA started putting this light line through here it was in the summertime. Business wasn't that great at the store and TVA was trying to hire laborers. I think they were paying 47 cents an hour. I told Harry, "Lord a mercy, if I didn't have a job I'd sure go to work with 'em." A bunch of boys hung around there all the time, you know, and just worked farm labor, and didn't do hardly anything. Harry told me "We're not too busy right now; if you want to go to work for them, go ahead."

So, I did. I went up to Chapel Hill and signed up and I went to work for them right then. That's when we first got electricity through here. I just dug holes for the poles – dead men's holes. I never will forget, for I'd been working for Harry for about two years eating crackers and pork and beans, you know. They put you out there cutting right of way out and in July and hot. You didn't have chainsaws then. I know they put me over yonder. Well, he was really nice though. The foreman told me – I think I started to work on Thursday – "I know you boys are not used to this kind of work. We'll be light on you for a while." And man, the first two days – if it had been more than two days, I would never have made it. I came in at night and I fell up on that porch and I laid there. I didn't even go to bed. But after that, I finally got better.

I'll never forget one day over yonder at Terry White's, I believe. I had to dig a dead manhole, and it was about 18 inches wide and four foot long, and I guess it was four foot deep. Had this big old maple tree there and I started digging. I got down about two feet. They would put you on the job and go off and leave you, you know. I got down about two feet and I hit this soft sandstone rock. You had to pick every bit of it up. Well, I'd done about give out – that was on that first Friday, I believe. So finally, the boss came around and wanted to know how I was doing. I said, "Well, I'm not doing too good." He said, "Well, get over there and sit down; let me help you a little bit." Well, that suited me fine I rolled over behind that pile of dirt there in that shade tree, and when I woke up, he was through. Ha! He didn't say a word though.

I don't remember where I went after that. When the TVA moved out of one area, they would hire a new bunch. I guess I went to my uncle. He bought out a little old grocery store over at Arno and I think I went to work for him somewhere about that time.

THE SKATING RINKS

I didn't tell you about the skating rink. Well, they had a portable. Some guy from Alabama came up here with a portable rink and set it up right there beside where Henry's grocery was, right next to the railroad track [in Franklin, where route 431 crosses the track now]. There's an antique shop there now. That thing was 50 by 100 feet long and under a tent. Man, it set the woods on fire! Well, after they stayed there a while a storm come through and blew it down. The people weren't able to buy a new tent and put it back. So, Henry, the man that ran the grocery store and rented them this piece of property, bought what remained of it from them. They went back to Alabama.

Well, a few years after that I was in that store. Mr. Henry said, "I've got something you need to buy." And I said, "What is that?" and he said, "a skating rink." Well, I wound up buying it. Crazy - and we think kids do crazy things this day and time! It was stored away in a building out there. This must have been about 1947 or 1948. So, I thought, I don't know what I bought the thing for, I'm telling you the truth! 'Course, I like skating and I knew I couldn't run it. Anyway, after I bought it I found out I was in trouble so I contacted the man in Alabama who used to run it for these other fellows. And luckily enough he was available, so he came up and talked to me. We made the deal, and he took over everything – getting it out of the storage, setting it up, hunting a place to put it, and all that kind of stuff. So, we set up on the old school ground there in Franklin and stayed there about two months or something like that. Didn't do too well.

So, he got out scouting around trying to find another place to put it. We went to Dickson. Of course, you've got to tear down. It took an 18-wheeler to haul all that stuff. You had your floor, and your blocks, and everything. We set up down there – that was before Clement was elected [governor of Tennessee]. He was campaigning at that time. He brought his two boys up there, I remember that. But we did pretty good down at Dickson. Man, it went over big down there. There was excitement in those days. And crowds, the floor was full of them; I guess there was a hundred couples out there. We had a PA system and we played records. There was a floor man who skated out there with them, and they would blow a whistle if you got to going too fast.

Stayed there a while, you know, and then we went to Gallatin one time, and we went to Columbia one time. But I began to get tired of it so I just about give my part away to get out of it. I was getting tired of it. I just went to Dickson on the weekends and stayed down there. I was working at the bridge company at the time. But it was quite exciting.

Then, after that, I had little enough sense to build this one up here at Chapel Hill. There was an old boy starting out – he lived up there at Jimmy Griggs' – he started out in some old building up there with, oh, maybe 15 or 20 people skating. I knew Jimmy's daddy real well and anyway, I carried a bunch of MYF [Methodist Youth Fellowship] kids up there. I had an old station wagon that held about 10 people, I guess. We carried them up there to skate and we got to talking and decided we needed a bigger place. So, we got together and had this one built down there at Chapel Hill. Big rink! I guess it was about 40 or 50 by 100, or something like that. I stayed in it a while, but when this old Griggs boy that run it for me got more out of it than I did, I saw it was time for me to get out. Sometimes he'd have trouble up there with some of the boys, and he would call me at night wanting me to come up there and get them straightened out – them boys from Wheel [another community]. The first opportunity I got I sold out to him. [Jessie met Charles skating – fell in front of him.]

Hugh: what would you pass on as words of wisdom for future generations?

Well, I guess work hard and be honest. Be fair with people and go to church. When I started in the well machine business there were already two or three other people. I didn't know how we would work out but I know I told my daddy, "The only thing I know to do is just be fair with a fellow and be honest with him, and I believe we will be all right." And we were never out of a job.

Bethesda as a whole is as good a place as any to live. I do a lot of looking and riding around and seeing other places. Some of the places I like, but then I get to thinking, I believe I'd rather be back here. Yeah, I'm satisfied here.

JEAN GARY SANDERS, 1926-2010

I've heard so many stories passed down from one person to another. I don't have anything written down. I should write it down for my children and grandchildren.

GRANDPARENTS

William Dabney Irvin married Laura Alice Alexander. He came in the covered wagon and lived down here above the store where the Taylor farm is. They were my grandmother and grandfather. There were several years difference in their age, he was her schoolmaster. I guess she was an attractive student, so he married her. And she always called him Mr. Irvin because she had become accustomed to this with him being her teacher. My grandfather was injured and carried a minie ball in the joint of his shoulder, so my grandmother ran the farm.

    This family had a good sense of humor. I hope people won't think we are rock foolish. My grandmother had a wonderful sense of humor. Remember, she was an Alexander and you have met Billy Alexander – he loves to tease. He has the same Alexander sense of humor. Part of the farm at that time lay across the road and part of it was a section of the Mt. Pisgah hill that lays to the right as you are going to Cross Keys. They kept the goats up there. It wasn't too long after they bought the farm that they walked up the hill and it looked so nice. It looked so nice and smooth where they were standing, and grassy. She looked at my grandfather and said, "Mr. Irvin, I want to just lay down and roll down that hill." He said, "Well, just go right on." So she laid down and began to roll. She wound up in the creek. She went over stumps. She was young, but she did get over it.

My grandfather had time on his hands since he wasn't into farm work. He had some sons to help out with that. But he was very interested in politics. He would [go] down to the store at Bethesda because he was reared down there. He never went to the Cross Keys store much even though their home was about halfway between Bethesda and Cross Keys. This would be in the very early 1900s. It was still a primitive community – no electricity, of course.

My grandmother had told him, "Now Mr. Irvin, I don't mind doing any work on the farm that I am capable of doing, but there is one thing I will tell you ... I will never chop wood. If you don't cut the wood for the cook stove, there won't be a meal cooked." Well, there was some candidate that was going to come through the community, and they were told previously that he was coming. So, grandfather got up and got off early to the store at Bethesda but, lo and behold, he forgot to cut the wood. At lunchtime, she looked out and here he came, and he brought the candidate home with him for lunch so he could carry on a deeper conversation, one-on-one. He came in – his pet name for her was Allie – and said, "Well, Allie, this candidate is here for lunch," and introduced him. She said, "Fine Mr. Irvin, give me just a minute." She went into the dining room, and she came back and said they could go right on in. They went in there... Ha!... and there was a glass of water and a toothpick at each plate.

William D. and Alice Irvin

Jessie: So that's where you get your meanness!

Right. Another tale they told on my mother was that grandfather another time brought a candidate home, but I'm sure they weren't fixing lunch that day. My mother was a pretty good size child by that time, and somebody looked out and said, "Well, I wonder what that man is running for?" And mother comes tripping up to the window, looks out, and says, "I don't see anybody running anywhere." She had not the vaguest idea of what they were talking about.

Oh, I remember another story. He was a member of the lodge; the lodge that is still in Bethesda. He was a big man and at that time could not buy shirts that fitted him comfortably. He couldn't keep his shirt tail in, for one thing. So, he came in one day and he had several yards of material. He said, "Allie, I don't know when you will have time, but I want you to make me some new shirts to wear to the lodge. I'll tell you what I want you to do. I want you to measure the sleeves by that door facing and the tail by that bed rail." She said, "very well, Mr. Irvin." And he came in several weeks later when it was time for a lodge meeting and said, "Allie, are my shirts ready?" "Why, yes, Mr. Irvin." And she brought out one of those shirts. He held it up and looked at it and said, "Ay, golly, Allie, I did think you had a little sense!" She had cut up that whole piece of material and measured the sleeves by the door facing and the shirt tail by the bed rail. I don't guess he ever gave detailed instructions like that anymore.

CHILDHOOD DAYS

I weighed 11 pounds when I was born. I call my baby pictures the Gerber baby. I was born in the Shiney Hargrove house on Cross Keys Road. In Shiney's family, there were five girls and two boys. Richard died of pneumonia during the Civil War.

Now, I can tell you some about the memories I have because, after all, I'm well into the senior citizen category. I lived with my grandmother and that was my world. I never saw my grandfather. He died before I was born. In fact, I never knew either of my grandfathers. When I walked, I was given quite a bit of freedom, until after they lost my older sister. She died from what at that time was an unknown disease. They had [brought] in baby specialists from Nashville and the way they described the symptoms [was that] it was either what today would have been pronounced polio or spinal meningitis. They lost her at age three when I was just one. I don't remember her, but they said I went all through the house calling her and looking for her. After that, they were sometimes overly cautious with me. In my immediate family, there were just two children – the sister I lost and me. So, I was reared as an only child. I lived with my grandmother, an aunt that never married, my mother, and Mary, a retarded lady who was boarding there.

I was a dreamer. I guess I have been rather artistic most of my life. Loved school and cried every year when it was out because this was my companionship. In those days you didn't have cars and things and if you did everybody was busy in the field. You didn't get to travel and play with a friend all afternoon unless they were within walking distance. So, I was lonely. Just really lonesome.

I couldn't climb Mount Pisgah. They wouldn't let me do that. Mount Pisgah is the hill more or less across the road on my grandmother and grandfather's home place, on Cross Keys Road. But I climbed up there anyway to see Bethesda and thought, "My goodness, I can see the whole world!"

It was really true. This was my whole world. Occasionally my father would go to the corncrib and get an ear of corn. We would shell it into a bag, and I got to go to Centennial Park in Nashville and feed the ducks on the lake. That was really an outing for me. I thought I had been hundreds of miles by the time I got there. We had a car ... a Model A Ford.

I was allergic to milk when I was small. People thought they spoiled me horribly. When I finally got to where I could take pure milk, the doctor told them to let me take my bottle as long as I would take it, because I needed the milk to build my bones. I'm not sure that I wasn't close to four years old and still taking a bottle. I can remember a pocket in the front of that car, and when we went to church on Sunday morning they would stick my bottle in that pocket, over on the side.

To this day, I am afraid of rushing water. I think it was because one Sunday we had a horrible rain, a huge spring rain. The creek that runs behind the Presbyterian church has several bridges over it now, but there were none back then. The road did not run where it is now, either. You just forded the creek, and if it was up, the sensible thing to do was wait. But we couldn't miss church. So, Dad drove right on through the creek, and it came up through the floorboard. My mother was petrified and naturally, I was too. To this good day, when I see rushing muddy water, I can remember that scene and I become petrified again.

Lots of Sundays, if it had rained and the creek got up while we were in church, we went up to my great-grandfather's home. He had two daughters that had never married who were living there. They would have lunch prepared. I think perhaps they leaned toward the Shaker faith. They did nothing on Sunday. They put the meal on the table, but they had prepared that meal on Saturday. By that time, they had a kitchen connected to the house and they also had a cook stove, but there was a huge fireplace in the kitchen that they had originally done their cooking on when the kitchen was added. The building is still standing. It is one of the log buildings there at the Taylor farm, the old kitchen that was totally separate from the house. They tell me that was done because of the danger of fire.

We attended the Presbyterian church. We came to America because of religious oppression. Those ancestors were braver than I was because if I had seen the ocean I would have stayed in Ireland. We were a Scots-Irish border clan, and because of religious oppression, we came to America. They landed in the northeast and lived there. I do not know which generation that was.

MARY

Mary, our retarded boarder, had a good mind in certain respects, and she was from a wealthy family. They would not accept her in an institution. She had private tutors, and she could play the piano, which I was never able to learn. She could read but I don't know how much meaning she grasped from her reading. But she loved magazines and we took lots of magazines. She would sit on the back porch in the summertime and stack the magazines in an old wooden wagon, which I still have in my home. It was Aunt Willie Irvin's wagon, but it made a wonderful place. She had her straight chair out there and she used a pointing stick [and] read all day every day. She would go to my grandmother – she loved to clean up the yard – and would say to her, "Miss Alice, can I expect ... " (she would say "expect" before everything she would say). "Can I pull some weeds?" And my mother would say, "No, Mary, it is too hot. You'll have to wait until the sun goes down." My mother took good care of her. She ate meals with us and ate exactly what we ate.

One day my grandfather passed by and Mary was industriously reading. She had the Bible instead of her magazine. He said, "Mary, what in this world are you reading about?" She looked up at him and said, "I 'spect its old man Jesus and his disciples." He didn't ask her that question anymore when she had the Bible in her hands. It shocked him in those days, but you wouldn't think too much about it today.

FAMILY STORIES

This is another memory. Our next-door neighbor was Mr. John Wallace and his wife, Miss Lottie. We did have a telephone, but lots of people did not. The Wallaces also had a telephone with, I think, eight parties on the line. My grandmother for some reason would shut her eyes tight when she talked on the telephone. She would describe what she was doing. They always kidded her about talking to Miss Lottie. They were talking about harvesting the turnip greens that had come up in the early spring. And she says, "Why, Lottie, I just grabbed that thing up this way with my hands and took the butcher knife and cut it off." Just like she could see her description of it.

One day grandmother heard that Mr. John was ill. They had grandchildren that lived with them; their mother had died. The father was unable to care for them by himself, so the boys went to Miss Lottie's and Mr. John's to stay. She called over and said, "Lottie, I've just made some salt-rising bread. How's John doing? Would he be able to eat some? Send Ellis over here and I'll send him some that is just hot – right out of the oven." Ellis came and got the loaf of salt-rising bread. Now, fresh salt-rising bread has quite an odor to it. Ellis got back home with it, in a little basket with a cloth over it, and he said, "Taff, you may be sick now but if you eat that stuff you are going to die!"

Dr. Core was a character too. He really was. My dad drove him after he got older. When I was born in 1926, he was well-established in this community. At that time his daughters were very close friends of my mother and my aunt. I just would give anything if I had asked more questions when I was growing up. I do recall that when he passed away, I cried like I had lost my very best friend. I was not the least bit afraid to go to him. I was sick all the time and still have some of the same allergies today. For instance, I got this horrible rash all over and my mother rushed me to Dr. Core. He said, "Mary, what are you bathing this child in?" She said, "Well, Lifebuoy soap." He said, "That stuff ought to all be destroyed. It causes more skin [problems] than anything ever did." So, I've never touched another bar of Lifebuoy soap. It has a horrible smell, anyway.

My Aunt Dena Stowers reared me after my mother's death. She thought that women who smoked were making a dreadful mistake and it disturbed her terribly. She got to thinking one day and said, "You know, Aunt Mary Cox smoked." I said, "Deedie" (my pet name for her), who was Aunt Mary Cox?" So, she explained all of this to me and said she remembered her saying when she visited her while visiting her grandmother and grandfather, "Child, come here and get me a coal from the fire to light my pipe, it's gone out." She smoked one of those long clay pipes and would sit on the edge of the hearth in her chair so the smoke would go up the chimney. Apparently, they didn't want smoking in their household, but they would allow her to go to her room and smoke the old clay pipe.

FAMILY HISTORY

It was the Steeles that I have the history on. There was bound to have been a land grant somewhere because my great-great-great-grandfather was an officer in the Revolutionary War. I never heard things like that discussed but a lady called me from Texas and said she had been given my name to contact. She understood that I had ancestors who were members of the Steele family. She said, "Alex Steele?" and I said, "Yes, he was my great-great-great-grandfather." She introduced herself and said she was also descended from these people. We corresponded and I copied the family genealogy I had and sent it to her, and she was happy to get that. She was able to tell me where Alex Steele was buried, in an old church ground in Boston. It hadn't been many years since I had been in Boston and followed the footsteps on the historic tour but didn't know to stop in that churchyard and look for my great-great-grandfather.

The stone house up there at Cross Keys was a land grant from the Revolutionary War. [Some men in that war were given land grants in the Bethesda area. Several Revolutionary War veterans are buried in a cemetery on Flat Creek Road]. I did not know until recently there were actually battles fought in the Civil War in this community.

I have a grandmother who, when she married, became Alice Irvin. She was Laura Alice Alexander, but she married an Irvin. My grandfather's sister was also Alice. So, we had two Alice Irvins since one never married. The Alice who didn't marry went to a female normal school, I believe in Clarksville.

In the Irvin family, there were two aunts whose men both went to war. The grandmother and the daughters ran the farm with the help of the one slave who remained there. He was old then. That is what is now known as the Taylor farm, in the heart of Bethesda. There was a little peephole in their attic and there was a ladder built up the wall in one of the upstairs bedrooms. It was built on the same plan as all of the old homes, but it has since been remodeled. There was a boys' upstairs and a girls' upstairs that were completely separate. The ladder was possibly on the girls' side. They brought with them my grandfather's sister. I don't know where she is buried but, undoubtedly she was widowed. She came to Tennessee with them. Her name was Aunt Mary Cox. This little ladder was in her room while she lived there.

I never asked when my ancestors came here. It was prior to the Civil War and one member of the family was an infant, I've been told. I didn't ask which one and should go back to the genealogy book. It rode in my grandmother's lap in the covered wagon in the chair that I now have. I don't know whether the chair just wore off – she was a rather portly lady – up to the first round or whether they had sawed some off of it to make it more stable. She had carried the infant, whoever it was, on her lap for that journey. I also have the rolling pin that they used on the trip, just a hand-carved rolling pin, smaller on the ends with no definite handles. They would have to stop, of course, and prepare meals. I can recall seeing the Dutch oven in that house, but so many of these things were sold to settle the estate.

GYPSIES

Gypsies. People were afraid of them because they would steal your chickens. They would come through in the daytime, but they wouldn't go too far. Then they would come back and visit again at night when you didn't know they were there. At least, this is the proposition.

My Aunt Willie loved flowers and had a flower garden in part of the front yard, in the left corner as you faced the house. I believe she milked the cows and fed them and shelled the corn for the pigs or got the corn out for the pigs. We were very self-sufficient. We had hog killing, my highlight in the wintertime, except for Santa Claus coming. She did the milking and got the milk strained up and I understand they allowed her to have the money from the milk that was sold. She bought a gypsy basket that stood on a stand off the floor. It had a beautiful handle.

Jessie: I remember it sitting in the front hall when I was seven or eight years old.

She would fix flowers in it, and it was used at the church quite often for special occasions. It was a nice basket, and I am sure quite cheap. I remember seeing them in Mr. John Wallace's lot that was right across from my grandmother's, just one time.

CURE FOR THE FLUX

The valley between your [Jessie's] hill and Mount Pisgah is called the Jimmy Hollow. There was a black couple, Uncle Jimmy and Aunt Parrah Lee Grimm. Aunt Parrah Lee came to see my grandmother one day and she said, "Miss Alice, I haven't been down here to see your new baby. How are you doing?" This was Dabney, my mother's brother. She said, "I'm terribly worried. You know, he's got a bad case of the flux and I haven't been able to find one thing that has helped him. I'm just afraid I'm going to lose him." I think diarrhea in those days was called flux. She said, "Alice, don't I smell cabbage cooking? You give me that baby and you go in the kitchen and bring me a cupful of that cabbage broth." She said, "For what?"

"I'm going to feed it to this child."

"Are you sure?"

She said, "Yes, you just do what I tell you."

She did that – she tried everything else, and it wouldn't work – and do you know, it cured the child. Boiled cabbage pot liquor, seasoned and everything!

Think about the different meanings that words we knew meaning one thing that have already changed today. Frontier people used old English. People used to say "tote" but that was a valid word for carrying. Also, a "tow" sack for a burlap bag.

EARLIEST SCHOOLS OF BETHESDA

Richard Irvin, Uncle Dick, who died in the Civil War was in training in Lebanon to become an attorney. I have letters at home where he made the trip there by stagecoach. He had to go to Franklin and had to take the stagecoach. He was belaboring the fact that they charged as much as they did for the candles to study by.

I have a letter where he was going to establish a private school here. That was undoubtedly prior to there being public schools here. My family and I went walking after we came back to the Bethesda community in 1954 and began to go through the back of the old Irvin home place. We came upon a log structure back behind the James Bond property that turns off Arno – Bethesda Road. I came back to the house and said to Aunt Dena Stowers, who was in her eighties, that I had found this interesting log cabin back in the woods and described where it was. I asked who she remembered who ever lived there. She said, "Nobody ever lived there. That was the black folk's schoolhouse." So, once schools were established there were schools for both. I don't know the exact time, but I do know that my mother – she was the youngest – completed part of her education in Nashville because my grandfather had died, and my Aunt Dena and Uncle Jim were living in Nashville and Mother lived with them.

The old store was a two-story affair where the present store is in Bethesda. That was used as a schoolhouse where part of them went to school. I understand that the lot that is between that and Dr. Core's house is where the original school was. The store was possibly the first school.

MY SCHOOL DAYS

I started to school here when I was seven, but Mother had taught me at home because I just had a terrible inquisitiveness. I asked questions and I wanted an answer. I found a copy of a story of my life that some teacher in elementary school had required us to write. That was when I found out that I weighed eleven pounds when I was born and as I told a friend, I haven't gained much since. I went on to say that I wanted to learn to read, and I had not been a healthy child because of allergies, basically. I still have a lot of them. I begged my mother to get me a baby-grade primer, and this was an outdated primer, but I had seen it on the shelf at the Cross Keys store. They got me that primer, but they decided that having to walk that distance to school I was too fragile and frail, and having lost my sister, they were overly protective. So, she taught me at home. I did learn to read that baby-grade primer.

As soon as I got through with that primer, I insisted that she buy me a lunch box. I got the lunch box and then I insisted that she get me a pair of scissors and something else that I don't recall. She asked what I needed with a pair of scissors. I said, "Don't you know, I'll be taking home economics." Needless to say, when I started to school, I found out that home economics was a good distance in the future. I did do this. I got the newspaper and my little blunt-tip scissors and decided I wanted to make something for myself. My mother sewed; she was an accomplished seamstress. I was fascinated by it. I cut out my own pattern and made myself a pair of pajamas. I was eight at the most.

But I remember I came to almost a disastrous end because I was hardheaded. Mother was helping me sew one day and you had door-to-door salesmen in those days. You didn't hesitate – Watkins man was one of them — never do remember what this young man was selling. I don't know whether it was just to be courteous or whether it was something she might be interested in. The other people in the household were busy elsewhere, so he came up and knocked on the door while she was giving me a lesson on the sewing machine. With the curiosity that I had, I went to the front hall, and they took their seats. I stood around a while to see if I was going to be interested in what they were talking about, and I wasn't. She had cautioned me when she left the machine, "Don't touch the sewing machine until I get back." Guess what. I decided I could do that; I know exactly what I am doing. I put my foot down here and I peddle, and I hold on to this fabric. Just hadn't noticed that you had to move your hand along. I kept sewing and I sewed through my finger and was so appalled at what I had done that I jerked my hand and broke the needle off in my finger. Went all the way through. The salesman was kind enough that my mother carried him a pair of wire pliers and he pulled that needle out of my finger. And guess what treatment they did. They stuck my finger in kerosene and it never did even get sore.

I was in school when it burned in 1935. That's when the schools met in the churches while the new school was being built. I remember getting down on my knees in the pews, and we used the pews as desks. To do our writing we got on the floor on our knees. I was in the Methodist church and the house that is across from the Taylors now was the high school. Charles Oliver was the principal and Jesse, his wife, taught economics. Aunt Dena and Uncle Jim had moved into my great-grandfather's home with his sisters, who had become unable to care for themselves. They rented their home to Mr. and Mrs. Oliver, which was convenient to them because it was right next door to the school. After the school burned, they continued to live there but taught the high school section.

We had I.Q. tests in those days just like they do today. I remember having to trek up the road; we had to go up there because the principal had to supervise those tests. I always loved math, but I didn't how all of the things you were supposed to work on were laid out. I kept going past my stopping point, and I got into the algebra section. I thought that didn't make too much sense to me, but I began to work and evidently got some of them right. I began to wonder why students would look at me strangely when I would come around. Then, somebody told me, "Do you know what Mr. Oliver told us?" I said that I had no idea, but that I was scared to death of the test. He had a very loud voice and was a strict disciplinarian. If I would hear him holler at somebody I would shake in my shoes. She said, "He was trying to explain algebra to us one day and we couldn't grasp it. He said wait just a minute, let me go in yonder and get Jean Gary; maybe she can explain it to you!" No wonder they looked at me strangely when I came around. I had no idea what I had done or what I had done to make enemies out of them.

And I called down to the store – someone dared me to do it – and said very sweetly, "Do you have Sir Walter Raleigh in a can?" He said, "We do." And I said, "Better let him out!" [Every generation thinks that is a new prank.]

CROSS KEYS

The dividing line between Bethesda and Cross Keys was just about my grandmother's house. We went in both directions. My dad would go to the Cross Keys store and play cards with the men that would congregate there. I can remember going with him. There was a gentleman in the neighborhood, Greasy Creswell, who was a big tease. My aunt had bought me this specially imported hat for me to wear to school, but I would wear it to the store when my dad would take me up there. I could get a whole bag of candy for a nickel if I could salvage me a nickel somewhere and catch Dad when he was going to the store. If Mr. Creswell would come in while I was there, he would come sidling up to me and grab that hat and say, "Oh, look, I've got me a pretty hat." And it would just make me furious because he had taken my wonderful cap off of my head.

I remember the Cross Keys community about as well as I do the people of the Bethesda community. But there was a dividing line. The funny thing was there were the churches and the Choctaw school house and they were a separate community altogether. They were our friends, and people would come to my grandmother. She must have been a fairly intelligent lady and had a lot of business sense. Apparently, even when my grandfather lived, she did the major portion of the running of the farm.

I guess the boys did the work; I know my dad did a lot of it after he came there. But times got so hard that Dad took a job away from home and would just come home on weekends. He was in construction and helped to build Milky Way Farm in Pulaski. You couldn't drive because you didn't have money for the gas; that would have taken all you earned. You went and stayed on the job and came home on the weekend. I remember him coming home. We had the telephone because the women were there alone. By this time my uncles were in business in Franklin, and I think they funded the telephone for us, for our protection.

TROUBLE IN THE CORN CRIB

I remember my dad coming in one night. There was one thing about the depression. You did not leave anything of value in a building that was unlocked. You went out about dark, once the chickens went to roost, and you locked the hen house. You did not necessarily keep a lock on the barn door unless you had a lot of harnesses, but you definitely locked the corn crib. We had a window where we pitched the corn in. I remember my dad getting home fairly late one night and he came up and pulled around this way. If the weather was bad, he sometimes parked the car in the barn, but the weather was not bad. He parked the car in front of the front yard gate but facing the barn, and his lights played on the barn wall. Someone had gone to the trouble and was hanging up there by main strength and awkwardness, by the window into the corncrib. They intended to go in that way, and I guess would have been there the next morning because they couldn't have gotten out. But with the light flashing on them, they dropped off and ran away. Apparently, they had chickens or hogs or something they were going to lose and did not have enough corn, or maybe they had hoped to sell it and get money to buy some food. We never knew.

I recall this. I had for a long time at my home a tattoo dye, more or less, that the county agent came up with. You raised your flocks' wings and in this flesh under the wings, you tattooed them with this dye. Everybody had their own mark and if somebody came along and stole all your chickens, all you had to do was look under the wings and see if they were your chickens. Now is not the first time that crime has come to the Bethesda area.

GAMES AND PIE SUPPERS

Games were played, but I'm not sure what. Some people were allowed to dance. But there was some in our family that thought that was sinful, and I wanted to learn to dance. I did have a little rhythm and I wanted to dance so badly, and they would not call me to go. People in the country were still having square dances as I grew up. A lot of families had dances, especially if anybody had musical talent that could play the fiddle for them. They just rolled the rugs up and had square dances. They had large rooms for the most part. The young men would come.

Then, they had pie suppers. You got a shoe box and – I can recall the older girls talking about this when I was just very small – you decorated this shoe box with tissue paper or crepe paper or wallpaper or anything to decorate it. Maybe even put wildflowers on top of it, but you had to do an elaborate job. One thing you did was make a pie, but I think you also packed sandwiches and this kind of thing in there. The thing was that the most popular girl in the neighborhood would normally – the young men would be against each other for the opportunity to eat with this particular girl. Of course, if several were struck on the same girl the bidding got wild. They would spend money they could maybe ill afford. Maybe spend all the allowance that they had. This was quite entertaining. It usually took place at the schoolhouse. Some called this a box supper, but you included pie as your dessert. Maybe they weren't sometimes as struck on the girl as they were on the food she produced, because we had some excellent cooks here. I think that the money was a cause for the school. The two churches in the area did not do this to raise money. I can remember having ice cream suppers back in my young days. It was homemade ice cream, and it was excellent.

SUGARCANE

Most people raised their own sugar cane. I remember on the Charlie Reed place, cane was grown down in the bottom, this side of the creek, from there out to the road. This was Miss Lola Glenn's parents and where she grew up. It was the Tom Giles farm, and her mother was Ruth Giles. She lost her mother when she was young, and my grandmother took over and helped Mr. Tom. Miss Ruth would come, and she and my mother were the same age. She would come oftentimes and spend the night. My grandmother would sew for Miss Ruth, so the families were always very close. Mr. Charlie would come to my grandmother for farming advice; I can recall that. She was considered kind of a sage in the community.

They raised sugar cane. I can remember many times coming along, and Jessie's brothers would be along. We'd walk up the road together to have company home from school. One of them might have a pocket knife, and we'd get over in the cane field and get us one cane, and we would suck the syrup out of the cane. It was good, but I guess if you ate too much of it it would probably make you sick. But the field would be minus one sorghum cane by the time we got past going home from school. You would cook off the molasses and everybody had this store of molasses, and sugar was not plentiful in those days. I guess this started during the Civil War because sugar was non-existent. If you had it, you had to hide it.

TAFFY

To make taffy, they would cook some molasses down to a certain degree. It was from experience that you knew when it was ready. You took it off and let it cool, and then you would butter your hands. Remember that you made your own butter then so there was plenty of butter. Couples, your boyfriend and you would work this candy. You would pull and pull, and lap it back over, and pull. Once it reached the right stage you would lay it down and let it season to just a certain stage. And you cut it. If you didn't get it cut, it would get too hard to cut. My grandmother would make such old-fashioned things as homemade gingerbread. They would often make a sauce to go over that. I don't remember the parties because there was sickness, there was death in the family and this kind of thing, and I missed them.

We had hard cider sometimes.

Jessie: did you ever drink any hard cider?

Yes, and furthermore there was a bottle that was covered with some basketweave. It was kept in a fruit closet under the stairway that was in my grandmother's room and was used for medicinal purposes. It was called blackberry cordial. It had a most delightful taste. Believe it or not, there was such a small quantity in there I would just get me a taste. I was considerate; I thought that somebody might get sick and need that. It is a good thing because I guess I could have got drunk. I really liked the taste of it, I really did.

CHILDHOOD MEALS

They would leave me. You know how old houses are heated – the fireplace in here and you went through a room or two and you got to the kitchen. If you kept a pretty good fire in the cook stove, then the kitchen was warm enough that you could endure if you had put on an extra sweater or two. Being the delicate thing that I was they left me in the bedroom with the fireplace while they went to the kitchen to prepare the evening meal, or to get it together. Right often I ate my evening meal after I started to school in front of the fireplace on a little stool-like table, and I had a tater that was baked in the ashes, homemade tomato soup made from whole canned tomatoes, and I had a peculiar appetite. I loved roasted duck eggs. You would crack the shell just a little bit, possibly tap it with a knife, and you would wet newspapers and wrap the duck egg and tuck it into the ashes and keep the hot ashes. It was actually a baked or roasted duck egg. I could eat that whole thing by myself, and they tell me they are so strong that the average person doesn't even like them. That was my favorite thing.

While they were in the kitchen preparing the meal, there were wonderful things to do in that bedroom. My grandmother had a rocking chair that is in my den today. It would walk when you would rock. Thank goodness it walked backward because I would put it right up to the edge of the hearth. The arms came up more or less in a circle at the front and were attached to the seat. I would plant a foot in each one of those circles and rock just as hard as I could rock and the first thing I knew I had walked all the way to the back of the room and was bumping the door that went into the entrance hall. So, I would patiently drag the chair back up there and start all over again. My grandmother had an oak bedroom suite – the prettiest bed and dressers and things were upstairs. The more modern things were downstairs. I understand that her son Dabney and his wife Laura had given her this bedroom suite. They had brought it back from California. They were apparently not successful there, so they came back to Tennessee. He was a druggist. This was one of the old-fashioned beds that had a high footboard and a yet higher headboard. The headboard went almost to the ceiling in that room. My grandmother's bedroom was the original log cabin that the home was constructed around. It had low ceilings. Just gave room enough for her to pull her quilts on the quilting frames up to the ceiling and have headroom.

They had two wells. The refrigerator well was behind the house and is still there today. They fastened on this chain they had buckets that the lids fit very tightly on, and they put the butter and I guess at times jello. The water was cold enough that it was equal to an icebox. I remember eating the jello in pressed glass bowls that had this gold edging on it. I was so fascinated by the sparkle of this jello in that gold that I would forget to eat the jello.

WADDEY CHAIRS

I don't know the time when the Waddey chairs were made, but it was before the turn of the century [about 1888 as the best calculation from genealogy]. The Waddey chair in the picture I have was a gift for Aunt Willie when she was born. They made ladder-back chairs that are quite collectible now, and they made caskets. We had enough chairs that we used in the kitchen, but they were a little low for our dining table. They were made in Bethesda – I've laughed and told some people it was in downtown Bethesda. I almost think it must have been close to the Presbyterian church but that is an awfully low field. Mr. Dick Waddey is Mr. Ira Waddey's daddy. He and Aunt Dena were real good buddies. He would come all the way to Bethesda to trade when Mr. Ira was running the store.

I got through history by memorizing. It didn't mean a thing to me then. Can you imagine anybody being so interested in family history and antiques now to have never liked history? I think it may have been some of the teachers I had.

WILLIE RUTH VEACH TAYLOR
1925-2014

Willie Ruth Veach Taylor

I was born May 17, 1925, at the homeplace of my grandfather, Morgan Veach, on Bethesda Road where the Joe Johnsons live now.

SCHOOLING

When I was just a small child, my parents moved to the Trinity Community on Wilson Pike in Williamson County. I started to school when I was five years old, at Pleasant Hill School, which was just a one-room schoolhouse. The first day or two I enjoyed it. The teacher was Mrs. Ezell, who would come by my house on her way from Franklin each morning and carry me to school. When I began to write some letters on paper, she picked up my paper one day and showed it to the class. I thought she was making fun of my writing, so from then on, I did not want to go back to school. Every morning when Mrs. Ezell came by for me, my mother would have to spank me to get me to go with her. I would even get under the bed to keep from going. Finally, Mother let me stay at home. I thought, "Oh, my goodness." I just didn't like that teacher at all. I thought she just did something terrible to me. But she really wasn't making fun. She just wanted to show the class my work.

When I was six, Mother started me to Trinity School, which just had three teachers. Trinity went through high school at one time. The teacher that I was under then had all the classes from the first to the fourth. You don't have anything like that now. I went there and finished through the first half of the eighth grade. During that time, I would ride a train to school sometimes because we lived next to a railroad station. From one station to the next was about three miles. I would get off at that station, which was but a few yards from the school. It just cost five cents from one station to the next. We rode to school and caught it coming back, for a dime. The train was really interesting, just a locomotive and the caboose on the back of it.

HIGH SCHOOL IN BETHESDA

My granddaddy's people had lived in Bethesda, and he wanted to come back; he was getting old and feeble. In 1939 my parents moved back to Bethesda.

I started to school at Bethesda. The one school had burned, and they had built a new one in 1936. I really did hate to come back to Bethesda because I didn't know anybody, and it was a high school. I was just killed. But then, after I got started, they soon wanted to know if I could play ball, or do this, or that. I really did like it.

In 1941 my parents bought a home in Peytonsville. That's where we lived until my father died several years ago. My mother is still living in Franklin. After we moved, I had to ride the bus to Bethesda then. The bus was made out of wood and put on the bed of a truck. It was called the "Cracker Box." The P.T.A. furnished the bus that I rode to school. That was the first time that I had ever ridden on a school bus, because before I walked to school. Now, children think you are crazy if you have to walk to school.

The old gym at Bethesda was made by people in the community. We had tin put on the outside. We had to go outside of the school to go to the gym. And it had big old box seats. The dressing rooms were under the seats and were heated by coal stoves.

Jessie: There by that door was where Mr. Adams taught me how to drive. He laid down matches and showed me the gears. He put those matches down and showed me how to change gears. First. Second. High. And I drove his car – never had been in a car and drove it to Thompson's Station and got a class ring. How daring I was! I said I thought I could drive so he let me drive around the school up there and said he believed I was ready. I didn't have a driver's license. That was my teacher that let me drive. When Billy Mae Johnson and W.L. Wilhoite got burned up – we were juniors then – I carried them all to the funeral in his car. I didn't even learn how to drive, really. I got my driver's license when Brenda was ten months old. All the time Charles was in the service I kept his car and drove and carried everybody around in the community to the doctor, and didn't have a license. I don't know when the law about licenses went into effect, but I know I didn't have one.

I graduated in 1943. That was during World War II. We had 12 to start with in my graduating class. Jim Eggleston was a senior who went into the service, so we only had eleven to finish.

I didn't learn to drive until later; I couldn't even drive when I finished high school. We didn't have a car at home then. I had to get a ride when we had plays and things at school.

AFTER GRADUATION

After finishing high school at Bethesda, I went to Draughon's Business College for a year. After I finished, I worked at the Metropolitan Nursing office as a clerk for a year. Then I worked as a payroll clerk at Montgomery Ward, at Fifth and Church in Nashville, until I married. We had a lot of friends in Bethesda, and I came back to ball games and other things while I was in Nashville, on weekends.

I lived in Nashville during wartime. It was hard to get anywhere because gas was rationed. I know that when I went to Nashville to board you had to have stamps to buy canned food, sugar, and gas. You needed stamps for 'most everything.

Most every weekend I would come home if I could get away. My parents did not have a car at this time. I had to catch a ride to come home.

WALTER

My girlfriend came home with me one weekend and we went over to our friend's house, Mrs. Ladd's. The Ladds lived over where Miss Annie is. We were always good friends, and I went to Miss Annie's often. It was on Sunday afternoon and Raymond and Walter were there. Raymond was just like a brother to me. I had known Walter for a long time, but he had just returned from the armed service in 1945, where he had spent four years. I just happened to get with him and that's where it started. We started dating then and went together about two years. In 1947 I married Walter, who was living up where I do now, with his father and mother.

After we married, we lived with Mr. and Mrs. Will Taylor, Walter's parents. Mrs. Taylor died June 10, 1976, and Walter died March 2, 1977. Mr. Will lost his eyesight several years before he died and could not get around very much. He died in 1989. I am still living at the same house now, after about 49 years.

Walter and I had three daughters. Elaine Holt lives at Arno; Jennie King lives in Bethesda; Sandra McCollum lives in Bethesda. Jennie and Sandra live in homes built on the Taylor farm.

Will Taylor of Bethesda

THE HOMEPLACE

My house is the white house on the hill [just north and east of and overlooking the intersection of roads at the store]. That house was moved over there – two rooms of it was moved – in 1847. The farmhouse originally sat elsewhere, but it was moved by twenty-yoke of oxen across rough land, called Preacher Horton's field, to a more accessible spot. There's been a lot added to the main house since we have had it. Mildred told me that it had sleighs (runners for moving the house).

Three landmark cabins are conveniently near the farmhouse and have been used by the families of two owners for 128 years. The middle cabin is where the old generation of the Irvins cooked and then brought the food into the main house. The far cabin is where, I understand, slaves were. We used the first cabin for a smokehouse, but now it is just used for storage. The notched corner of a slave cabin still shows the careful work of long-forgotten hands that took pride in the art of chinking and mortaring the hand-hewn logs. The log cabins are among the oldest in middle Tennessee and are still in good repair.

I don't know how long it took when they moved the main house, or when they had those cabins put there. I don't know if they put the cabins there later, or they moved the house there and the cabins were already there.

My sister-in-law, Mildred, told me that the attic of the house, which has never been completed, has little windows in it, up above. That's where, it is said, they peeked out to watch during the Civil War. We never found anything about the Civil War or slaves on the place. Several people wanted to come out and check but if they found anything I never did know it.

HISTORY OF THE HOMEPLACE

The people that owned the place, as far back as Mr. Taylor told me, were the Horton's and the Irvins. In 1936 Mr. Alex and Mr. Shearer Irvin bought the Irvin place, which was their granddaddy's and had then belonged to Irvins for 103 years. The Irvin brothers ran the Roberts Store in Franklin. The way I understand it, old ladies lived there ... old maids ... about four of five of them. In 1936 Mr. and Mrs. Taylor were living down there where Jean was.

Mr. Will Taylor began renting the place in 1939 from the Irvins and lived in the tenant house just beyond the main house. When Walter and I first moved here after we were married, Mr. and Mrs. Taylor were still renting. We also rented the farm next to it across the street. They had cows and milked them on the share, and they had hogs and things. Mr. Taylor would kill hogs and carry their part of the meat to the Irvins. Mr. and Mrs. Taylor were real nice to the Irvins, and when they got ready to sell the place they sold us everything they had and what they had on it.

R.A. Irvin

Shearer Irvin, Sr.

The Taylors had electricity when we first came there in 1947, but we just had electric lights. We didn't have a refrigerator, an electric range, or electric iron. Mr. Taylor wouldn't talk about an electric stove and there were a lot of things he didn't want. We used the wood stove in the kitchen for a long time. We had our first TV in 1953. We had a well-house. To keep our milk and butter from spoiling we would put it in a large bucket and lower it into the well to keep it cool and from spoiling. When the children were little – Lane was a baby – we kept our milk that way. It was cool down in the well.

When ironing, we put heavy metal irons on the stove to heat them. We did not have a washing machine. We did the washing on a washboard, which was a hard job. I wish that some of these young people could go back and just see how things were. They just can't believe it.

In 1952, when Mr. Taylor and Walter bought the place, the Irvins had gotten to where they couldn't take care of it and wanted to get out of the responsibility. They sold everything with the farm; cows, hogs, tools, and 184 acres for eighteen thousand dollars.

THE OLD MAIDS

I remember Mrs. Taylor used to sit with the old maids. One of them was in bed for a long time, and she helped her until she died. There were four rooms upstairs, two rooms over the front and two rooms in the back. They said that each one had a room. Jean Sanders can tell you a lot more about the old ladies because they are her great-aunts or great-great-aunts.

DAIRY FARMING

After buying from the Irvins the land was chiefly used for pasturing sixty head of dairy cattle and heifers.

Jessie: Didn't you have the first milk barn around here?

They milked by hand before they built the milk barn. The milk trucks came by at the end of the road. We'd have to carry the milk out in cans to a little milk stand we had beside the road. Walter made a wagon to take three or four cans at a time, every day. They would carry the milk out to the road on the wagon for the trucks to pick up.

Then in 1950, a grade A milk barn was built, and we began selling grade A milk. I know we were really proud when we sold the grade A milk. We milked about 40 cows at one time.

When we got our barn, we had a tank, and the milkman didn't come every day. The tank kept the milk cool all the time. It was run by electricity and held 500 gallons, which is a lot of milk. There were vats and automatic washers to wash the tank and everything. One room held the strainer and other equipment, and there was another room for the cows to come in.

From the first, we had milking machines, but later we went to a pipeline that ran the milk directly from the machines into the tank. Then, all you had to do was wash the cows and put the cups on them. It was really amazing to see how the milk went to the tank. Trucks would come in and pick the milk up from the tank.

We had about the only milk barn except for James Bond, and later on John Williams, and the McMillans. Now, nearly everybody is out of the business except the Bonds and Everett Hayes. Mr. Taylor told me that he told James Bond what kind of cows to get when he got into the milking business. I don't know if James had milked before or not.

END OF THE MILKING BUSINESS

I milked for nine years, by myself with Richard's help. One morning the last year, in 1985, everything was frozen up and Richard was sick. Snow was up over my ankles, and I thought, "Lord, if you will just let me live through this I'm going to quit!" Mr. Taylor kept after me saying, "You're going to fall out there at the barn." I loved it and I miss it, but I couldn't do it now, anyway. After you have been used to something for so many years you just like to do it.

I have missed it, but I don't have any cows. Richard has all the cows now. I did have some that we sold calves off of until last year, but I told him to take what I had left and do whatever he wanted to with them. We were talking here a while back about dairy farming being a gamble. You don't ever know. Cows die.

Jessie: Well, that is about five or six hundred dollars. Several cows have died in the Bethesda area within the week before this interview and something in the grass that was now coming up was suspected by a vet.

You have lost a lot, and you never know when a cow is going to get sick. They don't generally pull out of it when they do. It's sad, really sad. A farmer doesn't get much for what he does now.

PRANKSTERS

Now they talk about the kids being bad, but there was a lot going on back then, too. It's killing now, but then it was more pranks.

Jessie recalled when Shorty (Marvin Lillard) and Squeaky (Clifford Grigsby) put forks in the piano and a lot of things like that. Mr. Lulu always wore a shirt with Hawaiian things on it. He would sit down to play, and the forks would go flying out of the piano amid strange plunks. The kids thought it was funny, and everyone would get into trouble because they all laughed. She also recalled when Shorty, Paul Williams, and some other boys got a blind pony and put it in a school room. When we got off the bus the next morning, everything was going on. We thought it was fun. But Cleo told us to get in that room, sit down, and not dare look out the window. We would go to looking out the window and she would go to hitting us in the head with a book because we wanted to see what was going on. Mr. Harris was the principal. Mean ... I mean, he was mean! Had to be!

We had a teacher that taught me math. I was talking to an old schoolmate recently who said, "Can you remember?" And I said, "Yes, mighty well. He was kinda' cross-eyed and you could never tell when he was looking at you." In study hall, I would think he was looking somewhere else, but he would be looking at me, and would say, "You are just worse than a worm in hot ashes! You just jump from one place to the other." My friend said that one time when they were having something up there at school, they jammed the teacher's car ... twisted it in between things ... to where he couldn't get in it. They did some mean things but nothing like they do today. When we used to get home, we would get a spanking for what we did.

Sometimes I kept my grandchildren. They later told me, "Nanny, you used to catch us in behind the house when we were carrying on. I said, "Let me tell you something. I almost had to whip you." I used to catch them and pull them apart and they would say, "Nanny, you've hurt us." Now they tell me they don't see how I kept them. I couldn't do it anymore.

THE GRAVEYARD

The graveyard close by on Bethesda-Arno Road is the Earlys and the Millards and some others; there's a bunch over there. I heard Mrs. Taylor tell about when they buried Brother Millard, who was a preacher. It was raining so hard, and the water had gotten in the grave. They had to push the casket down and hold it down in the water. It's a shame that the graveyard is grown up. They used to have somebody to clean it off. They put a fence and bulldozed it off, but it still needs work to fill up the graves. Jane's little sister is buried up there.

They had a group that went around trying to find all these old graveyards. They never did have this one on their records. I knew it was there because it was fenced off. We have fenced it closer in now because nobody else will be buried there. We asked Jean about it and she said there might be some graves on the outside that were colored or slaves. Some of the graves don't have tombstones. You know, slaves didn't have tombstones.

RURAL LIFE FOR ME

Jessie: What do you think about living in one community all your life?

I think it is nice. I still wouldn't want to live in town. I'm close enough. A lot of people wanted me to sell off some of my land but I said, "No, as long as I live, it will never be sold." Several years ago, one of our preachers said, "That lot out there in the front of the school would be a fine place." We still have 151 acres. It runs way back into the woods. We had 184 acres 'til we sold 19 acres off, over where you go to where William Marlin and Pat Marlin live. All that went with this place originally.

CHANGES IN BETHESDA

Jessie: Tell us about the changes that have been in Bethesda in the last 50 years.

There have been lots of changes since I have been living in Bethesda. Three stores were present at one time. One, owned by Williams, burned. One, owned by J.O. and Clifford Grigsby, went out of business. The store that is operating now is at the location of the one that burned in the 1980s.

A new Bethesda United Methodist Church was built on Bethesda Road in 1960. The old church was on Bethesda-Duplex Road. A Masonic Lodge was built where the old church was.

There has been a new school built – just a grade school, kindergarten through the fifth grade. Part of the old school is being used as a senior citizen center, a library, a museum, and a fire hall.

As far as the community is concerned, we have had so many new people move in. Houses have been built. I used to recognize everybody's car that drove up to the store. Now I don't know anybody. When I am out, I see people that I don't know. I went to the ball game last night but didn't know anybody there.

SOME FINAL THOUGHTS

Mr. Taylor told me some other things before he died that I wrote down on a piece of paper that I put away somewhere. He told me some of the things that were in the *Tennessean* paper before he got sick. They came out from the *Tennessean* and made a picture of him. They wanted to show a picture of the ham that we had in the smokehouse and had him stand and hold it on a stick.

It's been a good life and it's been a bad life too. I have loved living in this community most of my life and I hope I can live the rest of my life in Bethesda.

JAMES TRICE, 1918-1999

Trice House at Cross Keys

MY YOUNG DAYS

I was born in the little white house across from the Bennetts. The doctor was probably Dr. Core. My parents farmed. They lived in the house where you [Hugh] bought. There used to be another house out the other side of the house. It burned up. Lincoln Binkley lived there at the time. We had a big barn that burned this side of our house, the old house that you bought.

My parents bought that place up there after I was born. I don't know how old I was when we moved up in the hollow. There were two places for sale. Joe Trice bought it all. My daddy, Charlie Trice, took the back place and they took the part on this side [south]. Momma was Fannie Biggers. [They lived on the other side of Pull Tight Ridge.] I had no brothers or sisters.

Our kitchen when I was growing up was in the back room of the house. I used to sleep on the side porch, winter and summer. We had a wood stove and a wood heater too. And coal oil lamps. The upstairs was just a loft. Nobody ever slept up there.

BETHESDA

I remember one thing. My granddaddy had a bunch of bees out there in front of the house. In the summertime, they would get in big lumps. I remember one time, just as well as yesterday, when I was a little bitty boy wearing a diaper. I went out there with a stick and punched in there and them things they liked to eat me up. They thrashed me out, I'll tell you.

My daddy got up one night in his sleep and thought someone had put a horse there and kicked it. He hit his foot against the rocking chair and broke his toe.

Jessie: Aunt Fannie tells that he saddled up his horse one time and when he got to the gate, the horse stepped on his foot.

I went to school at Choctaw part of the time. Choctaw was a one-room school. My teachers - Miss Louise Sawyer was one and Miss Nell Smithson was one. There used to be a little icehouse up here at this store. I'd ride behind on a horse. I'd get up on that icehouse porch and Miss Smithson would ride beside me. She lived over Pull Tight. She would come by, and I would get on and ride to school.

Then I went down to Bethesda, down where the store is. I walked or run. From up there where you lived, I would run to school every morning, run back that evening, run back that night and practice basketball, and run back home.

When I was a boy, I helped a fellow run a cream route to Murfreesboro. We'd get ice cream up at the center. When we were done loading the cream we come back there, and we'd get a gallon of ice cream for eighty cents. We'd stop out there at Stones River, me and T.R., and get up under there and eat it. Later I didn't do much of nothing but work with T.R. Clendenen in the sawmills.

We didn't have electricity until way up in the forties. We had Aladdin lamps, with the little wicks. I believe we had a battery radio before we got electricity. Big old long Philco, I believe. We bought one from an old man who runs an electric place here in Franklin when they put electricity in. I don't guess we listened to anything but WSM.

We killed hogs. Everybody would go in right up here at the rock house up here on that creek. They had a big gamboling pole they would hang the hogs up on. Everybody in this country killed hogs up there. And they killed a big bunch over at the white house where my granddaddy Pappy Will and Mammy Kate Trice lived. But nobody kills hogs no more.

CROSS KEYS

When I was young, I played horseshoes. That was the biggest game in this country! Up here where the old store was [at Cross Keys, where James' house is now], where the old locust tree is now. There was a big store there on the right-hand side. I tore it down when I bought where I am now.

They had a barber shop upstairs, and tested cream and stuff downstairs in that little side room. They bought possums, polecats, rabbits, and everything and had chickens. They carried them to Nashville. I've seen Trav Wallace, who run the grocery store, back his big International truck up there one day and put 100 cases of eggs in that thing, that he got in one week from people in this county.

I have heard them tell how things around here started. Over at Flat Creek in front of that old store out there on that creek, there is a big flat rock. There used to be an old store there and a barber shop, and they made twist tobacco and they done everything at that place. Had a post office there. But I have heard them tell about who started down here in Bethesda.

I guess the old store house close to me is the oldest one around, Laban Hartley's [Jessie's great, great, granddaddy] house. Laban Hartley had slaves up there. Way back in the 1800s. He lived in that house with slaves. This side of there, they made whiskey and everything at that place then. That thing used to be full of barrels and old counterfeit money. On this side of the road was a saloon where people went to drink in there.

The old store across from my house used to be a service station and everything. [They] sold Cities Service gas, sold white whiskey on the inside, and upstairs they gambled. T.R. and Russell Runnels run it. That was way back in the first of the thirties. [Now, there is a one-story building that was once a store at that location.]

Cross Keys Tavern

There was a funeral home up on the hill – a big red building. You could go up there and buy the casket, handles, and screws all for $25. You would put them together yourself; they were made like a fiddle, with a tapered end.

Where my garage is now is where the man that run the store had a scale. They would bring calves and sheep down there and separate them from the lambs. They would load the lambs up in a truck and take them to Nashville – calves and everything. You had pens you could drive them in and separate them all out.

Roads were just dumb old dirt roads. Across the creek, there used to be rails and poles laying there that you walked across on. There weren't any road bridges then. You had to ford the creek.

I've heard them tell how Cross Keys got its name. A man lost his keys up there one day, and he found them. They were crossed and they named it Cross Keys. That store where my house is, over a hundred years ago, used to sit long ways there. That was before they ever built that little one. John Trice run it.

Have you ever seen this cheese cutter down at the Bethesda store that they cut cheese on back there? That's mine. Aunt Carrie said when she was a little bitty girl, they had that thing up in this old store to cut cheese on.

THE PICTURE SHOW

Out there where Mr. Nichols's barn is there used to be a theater. A picture show come here every year. But it didn't make no sound. They put up a big tent. I'll tell you what. We'd be up there in that hollow and we could always tell. When you heard chickens squalling all over this country, people were taking their chickens to sell to go to the show. They had a little box of candy for a nickel, but there wasn't no use to sit there and look at the picture. There wasn't no sound to it.

That was back in the 1920s.

THE ICEHOUSE

Joe and Bettie Creswell at Cross Keys

They got the ice for the icehouse at Cross Keys from Franklin. They would cut a twelve-pound block and sell it to people. Roy Creswell lived in the hollow the other side of where you live over there. He would go to Franklin every Saturday, and he would bring back ice. He run an ice route. He'd stop and leave fifteen cents worth or a dimes-worth, or whatever you wanted. People had boxes with sawdust in them, you know, to keep the ice. He would bring the store two or three blocks to put over in the icehouse and the sawdust would keep it. Some people had an icebox to put the ice in. But a lot of people dug a hole in the ground and put sawdust in there. Put the ice in it and put the sawdust back over it. It would keep a long time. Just put the ice in on the sawdust. Chip you off a piece when you wanted it.

SPORTS

We had a basketball team and a baseball team too. We had a real baseball team. Ward Taylor was the back catcher and John Williams – they were the back catchers. I was the pitcher. I don't know who all played on it. Watson Wally did but he got killed. We played right there beside the store [in Bethesda]. That store has burned up four times down there. We played at Arno and Rudderville.

Cross Keys had a ball team. Right here where the Cross Keys Baptist Church is, that used to be Cross Keys diamond. I remember one time they were playing down there, and Howard Robertson was on third·base and Owen Farrar was back catcher. They got somebody in the hot box [a rundown between third and home]. Owen throwed Howard a hard one; he always slapped at the ball to catch it, but he slapped too late. The ball hit him in the mouth. He had to reach up there and take both hands to pull that baseball out of his mouth.

THE HOMEPLACE

Note: Hugh bought the farm and house that James was raised in, in 1991. Over the years many remodelings and additions had been made. The cabinets in the kitchen are those that were removed from the kitchen of Dolly Parton when it was remodeled.

I don't know when that house was built. It's way over two hundred years old. Old Dr. Bennett used to live there. Had a doctor's office there. He married old man Charlie Anderson's aunt. You know there was a big graveyard in front of that house up on that hill there, on the other side of the road. They dug phosphate up there twice. I've been up there and picked up casket handles and tombstones, and everything.

There is also a cemetery up on Rabbit Hill [the hill up the hollow behind the home place]. Miss Erma Creswell that lived up where the Hagewoods live, she was raised up on top of that hill.

There used to be a road that come out that ridge and come off down there at their house.

And then there used to be road off of there that went on out that ridge and come out over at the Arno-Allisona Road.

There was another house up in the hollow behind my home, just on the left-hand side of the spring there. That's where I saw one brother kill the other right there. It didn't kill him right then, but he was never right before he died. These boys were going to haul gravel to gravel the road with and I was walking on up there with them. They got up there and they got into a fight. One of them drawed back to throw a rock to hit the other one. The other one was too fast; he hit him up the side of the head. Carried him up to the spring and I run over to get his daddy. Mr. Creswell was to go over there. The first thing, he reached and got his gun. He said, "I'll kill that son of a bitch."

He talked to the other boy, but he didn't ... to the other boy. He got over there and seen that Bill had hit Roy and he didn't say anything, but if Roy had hit Bill, he would have killed him right there. He laid there for months before he died. Their momma and daddy – Miss Erma Williams, her daddy was a captain in the Civil War, and they moved out and bought that place up there in 1878 where Hagewood lives.

The house up by the spring [up in the hollow] was there somewhere about 1924 or 1925. There were two houses, the one I lived in and the one by the spring. Lincoln Bennett lived in the one by the spring, but they had gone off over to Little Texas where they were from. There was a big snow on the ground. The house caught afire some way. On the left-hand side of the spring, there was a big rock that water came out of when it rained. There used to be some big locust trees right there and that's where that house was. It was a two-room house and had steps to go up to it. The house was right by the big rock, sitting on rocks.

James Edward Crafton, 5th U.S. Cavalry

Joe Biggers bought that when I left home [after 1959]. He bought that up there and sold the timber off to the co-op. They went up there in the hollow on the left-hand side and cut that timber.

Back in the hollow, just over the fence seven or eight feet, there are seven springs. They run all the time, but they don't run much. And there used to be a big spring above our house, back up in the hollow next to Jack Webster's place.

The spring right in back of our house went dry. [Until 1996 it had big rocks in the bottom and a cooling ditch in it, and there was a little water coming out. A frame shed still covered

309

it.] We got Flooky Buford to come over and dig a ditch. We didn't have any water. They dug a ditch out and struck that spring where it is at right now, just a few feet away from the old spring.

There was phosphate mining up there in the hill in front of my home place. Way back years ago, and then they came back again. They dug phosphate with picks and shovels and hauled it to Thompson Station to the train. Old man Hackney and Malcolm West hauled it on wagons.

In the Civil War, that road came around off that hill around by Hagewood's house and around the other side of Bald Hill and come out down here by the Lynch's. That's where the road came out.

G.W. Creswell at Cross Keys

BEAR HOLLOW

That hollow up there is Bear Hollow. Up where that spring is somebody cut a big sycamore tree and some man had been up to the house on the hill there and started back down off the hollow here. And this bear was laying up there on that stump. And he killed him and that's where the name of Bear Hollow came from, according to Miss Erma Creswell. That is supposed to be the last bear killed in this area.

BALD HILL

I was going to tell you about this Bald Hill. [The hill across the road from where James was raised; today it is grown up with lots of cedars and other trees.] On the left-hand side there, my granddaddy had that fenced off and there were plum trees. He would put his hogs in there every fall and feed them corn and them plums. Man, he'd have some fat hogs. That Bald Hill used to be like that yard out there when I was a boy. They raised corn about halfway up that hill, and they would start a row of tobacco and would go round and round and round the hill 'til they got to the top with tobacco. When I lived up there in the hollow where you [Hugh] own now you could sit up there and see all over this country because there wasn't a bush in there. You could see this whole country. Back in those days people just raised a little tobacco and what they could eat.

Jason used that big hillside. That used to be a big orchard up there. You would get a cider mill and haul it up there to grind apples and make cider, in the fall, and have vinegar all year. Made it by the barrels. Made it up in the orchard. The mill was hand-operated.

ARMY DAYS

I quit school and went to work at TVA. Then the army got kinda hot and I quit and joined the army. They wrote me after I got out of the army and wanted me to come back, but I didn't go. That's what I ought to have done.

I saw foreign service and was in six years, two months, and eleven days, I believe it was. I had a cousin who lives up there in that old red house. He was to go the next day to the army, and they had a party for him, a big supper and everything. He was crying cause he was having to go by himself, and everybody was about two-thirds drunk. I told him if you'll just be quiet, I'll volunteer and go with you tomorrow. He said, "You won't do it." I said, "I will." He made me stay all night. He slept with his arm around me like this, cutting my wind off so I could hardly breathe. We come down the next morning and borrowed old man Sam Anderson's car and Black Creswell drove us to Franklin. I passed and he didn't. He didn't go.

I went to Nashville. Rode that old steel tired interurban from Franklin to Nashville. First time I ever rode it. It might have been the first time I was ever in Franklin. Then went to Fort Oglethorpe, Georgia. And from there to Fort Jackson, South Carolina. I was in the Tennessee Old Hickory Division and saw battle conditions. Yeah, I talked to Eisenhower, General George Marshall, head of the army at that time, and all of them. I talked to a whole bunch of them; I've seen them all. I volunteered the 18th day of December 1940 and left January 20. They let me stay out for Christmas.

AFTER THE ARMY

When I got out of the service I married. We didn't live too long together. And then I married Leo Crafton who lived over Pull Tight. We lived together twenty-five years, or thirty, somewhere around there. We lived in the house on Lane Road with my daddy for a while, and then we moved down to a house on the Graham place on Pull Tight Hill Road. But they tore that house down about 1959.

Me and Leo, we had five children. Stan is over in Choctaw, one is down in Chapel Hill, one is in Smyrna, two are in the Rudderville community. We have four grandchildren.

The first car I ever owned was a forty-one, it seems like, Mercury – a four-door. I don't even know who I got it from. That was after I got out of the army. I don't think I paid much for it because I didn't have much to pay with.

JAMES TRICE, 1918-1999

THE FORTUNE TELLER

Man, there was big snow on the ground. This boy on Flat Creek, up in Cobb Hollow there, he had killed a woman and somebody else and himself off. He killed himself in the smokehouse. They couldn't find this woman over there and they went to Simon Warner, a fortune teller in Shelbyville. He said you go back to that boy's house, and you go 100 yards down the creek and you will find her in a brush pile. Her aunt was the one who found her. Her toes had melted the snow off of them a little bit and they found her under a brush pile. They never found the other one.

THE CROSS KEYS GRAVEYARD

Over here at the graveyard in Cross Keys [across from the Bennetts], the apple tree used to be on the outside of the fence. They were horse apples, a great big apple; the best you ever ate. They built that fence and put that apple tree over on the graveyard side so no one would bother it. The name of it is the Hartley Community Cemetery. Laban Hartley was the first one buried there.

Some Hartleys are buried right across from R. C. Edmonson's. His daughter is, but it doesn't say anything about his wife. There are rocks piled up that you can see from the road. You go over to Flat Creek and turn to the right and make that little dip at that big oak tree that is there. Look down there. One of them died in 1843, and the other I don't know when. But he and his girl are buried there. I don't know where his wife was buried.

I don't know who was buried in the cemetery across the road from where I grew up [on Lane Road]. There used to be some big tombstones in there. I've picked up handles up there.

The ones who ran the funeral home on the hill were the same family as the Chapel Hill Lawrences. When they moved up there, they changed the name to Lawrence instead of Lavender. The Lavenders ran the one in Cross Keys. There was a blacksmith shop right on the other side where the road turns to the right. Used to be a great big place there. Blacksmith shop, Ralph Simmers and Reed Walker used to trade horses all the time. There was a bunch over there all the time playing horseshoes and trading horses and getting horses shod.

NATHAN

I bought the house I am in from Earl Gatlin. Nathan McClain, a black man, used to rent it. He was the blacksmith. Besides shoeing horses, he sharpened plow points and did any kind of metal work. Fixed buggies. Put rubber tires on them. He was a handyman. He had a wreck out this side of Franklin Road. It wasn't even his fault, but he killed someone, and they sent him to the pen. One day I got a letter from the penitentiary, and I said, "Who in the devil is that!" They were wanting me to get a bunch of people to sign to get him out. I said I would sure do it. I got me two or three cases of beer and every house I would go to, I'd give them three or four beers. A whole bunch signed it and I sent it back. In a few days, Nathan came home.

But I used to read the *Williamson County News* every week. They sent me the *News* and I was reading one day where they caught Nathan driving, drinking a quart of beer, and driving with his feet.

SOME OTHER STORIES

Me and T.R. Clendenen always wanted to see a rattlesnake [they had never seen one in the Bethesda or Cross Keys area] and we were fishing in Hickman County. We told old man Charlie Pruitt if he would ever catch one to write us a letter and someone would come and get him. One day we got a letter. We made T.R. run the store and Marvin Clendenen and George Earl Creswell went down and got that rattlesnake. We set that locust tree next to my house out that day while they were gone. That's where that locust tree come from.

Mr. Ross, who lived up there back of Pull Tight church in that log house, had a sister. One day she was coming down the road and everybody was sitting on the porch – John William Beasley, O. C. Farrar, John Grimm, and who all were sitting there. We were all guessing who it was. She come on down and she walked over there and told us who she was. She said, "Would you all mind if I make a picture of you? I work for the television station in New York." She made a picture of all of us and put it on television. The other day she came back down the road. She walked up to me and said, "Do you remember me now?" I said, "No, I don't." She said it had been several years since she had been down here, and she told me what she had done. I said, "Every one of them is dead."

Hugh: What words of wisdom do you have to pass on?

Be Good and Sit on the Front Porch. I went to this store in Chapel Hill the other day. A new man has bought the grocery store. One of the fellows working in the store called me back there and introduced me to him and said, "Now this is one of the finest fellers you've ever seen. He buys all kinds of stuff and takes it and gives it to people around where he lives – poor people. That new man said, "I'll tell you what, you're a Baptist." I said, "You're right! That's what a good Baptist will do. Help people like that."

JERRY WATKINS, 1909-1997

Jessie: Tell about the giant.

They found him in a well over here on Route 431. They dug a well. They started on solid rock, and they hit a cave down there. That's where they found a giant. He was about nine foot tall. Just the bones. Ward Daniel and some other man dug the well. Fleming West, he owned the place. If he was living, he could tell you about that giant. He never did have no whiskers. They shipped the giant's bones overseas, but the ship got sunk or something. I don't know why they were shipping the bones overseas. They might have been going to experiment.

My grandma came from West Virginia. Her name was Perry Lee Daniel and was a Cherokee Indian. She used to tell me I wouldn't live to be very old. But I'm 88. My birthday is in May.

Judy: They had so many children back then that they didn't keep up with birthdays. There were two families and a total of twenty-plus children in his family. The year he was born in is known because a neighbor had a baby at the same time. He put down September 15 as his birthday when he went to sign for Social Security, but it is really in May. He has two birthday parties a year that way. Ha!

I was not born in Bethesda. We lived down in what was called Callie on Route 431. We lived back over in the hollow in an old house that we had for years.

OLD TIME MEDICINE

I got the itch one time when I was a kid. I cured it with poke leaves. Take it and boil it to get the juice out of it and wash off in it. I went and got me a sack full. It was just as red. I got me a tub and got in the kitchen and throwed that water all over me. It killed that itch! I imagine I learned that cure from my old grandma. I bet my granny made 50 gallons of butterfly root for me. But I don't know what it was for. My grandma took the fat off a polecat and cooked it down to get the grease to put on sores. But it didn't smell like polecat.

THE FROG

My grandmother stayed with us a lot. She caught her a frog in the spring down beside the road. I went down and took an old trap. I was just a little boy. I set the old trap there and I caught a frog. The old frog would holler, and she thought a snake had him. She was crippled in one foot. She went down there, and I had a frog in the trap. Oh, if she didn't fuss, and said, "I'm going to make Daddy wear you out." But Daddy was glad I caught him. Every time he would come to the spring, the old frog would jump in there and make it muddy.

Leon saw the same frog forty years later, or thought it was. He was still up there on the hill.

Judy: You told us that it was the same frog because it had a cut on its stomach where the trap had caught him. And you said that frog could jump forty feet.

I figure he could. Me and John got after him and we couldn't catch him. He was in some bushes and briars.

The same frog?

Probably was, yeah.

CHILDHOOD MEMORIES

When I was a little boy my daddy made us work. I grew up on a farm in Callie. For a vacation we would go to the Harpeth River and fish. My daddy bought an old sow from Lee West. I had to feed the hog. I had to cook a big pot of hominy every day to feed the hog. We had to cook it because the hog didn't have no teeth. To make hominy you put corn in a big kettle and cook it, and put a few ashes in it. Cook it all up for half a day.

What happened to the hog's teeth?

Well, the old hog eat walnuts and everything and broke them all out.

Susie Lee, my sister who just turned 90, and I had been to the grocery store at Callie. We saw a big pear in a pear tree and Susie Lee clumb up there to get it. I saw old Mrs. West coming around the hill, walking with a big stick. I got my groceries and took off and got off of that place and left Susie Lee up in the tree.

JERRY WATKINS, 1909-1997

I went to school at Harpeth. My teacher was Susie Scales. I didn't learn a thing. I went to school four or five years but didn't learn to read or write. I can sign my name on checks. I was one of 13 kids. Lizzie was the oldest. She married Joe Lynn Davis. Billie was next.

Judy: He died at age 95 a few years ago, Luke is 93, a sister 90, then Daddy is 88. ... He was a neighbor of Virginia McGee. Daddy never did learn to read or write because he didn't get to go to school. He was about five or six years older than my mother, Johnny. Mother used to write letters for him to Virginia, and he talked to Virginia for about five years.

Susie Baugh Scales

I liked her. Still like her.

But her family made her dump Daddy, and she was told she couldn't talk to him anymore. Mother was just about 12 or 13 at the time. The day that Daddy was told he couldn't talk to Virginia any more ...

I cried. I come up to Johnny's. Prentice Maupin was a buddy that I run around with. I come up crying and he said he believed I needed a drink. I went out on the porch and Johnny was sitting out on the porch. I laid my head in her lap and she asked me would I marry her.

Daddy said one time, "I work fast; I got dumped and engaged all in about three hours." They married, lived together for 66 years, and had four children. Mother was always jealous of Virginia. Now Virginia's husband and Mother have both passed away, so they visit together again. He refers to her as his woman.

MARRIED LIFE

The day I got married my whiskers were about two inches long. I washed off a little the day I got married. Charlie Teasley shaved me and cut my hair, the next day. I reckon I actually started to hippie! Ha!

Judy: He said he didn't have time to take a bath and shave. Johnny was only 13 when she got married, she had two children when she was 15. She used to say her children were almost as old as she was. Her name was Johnny, and his name is Jerry, so their first child was John Jerry.

Judy, you get me into something all the time!

Our house when we were first married was in the middle of a cornfield. When we heard a car, we climbed the peach tree in the yard to see who was coming. L.T. climbed up in that tree. We had peaches right on my porch. We cleared new ground for tobacco. Take and cut it off and burn the brush. We plowed up the roots. A man over at Hillsboro made what you call a new ground plow. It had a "colder" on it to cut the roots. It broke them more than cut them. I had a couple of acres at the start but about six acres later.

*Judy: He had a tobacco crop on what they called N*****bone Hill, because that is where they said they hung some blacks. I was five or six and don't know why daddy wanted to have tobacco on that hill, but they slid the tobacco at harvest time down the hill on a wire and someone had to catch it.*

I took baths in the creek. There was a big old snake lived in there. I'd plow all day – talk about dirty, you'd be dirty then. The water was cold, and that big old water moccasin was there. He was as scared of me as I was of him and crawled on off

Judy: Daddy never did discipline. Mother always disciplined.

I whipped you one time with a little old straw.

Judy: He told me not to let the hogs get around the cream can where we were milking, and I didn't pay any attention to him.

Jessie: Tell about how you started dancing the country two-step at age 86 and going to dance at Spring Hill wearing loud boots and loud clothes. Did you like that?

No!

Jessie: Tell us about it.

I went to see my girl the other day and had to use the bathroom. That was embarrassing! What I liked best about dancing was the music and I got a lot of hugs – these women would hug me. I put on a pair of hee-haw pants and a cowboy hat.

My woman says we are too old to get married again.

Judy: I took him up to see Virginia a few days ago and she had a lift chair. She lifted him up and down in it and said he needed one.

Hugh: what would you say is your philosophy of life?

I lived a pretty good life. I've done a lot of walking. Walk and don't worry too much about anything.

BILL WILEY 1910-2005

I was born in 1910 in the Flat Creek community. We moved to Bethesda community when I was one year old, to the T.C. Bond farm. We lived in the house over the hill from where you [Hugh] live now. It joined the old Will Creswell farm. [It is now owned by the Hagewoods.]

They moved the old house out that we lived in. It was over on the back side and the farm we lived on joined the Roy Creswell place. I started to Bethesda school in 1916.

We lived up in the valley 'til I was ready for the seventh grade, and then we moved. And then we moved back there. We stayed away for eight years and moved back and stayed there four more years. I spent my entire early life within ten miles of Bethesda. My father was a farmer. He wasn't into milking; he was just a general farmer. Raised tobacco, corn, and stuff like that, and worked on the farm.

There were ten children in my family, six girls and four boys. I had two girls and one boy and three grandchildren, one of them dead.

CARPENTRY

I was a farmer 'til I was about 50 years old, and I started carpentering. That's what I did the rest of my career. General carpentry. Building houses.

Jessie: And every cabinet in Bethesda probably, every home, just about.

Just about. Miss Loreen Bond asked me one time when I was building cabinets in Billy Giles's vacation house and she was standing there watching me, "Where did you learn that?" I said, "Miss Lorene, going to school to Bethesda. Didn't you learn nothing out of that?" She said, "Nothing like that!" Ha!

I guess I just decided to do something else and started carpentry. When I was farming my main sources of income were raising tobacco and running a dairy. I run a grade-A dairy my last farming years – John William Beasley and myself – over on Byrd Lane where Dwight Lynch lives, right around from Miss Leo Bond's, the next house and barn on the other side. When I left there, I went to carpentry. I lived there four years. I just picked carpentry up. I went to work with other carpenters who taught me a lot. Then I went out on my own and had my own crew. John Neal and Henry Wiley worked with me. I worked with Jimmy Maxwell. In fact, I went to work with his daddy, Mack Maxwell.

Jessie: He built our house.

Jimmy was just a boy. I worked with them and after Jimmy took the business over, I worked for him. [As of this writing, Jimmy's son has since taken over most of the business.] After I quit working for them, I worked for myself. During the time between him and his daddy, I did have my own crew, but then Jimmy would call me, and I'd go back and work for him. Then I retired when I was 65 and stayed retired about six months, I reckon, and went back to work and I worked on until I was 77. I worked for Ralph Gedding. We did finish work in houses.

One thing about the Maxwells: Jim and his daddy and Jimmy and all of them – whatever they tell you, you can depend on. I told some people if you want a house built, just turn it over to them and go on to Florida or somewhere else and stay away from it. And when you come back, they will have it ready for you to move in and there won't be a nail left out of it. Everything will be in it and just a little bit more than they promised they would. But you don't find all builders that way.

John Lorenzo McGee with his grandson Jim Maxwell

Hugh: They certainly did a fantastic job on the house they built for us.

OLD BETHESDA SCHOOL

I remember about the old Bethesda school. Back then there weren't any automobiles. We all walked, rode horseback, or went in buggies. There was a row of stables that ran from the back of the school plumb down to the other line, just stable after stable. That row of stables separated the boys and the girls. The boys stayed on their side of the stables and weren't allowed on the other side. The girls stayed on their side when they were outside. Boys and girls didn't play together.

The stables were set back away from the road, and there was an old store over there, Jim Grigsby's old store. The row of stables split the school property just half open. Each side had a basketball court – they played basketball outdoors. The team that I remember was Miss Leo, Miss Cleo, and Miss Ella Francis (Miss Leo's sister), Miss Bessie Mosley, and my sister. They were the main team. The reason I remember that was that they didn't lose a game all year. They played other schools, just like they do now, but they played on this open court.

The old school had three rooms to it, and three teachers. There was an auditorium downstairs, that was the principal's office. The principal taught then just like other teachers. We didn't have just a principal that set back in his office – he was a teacher. The first four grades went upstairs. After you finished that you came down and went in over here in this wing for four years, through the eighth. And then you went on into the principal. Most of the time the teachers were women and the principal a man. Mr. Marvin Clendenen was the only man teacher that I remember who taught the middle grades. There was a little old small music room in addition to those three rooms. Miss Elizabeth Houser was the music teacher, I believe. She didn't marry until she retired. Her husband died last year.

The water came from a spring down to the back of the old Dr. Core place. We carried water from there. The spring branch ran from there out into the creek that is there. I am sure the spring is still there, but I don't know if it is still kept up. There was a spring house with walls of limestone rock. The schoolchildren would go and get the water. We would carry it in buckets, and then we had coolers. Of course, we didn't have ice, but we would bring it up and put it in those coolers. They were insulated and would keep the water the temperature that you brought it from the spring.

All of the rest facilities were outhouses. We didn't have any indoor toilets. The outhouses were two-holers, usually. One outhouse was on each side of the row of stables.

The heating of the school was done with pot-bellied heaters. They burned coal. You would have a student appointed to go early and build fires in all the rooms; each room had a pot-bellied heater. Children come in frozen, some of them with their hands aching and a-crying. The teachers would have to baby them and get their hands warmed up.

SCHOOL DISCIPLINE

Jessie: Did you ever get any spankings?

Did I! You couldn't do things today like they did then. If you did just a small thing, your teacher could handle it. But if it was sort of a major problem, they sent you to the principal. A small thing might be talking or throwing paper wads or something like that or setting down a pin for somebody to set down on. That might get you two or three licks. Most of the women teachers would hold your hand back and take a foot ruler and hit you a few pecks in the hand. Of course, that didn't hurt, but if you had to go to the principal you didn't want to go there anymore. Ha! I never did have to go to the principal in Bethesda, but after I transferred to Harpeth – down here where the Harpeth Baptist church is, and where I went in about the seventh or eighth grade – Miss Bessie Bond gave me a whipping. She ate me up pretty good. Preston Scales was the principal there then, and she sent me and another boy to him one day. He had a paddle that he used on you. He would take you by the back of the neck and bend you over and when he turned you loose, you didn't want to go back in there no more. You couldn't do that anymore, but that was the way then.

Elizabeth Houser

W. Preston Scales

I remember one incident. They had a rule at school that if you came by the school and used some sort of a foul name for the school, they would catch you and carry you to the creek and dunk you. The schoolteachers supervising would do this. Garrett Reed was the teacher at the time of this incident, and Owen Farrar came by in a buggy. He repeated some of this stuff that they didn't allow, and the older boys – James Bond, Leonard Grigsby, Bill Eggleston and a bunch of them – got on horses and run him down. He was in a buggy. They caught him over here somewhere and were going to take him to the creek and give him a ducking. Well, he begged off. He was going to Franklin to get his wife some medicine. He said he would come down someday and take his medicine.

He knew that was the school rules. So, one day, they called from up there at Cross Keys store. He said, "I'm up here at the store; come on up here and we'll go to the creek and get it over with." Well, they went and they had a gang ready for them. These schoolboys came out with wet tails. Owen had a bunch of boys – George Ladd, Charlie Trice, Grover Trice, Laban Daniels, and all of them. Jessie, your daddy was in on this; he got ducked. And that bunch ducked these boys. It didn't matter who talked against the school, whether they were a student or not. After that, you see, they caught them one at a time. If they ever came to Bethesda, they would get them.

There is a place right down here where you turn off to go down to Miss Bessie Mosley's. They called it the Beech Hole. They would carry them down there and four boys would get them by their legs and arms and give them a swing, and whop them off in there, you know.

The teacher and the whole school – they would turn out the school to go down and watch them. They had a picnic out of it! Talk about Grover Trice, he brought him some extra clothes and said, "C-C-C-Come on boys and-and-and I'm ready for my medicine." They went down there, and he did. They let him go 'round and change clothes before he went home. And nobody got mad about it. But they would kill you now if you did that.

PHOSPHATE MINING

They mined phosphate up there on the old Crafton place. That was before my time. The old signs were still there where they mined it. Later years in the forties they started mining it again, a different type. I do remember my daddy saying that Mr. Joe Harmon lived down here at Duplex.

He used his wagon and would haul phosphate. They said he was always late getting there. He told them one morning, "The reason I was so late, I wake my wife up and every one of my children and kiss them good-bye before I leave." There was an old Negro there who said, "Mr. Joe, that's the reason you is always so late. Takes you a long time to get around to kissin'."

THE ROADS IN BETHESDA

I started out walking and then I finally got a horse and buggy. At times I would walk ten miles. I rode a mule lots of miles. I was living down here where Lundy "Beater" Crafton lived. It was Jimmie Core's (Dr. Core's wife's) place. She was born and raised there. I was walking when I started courting but my main courting days were done in a horse and buggy. My wife lived over in Maury County. We went places that some people wouldn't think about going in an automobile now. Oh, that is too far. It didn't get too far. I would hitch up a horse and go to Columbia.

The roads were just gravel roads. They had a certain fellow appointed over the roads. He took his so many miles of the road. Then, people would haul gravel out of the creek. This creek right down here [Beech Creek] must have had millions of wagonloads of gravel hauled out. Through the summertime, after the farmers would get caught up with their crops, they would hire this superintendent to haul gravel out of the creeks. They would stockpile gravel along the roads where they could get to them all the winter, to keep the roads up. That was the way we would make a little extra money through the summer after the crops were caught up. Back then you had to pay a poll tax to vote – I think it was $4 – or you could work on the road four days, and you didn't have to pay that. That was the way you paid your poll tax. If you owned a wagon and team you could use them and get your time in earlier, by using your wagon and team. But you either had to pay that poll tax or have a receipt that showed that you worked the road so many days, to vote.

Right over here on the hill on the other side of Reed Road, there was a tollgate. You never saw a tollgate like that. It was an old pole, a post with a big bar through it pulling down over the road. A fellow, Mr. Bruce, set there and kept it. When people come along, he charged you a dime to get under. That was what they took to pay for keeping the road up.

WEDDINGS

What was a wedding like? The couple either went to a magistrate or a preacher – just went to their home and he performed a ceremony. They didn't have anything else. The only church wedding that I remember was Mr. Gordon McCord and Miss Mary. They had theirs at the Presbyterian church. They turned school out and let the whole school go up there. That was the only wedding like that.

Boys and girls back then would go to magistrates – I think they called them something else now – and they performed the marriage.

Jessie: Did they have any kind of celebration after that?

Why, no! They went back to work – they didn't have any money. There wasn't any money, and everybody had to work. I got married on the Saturday before Easter and Monday morning I went right on back to work just like I did the other days. There wasn't any money. That was in the depression.

Didn't anybody have any money to take trips or anything like that on. Ninety percent of them married and didn't even give the girl a diamond. Some of them made homemade wedding bands. Lots of people got married and after being married got able and bought the rings.

Those were what they called the Hoover days, with the Republican president. Mr. Lemming Marvin was working at Franklin at the farm store. He said that Christmas was coming on and the boss told him that they had a case of ammunition coming in – gun shells and stuff like that – for Christmas. There had just been an election and another Republican president had been elected.

Mr. Lemming told the boss, "Save me a case of those shells." When he was asked why he wanted so many, he said, "Well, I had to run my rabbits down during the Hoover days, I don't want to have to do that again." Haha! Now those were rough days. They were good in a way.

CHRISTMAS

At Christmas, we got a little fruit and maybe a couple of little toys. That was it. I remember getting up and going out and finding reindeer tracks in the snow and the sled tracks. I came back in and said, "Yeah, I saw where they went around the house." A little fruit and maybe a toy or two to play with, that was it. We didn't have any trees like they do now. We did hang up a stocking.

Children wore long black stockings back then. You would hang that stocking up and you would have the fruit and stuff in there in the morning. If you had been sort of a naughty boy there would be a switch sticking down in there. Ha! That was about the way the Christmases were. They always had a big family get-together on Christmas. Big dinner. Some of the children may have married and left or whatever, but you always had that big Christmas dinner. A typical dinner was maybe twelve or fifteen people. Dinner was about like it is now; beans and potatoes and whatever, always had cake, and always had ham. Of course, farmers always raised their own hogs and killed their own meat, you know. We'd always have a ham for Christmas and might have a turkey or chicken.

DOCTORS AND HOSPITALS

My first child was born at home. There wasn't a hospital this side of Nashville. Old Dr. Woodward delivered my first one, Willene. Twenty-five dollars was his fee. Five years later Dale was born. Williamson County had a hospital at the time. Dr. Guffee was the doctor. The hospital bill was thirty-five dollars. Fulton Beasley was at the time working at the funeral parlor that Mr. Cotton owned, right across from the old hospital. Fulton had an ambulance and I asked him what he would charge me to carry my wife and baby home, ten miles out from Franklin. He said three dollars. And when we got home, he even carried the baby in the house. I remember that just as well. Linda, my youngest one, was born in Williamson County Hospital.

Williamson County didn't have a hospital then. We married in 1933 and had been married a couple of years and were living where Billy Giles lives when my wife got sick and had to go to a hospital.

Dr. Eggleston and Mr. Tom Beasley came and carried her to the old Protestant Hospital, which is Baptist Hospital now, to take care of her that night. That was the fall of 1935, and there was not a hospital at Franklin then.

ROOSEVELT DAYS

After Roosevelt was elected everything completely changed. He set up projects called CCC

[Civilian Conservation Corps] camps. Boys who weren't in school joined the CCC camps and cleared right of way for roads and stuff like that, to give them something to do and to make a little money. If a man had a family, they would let him work on these roads. According to the size of his family, you got to work so many days. If it was just a man and his wife, they would let him work two days. They paid I think $4 a day. Then $8 a week would buy them enough groceries at that time to carry them a week. If you had three or four children maybe, you would go to work three or four days. You could make enough to feed your family. They had camps for the boys. If you had a family, you just stayed home and worked in your area. They built the Cross Keys Road from Cross Keys through to Flat Creek Road during that time. People in that area got to work on that road.

Hugh: Were there other projects in this area?

Ha! You were talking about the outhouses. People who were just renters like we were didn't have a decent outhouse. They set up a place and they built these little outdoor toilets, and they gave them to people. That was part of the project that Roosevelt started. Then, you did some kind of improvement to your farm to match it. That was the way it was. Ok, that's when they first started to put so much of your land in what they called the "soil bank." People had to work the land to death back then to have enough tillable land for the farmer to make a living. Roosevelt set up a fund and the government would pay you so much if you would rest the field. You set the field aside, sow it in grass or something, and let it rest. The government would pay you a percentage on that land while you were resting it.

My son and I had a farm down in Hickman County a few years ago. There was one blacktop road down there, Gray's Bend Road, the only rural asphalt road down in there. They said the CCC boys built that road. There were no camps around Bethesda; I don't know where the closest one was. It wasn't in Williamson County, anyway.

The toilet business was WPA [Works Progress Administration]. They also had projects where women would get together and can food, to be distributed out to people.

Privies furnished by the WPA. in Franklin

BILL WILEY 1910-2005

Jessie: I remember my mother doing some canning at Flat Creek School when I was little.

They would pay them to do the canning. It was another project to help poor people get on their feet. All the projects were to keep people from starving to death.

They had a program that they would lend you money to buy a farm with. The government would lend you money and you would pay it back as you made it on the farm. They didn't just bind you down; you just paid so much and so much interest. It was all figured in to start with. It had the payments down to where you could afford to do it. That's the way a whole lot of people got on their feet and own farms today, big farmers who would never have had a farm if it hadn't been for that.

Hugh: That may have been the NRA, National Recovery Act.

We had two stores in Bethesda in about the twenties. Mr. Jim Grigsby ran one of them. Mr. Leonard Grigsby ran the main store, the bigger store.

Hugh: And how would you sum up your philosophy of life?

Just to be honest with everybody. I don't guess you'll have this in the book …

Jessie: Ever what you are saying we put it in that book.

… but I heard on TV two guys were talking and one said to the other that he had decided that the best policy in life was to be honest with everybody. The other guy said, "Why, man, I'm a used car salesman!" Hahaha! He couldn't do that. He couldn't be honest.

But I'm trying to be like that. I'm trying to be honest with everybody in all of my dealings.

Irvin Store 1914. Dr. Core in chair on porch.

Reflections of Joyce Smith

What an excited feeling I felt when my husband Russell approached me about moving back to my home community, Bethesda. That was 24 years ago. As I sit and reflect on the past years of my life, I count my blessings for having been raised in the Bethesda community in a loving and caring family.

At the age of four, I, along with my eight brothers and sisters, lost our father to a car wreck. Our mother, the late Vivienne Grigsby Watson, moved into the home of her parents, Ollie and Ida Grigsby, and sister Cleo Grigsby, along with all of us.

My mother took a job as librarian at Bethesda (at that time it was grades 1 through 12 until she received her certificate to teach. My brother Ralph and I were allowed to go to school with her, and I recall taking naps on the floor of the library. During the years Miss Frances Hatcher, first grade teacher, would send for Ralph and me to take part in school parties or to go outside and play with them.

When I became of age to attend school, I not only had Miss Frances as my teacher but mother, Aunt Cleo, and Cousin Bess Eunice Bond.

I recall an incident that has "stuck" in my mind for years. We were not allowed to take candy to school, but during the day someone would ride their horse to the Bethesda store to get supplies for teachers and other students. I had slipped some money from home, so I left the classroom to give it to Herbert Giles, who was going to the store. I also gave him another student's name rather than mine. When he returned, I rushed to meet him thinking I could get my candy, but he told me he had to take everything to the teacher for her to give out. So, naturally, I did not get my candy.

As I grew older, I was in Aunt Cleo Grigsby's classroom with Grace Tomlin Glenn and Jimmy Bond. I remember writing a "love letter" and Aunt Cleo coming by my desk and taking it away from me. She carried it home and gave it to Mother, and said, "This is the type of work your daughter is doing for me." Of course, Mother sat me on the "wood box" and started lecturing me. (For those that don't know, the wood box held the wood for the stove.) The whole time she was lecturing me I was praying she would get a piece of that wood and spank me so I could leave, but the lectures did more good.

There were times when there was no water at the school for the students to drink. There were a number of times when Mr. Billy Alexander would bring milk cans filled with water. We would make our own cups from notebook paper and stand in line just to get a sip of water.

My fondest years were those of high school. I remember teachers such as Jessie Bourne, Clyde Adams, and Principal Nelson Jones. Mr. Jones was also my literature teacher. I remember him reading Shakespeare and then commenting, "Isn't that a beautiful thought!" O.L. Garner and I still talk about the wonderful years with Mr. Jones.

I was a member of the Bethesda Dragons basketball team. When we had "away" games we would stay at school and the late Mrs. Carrie Trice would stay and prepare the best grilled cheese sandwiches that anyone could want, for us to eat before going to the game. She was cafeteria manager.

Clyde Adams

Graduation came in 1954 with twelve boys and four girls receiving their diplomas. Over the past forty-plus years we have remained in touch with each other as well as other classmates we started with. We try to have a class reunion every five years, and more often when possible.

My religious background was one I thank God daily for. We were members of Bethesda United Methodist Church, which at one time was located where the Bethesda Masonic Lodge is, but we also attended the Bethesda Presbyterian Church. We would alternate

Sundays for preaching. I remember sitting in church with Mrs. Annie Lou McCord and trying to put her long gloves on my tiny fingers. She had so much patience with me. Revivals were attended by all in the community. There were services in the morning as well as at night. The preacher would go home with a family in the community for a large noon meal and then would visit in the homes of community people before going back at night for services.

Vacation Bible School was also held jointly. One year we would have it at the Methodist Church and the next year at the Presbyterian Church.

Bethesda will always have a special place in my heart. I wish space would allow me to list all the names of people who have influenced my life and have been an example to me, but there are so many that it just lets you know what a wonderful community Bethesda is. That is why we are growing so. We now have our own public library, an excellent museum, and a senior citizen center.

The following poem was sent to me by Aunt Cleo Grigsby in 1975, but I find it fitting for the community of Bethesda.

You're Somebody Special
You're "somebody special"
Who has a true knack
With the niceness and warmth
That a lot of folks lack.
You're one of a kind
And it seems from the start
You capture a place
In everyone's heart.
You're "somebody special"
What more can I say
Except that I "thank you"
For being that way.

REFLECTIONS OF JESSIE TRICE BENNETT

I was born in Cross Keys and have lived there all my life. There were seven in my family. We were raised poor, but very happy. My parents, Grover, and Carrie Trice raised all we ate. My mother made my clothes out of old shirts and feed sacks.

We never had a car because as far as we went was to Bethesda and Cross Keys. As I got older, I rode to Franklin with my uncle and aunt, Chubb and Louise Hargrove. We had lots of cousins. I visited my grandmother, Kate Trice, who lived across the road.

My special cousin was Billie Jean Hargrove (now Lillard). Billie Jean and I would walk to the Cross Keys store and carry eggs to sell for our grandmother. One time we spent some of the money. We told grandmother we fell and broke some eggs. She was smart enough and kept asking us about it. We finally told her we spent some of the money. She was going to whip us and I ran home. Billie Jean lived with her. She always got into trouble.

The preacher came one time. Grandmother told us to be good. We got tickled and I would look into the mirror and make faces at Billie Jean. I was always mean. When the preacher left, Grandmother did not say a word. She got a long stick she kept on the porch and gave Billie Jean one hard lick, and me two. I asked her, "Why two?" and she said for the eggs. That was my last time to not mind her.

The only thing I ever took was a nickel I took from my aunt. I got it out of a little glass hen and stopped at Cross Keys and bought ice cream. I told my sister Peggy about it and she cried and told Mama. She got a nickel and a switch and whipped me all the way to my aunt's. Then she gave me the nickel to give her. So I was broke young.

All my brothers and sisters along with cousins and friends walked to church. We carried shoes and changed at the crossroads in Bethesda. I was next to the baby in the family; it was hard growing up. My mother worked in the lunchroom in Bethesda, so I had it made in getting plenty to eat.

I went to the first grade at Choctaw school, which is still standing and rode horseback with my teacher, Lola (Reed) Bowersox.

My special friends at Bethesda were sisters, Grace (Tomlin) Glenn and Sara (Tomlin) Mosley. They would spend the night with us. We always went to the "old apple tree" and sat up in it to eat apples and talk. We made playhouses on big rocks. My mother would call us to come and eat.

We are all still good friends. That is why I like living in a small community.

While I was in high school, I had a lot of fun. I was always into everything. I had a very special teacher, Clyde Adams. He taught me to drive with match sticks that he laid out in the "old gym" to show me how to change gears. (I still don't know how. Ha!) I drove to get our class rings at the Thompson Station post office. If anyone got sick at school or needed things at the store, I got the job to drive.

When we were seniors, I had bangs and thought all the girls needed bangs to go on the senior trip to the Smoky Mountains. So, I carried my scissors and cut bangs in the gym. I cut one girl's too short. She was a lot bigger than me, so she had it in for me. On one class trip, we decided to smoke in the motel room. It didn't take me long to know I couldn't smoke. My eyes burned and the next day they were swollen together. I didn't get to go on the morning trip, so guess what. That girl whose bangs I cut short told on me. Thank goodness I was ready to be out of school.

Charlie Bennett

I went 11 years to Bethesda school and finished in 1952. I also was married that same year to Charlie Bennett. I met him at a skating party in the old Bethesda gym. We have two daughters, Connie, who married Tim Marlin, and Brenda, who married Dan Wooten. Our one son Rodger married Lynn King. We have five grandchildren: Jason and Jessica Daniel, Kyle Marlin, and Buck and Tanner Bennett. They all have gone to Bethesda school.

We built our home, 34 years ago, in the old pea field where I grew up on my parent's place. I still go to the same church, Bethesda Presbyterian. The building is over 100 years old.

I love living and working in the Bethesda Community. This is a dream come true to work in the Bethesda Museum and help write this book with my friend Hugh Keedy.

Brief Biography of Hugh Keedy

I was born in the eastern panhandle of West Virginia to parents who were struggling on a small farm. Within a year they moved to the Baltimore, Maryland area where my father worked as caretaker for Mr. Hinds, the inventor of Bromo-Seltzer, on his estate. We weren't rich but the depression did not affect us much there. Dad received $75 a month, a comfortable house on the estate, and food from the garden. Mr. Hinds died in 1935 and Dad worked in various places as a caretaker until he got permanent work in 1938 in a steel mill in Baltimore. We moved often during this period. When we located in Baltimore, I began the seventh grade in the 12th school that I had attended. I did stay there for three years and three years at one high school. Dad and Mom lived in a "row house" in Baltimore from 1938 until the mid-1980s when they both entered a nursing home. During this time, our country roots in West Virginia were kept very much alive by frequent visits to and visits by our country relatives. So, I grew up knowing about both the city and the country, but without the chores that many country boys had.

World War II was in progress when I graduated from high school and within six months I was in the army. I went through Surgical Technical School there, traveling to Texas, Missouri, Colorado, Kentucky, and South Carolina. By the time my training was complete, the wars with Germany and Japan were both over but I was sent to Cairo, Egypt for eight months to help close down a station hospital that had been there during the African campaign. When that was done, we returned to the States and I was discharged after 19 months and 8 days of service, on August 22, 1946.

I enrolled at David Lipscomb in Nashville and began in January 1947, staying through the summer quarter. During that time, I met Marjorie Bomar, my wife-to-be, whose home was in Shelbyville. I left Lipscomb one year to the day from my discharge from the army and returned to Baltimore where I began working as a draftsman for Koppers company. Two years to the day after my discharge from the army, Marge and I were married. She had finished her degree at Peabody and taught in Baltimore the first year we were married. During that year I decided to use my GI Bill and return to Nashville to attend Peabody.

I was able to finish my undergraduate work in two years by taking heavy loads and going year around. Those days, with only a meager GI stipend as income, were the toughest we have had, but they still were enjoyable in many ways. Marge worked, as did I some. We still talk about going to the corner grocery and standing there, discussing what we could get for 25 or 50 cents for supper.

By the summer of 1951, I had actually had some graduate work, my GI entitlement was running out, and I was beginning to wonder what I was going to do. God's providence took over, as it has so often for me. One day, when I went to class, the teacher said there was someone outside the room who wanted to see me. It was the department chairman of Engineering Mathematics at Vanderbilt. There was an opening and my name had been given to them, based on my math major, physics minor, my drafting experience, and the pre-engineering subjects I had taken. I began teaching engineering math classes in the fall of 1951 and remained a faculty member until my retirement on the last day of December 1989, a period of 38 1/2 years.

We bought a house, which was right in the middle of what is now Briley Parkway in Nashville and lived there several years. With a change of Deans at school, I was urged to get a doctoral degree and was assisted greatly in that by Vanderbilt and a National Science Foundation grant. By this time, we had a daughter, Susan, and a son, Bruce. In January 1961 we moved to an icy, cold, snowy Ann Arbor, Michigan and I began work at the University of Michigan. Despite the cold winters, we all thoroughly enjoyed the five years that we spent there.

When I returned to Vanderbilt, my teaching shifted from mathematics to engineering subjects and to interests in engineering education. I became quite active as a member and officer of ASEE, the American Society for Engineering Education. I developed several new courses and headed the freshman engineering program for nearly the last 20 years I was at Vandy. The freshman computer drafting course we began in 1985 was the first of its kind in the country.

When I retired at the start of 1990, we were living in Nashville but began to look for a place in the country. Marge grew up on a farm close to Shelbyville, so we both had roots in country living and enjoy the outdoors. Our daughter-in-law, Pris Keedy, found a place on Lane Road that was for sale and told us about it. They were living on Bethesda-Duplex Road at the time. So, in April 1991 we bought the Trice place, the home place of James Trice, with its old house and 53 acres.

For the next year, we spent about half our time on Lane Road, working on the house and planning a new house. The rest of the time we spend in our Nashville house. In August 1992 we sold our Nashville house and moved into what had become known as the "little blue house." The paint was sold to us as a grey, but you would never know it by looking at it. The Maxwells started our new house on the hillside up in the valley that same summer, and we moved into it on February 10, 1993.

Our daughter, Susan, her husband Andy Reese, and their four children (Amelia, Austin, Evan, and Nicholas) moved into the little blue house almost immediately. They had sold their house in Nashville and were deciding what their next move would be; living in the little blue house gave them some thinking time. It also made them develop a love for the country. However, Andy travels extensively and found the trip to the airport too long, so they bought another house in Brentwood. Meanwhile, Bruce and Pris had sold their house on Bethesda-Duplex and moved into the little blue house almost before Susan and Andy had moved out. They and their three children (Daniel, Sarah, and Joel) stayed there for about a year, during which time they purchased a farm on Route 431, where they now live. Having the grandchildren as close as they have been, and still are, is a luxury not too many can claim.

Since moving to Lane Road, Marge and I have become more involved with community activities, in Bethesda, Flat Creek, and College Grove. We both spent our early days in the country and are now enjoying our retirement days in Bethesda, which we both love. You might say that our lives have been "country to country" with lots of city in the middle.

In Miss Jessie's Footprints, by William T. Byrd

William Thomas Byrd, affectionately known as T-Byrd to friends

It was an honor and a pleasure to be born in the Dan German Hospital in October of 1955 and to grow up on James Avenue in Franklin. I was raised by my mother, Jean Langley Byrd, along with a brother and sister. Another blessing in my life was living across the street from Miss Jessie Trice Bennett, her husband, Charlie, and their daughter, Brenda, during my early childhood days. When I was in Elementary School, the Bennetts left Franklin for Bethesda and a better life in the country. They settled in a nearby community called Cross Keys. Over the years, we stayed in touch when visiting friends and relatives in the area.

When I retired from CSX Railroad after 32 years as a train engineer, I knew exactly where I wanted to live… anywhere in or around Bethesda. I eventually settled in the community of Cool Springs and now have the honor of being the director and curator of the Bethesda Museum, a position that Miss Jessie previously held. It brings me great pleasure to think that I am carrying on the tradition by following in Miss Jessie's footsteps.

About Byrd Lane

The family of Hugh Lovins Byrd came from South Carolina and settled in Williamson County in 1826. Here he married Susan Crane, and they raised their ten children. Hugh, a carpenter by trade, worked in the surrounding counties and eventually bought a farm on Bethesda Road. With Hugh's permission, the county went forth with a cut-through road from Bethesda Road to Bethesda-Duplex Road. Today, this road is known as Byrd Lane. His family members are buried at Mt. Carmel Cumberland Presbyterian Church at Duplex. According to the Beers map of 1878, those living on what would become Byrd Lane were Mrs. J. Chrisman, W.M. Knott, J. Sprott, M.R. Hudson, A.J. Chrisman, D.C. Padgett, Mrs. T.A. Blythe, and W.H. Wiley.

Neighbors of Hugh Byrd who lived along Byrd Lane: Andrew Irvin, Edward Eggleston, Thomas Irvin, Robert Irvin, John Henry Byrd, William Almer Byrd, William Blake Byrd, Andrew Chrisman, James Chrisman, George Ingram, William Ingram, Alexander Hargrove, and Pomp Watson.

Faces of the Past

Sprott-Alexander Family Reunion, 1904

Seated: Fred Sprott, Ebb Alexander, Brown Evans, Jessie Johnson, Tom Stammers, John B. Bond. standing: Nora Sprott Hall, Lillie Sprott Alexander, Sally Sprott Evans, Ophelia Sprott Johnson, Virge Sprott Stammers

Sprott-Alexander Family Reunion, 1904

From left: Lee Alexander with banjo, Haley Hall, Louise Alexander, Margaret Evans, Julton Hall, Leonard Bond, John Hall, Elise Sprott, Lucille Bond, Horace Sprott, Gladys Bond, Thomas Evans; 2nd row: Evan Sprott, Elizabeth Evans, Virginia Evans, Naoma Alexander, Pink Johnson, Ebb Alexander, Jessie Johnson, Tom Stammers, John Bond, Brown Evans holding Roy Evans; 3rd row: John Evans, Alvin Alexander, Jimmer Parks, Virge Parks, Claude Alexander, Lillie Alexander, Nora Henson, mother of Hall children, Clarence Alexander, Ophelia Johnson, Virge Stammers, Fred Sprott, Maude Stammers, Grigg Johnson, Nettie Alexander, Sally Evans, Luther Alexander, Jessie Evans, Kit Evans, Sara Alexander, photographer Johnnie Alexander McCall.

Johnnie, Sarah, Pete, Naoma, Lee, children of Ebb and Lillie Sprott Alexander

Emma Catherine Sprott, Leonard, and John Bryan Bond

Lelia Steele, Mrs. A.B. Fleming

Susan Steele Petway, wife of J.T. Petway

Molly Chapman Anderson

Kate Pollard Hatcher 1872-1962, mother of Frances Hatcher

Mary Elizabeth Steele Bond (1831-1911) wife of W.A. Bond

Virginia McCall, 1861-1910, daughter of Lycurgus McCall

Irene Steele Bond (Mrs. T.C.), Bettie Bond Anderson (Mrs. Walter), Cora Steele Bond (Mrs. W.C.)

Rachel Steele Rucker (1838-1914) and granddaughter Cora Rucker (1888-1956)

William S. Rucker 1862-1913

Louise Bond Ferrell, daughter of Tom Lafayette and Cora Bond

Malinda Hartley, daughter of J.W. and E.A. Hartley

Preston Wiley, Co D 59th VA Inf, CSA, and Suedie Wiley

James Wilson Williams, Co F, 4th TN Cav, CSA

Tennessee McCall 1859-1890, Laban Hartley McCall 1838-1883, Virginia McCall Buntin

Thomas Perkins Giles, Co A 45th TN Inf, CSA

FACES OF THE PAST

Walter Lee and Tena Poteete Deason family: Charles Deason, Lera Tomlin, Lelia Goins, and Ada Bennett

Charlie Trice, Sam Trice, Grover Trice, A.F. Hargrove, and Louise Trice Hargrove

Eggleston Brothers – Edward Everett, William Clyde, Josiah Carr, James Fleming, and Robert Waller

John Doss Tomlin and Lera Mai Deason Tomlin

John A. and Samuella Scales McCall

Butch King, Barry, Robert Tomlin, Josie Tomlin, Leon Poteete

Butch King, Susan Bennett Tomlin, and Josie Tomlin

J.W. Poteete, Doss Tomlin, Bill Tomlin, Oakley Tomlin

J.W., Leon, and Ruby Poteete

FACES OF THE PAST

Naoma Alexander and Lawrence Bond

Robert Lycurgus McCall

Lou McCall Crafton, William L. McCall, and Anna Laura McCall Chest

Samuel Lycurgus McCall, Nancy Crafton McCall, Carrie, Bessie, Jim and Jessie Marion McCall

David Ebenezer Comstock 1830-1909

Nancy Marenda "Rendy" McCall (Mrs. R.S. Sampson) and Delia Sampson

Jack Crafton, Dora Myrtle McCall Crafton, and Jimme Lou Crafton on Cross Keys Road

William Cicero Bond (1862-1928)

Cora Steele Bond, wife of W.C. Bond

Mary Bond

Lorene Bond

Christopher "Kit" Giles, Co A 45th TN
Inf, CSA, and Mary Graham Giles

J.W. and Ellie Marshall Beasley

C.K. McLemore, County Surveyor

Wallace McCall

Perkins Jordan (1848-1914) was an ex-slave who owned a large farm on Owl Hollow Road in the Duplex community. He is seen here with his prize horse. His descendants were honored as a Pioneer Family at the Black Tie Affair in 2013.

Perkins Jordan

Dr. Harry Guffee with Bill and Mary Dorton's family

Dr. Harry Guffee (1913-1996), son of Bert and Janie McGee Guffee of the Callie community, was undoubtedly the most beloved man in Williamson County. On horseback, he is seen here visiting ."

FACES OF THE PAST

These were once familiar faces of members of the One Gallus Fox Hunters Association of Williamson County. These men loved their dogs and the sport of chasing the Red Reynard across the rural countryside.

William Franklin Byrd "Frank" (1882-1965) with his fox hounds

Gilbert and Lewis Edgmon with their winning hounds.

350

Champion fox hunters included the Edgmon brothers – Gilbert, Lewis, and Wallace of Callie, Otto Green of Hillsboro, and Frank Byrd of Bethesda. Sadly, the sport has dwindled in numbers due to the deaths of the old-timers and the lack of open space in the countryside.

Wallace Edgmon, Gilbert Edgmon, and Otto Green showing their winning hounds with pride.

The One Gallus Fox Hunters Association Field Trials in 1949

Index

4th Tennessee Cavalry
  Co. F, 343
  CSA, 79
12th Civil District, vii, 1, 3, 12–13, 95
12th Civil District of Williamson County, 3, 28
20th Tennessee Regiment, Co. D, CSA, 70
24th Tennessee Infantry, CSA, 199
24th Tennessee Regiment, Company D, CSA, 77
32nd, Tennessee Infantry, Company D, CSA, 76
32nd Tennessee Infantry
  Company D, CSA, 76
  Company H, CSA, 71
32nd Tennessee Regiment, CSA, 145
45th Tennessee Infantry, CSA, 95, 343
  Co. A, 348
4,800-acre North Carolina land grant, ix

A

Aaron, 217
Aaron, Sam, 150
Adams, Clyde, 50, 62, 297, 330, 333
Adams, James, 47
African campaign, 336
Air Corps, 112, 131
Air Force, 273
Alabama, Marion County, 9, 188, 266, 277–78
Alabama Line, 7
Alamen, Mrs., 208
Alexander, 2, 4, 8, 38, 83, 105, 219, 251, 280, 341
  Alexander, Alice, 76
  Alexander, Alvin, 102, 341
  Alexander, Antoinette, 145
  Alexander, Bill/Billy, 47, 177–78, 180, 182, 184, 186, 188, 281, 330
  Alexander, Clarence, 100, 103, 341
  Alexander, Claude, 341
Alexander, Donald, 1st Lt., 131
Alexander, Ebb, 103–4, 340–41
Alexander, Elizabeth, 8
Alexander, Eva, 188–89
Alexander, Horace, 105
Alexander, John Ebb, 341
Alexander, Johnnie, 38–40
Alexander, J. Wallis, 8
Alexander, Laura Alice, 286
Alexander, Lee, 38, 341
Alexander, Lillie Sprott, 340–41
Alexander, Louise, 39–40, 341
Alexander, Lt. Donald, 131–32
Alexander, Luther, 341
Alexander, Margaret Daniel, 131
Alexander, Mary, 76, 131
Alexander, Mattie, 63, 219
Alexander, Mattie Sue Ware (Mrs. C.E.), 100, 102, 104
Alexander, Miss Willie, 185
Alexander, Nettie, 341
Alexander, Rachel, 105
Alexander, Rachel Sprott, 103
Alexander, Richard, 76
Alexander, Ross, 105
Alexander, Susanne, 188
Alexander, William, 69–70, 80, 145
Alexander, William Hatcher family, 96
Alexander, Willie Hatcher, 102
Alexander place, 225
Alice, 76, 147, 153, 286
Alice, Miss, 284, 287
Alice Paulette, Miss, 202
Allen, Catherine [Sprott], 9
Allied Arts Club, 169
Allisona, 3, 77, 113
Allisona Road, 242
Alta Mai Williams, 62
Anderson family, 16
Anderson, Bess, 117
Anderson, Brownie, 117
Anderson, Chapman (Chap), 106, 108, 110, 116, 142
Anderson, Charlie, 308
Anderson, Elizabeth Rivers, 112
Anderson, Fannie, 5, 242
Anderson, Fannie Creswell, 113
Anderson, Frank, 110, 116–18
Anderson, Frank M., 106, 108, 110
Anderson, George, 50
Anderson, Hartley, 112
Anderson, Herman P., 45, 112–14, 238
Anderson, James, 63
Anderson, Lewis, 63
Anderson, Mary Frances Cowles, 106–7
Anderson, Mary Thomas, 106, 108–9
Anderson, Molly Chapman, 342
Anderson, Mrs. Walter, 342
Anderson, Rosa Dean, 63
Anderson, Sallie, 112
Anderson, Sam, 5, 113–14, 238, 242, 311
Anderson, Sam F., 21, 111–12, 114, 243
Anderson, Thomas, 63, 108
Anderson, Thomas P., 106
Anderson, Thomas Page, 107, 116
Anderson, Tommy, 117
Anderson, Walter, 63, 106–8, 115–18
Anderson, Walter, Jr., 117
Anderson, Walter Bond, 108
Anderson, Walter "Buddy" Jr., 117, 151, 316
Anderson, William, 107, 115
Anderson family, 16, 108, 117
Andrew Blythe place, 103
Andrews, Ephraim, 67
Andrews, Mark Montgomery, 66–67
Andrews, Mary, 169
Annie, Miss, 297
Annie Lou, Miss, 255
Annie Margaret, 61
Arnold, Sallie, 56
Austin Peay College, 208

352

B

Basketball, 47
Battle of Culp's Farm, 145
Baugh, Susie Mai, 63, 142, 148, 166
Beard, Elizabeth, 44
Beasley, Mary "Bunny", 44
Beasley, Ellie, 258
Beasley, Ellie Marshall, 51, 273, 348
Beasley, Fulton, 326
Beasley, Lera, 41
Beasley, Marshall McCoy, 219
Beasley, Mary "Bunny," 44
Beasley, Mildred, 4
Beasley, Thomas Edgar, 46
Belle of Bethesda, 146
Bennett, Charles, 241, 266
Bennett, Charlie, 334, 338
Bennett, Daisy, 44
Bennett, James, 4
Bennett, Jessie, viii, 37, 174–76, 241, 264, 266
   Bennett, Jessie Trice, 338
   Bennett, Jewell, 46–47
   Bennett, Jimmie D., 70
   Bennett, Jimmy D., 70, 243
   Bennett, Lincoln, 309
   Bennett, Paris, 186
   Bennett, Rodger, 334
   Bennett, Shela, 238
   Bennett, Tanner, 334
   Bennett, William Y., 29
   Bennett Hardware Company, 109, 131
   Bethesda High School, 45, 54, 137, 172, 194, 260
   Bethesda School, ix, 33, 36–44, 46, 51, 55, 121, 123, 186, 191, 193–94, 321, 334
   Beulah, Miss, 215
   Biggers, Lera McCall, 42
   Black students, 13
   Blythe, Richard Anderson, 30
   Bolton, Geneva Anne McCall, 58
   Bomar, Marjorie, 336
   Bond, 83, 123, 207, 243
   Bond (Tom) place, 75
   Bond, Bess Eunice, 330
   Bond, Bessie, 49, 98, 322
   Bond, Betty, 115
   Bond, Betty Ruth Parker, 207
   Bond, Bryan, 341
   Bond, Carol, 198, 202
   Bond, C.C., 19
   Bond, Charles, 84, 122
   Bond, Charley, 119, 122, 198, 206
   Bond, Cicero, 84, 103, 117, 207
   Bond, Cicero Columbus, 84, 120

Bond, Cora Steele, 80, 191, 342, 347
Bond, Cora Steele and William Howard, 80
Bond, Danny, 84, 119, 122–23
Bond, Elizabeth, 84
Bond, Elizabeth Bryant, 98
Bond, Elizabeth Preston, 81
Bond, Franklin, 80, 187, 190, 192, 194, 196, 218
Bond, George, 117
Bond, Gladys, 40, 74, 341
Bond, Howard, 39–40, 80, 89, 103, 141
Bond, Irene Steele, 39
Bond, James, 3–4, 40, 84, 260, 288, 300, 323
Bond, James W., 84, 119, 207
Bond, James W., Jr., 119–20, 122
Bond, Jane, 197
Bond, Jemima Chriesman, 81–82
Bond, Jim, 117, 202
Bond, Jimmy, 330
Bond, J. Lawrence, 90
Bond, John, 40–41, 79, 81, 83, 120, 341
Bond, John B., 74, 340
Bond, John Preston, 81
Bond, J.W., 3, 103, 120
Bond, J.W., Jr., 84, 90, 123
Bond, J.W., Sr., 84, 103
Bond, J.W. III, 123
Bond, Lawrence, 38–40, 74, 346
Bond, Leo, 38–40, 123, 206, 320–21, 341
Bond, Leo Grigsby, 42, 44, 119, 121, 123, 167–68, 198, 200, 204, 206, 208, 210
Bond, Leonard, 341
Bond, Lorene, 3, 39–40, 80, 89, 104, 237, 320, 347
Bond, Louise, 40, 74
Bond, L.P., 2
Bond, Lucille, 39–40, 74, 341
Bond, Martha Frances, 44
Bond, Marvin, 40, 74, 81, 98, 105, 196
Bond, Mary, 40, 80, 104, 237, 347
Bond, Mary Elizabeth Steele, 342
Bond, Mary Frances, 117
Bond, Mary Steele, 120
Bond, Marvin, 98
Bond, Mattie Elizabeth, 120
Bond, Naoma Alexander, 90
Bond, Nettie, 41
Bond, Rachel Chrisman, 117
Bond, T.C., 3
Bond, Thomas C., 121

Bond, Thomas Lafayette, 81–82
Bond, Tom, 79
Bond, Tom C., 231
Bond, Tom Lafayette, 74, 343
Bond, W.C., 347
Bond, William C., 191
Bond, William Cicero, 80
Bond, William W., 19
Bond Brothers Dairy, 93
Bond family, 83–84, 120, 123, 207, 243
Bond Farm, John P., 82
Bond Home, Thomas C., 90
Bond place, 103, 122
Bond's Creek, 218
Bourne, Jessie, 104, 330
Bowersox, Lola Reed Glenn, 211–22, 333
Bowman, Capt., 73
Bowman, Virginia McDaniel, ix, 66
Britain, Mr., 262
Brittain, John H., 78
Bronze Medal, 132
Broom factory, 200, 230
Brother Millard, 163, 302
Brother Miller, 220
Brown, Addie, 124
Brown, Duncan, 23
Brown, Samuel, 12
Brown Evans, 340
Bruce, Michael, 65
Bruce, Mr., 325, 336–37
Brumbach, Margaret James, 45
Bryant, Elizabeth, 83
Buchanan, Fred, 47
Buchanan, Gracie, 45
Buford, 53, 125, 128
Buford, Clarice, 63
Buford, Flooky, 310
Buford, Gertrude, 63
Buford, Louise, 63
Buford, Virginia, 62–63
Bugg, Allen, 19
Buida, John, 200
Bullington, Charles, 131
Buntin, Virginia McCall, 343
Burkhart, Lillian, 249–50
Burrow, Olly, 52
Burwood, vii, 128, 275
Buses, first automobile-modified, 54, 187
Business, 33–34, 104, 110, 169, 199, 235, 276, 290, 300, 303, 320
   Iron manufacturing, 12
   Businessmen/man, 5, 88, 110

INDEX

Byrd, unknown, 40, 338
Byrd, Blake, 40
Byrd, Carry, 40
Byrd, Frank, 351
Byrd, Hugh, 339
Byrd, Hugh Lovins, 338
Byrd, Jim, 38
Byrd, Shannon, 40
Byrd, William T., viii–ix, 176, 338
Byrd, William Almer, 339
Byrd, William Blake, 339
Byrd, William Franklin "Frank," 350
Byrd, William Thomas, 338
Byrd Lane, 71, 73, 91, 96, 206, 320, 338–39

C

Cafeteria manager, 330
Callie box, 142
Callie community, ix, 10, 12, 14–16, 314–15, 349, 351
Callie Giant, the, 16
Callie Post Office, 14
Callie Store, 14–15
Calvert, Joyce, 50
Cameron, George, 136
Cameron, Mrs. George, 169
Campbell, Fredrick, 62
Campbell, Hassell, 62
Campbell, Mack, 11
Campbell School, 110
Campbell's Preparatory School, 117
Camp Boxwell, 156
Camp Breckenridge, 249
Caney Fork, 8
Cannon, Newton, 88
Carey, Matthew, 7
Carlisle, W.O., 152
Carpenters, 249, 274, 320, 338
Carpentry, 107, 320
Carr, Josiah, 344
Carrick North, 108–9, 116, 118
Carson, unknown, 38
Carson, Jim, 38
Carson, Robert, 38
Carson, Virginia, 166
Carter House, 68
Carter's Creek Pike, 125
Carter's Creek Road, 116
Carthage, 194
Cartwrights, the, 218
Casey, Dudley, 127
Casket maker, 294
Caskey, George T., 6, 12, 33

Catechism, 200–201
Cathey, Buford, 59
Cathey, Dee, 59
Cathey, John, 8
Cathey, W.B., 22
Cathey family, 22
Cattle, beef, 191, 229
Cattle business, 191, 243
Caves, 9, 206–7, 314
CCC, 324, 326-7
Cecil, 240
Cedar Hill School, 13
Cellars, 78, 127, 151, 229
Cemeteries, 18, 70, 87, 96, 286, 308, 312
Chair, Chairmaker, 173
Channing, William Ellery, 173
Chapel Hill, 245, 277–78, 311–13
Chapman, Benjamin, 70
Chapman, John, 76
Chapman, Philip, 3
Charlie Reed Place, 222, 292
Charlie Trice place, 206
Cheairs, Nathaniel, 73
Cherokee Indian, 314
Chest, Enoch, 171
Chicken house, 86, 266
Childress, Virginia, 45
Choctaw, 54, 213, 215–16, 305, 311
Choctaw School, 54–58, 213, 215–16, 290, 305, 333
Chriesman, Jemima, 81
Chriesman, Lizzie, 103
Chriesman, Lula, 103
Chrisman, A.J., 339
Chrisman, Andrew, 339
Chrisman, Arthur, 179
Chrisman, Bess, 41
Chrisman, brother of Henry, 200
Chrisman, Eunice, 4
Chrisman, Farrar, 42
Chrisman, Fern, 41
Chrisman, Harvey, 40
Chrisman, Henry, 200
Chrisman, James, 339
Chrisman, Jim, 39
Chrisman, John, 104
Chrisman, Liz, 39
Chrisman, Lizzie, 38
Chrisman, Mary, 38–39
Chrisman, Monroe, 41
Chrisman, Mrs. J., 339
Chrisman, Orr, 179, 182
Chrisman, Stella, 5
Chrisman farm, 9
Christmas dinner, 326

Church, Fross, 143
Church of Christ, 25, 133
Church of Christ Girls' Home, 131
Church picnic, 230
Cicero, 84, 97, 117
Cicero Bond House, 83
Cicero Sanford Home, 97
Civilian Conservation Corps (CCC), 327
Civil War, 101, 103, 107, 113, 116, 159, 164, 286–87, 292, 298, 309–10
Clark, Irene, 52
Clark, Sheffield, Jr., 142
Clendenen (merchant), 33
Clendenen, Mack, 202
Clendenen, Marvin, 41, 313, 322
Clendenen, Marvin "Mack," 202
Clendenen, M.F., 2, 5
Clendenen, T.R., 232–33, 238, 276, 305, 313
Clendenen family, 33
Cobb Hollow, 312
Cock, Thomas, 67
Coleman, Mr., 261
College Grove, 54, 77, 105, 120, 186, 202, 264, 272, 337
Color-bearer, 76
Columbia, Tennessee, 121, 163, 168–69, 184, 243, 278, 324
Columbia Avenue/Highway, 116, 127-8, 151, 259
Commissioners of the County, 7
Community Center, 14, 37
Community Center/Club, 4, 139, 153, 156, 186–87, 230
Community Fund, 241
Comstock, David Ebenezer, 346
Comstock clan, 33
Comstock Road, 33, 35, 154, 218, 245
Confederate Army, 77
Confederate money, 145
Confederates, 116, 160
Confederate soldier, 71, 79, 135
Confederate veteran, 102
Continental Army, 8, 67, 85
Continental soldiers, 7
Cook, Marshall, 54, 187
Cookeville, 210
Cool Springs, 338
Cool Springs Primitive Baptist Church, 97
Cool Springs Road, 95, 97
Cool Springs School, 171
Coon hunting, 179
Cooper, Roy, 255
Copass, Mrs., 169

Core, Addie, 139
Core, Debbie, 38–40
Core, Dr., 30, 133, 166, 177, 220, 223, 225, 257, 265–66, 269, 285
Core, Dr. J.B., 31, 103, 220
Core, Elise, 38–40
Core family, 15
Core, Frank, 38
Core, J.D., 28
Core, Jimmie, 324
Core, Jonathan Dickerson, 30
Core, Rebecca, 38–40
Core, William, 30
Core family, 15
Core house, 273
Core office, 273
Core place, 192, 265, 322
Core's barn, 266
Core's home, 269, 288
Corinth, 70
Cotton, Henry Matt, 142
County Commissioner, vii
County Council, 139
County Court, 117
County Highway Department, 136
County Special Education Center, 54
County Surveyor, 348
Courtney, Wirt, 101
Cove Section, 77
Cowles, John, 24, 67
Cowles, Macon, 149
Cowles, Mary Jane King, 67
Cowles Chapel Methodist Church, 14–15, 24, 67, 148, 150
Cowles family, 14, 149
Cowles School, 117
Cox, Mary, 285
Cox, Mary Irvin, 75
Cracker Box, 187, 194, 296
Cracklins, 251
Crafton, 16
Crafton, Alice, 58
Crafton, Buford, 125, 128
Crafton, Clara, 38–39
Crafton, Cora, 125
Crafton, Doc, 246
Crafton, Dora Myrtle McCall, 347
Crafton, Elbert, 204
Crafton, Eula, 58
Crafton, Ewing, 38
Crafton, Fannie, 125
Crafton, Fannie Bell, 43
Crafton, Frances, 125, 128
Crafton, Grace, 63
Crafton, Inez, 125

Crafton, Jack, 347
Crafton, J.E., 26
Crafton, Jody, 58
Crafton, Joe, 58
Crafton, John Thomas, 125
Crafton, Kimmie Lou, 56
Crafton, Laura, 45
Crafton, Lee, 235
Crafton, Leslie, 125
Crafton, Lou McCall, 346
Crafton, Lundy "Beater," 324
Crafton, Martha, 63, 125, 128
Crafton, Martha Beth, 43
Crafton, Martha Johnson, 125
Crafton, Mary, 43, 125
Crafton, Mattie Sue, 2
Crafton, Modee, 235
Crafton, Mrs. J.E., 2, 4
Crafton, Myrtle, 58
Crafton, Odeline, 56
Crafton, Raymond, 57
Crafton, Rosie, 125
Crafton, Roy, 58
Crafton, William "Toby," 38
Crafton, T.P., 124–28
Crafton, W. L., 21
Crafton family, 16
Crafton place, 324
Craine, Thomas A., 9
Crane operator, 274
Crawford place, 127
Creek Indian War, 73
Creek line, 7
Creswell, 16, 30–31, 156, 196, 239, 290, 309–10
Creswell, Bessie, 56, 239
Creswell, Bettie, 307
Creswell, Erma, 308, 310
Creswell, Frances, 57, 156
Creswell, George Earl, 313
Creswell, Greasy, 290
Creswell, Laban, 21
Creswell, Leslie, 20
Creswell, Louise, 56
Creswell, Maynard, 112
Creswell, Mildred, 155
Creswell, Murry S., 156
Creswell, Roy, 56, 196, 238, 307
Creswell, Ruth, 56
Creswell, William, 113
Creswell, Willie Mai Culverson, 155
Creswell farm, 319
Critz Lane, 24, 245
Cross Keys, 8, 10, 12, 14, 16, 20–21, 33–34, 85–86, 113–14, 195–96, 222, 233, 238–39, 275–76, 281, 290, 304–8, 312, 332–33, 338
Cross Keys and Choctaw Road, 95
Cross Keys Baptist Church, 20, 91, 308
Cross Keys Graveyard, 312
Cross Keys Road, 85, 98, 282–83, 327, 347
Cross Keys Store, 233, 275
Cross Keys Tavern, 306
Crosslin, 276
Crosslin, Mr., 232
Crosslin Lumber, 276
Crosslin's Portable Store, 276
Crossroads, 12, 28–29, 32–34, 36–37, 92, 333
Crowder, Leslie, ix
Crowley, Miss [Lois], 104
Crunk, Elizabeth McCord, 250, 252
Crunk, Eugene, 45
Crunk, Herbert, 45
Crutcher, Rebecca Wiley, 42
Crutcher, Sarah, 96
Crutcher, Willis, 9
Crutcher family, 22
CSA, 76, 95, 343, 348
CSX Railroad, 338
Culberson, Claiborne, 59
Culberson, Elsie, 58
Culberson, Fronie, 45, 59
Culberson, James, 59
Culberson, Louise, 59
Cumberland Crossing, 8
Cumberland Presbyterian Church, 18
Cumberland River, 8, 115
Cummins, Mrs. H.D., 164
Cunninghams, the, 201
Curtis, C.C., 27

D

Dairy business, 208
Dale, Rev. W.T., 22, 72
Dalton, Glothine, 57
Dalton, Mary Lyell, 67
Dalton, Maxine, 57
Dalton, Ross, 57
Daniel, Charlie, 131
Daniel, Edward, 133, 169
Daniel, Eliza Hardison, 133
Daniel, Fannie, 102, 129–33
Daniel, Felix, 131
Daniel, Hannah, 38, 40
Daniel, Jessica, 334
Daniel, Kenny, 232

INDEX

Daniel, Lucy Smithson, 102-3, 129-30
Daniel, Margaret, 131
Daniel, Mary, 131
Daniel, Nannie Mai, 102, 129-32, 263
Daniel, Perry Lee, 314
Daniel, Punch, 133
Daniel, Thomas A., 102, 129-30
Daniel, Tommie Lou, 38
Daniel, Ward, 314
Daniel children, 131-32
Daniel family, 130
Daniels, Edward, 133
Daniels, Laban, 323
Daniels, Nannie, 263
Daniels, Nannie Mai, 130
Dave Crawford Place, 127
David Lipscomb College, 336
Davidson, Doug, 254
Davis, Jimmy, 63
Davis, Lizzie Watkins, 316
Davis, Lynne Laughmiller, 90
Davis, Sam, 63
Davis, William M., 6, 12, 33
Deason, Charles, 344
Deason, Charlie, 63
Deason, Joe, 40
Deason, Lena Wade, 63
Deason, Minnie, 124
Deason, Tena Poteete, 344
Deason family, 14
Deed of Gift, 19
Delco lighting plant, 37, 178, 194
Dement, Cyrus, 63
Democrat, 114, 142
Demonstration Club, 123
Derryberry, Jane, 254
Dick, 150, 170
Dickey, Robert, 11
Dickson, Tennessee, 278
Dodson family, 14
Dolly, Ms., 259
Donelson, Fort, 70
Donelson, John, 67
Donnelly, James, 50
Dorothy, 250, 252
Dorton, Bill and Mary, 349
Douglas Church, 7
Douglas community, 151
Dowell, Jefferson, 183
Draughon's Business College, 297
Drury, Ralph, 269
Drurys, the, 220
Duck River, 127, 260
Duck River Ridge, 8, 23

Duplex, 10-12, 14, 16, 18, 33-4, 37, 71, 145, 160, 162, 324, 339, 349
Duplex Post Office and Postmasters, 6, 12
Duplex Road, 13, 206

E
Eagleville, 232, 276
Early, Vashti, 108-9, 142
Early graveyard, 302
Eastern Star, Order of the, 4
Ebb Alexander house, 92
Eddington, Glen, headmaster, 156
Edgmon family, 15
Edgmon, Carl, 63
Edgmon, Donald, 136
Edgmon, Ethel, 62-63, 136
Edgmon, Gilbert, 63, 350-51
Edgmon, Hazel, 62
Edgmon, Horace, 15, 62
Edgmon, Leonard, 63
Edgmon, Lewis, 62, 350-51
Edgmon, Martha Guffee, 134
Edgmon, Mary Jane Guffee, 134-35
Edgmon, Miss, 62
Edgmon, Mrs. Samuel Perkins, 136
Edgmon, Murray, 63
Edgmon, Reedy, 62
Edgmon, Sam, 14
Edgmon, Samuel Perkins, 134-36
Edgmon, Wallace, 63, 351
Edgmon, Willie Lee, 62
Edgmon brothers, 351
Edgmon family, 15
Edmondson, Luther, 58
Edmonson, unknown, 56
Edmonson, Buford, 58
Edmonson, Claude, 56, 58
Edmonson, Clyde, 56
Edmonson, Grace, 56
Edmonson, R.C.
Eggleston, unknown, 39
Eggleston, Addie, 3-5, 40, 46, 51, 103, 137-39
Eggleston, Andrew, 38
Eggleston, Bill, 3-4, 40-42, 103, 323
Eggleston, Dr., 177, 263, 326
Eggleston, Edward, 339
Eggleston, Edward Everett or E.E., 139
Eggleston, Jim, 38-39, 192, 297
Eggleston, Joe, 3, 38
Eggleston, Julia, 3, 5, 40, 45, 51, 139
Eggleston, Lizzie, 139, 241
Eggleston, Ned, 45
Eggleston, Robert, 4
Eggleston, W.C., 31

Eggleston, William Clyde, 30, 344
Eggleston and Blythe families, 139
Eisenhower, Gen., 311
Electra, 5
Ellie Marshall's Place, 257
Elliot, Seth, 19
Elliott, Allein, 149, 151
Elliott, Elizabeth, 45
Elliott, Jake, 45
Ellis, 284
Ellis, Dr., 245
Ellis, James, 161
Elsie, 245
English, Gore, 44
Epps, Porter, 8-9
Epworth League, 206, 270
Esperanza Church, 14, 25
Eugene McMillan's Place, 179
Evans, Brown, 340-41
Evans, Elizabeth, 40, 341
Evans, Gus, 8
Evans, Hannah, 129, 131
Evans, Jessie, 341
Evans, John, 341
Evans, Kit, 341
Evans, Leon, 131
Evans, Margaret, 40, 341
Evans, Roy, 341
Evans, Sally, 341
Evans, Sally Sprott, 340
Evans, Thomas, 40-41, 341
Evans, Virginia, 341
Everett, Edward, 344
Evergreen School, 13
Ewin, Mr., 142
Exxon Convenience Center, 14
Ezell, Mrs., 296

F
Fagley, Sarah, 85
Fannie, 102, 125, 129, 131-32
Fannie Anderson, Fannie, 232
Fanny, Miss, 242
Farm Bureau and Community Club, 153
Farming, 3, 101, 117, 127, 130, 172, 185, 199, 320
Farrar, Joe, 237
Farrar, O.C., 57, 313
Farrar, Owen, 58, 235, 240, 308, 323
Farris, Margaret, 50
Father's Day, 124, 128
Faulkenberry place, 9
FBI, 166
Federal prison, 76
Federal soldiers, 77

356

Felix Truett's Place, 143
Ferguson, M.J., 9
Fisher, Steven, 54
Fisher, Susan, 264
Fishing Creek, 70
Flat Creek, 33, 86, 112, 121, 125, 167–69, 194, 205, 306, 312, 319
Flat Creek Road, 33, 35, 86, 217, 249, 286, 327
Flat Creek School, 155, 167, 205, 328
Fleming, Fillmore, 149
Fleming, Millard F., 6
Fleming, Mixey Thompson, 87
Fleming, Mrs., 88
Fleming, Sam, 87
Fleming, Samuel, 87
Fleming, Samuel M., 6, 34, 88
Fleming, William, 87, 241
Fleming Jefferson, 62
Fleming Place, 150
Fleming's business, 88
Fleming's home, 88
Fleming Susan Steele Petway, 342
Flippen, Robert A., 33, 233
Flippen family, 33
Flour mill, 3
Fly, Lora, 161
Food, home-cooked, 236
Ford, 228, 268, 283
Ford, 1930s, 228
Ford, Model A, 283
Ford, Model T, 114, 182, 206, 268
Ford 8N tractors, 193
Fords, old, racing, 121
Forrest [Nathan Bedford], 70
Fort Glenn, 59
Fort Jackson, South Carolina, 311
Fort Oglethorpe, 311
Fort Pillow, 77
Fortune teller, 312
Fox hounds, 136, 350
Fox hunters, 141
Fox hunting, 125
Frances, 125, 128, 150–51, 156
Frank, 78, 106, 108, 110, 116–17, 172, 350
Franklin Courthouse, 14
Franklin Elementary School, 165, 169
Franklin High School, 105, 113, 172
Franklin mailmen, 14
Franklin Manor, 259
Franklin merchants, 102
Franklin Presbyterian Church, 110
Franklin's postmaster, 116
Fraternal orders, 26, 28

Fred Lee Williams, 45, 62
Frigidaire, 127, 131, 154, 231
Frontier people, 287
Fulton, 233, 326
Funerals, 159, 254, 297

G
Garner, O.L., 330
Gary, Jean, 222, 289
Gary, Mary, 3, 285
Gary, Ross, 270
Gas, Cities Service, 306
Gatlin, Earl, 312
Gatlin, Katie Lou, 64
Gedding, Ralph, 321
Geers, Ed "Pop," 11
Gertrude, 271–72
Gettysburg, Battle of, 164
Ghee, Dewees, 42
Giant of Callie, 16
Gifts, 19
Gilbert, 350–51
Giles, 16, 23, 33
Giles, Alice, 264
Giles, Alma, 45
Giles, Billy, 326
Giles, Charles, 257–59
Giles, Christopher "Kit," 348
Giles, Hawkins, 38, 243
Giles, Hawkins H., 58
Giles, Herbert, 330
Giles, Howard, 44
Giles, Jane Bond, 197
Giles, J.C., 44
Giles, Kit, 41
Giles, Larry, 29
Giles, Leonard, 44
Giles, Mary Graham, 348
Giles, May Alice, 236
Giles, Ross, 53
Giles, Ruth, 38, 40, 292
Giles, Thomas J., 27
Giles, Thomas Perkins, 343
Giles, Tom, 292
Giles, Watson, 41
Giles, Will, 105
Giles family, 16, 23, 33
Giles Place, old, 222
Gillespie, 22
Gillespie, Dot, 123
Gillespie, J.E., 45, 47
Gillespie, Musie, 45
Gillespie, Sam, 2, 111–14, 135
Gillespie, W.H., 27
Gillespie family, 22
Glenn, Alma, 211

Glenn, Burney, 41
Glenn, Carl, 40
Glenn, Edwin, 40
Glenn, Grace Tomlin, 330, 333
Glenn, Leon, 220
Glenn, Lola, 49, 55, 155, 211, 292
Glenn, Lola Reed, 54, 57
Glenn, Mattie Bond, 42
Glenn, Mildred, 57
Glenn, Thelma, 221
Glyndon, 220, 222
Goins, Lelia, 344
Gooch, Mary, 41
Gordon McCord House, 71
Gosey Hill Road, 64
Government, Federal, 216, 327–28
Graham, 177
Graham, C.C., 26
Graham, Dr., 177
Graham, Dr. Walter W., 30
Graham, Dr. W.W., 31
Graham, Elsie, 58
Graham, John F., 27
Graham, Nannie T., 58
Graham, Robert, 27
Graham, R.T., 21
Graham, Walter W., 30
Graham, W.J.S., 26
Graham, W.W., 30
Graham place, 311
Grassland community, viii
Gray, Frank, 101
Gray, John B., 101
Gray Drug Company, 101
Graystone Quarry, 14
Great Western Land Pirate, 14
Green, Bill, 57
Green, Mary, 156
Green, Robert, 57
Greer, Joe, 127
Greer Farm, 151
Griggs, Fred, 42
Griggs, Jimmy, 278
Griggs boy, 278
Charles, 257, 259, 266
Grigsby, Aba, 74
Grigsby, 30, 73, 83, 218
Merchant, 33
Grigsby, Alice, 74
Grigsby, Alma, 74
Grigsby, Booker, 74, 101
Grigsby, Booker P., 73
Grigsby, Booker Preston, 74, 224-5
Grigsby, C.F., 74
Grigsby, Charles, ix, 12, 37, 42, 74, 77, 166, 168, 199–200

Grigsby, Charles F., 37, 78, 122
Grigsby, Charlie, 5, 78, 101–2, 263
Grigsby, Charlie F., 165
Grigsby, Cleo, 2, 4–5, 40–42, 49, 54, 73–74, 219, 224, 226, 228, 230, 259–61, 329
Grigsby, Clifford, 257, 301, 303
Grigsby, Cora, 74
Grigsby, Elise, 74
Grigsby, Elizabeth, 74
Grigsby, Elizabeth Sprott, 225
Grigsby, Ella Frances, 41, 74
Grigsby, Ella Francis, 321
Grigsby, Ella Scales, 78, 166
Grigsby, Ethel, 39–40, 74
Grigsby, Geraldine, 74
Grigsby, Glenn, 2, 43, 74
Grigsby, Harry, 45, 166, 178, 233, 272, 274
Grigsby, Ida, 74, 329
Grigsby, Jessie, 42, 74
Grigsby, Jim, 74, 265, 269, 321, 328
Grigsby, J.O., 3, 104
Grigsby, J.O., Jr., 104
Grigsby, John B., 74
Grigsby, Julia, 46
Grigsby, Katherine, 45
Grigsby, Leo, 40–41, 44, 51, 74
Grigsby, Leonard, 42, 74, 323, 328
Grigsby, Maggie, 74
Grigsby, Marion, 2, 4, 43, 51, 167, 169
Grigsby, Mary Elizabeth Sprott, 73, 225
Grigsby, Mary Kate, 74
Grigsby, Mebane, 41
Grigsby, Miriam, 43
Grigsby, Mr. and Mrs. O.T., 2
Grigsby, Mrs. J.O., 104
Grigsby, Ollie, 73–74, 102, 329
Grigsby, O.T., 2
Grigsby, Sallie Turner, 73
Grigsby, Scales, 40–41, 74
Grigsby, Suzie, 74
Grigsby, Suzie Lee, 74
Grigsby, Vivienne, 40, 74
Grigsby family, 73, 83, 218
Grigsby Store, 30
Grimm, John, 313
Grindstones, 68, 86, 250
Grover, 240, 332
Guernsey cows, 232
Guffee, Bert, 15
Guffee, Dr. Harry, 326, 349

H

Hagewoods, the, 308–9, 319
Hall, Haley, 341
Hall, John, 341
Hall, Nora Sprott, 340
Ham, Thomas, 271–72
Hamilton, J.A., 152
Hamm, John, 47
Hardeman, Paul, 63
Hardison, Fannie, 129
Hardison, Murrey, 42
Hardison's mill, 226
Hardware business, 104, 109, 275
Hargrove, 16, 22, 33, 46, 56
Hargrove, A.F., 344
Hargrove, Agnes, 33, 232, 234–38, 240, 242–44, 246
Hargrove, Alexander, 339
Hargrove, Billy, 253
Hargrove, Buddy, 58
Hargrove, Chub, 91
Hargrove, David, 217, 222, 240, 242
Hargrove, Earlene, 42
Hargrove, Erlene, 41
Hargrove, Frank, 43
Hargrove, Grandma, 232–33
Hargrove, Herbert, 56
Hargrove, Howard, 40, 42, 206
Hargrove, Jake, 215
Hargrove, Katherine, 42
Hargrove, Lizzy, 262
Hargrove, Louise, 332
Hargrove, Louise Trice, 344
Hargrove, Myrtle, 40–41
Hargrove, Roy, 40
Hargrove, Ruby, 43
Hargrove, Shiney, 282
Hargrove family, 16, 22
Harmon, Annie Lee, 61
Harmon, Charlie, 61
Harmon, Joe, 258, 324
Harmon, Murry, 61
Harmon, Roy, 61
Harmony Lodge, 17
Harper, Everett, 150
Harper, Frances, 150
Harpeth, 10, 12, 14, 16, 25, 35, 54, 87, 121, 316, 322
Harpeth Baptist church, 322
Harpeth community, 10, 12, 14, 16, 24–25, 34–35, 68, 87–88
Harpeth Lick, 77
Harpeth Lick Cumberland Presbyterian Church, 112
Harpeth-Peytonsville Road, 13, 34–35
Harpeth River, 315

Harpeth School, 15, 25, 54, 62–63, 121, 136, 142, 148, 316, 322
Harpeth School Road, 14
Harris, Earl, 243
Harris, Jon, ix
Harris, Michael, 54
Harris, Mr., 301
Harris, Tom, 50
Harris family, 263
Harry, 166, 276–77
Hartley, 33, 112, 312
Hartley, Albert, 40, 266
Hartley, E.A., 343
Hartley, Frances, 46
Hartley, Hershel, 57
Hartley, John, 46
Hartley, Laban, 16, 85–86, 306, 312
Hartley, L.C., 21
Hartley, Malinda, 343
Hartley, Mary Beth, 58
Hartley, Napoleon B., 6
Hartley, W.L., 21
Hartley-Anderson home, 86
Hartley Community Cemetery, 312
Hartley Tavern, 16
Hatcher, "Buck" Jim, 38, 62, 334
Hatcher, Charles, 3
Hatcher, Charlie, 74, 104
Hatcher, Edgar, 158, 161
Hatcher, Ellis, 72
Hatcher, Everette, 161
Hatcher, Frances, 2, 4, 40, 49, 51, 54, 74, 123, 329–30, 342
Hatcher, Jim "Buck," 38
Hatcher, John, 38, 40
Hatcher, Johnny, 249
Hatcher, Kate, 74
Hatcher, Lawrence, 161
Hatcher, Lula, 161
Hatcher, Mack, 161
Hatcher, Sara Lou, 161
Hatcher, W.D., 102
Hatcher, William Dodson, 96, 102
Hatcher, Willie, 38–39
Hawkins, 33, 58
Hawkins, Hugh, 233, 243
Hawkins, Marilyn, 201
Hawkins, Peter, 201
Hayes, Everett, 300
Hayes, Jim, vii
Hayes, Judy, vii, ix
Hayes, Leon, 45
Hazelwood, 22, 33
Hazelwood, J.W., Store, 35
Hazelwood, Mattie Sue Cathey, 33
Hazelwood, Minnie, 252

Hazelwood, Minnie and Joe Will, 252
Hazelwood family, 22
Hazelwood Store, 33
Heithcock, Gene, 63
Heithcock, Noble, 63
Heithcock, Robert, 63
Henderson, James G., 6
Henpeck Lane, 15
Henry, 62, 109, 248, 277
Henry, Mr., 278
Henry's Grocery, 277
Henson, Nora, 341
Henson family, 22
Herbert McCall, 153
Hereford cattle, 154, 243
Hickman County, 313, 327
Hicks, Edward, 62
Hicks, Raymon, 62
Highland Rim Schools, 212
High School, 3–4, 166, 168, 178, 186–87, 194, 202–3, 228, 270, 296–97, 330, 333, 335–36
Highways, 15, 34, 194, 205, 212, 268
Macadamized road, 117
Hillsboro, 317, 351
Hinds, Mr., 335
Hispanic congregation, 14, 25
Historic artifacts, 68
Historic names, 14
Historic places, 34
Hodge, Bob, 141
Hog killing, 113, 226, 250, 286, 305
Holly, Ethel, 263
Holt, Elaine, 298
Home Demonstration Agent, 166
Home Demonstration Club, 104
Hominy, making, 226
Hood, Charles Edward, 143
Hood, Clayton, 62
Hood, Dalton, 62
Hood, Filmore, 63
Hood, Frances, 142
Hood, Frances Jefferson, 150
Hood, Fred, 62, 150
Hood, George, 63
Hood, Gerald, 62
Hood, Hattie, 141
Hood, Henry, 63
Hood, Howard, 15, 63, 140, 142–43, 150
Hood, Howard III, 15
Hood, Howard Jr., 142
Hood, Inez, 62
Hood, James, 264
Hood, James William, 142
Hood, Jefferson, 142
Hood, Katherine, 62
Hood, Logan, 15
Hood, Mable, 62
Hood, Margaret, 62
Hood, Morgan, 44
Hood, Morris T., 62
Hood, Nettie, 63
Hood, Reba, 142
Hood, Roberta, 63
Hood, Rosa Mai, 62
Hood, Tommy, 141
Hood, Walter, 141
Hood, Willie, 62, 141
Hood place, the old, 264
Hoover, Mike, ix
Hoover Days, 325
Horseshoes, played, 305
Horton, Henry C., 17
Horton Park, 221, 226
Hortons, the, 299
Horton's Field, 75
hospital, the old, 326
Hospital, Baptist, 326
Hospital, Dan German, 338
Houghland, 244
Hounds, 350–51
Houser, Elizabeth, 49, 64, 322–23
Houser, Nannie Lou Hatcher, 123
Howlett, Alice, 75
Howlett, Maxie, 75
Hoyte, J. W., Rev., 19
Hudson, Betsy [Sprott], 9, 26, 339
Hudson, John, 101
Hudson, Thaddeus, 2
Hudson, William A., 6
Hudson Alexander, 30
Huff, James, 74
Hugh, 175–76, 182, 189, 192, 195–96, 304, 308, 310, 313, 318–19, 321, 327–28, 338
Hurt, Eva Lois, 60
Hurt, Lois, 4

I

Ingram, Fronie, 41
Irene, Miss, 255
Iron manufacturing, 12
Irvin, 29, 37, 40–41, 58, 75–76, 101–2, 145–47, 259, 280–82, 286, 298–300
Irvin, Alex, 75–76, 102, 145–46, 299
Irvin, Alice, 75–76, 102, 144-147, 183, 222, 281-2, 286–87
Irvin, Andrew, 339
Irvin, Catherine, 75–76
Irvin, Catherine Steele, 146
Irvin, Dabney, 76, 146, 287
Irvin, Dena, 76, 145
Irvin, Elizabeth, 76
Irvin, Jessie, 40
Irvin, John S., 6
Irvin, Katherine, 75
Irvin, Leslie, 40
Irvin, Margaret, 76
Irvin, Martha, 75
Irvin, Mary, 39–41, 76, 145
Irvin, Matthew Dabney, 75, 146
Irvin, Minnie, 40–41, 58
Irvin, Richard, 76, 145, 287
Irvin, Richard A., 76
Irvin, Robert, 41, 339
Irvin, Shearer, 76, 102, 145, 202, 262–63, 299
Irvin, Thomas, 44, 339
Irvin, W.G., 28
Irvin, William D., 76, 144, 281
Irvin, William Dabney, 76, 145–46, 280
Irvin, Willie, 38–39, 76, 145
Irvin brothers, 299
Irvin family, 3, 286
Irvin heirs, 19
Irvin home, 3, 75, 232, 287, 299
Irvin's arrival, 75
Irvin farm, 8
Irvin sisters, 147
Irvin-Taylor-King Farm, 92
Ivy, David, 243

J

Jefferson, Alene, 62
Jefferson, Brown, 62, 148, 150, 152
Jefferson, Dick, 62, 150
Jefferson, Elizabeth, 62, 150
Jefferson, Elizabeth Anderson, 118, 148
Jefferson, Elliott, 148
Jefferson, Fleming, 62, 150
Jefferson, Frances, 151
Jefferson, Henry Dickinson, 148
Jefferson, Margie, 151
Jefferson, Stillman Alva, 151
Jefferson, Sue, 151
Jefferson, Virginia, 151
Jefferson, Virginia Carson, 169
Jefferson Walter Lee, 151
Jennette's Market, 151
Jersey cattle, 116
Jimmy Hollow, 287
John Bond brick house, old, 84
Johnson, Grigg, 341
Johnson, Ophelia Sprott, 340

Johnson, Pink, 341
Jones, Ellis, 71–72
Jones, Nelson, 48, 54, 123, 330
Joneses, the, 71
Jordan, Elmer, 61
Jordan, Perkins, 349
Jordan, Robert, 149
Jordon, Sgt. R.A., 70

K
Keedy, Daniel, 337
Keedy, Hugh, 175–76, 182, 189, 192, 195–96, 304, 308, 310, 313, 318–19, 321, 327–28, 334
Keedy, Marge, 336–37
Keedy, Pris, 337
Keedy, Susan, 336
Keith, William E., 6
Kelvinator, 185
Kentucky, Adairville, 7
Kentucky line, 7
Kerosene refrigerator, 208
Kerosene stove, 207–8
Ketchum, Josephine, 255
Ketchum family, 23
Kincaid, Paul, 44
Kincaid, Robert, 44
King, Butch, 345
King, David, 33
King, Jennie, 298
King, Jimmie D., 116
Kingfield community, 33
Kingston Springs, 156
Kinnard, Brown, 116
Kinnard, Margaret, 117
Kinnard, Martin Smithson, 42
Kinnard, Walter Cannon, 117
Kirkpatrick, Thomas E., 19
Kittrell, Minnie Claire, 149
Knott, Thomas, 6, 12
Knott, W.M., 103, 339

L
Laban Hartley house, 85, 250
Ladd, Clifton, 44
Ladd, George, 323
Ladd, Raymond, 297
LaFollette, Harvey, 20
Landis, Addie, 40
Landis, Mr. and Mrs. R.C., 40
Landmark cabins, 298
Landmarks, 8, 56, 69, 75, 77, 88, 102–3
Langley, Clarence, 62
Lavendar, Paralee Sprott, 71
Lavender, 14, 40

Lavender, Allie, 40, 63
Lavender, Anthony, 159
Lavender, George, 159
Lavender, H.W., 34, 88
Lavender, Margaret, 62
Lavender, Mary, 62
Lavender, Milburn, 40
Lavender, Nelson, 96, 105
Lavender, Nettie, 40
Lavender, Teddy, 63
Lavender, Willie, 40
Lavender family, 14
Lavender Place, 9
Lawrence, 90, 104, 161, 312
Lawrenceburg, 145, 172, 194
Lawrence of Chapel Hill, 312
Laws, Dr. H.A., 135
Lea, Mrs. R.M., 51
Lebanon, Tennessee, 287
Lee, 172, 341
Lee, Annie, 252, 255
Lee, Charles, 12
Lee, Claude, 3
Lee, Ed, 125, 128
Lee, Jack, 13
Lee, John W., 11
Lee, John W.N., 13
Lee, Laura, 13
Lee, Mona, 13
Lee, Samuel, 12, 77, 134
Lee, Samuel B., 13
Lee, Susie, 315
Lee, Walter, 151
Lee-Buckner School, 13
Lemming, Mr., 325
Leo, 121, 123, 167–68
Leo Grigsby Bond, 42, 120, 198, 200, 202, 210
Leon, 220
Leonard, 341
Leonard, Lawrence, 105
Leslie, Mr., 125
Lewis, 259, 351
Lewisburg, 184
Lewisburg Avenue, 100
Lewisburg Pike, 7, 12, 14–15, 18–19, 24–25, 33–35, 54, 60, 66, 88, 94
Lewisburg Road, 108, 116–17, 134–35, 149–50, 152
Library, 4, 157, 303, 329
Lillard, Bernice, 52
Lillard, Bill, 53
Lillard, Billie Jean Hargrove, 332
Lillard, Marvin, 301
Lillard, Mary Amy, 46
Lillie, Pryor York, Jr., 147

Lincoln, H.B., 19
Linnie and Joe, 201
Linsey-woolsey, 84
Lion's Club, 169
Little Texas, 232, 309
Lockton School, 169
Lodge, Mason, 142
Lodge Hall, 28–29, 36, 270
Lodges, Masonic and Odd Fellows, 28–29, 194, 220, 230, 269, 282
Loftin, Laura, 259
Log building, crude, 17
Log cabins and building, 17, 78, 83, 130, 256, 258, 288, 293, 298
Log church, 23, 219
Log homes, 66-7, 70, 83-4, 96, 98, 101, 103, 126, 172, 258, 260, 265, 269, 313
  Hand-hewn, 68, 126, 130, 298
Logs and log buildings, 75, 81, 101–3, 126, 129, 132, 146, 154, 159, 207, 233, 257, 260
Log smokehouse, 75, 130
Log Stools, 260
Longview (Walter Anderson House), 116
Lottie, Miss, 284
Lover's Lane, 206
Lowe, grandfather, 173
Lowe
  Gabriel, 170
  Viney, 171
Lulu, Mr., 301
Lyell, Jonathan, 67
Lynch family, 310
Lynch, Dwight, 198, 320
Lynchburg Female Academy, 163

M
Machine, drilling, 274
Machine, well-digging, 274
Mack, Clay, 145
Mack, Ronnie [McMurtry], 188–89
Mack truck, 271
Magistrates, 3, 95, 249–50, 325
Mail, 3, 14, 199, 234
Mail routes, 14, 113, 245
Malone, Daniel, 67
Maplewood Farm, 12–13
Mark Andrews place, old, 87
Marlin, 14, 33, 62, 88
Marlin, Billy, 179
Marlin, Dorothy, 35
Marlin, Joe M., 61
Marlin, Kyle, 334
Marlin, Pat, 302
Marlin, William, 183, 233, 302

married Adalyn Weakley, 117
married Booker Preston Grigsby, 73
married Catherine Louise Steele, 75
married Charles Bullington, 131
married Cora Belle Grigsby, 81
married David Deason, 128
married Elizabeth Brooks, 87
married Elizabeth Helm, 69
married Elizabeth Patton, 73
married Emmett Jennette, 257
married Fred Kinnard, 117
married Hazel Hall, 172
married James Bond, 167
married James O'Neely, 105
married Joe Lynn Davis, 316
married John Glenn, 120
married Kate Gant, 172
married Laura Alice Alexander, 280
married Leo Crafton, 311
married Luther Alexander, 131
married Lynn King, 334
married Maggie Stephens, 172
married Mark Puryear, 117
married Mary Cowles, 116
married Mary Elizabeth Sprott, 225
married Mary Hatcher, 131
married Mary Ratcliffe, 77
married Mary Tennessee Lavender, 71
married Mary Wallace Millard, 71
married Matthew Dabney Irvin, 70
married Matthew Wilson, 77
married Miss Annie Calvert, 110
married Miss Bettie Bond, 117
married Miss Cynthia Cannon, 88
married Miss Ellie Clayton Morton, 163
married Miss Fannie Creswell, 113
married Miss Willie Eve, 109
married Neil Skinner, 112
married Rachel Blythe, 73
married Rachel Webber, 70
married Rebecca Malone, 67
married Rosa Tennessee Tomlin, 126
married Sallie Belle Tomlin, 126
married Sally North, 66
married Sarah Akers, 69
married Susan Crane, 338
married Susan Napier, 12
married Tim Marlin, 334
married Veral Harrell, 150
married Walter, 298

married William Cicero Bond, 80
married William Pillow Rucker, 70
married Winfred Lyell, 67
Marshall, Gen. George, 311
Marshall, German McEwen, 101
Marshall, Martha, 5, 72, 158
Mary, boarder, 282, 284
Mary and Margaret, twins, 131
Mary Frances Cowles Anderson, 106–7
Masonic Hall, 219
Masonic Lodge, 4, 17, 29, 114, 178, 303
Masons, 28, 152–53
Mathis, Agnes, 42
Mathis, Braden, 42
Mathis, Jimmy, 41
Matthew Dabney Irvin House, 75
Matthew Dabney Irvin-Taylor House, 75
Maupin, Prentice, 316
Maury County, 11, 86, 103, 133, 190, 324
Maxwell, Jim, 321
Maxwell, Jimmy, 320
Maxwell, Mack, 320
Maxwell family, 321, 337
Maxwells, 321, 337
McCall, 156
McCall, A.L., 153
McCall, Alice Smithson Herbert, 155
McCall, Bessie, 58, 346
McCall, Bob, 3, 74
McCall, Bud, 233
McCall, Carrie, 346
McCall, Carrie Obera, 58
McCall, Curd, 264
McCall, Eva, 63
McCall, Herbert, 3, 40–41, 123, 153–56, 206, 264
McCall, Jim, 58
McCall, John B., 155
McCall, Johnnie Alexander, 341
McCall, Laban Hartley, 343
McCall, Lizzie, 74
McCall, Luther, 154
McCall, Lycurgus, 95, 155, 157, 342
McCall, Mrs., 156
McCall, Nancy Crafton, 346
McCall, Nancy Marenda, 346
McCall, Rainey, 43
McCall, Robbie, 74
McCall, Robert L., 6, 27
McCall, Robert Lycurgus, 346
McCall, Sally, 74

McCall, Sam, 5
McCall, Samuella Scales, 344
McCall, Samuel Lycurgus, 346
McCall, Tennessee, 343
McCall, Thomas, 154–55
McCall, Travis, 155
McCall, Virginia, 342
McCall, Wallace, 262, 348
McCall, William L., 346
McCall, William Lafayette, 98
McCall family, 155–57
McCall's Corner, 55
McCaul, Robert F., 6
McClain, Nathan, 312–13
McCollum, Sandra, 298
McCord family, 22
McCord, Annie Millard, 39
McCord, Billy, 44
McCord, Clifton, 61
McCord, Clyde, 61
McCord, Dale, 72, 254
McCord, Davis, 164
McCord, Dorothy, 46–47
McCord, Earnest, 47
McCord, Elizabeth, 45, 59
McCord, Ellie Marshall, 101
McCord, Ernest, 72
McCord, Floyd, 248
McCord, Gordon, 3, 71–72, 103, 158–59, 161, 164, 325
McCord, J.A., 101, 117, 160
McCord, J.A., Professor, 60, 158
McCord, James, 71
McCord, James Allison, 72
McCord, J.A. Professor, 60
McCord, Jessie, 43
McCord, Lera, 72, 158
McCord, Lera and James Allison, 72
McCord, Lida, 72
McCord, Llewellyn "Boo," 45
McCord, Lora, 72, 158
McCord, Lorene, 61
McCord, Ma, 161
McCord, Martha Ellis, 71, 72, 158
McCord, Marvin, 4
McCord, Mary, 5, 45, 72, 325
McCord, Mary Millard, 159
McCord, Mary Tennessee, 71
McCord, Milton, 8
McCord, Mr., 164
McCord, Mrs., 159, 161, 249, 254
McCord, Pauline, 61
McCord, Richard, 72, 145, 170, 172–73, 301
McCord, Rodney, 47, 72

INDEX

McCord, Roy Dale, 44
McCord, Talmadge, 72, 158–59, 161
McCord, Tennie, 71–72, 103, 161
McCord, Tennie Lavender, 158, 160
McCord, Tennie, family, 158, 161
McCord, Walker, 249, 255
McCord, William, 72
McCord family, 22, 71, 158, 161
McGee, Frank, 62
McGee, James, 46
McGee, Jane, 65
McGee, Rachel, 62
McGee, Richard, 62
McGee, Virginia, 62, 316, 318
McGee, Wade, 4
McGuffie, Bert, 349
McKay, Anna, 117
McKay, Cliff, 192
McLemore, C.K., 135, 141, 348
McLemore Lane, 148
McMillan, 15
McMillan, Annie, 39
McMillan, Callie, 14
McMillan, Eunice, 39–40
McMillan, Hardy, 180
McMillan, James K., 14
McMillan, Jim, 14
McMillan, L.G., 26
McMillan, Ottie, 41
McMillan family, 15, 300
McMillan Farm, 92
Memories of Christmas, 201, 247, 315
Memories of homelife, 225
Merchandise, general, 3, 234, 236
Merchants, 5, 32–33, 77, 101, 104, 122, 172
Methodist Church, 2, 24, 102, 105, 123, 169, 178, 194, 219, 220, 230, 289, 303, 331
Methodist Episcopal Church, 19, 21
Methodist parsonage, 104, 200, 273
Methodists, 2–3, 14, 19, 25, 37, 200–201, 219–20, 230
Methodist Sunday School Picnic, 183, 230
Methodist Woman's Missionary Society, 2
Methodist Youth Fellowship, 270, 278
Middle Tennessee State College, 168
Middle Tennessee State University, 203
Mildred, 155, 266, 298

Military Line, ix, 7–8
Military Reservation, 8
Milk, 113–14, 116, 119, 125, 127, 154, 183–84, 191, 221–22, 229, 242, 269, 283, 287, 299–300
Milk barn, first, 300
Milking, 121, 125, 154, 208, 221, 229, 232, 242, 252, 317, 320
Milking business, 184, 300–301
Milky Way Farm, Pulaski, 290
Mills, cider, 311
Mills, gas engine, 271
Mills, grist, 107–8, 179–80, 221, 226, 240, 265, 270
Mils, motor, 265
Mills, the old, 180, 258
Mills, planing, 3
Millard Graveyard, 302
Millard, Annie, 38–39
Millard, Ellie Clayton Morton, 162, 164
Millard, Ernest, 2, 39–40, 163
Millard, John, 2
Millard, Marshall Wallace, 72
Millard, Mary, 38, 40
Millard, Mrs. Recollections of the Civil War, 164
Millard, Ernest, 163
Millard, Mrs. M.W., 162
Millard, Rev., 72
Millard, Rev. and Mrs., 163
Millard, Rev. and Mrs. M.W., 104
Millard, Rev. M.W., 2, 19
Miller, Mrs., 219
The Millet King of Franklin, 88
Millstones and grindstones, 86, 171
Millwood, 183, 230
Mincy, Bessie, 58
Ministers, 2, 19, 23, 72, 162, 201, 219–20
Missionary Ridge, 70
Molasses, 248, 258, 292
Money, 178–81, 185–86, 159, 188, 191, 241, 248, 250, 259, 287, 290–92, 325, 328, 330, 332
Montgomery Ward, 297
Montrose, 73–74
Mooney School, 108
Moore Field, 112
Moore's Station, 152
Moran House, 107
Morris Mill, 127
Morris Williams Store, 33–34
Morton, Earl, 63
Morton, Ellie Clayton, 162
Morton, Elvira Clayton, 72

Morton, Horace, 63
Morton, Mary Lois, 63
Mosely, unknown, 41
Moses Steele Place, 69
Mosley family, 14
[Mosley], Henry, 266
Mosley, Bessie, 256-267, 273, 321, 323
Mosley, Gertrude, 123, 268, 271–72
Mosley, Gertrude and Lester, 269
Mosley, Henry, 270
Mosley, Lester, 33, 45, 123, 200, 219, 268–78
Mosley, Lewis, 259
Mosley, Nelle Smithson, 42
Mosley, Sara Tomlin, 333
Mosley, Willie Alice Reed, 42
Moss, Charley, 39
Mossy Creek, Tennessee, 163
Mount Carmel Church, 22
Mount Pisgah, 145, 283, 287
Mt. Carmel, 12, 18, 60, 145
Mt. Carmel Cumberland Presbyterian Church, 12, 18–19, 60, 161, 339
Mt. Carmel School, 54, 60–61
Mt. Pisgah, 7–8, 281
MTSU, 203
Mt. Zion Methodist Church, 21, 114
Mt. Zion Methodist Episcopal Church, 21
Mud Creek, 34
Mule, blind white, 142
Murfreesboro, 113, 121, 138, 145, 150, 168, 184, 203, 228, 305
Murfreesboro State Teachers College, 179
Murphy, Ann, 47
Murrell family, 87
MYF (Methodist Youth Fellowship), 270, 278

N

Naomi School, 212, 214–15
Napier, Jane, 169
Napoleon, 248
Nashville Bridge Company, 274
Nashville Presbytery, 19, 23
National Recovery Act, 328
National Register of Historic Places, 34
National Science Foundation grant, 336
Naval Training Station, 151
Neal, Hap, 255
Neal, John, 320

Neal family, 22
Negro, 85-6, 143, 324
Nelson, Robert, 67
Nelson Lavender Home, 96
Nelson Lavender homeplace, old, 34
Newcomb, Evelyn, 57
Newcomb, Irene, 57
Newcomb, Mildred, 57
Newcomb, Robbie Jean, 57
Newcomb family, 20
New Hope Church, 19, 72, 108, 152, 192, 249
New Hope Presbyterian Church, 19, 23, 118, 143, 150, 162
Nichols's barn, 307
Nickajack Road, 58
Nolen, Dr., 213
Normal School, 203
Normandy Invasion, 131
North, Elisha, 67
North, Frank Anderson, 110
North, Henry, 109
North, Mary Thomas, 118
North, Rhoda, 67
North boundary line, 7
North Carolina, 7, 9, 73, 83, 85
North Carolina, Penland, 168
North Carolina, Snowhill, 85
North Carolina, Union County, 73
North Carolina grant, 67
Northern Ireland, 75
Notable Homes, 89–90, 92, 94, 96, 98
NRA, National Recovery Act, 328

O
Oak Ridge, Tennessee, 238
Oakview School, 194
O'Connor, Billy, 9
O'Connor, the Irishman scholar, 9
Odd Fellows Lodge, 36
Oldham, Robert, 68
Old homes, 66, 68–72, 74–76, 78–80, 82, 84, 86, 88, 102, 139, 202
Old Maids, 237, 299–300
Old mill building, 180
Old North State Legislature, 7
Oliver, Charles, 4, 45, 47, 51, 54, 137, 168, 187, 289
Principal, 54, 187
Oliver, Charlie, 48
Oliver, Jessie, 45, 51
Oliver, Mr. and Mrs., 289
One Gallus Fox Hunters Association, 350–51

Orchards, 86, 229, 248, 311
Otis and Marie, 266
Overton, Edmond, 139
Overton, Robert, 44
Overton, Vernon, 272
Owen, Carl, 3, 48, 54
Owen, Jane, ix
Owen, Jane Bowman, 99, 308, 323
Owl Hollow Road, 349

P
Padgett, Henry, 94, 339
Page, Dee, 14
Page, Fred J., 214
Page High School, 54, 227
Page School, 214
Pantall, H.M., 4
Pantall, Jean, 62
Pantall, Mrs. Floy, 5
Pantall, Oliver, 62
Parent-Teacher Association, 4
Parker, Rev, Mrs., and Betty Ruth, 207
Parkes, Joe, 152
Parkes, W.J., 64
Parks, Virge, 341
Parks, Walter, 64
Parrish family, 68
Parton, Dolly, 308
Pastureland, 183
Patel, Mike, 33
Peabody College, 138, 203, 336
Pearce, Marie, 50
Pearl Harbor, 169
Penn, William, 157
Peoples, Greer, 154
Petway, John C., 95
Petway, J.T., 342
Pewitt, Clyde, 62
Pewitt, Lyn Sullivan, ix, 14
Peytonsville, 121, 194, 296
Peytonsville Road, 15, 64
Peytonsville School, 54, 64–65
Peytonsville students and teachers, 54
Phones, 243, 245
Phosphate, 258
Phosphate mining, 310, 324
Photographs, aerial, 33
Physicians, ix, 30
Pierce, 58
Pie suppers, 291
Pillow, William, 77
Pinkerton, Joe, 212
Pinkerton, John, 112
Pinkerton, Miss Nelle, 112

Pinkerton, Tom, 112
Pioneer Architecture, 68
Pioneer families, vii, ix, 117
Pleasant Hill School, 295
Plymouth Rock Chickens, 122, 127
Pointer's Corner, 110
Polio, 282
Postmasters, ix, 3, 5, 12, 14, 34, 77, 101
Postmasters, Harpeth, 6
Post Oak School, 214–15
Post Office, 3, 11–12, 14–15, 199, 229, 306
Poteete, Leon, 345
Poteete, Mary, 62
Poteete, Ruby, 345
Poteete, Willie Mae, 41
Poteete family, 14, 345
Potts, 58
Powell, Miss, 248
Pratt, Eaymond, 136
Pratt, Eunice, 63
Pratt, Sam, 9
Pratt, Tony, 65
Presbyterian, 2, 14, 23, 25, 201, 219, 230, 254
Presbyterian Church, 2–3, 146, 152, 200, 206, 213, 218–19, 230, 267, 270, 283, 325, 331
Bethesda, 191
Presbyterian Church building, 219
Presbyterian College, 209
Presbyterian Ladies Auxiliary, 3
Presbyterian manse, 104
Presbyterian minister, 204
Presbyterian School, 209
President Adams, 87
Preston, John, 81
Prince, Stella, 45
Prince Edward County, Virginia, 163
Prospect Methodist Church, 24, 67
Protestant Hospital, 150, 326
Pruitt, Charlie, 313
PTA buses, 191
Puerto Rico, 105
Pulaski, Tennessee, 2, 194, 290
Pull Tight, 204, 237, 242, 305, 311
Pull Tight church, 313
Pull Tight Hill, 16, 21, 33, 68, 204
Pull Tight Hill Road, 232, 242, 311
Pull Tight Ridge, 304

Q
Quilting, 226, 245, 249, 264, 293
Quirk, Mr., 243

INDEX

R
Rabbit Hill, 226, 308
Ragland, C.B., 235
Raising cotton, 227
Raising hogs, 136
Raising livestock, 12, 120
Raising wheat, 109
Ralston, Rev. C.N., 104, 192
Rascoe, Tyler, 143
Ratcliffe, Francis, 77
Ratcliffe, Martha Reams, 77
Ratcliffe, Mary, 77
Ratcliffe Cemetery, 78
Reams, Henry, 24, 66–68
Ream's Chapel, 67
Reams family, 14, 68
Reconstruction days, 84
Redford, Miss, 212–14
Reed, 261
Reed, Alma, 47, 220–22
Reed, Annie Lou, 248
Reed, Buford, 38, 248
Reed, Charlie, 212, 248, 266, 273
Reed, Classie, 56
Reed, Cora, teacher, 58
Reed, Ease, 56
Reed, Eunice, 58
Reed, Everett, 43
Reed, Fannie, 248
Reed, Floyd, 40
Reed, Frank, 57
Reed, Garrett, 323
Reed, Glenda, 220, 222
Reed, Glyndon, 46–47
Reed, Gusty, 58
Reed, Henry, 247–48
Reed, Hershel, 41
Reed, J.C., 21
Reed, L.C., 57
Reed, Leon, 44
Reed, Lera, 43
Reed, Lola, 45, 333
Reed, Luther, 218
Reed, Mr., 261
Reed, Ode, 58
Reed, Ross, 215
Reed, Ruth, 39, 104, 212
Reed, Sam, 244
Reed, Scott, 113, 216, 238
Reed, Terry H., 44
Reed, Willie Alice, 41, 248
Reed Road, 325
Reese, Evan, 337
Reese, Nicholas, 337
Reese, Susan Keedy, 337
Regen, Clare, 185
Review-Appeal, The, ix, 2, 7, 11, 58, 99–100, 106, 111, 134, 137, 140, 158, 162, 165
Revolution, the, 67, 73
Revolutionary soldier, 67, 70
Revolutionary veteran, last living, 16
Revolutionary War, 69, 285–86
Revolutionary War veteran, 16
Reynolds, Fred, 110
Reynolds
Reynolds, Mitchell, 61
Reynolds, Murry Jim, 61
Reynolds Cemetery, 86
Reynolds family, 23
Rice, Robert, 42
Richland Presbytery, 23
Ridge Meeting Church, 14
Ridge Meeting House, 23
Rigsby, Charles, 243
Ringstaff, James, 50
River Bend Nursery, 94
Road, Arno, 54
Road, Franklin, 28, 312
Road, Jordan, 70
Road, Lane, 311–12, 337
Road foreman, 242
Roane County, Tennessee, 135
Roberson family, 22
Roberson, Annie, 59
Roberson, Effie, 59
Roberson, Howard, 59
Roberson, Lera, 59
Roberson, Mary Lee, 59
Roberson, Willie Mai, 59
Robertson, Howard, 308
Robertson, Jimmie, 243
Robertsons, the, 255
Robinson, B, 65
Robinson, Lulu, 254
Rock City Construction, 12
Roop, Mary, 38
Roosevelt, President, 326–27
Rose, Dorothy, 142
Ross, Charlie, 131
Ross, Mr., 313
Roy Creswell Place, 320
Ruby, Rev. and Mrs. C.O., 104
Rucker, 70, 77
Rucker, Capt. William, 70
Rucker, Cora, 342
Rucker, Lt. A.D.A., 70
Rucker, Mrs. Will, 110
Rucker, Rachel, 70
Rucker, Rachel Steele, 77, 342
Rucker, William, 70
Rucker, William S., 342
Rucker, William Steele, 77
Rucker, Willie Anderson, 148
Rudderville, 172, 186, 227, 231, 308
Rudderville community, 311
Runnels, Russell, 306
Russell, Richard F., 6
Russell, Thomas, 3
Rutherford, Gen., 8
Ryan, George, 45, 47, 274
Ryan, Mary, 46–47

S
Sam Anderson House, 85
Sam Fleming Place, 150
Sampson, Delia, 346
Sampson, Mrs. R.S., 346
Sampson, William B., 6, 12
Sanders, Jean, 222, 232, 300
Sawmill, 3, 107–8, 182, 184, 186, 218, 230, 243, 274, 305
Sawyer, Bill, 48, 54
Sawyer, Louise, 305
Scales, 2–5
Scales, Charles, 78
Scales, Charles F. and Ella, 78
Scales, Ella, 74, 78
Scales, Frank, 78
Scales, Marion, 78, 200
Scales, Mary Ratcliffe, 166
Scales, Mr., 78
Scales, Mrs. W.P., 62, 148
Scales, P.D., 28, 122, 199
Scales, P.D. Store, 199
Scales, Pleasant, 77
Scales, Pleasant D., 6, 101, 199
Scales, Pleas D., 101
Scales, Preston, 77, 117, 322–23
Scales, P.W., 104
Scales, Stella, 58
Scales, Susie, 316
Scales, Susie Baugh, 316
Scales, Susie Mai, 62
Scales, Thelma, 50
Scales, W.P., 51, 62, 166
Scales-Grigsby store, 33
Scales Grocery, 5
Scales House, viii, 77–78
Scales Mrs., 78
Scales' Store, 78
Scales Stores, 37
School, elementary, 137–38, 288, 338
School, first free, 101
School, largest, 36

School, new, 37, 92, 178, 270, 273, 289, 303
School, one-room, 155, 204, 215, 263, 296, 305
School, one-teacher, 201
School, original, 288
School, public, 4, 287
School, three-teacher, 201
School, two-teacher, 64, 212, 214
School, Douglas, 15
School, Naomi, 212
School board, 37, 54, 137
Schoolboys, 232, 323
School building, 4, 201, 262
School, elementary, 104
School bus, 186-7, 191, 234, 237, 296
School bus driver, 190
School buses, 104, 187, 191, 194–95, 205–6, 296, 301
School children, 322
School Christmas Tree, 215
School commissioners, 262
School discipline, 322
School duties, 165
School girls, 234, 236
Schoolhouse, black folk's, 288
School library, 4, 168
Schoolmaster, 60, 280
Schools, 36, 38, 40, 42, 44, 46, 48, 50, 52, 54, 56, 58, 60, 62, 64
Schoolyard, 217
Scots-Irish border clan, 283
Scotland, 73
Scots border clan Presbyterians, 75
Scots-Irish descent, 133
Scots-Irish grandfather, 115
Scott, Lizzie, 43
Scoutmaster, 156
Seay, Evelyn, 167
Seed, Evins, 199
Sharp, Willie Lee, 59
Shearer, 76
Shelby Park, 272
Shelbyville, 312, 336–37
Sherfield, Luddie, 59
Shiney, 238, 240, 242, 244
Shipley, Charlie, 48, 54
Shriner, 153, 156
Shumate Farm, 16
Simmers, Ralph, 312
Simmons, J.W., 27
Simmons Hill, 204–5
Skinner, Effie Mai, 59
Skinner, Eunice, 59
Skinner, Jerry, 65
Skinner, Naola Mae, 58

Skinner, Willie Mai, 59
Skinner family, 23
Slave cabin, 75, 298
Slave quarters, 130
Slaves, 82, 103, 113, 159, 252, 286, 298, 302, 306
Smith, Fannie Myrtle, 168
Smith, Jimmy, 274
Smith, John, 142
Smith, Mrs. W.L., 3, 104
Smith, Rev., 3
Smith, Rev. W.L., 2–3, 163, 191
Smith, Tommy, 40
Smithson, Agnes, 47
Smithson, Alda, 59
Smithson, Alice, 153
Smithson, C.C., 26, 28–29
Smithson, Charles, 6, 133, 153
Smithson, Charles T., 154
Smithson, Herman, 42
Smithson, James "Jake," 45
Smithson, Joe, 45
Smithson, Leslie, 57
Smithson, Lizzie, 39
Smithson, Lucy, 130
Smithson, Mary, 38–39
Smithson, Mary Wilson, 133
Smithson, Millard, 43
Smithson, Miss, 305
Smithson, Nell, 305
Smithson, Nellie, 57
Smithson, Roy, 263, 266
Smithson, Thelma, 45
Smithson, Url, 3
Smithson, W.H., 27
Smithson, Woodard, 45
Smithson, Woody Junior, 271
Smithson family, 20, 23, 133
South Carolina Ancestors, 338
South Pacific, 179
Sowell, Filmore, 63
Sowell, Mrs. Will, 149
Spears, Hickman, 232
Spencer Waddey's place, 9
Split-Log School, 159
Spratt-McCord Place, 159
Spring Hill, 6, 11, 73, 195, 224, 257, 266, 317
Sprott, 8, 83
Sprott, Andrew, 9, 67, 102
Sprott, Elise, 341
Sprott, Emma Catherine, 341
Sprott, Evan, 341
Sprott, Fred, 340–41
Sprott, Grant, 225
Sprott, Horace, 341

Sprott, J., 339
Sprott, Jane, 73
Sprott, John, 9
Sprott, Joseph, 9, 71
Sprott, Martha Jones, 71
Sprott, Mary Elizabeth, 73
Sprott, Minnie, 104, 227
Sprott, Rachel, 103
Sprott, Rachel and Blythe, 73
Sprott, Roy, 61
Sprott, Samuel, 9, 73
Sprott, Samuel Blythe, 73
Sprott, Susie May, 61
Sprott, Will, 201
Sprott, William, 9
Sprott-Alexander Family Reunion, 340–41
Sprott children, 8
Sprott family, 73, 83
Sprott home, old, 198
Srygley, H.F., 48, 54
Stammers, Maude, 341
Stammers, Tom, 340–41
Stammers, Virge, 341
Stammers, Virge Sprott, 340
Stanfield, Mattie Sue Crafton, 42
Stanford, Cicero, 97, 171
Stanford, Virginia Waddey, 97, 171
Stanfords, the, 97, 145
Stan's Restaurant, 195
State Legislature, 5, 115
State Teacher's College, 113, 121, 138
Steele, Alex, 285
Steele, Cora, 80
Steele, Daniel, 122
Steele, Ella, 80
Steele, H.M., 19
Steele, Irene, 38–39
Steele, Lelia, 342
Steele, Margaret, 69
Steele, Mary Elizabeth, 70, 79–80
Steele, Moses, 3, 69–70, 75, 77, 79, 83
Steele, Mrs. William Alexander, 79
Steele, Rachel, 70
Steele, Rachel Webber, 70
Steele, Sarah Ruth, 70
Steele, Susan Moore, 79
Steele, W.A., 19
Steele, William, 3, 70
Steele, William Alexander, 69–70, 79–80
Steele family, 70, 83, 285
Steele family genealogy, 285
Steele Home, 190
Steele homestead, original, 104

INDEX

Stem, Mary, 52
Stem family, 22
Stephens, 22, 172
Stephens, Alcenia, 61
Stephens, Buford and Evelyn, 53
Stephens, Clara, 61
Stephens, Clyde, 61
Stephens, C.W., 45
Stephens, Emilly Giles, 172
Stephens, Evelyn, 53
Stephens, James W., 44
Stephens, Joe, 171
Stephens, John, 22, 159
Stephens, Joyce, 61
Stephens, Lawrence, 61
Stephens, Lera, 161
Stephens, Leslie, 61
Stephens, Maggie, 171, 173
Stephens family, 22
Stephenson, Jim, 44
Stephens-Roberson-Woodside House, 93
Stephens-Roberson-Woodside House on Ash Hill Road, 93
Stevens, Gene, 240
Stevens, Leslie, 240
Stevenson, 23
Stevenson, Rev. R.R., 123
Stevenson family, 23
Stoddard, Oliver, 15
Stoddard, O.R., 4
Stoddard, Susie, 15
Stoddard, Thomas, 63
U.S. Navy, WWII, 15
Stoddard Farm, 15
Stone, Odell, 62
Stones River, 305
Store, Callie, 15
Stowers, Dena, 285
Stowers, J.W., 3, 104
Sullivan, Gladys, 49
Sullivan, Mr., 212–13
Sunday School, 2–3, 118, 139, 146, 150, 152–53, 161, 164, 192, 219, 230
Sunnyside, 87
Surgical Technical School, Army, 336
Swan, Miss Foster, 43
Sykes, James, 54
Sykes, J.B., 48

T
Talmadge, 72, 158
Tavern, 86
Taylor, 22, 289
Taylor, Bertha, 257
Taylor, Bessie, 41
Taylor, Bill, 3
Taylor, C.C., 26
Taylor, Mary Sue, 257
Taylor, Mattie Sue, 43
Taylor, Mildred, 44
Taylor, Mr., 300–301, 303
Taylor, Mr. and Mrs. Will, 298
Taylor, Mrs., 300, 302
Taylor, Mrs. Will, 298
Taylor, Ruth, 270
Taylor, Sandra, 298
Taylor, Walter, 45, 47, 76, 123, 194, 297–300
Taylor, Ward, 308
Taylor, W.C., 27
Taylor, Will, 38, 76, 298–99
Taylor, Willie Lee, 46–47
Taylor, Willie Ruth Veach, 295–96, 298, 300, 302
Taylor family, 22
Taylor farm, 274, 280, 283, 286, 298
Taylor house, 183, 289
Teacher retirement, 208–9
Teachers, 14, 02, 104, 117, 139, 148, 165, 202, 215, 329
Teaching, 138, 164, 166–67, 169, 202, 204–5, 207–9, 212, 227–28, 230, 262, 336–37
Teasley, Charlie, 316
Television, 210, 238
Tennessean, The, 303
Tennessee and Williamson County Bicentennial Committee, vii, ix
Tennessee Capitol building, 12
Tennessee Conference Methodist Episcopal South, 21
Tennessee Old Hickory Division, 311
Tennessee River, 8
Tennessee Tech, 203, 208–10
Tennison family, 68
Thackston, James, 67
Thomas, Seth, 131
Thomas Johnston Place, old, 127
Thompson, 14
Thompson, C.C., 33–34
Thompson, C.C., Store, 12, 34
Thompson, Clinton C., 12
Thompson, Elise, 258
Thompson, Gracie, 61
Thompson, James, 34–35
Thompson, Lemuel G., 28
Thompson, L.G., 28–29
Thompson, Mickie, 142
Thompson, Mrs., 169
Thompson, R.C., 19
Thompson, Rev. G.E., 19
Thompson, Roy, 61
Thompson, Ruth, 32, 61
Thompson family, 14
Thompson Lake, 34
Thompson's Station, 6, 206, 297
Thompson Station, 13, 54, 112, 117, 125–28, 135, 150, 159, 205, 310, 333
Thompson Store, 34–35
Tobacco, 109, 114, 122, 127, 139, 141, 154, 172, 179, 180–83, 196, 267, 306, 310, 317, 320
Tobacco raising, 12, 154, 179–82, 196, 310, 317, 320
Tobacco barns, 180, 182, 259
Tohrner, Martin, 253
Toilet business, 327
Tollgate Hill, 166
Tollgates, 15, 263, 325
Tom Giles Farm, 292
Tom, Mary, 264
Tomlin, 14, 22
Tomlin, Alma, 62
Tomlin, Bill, 345
Tomlin, Dorothy, 62
Tomlin, Doss, 345
Tomlin, Effie, 63
Tomlin, Frank, 3
Tomlin, Gladys, 63
Tomlin, Grace, 333
Tomlin, Henry (Buck), 62
Tomlin, Henry "Buck," 62
Tomlin, Herman, 63
Tomlin, James, 62
Tomlin, Josie, 345
Tomlin, Lera, 344
Tomlin, Lera Mai Deason, 344
Tomlin, Lou Ellen, 40
Tomlin, Louise, 63
Tomlin, Luster, 62
Tomlin, Mary Thomas, 63
Tomlin, Maxie, 63
Tomlin, Milton, 62
Tomlin, Myrtle, 63
Tomlin, Oakley, 345
Tomlin, Reese, 4
Tomlin, Robert, 345
Tomlin, Rolfe, 63
Tomlin, Sara, 333
Tomlin, Susan Bennett, 345
Tomlin, Vashti, 62
Tomlin family, 14, 22
Tommy, 117, 141
Trevecca College, 203

Trice, 16
Trice, merchant, 33
Trice, Alexanie, 218
Trice, Alexine, 43
Trice, Carrie, 52, 250, 330, 332
Trice, Carrie Layne, 104
Trice, Charlie, 58, 249, 304, 323, 344
Trice, Charlie and Fanny, 249
Trice, Donald, 44
Trice, Dorothy, 45
Trice, Emma, 43
Trice, Ewell, 103
Trice, Gentry, 216
Trice, Grover, 20, 38, 58, 104, 240–41, 323–24, 344
Trice, Grover and Carrie, 332
Trice, James, 233–34, 304, 306, 308, 310, 312, 337
Trice, Jessie, 57
Trice, Joe, 43, 103, 110, 233–34, 304
Trice, John, 231, 307
Trice, Johnny, 57
Trice, Kate, 332
Trice, Leo, 311
Trice, Lois, 218
Trice, Louise, 56
Trice, Mammy Kate, 305
Trice, Margaret, 46
Trice, Mary Blythe, 56, 58
Trice, Mike, 237
Trice, Sam, 344
Trice, Sara, 47
Trice, Stan, 311
Trice, Sue, 57
Trice, Wallace, 58
Trice family, 16
Trice House, 196, 304
Trice Place, 196, 337
Trinity, 121, 227–28, 296
Trinity Community, 295
Trinity School, 228
Turner, 33, 233
Turner, Buddy, 105
Turner, Clarisa, 58
Turner, John, 233
Turner, Rich, 58
Turner store, 33, 233
Tusculum College, 209
TVA, 276–77, 311
Twelfth District, 145, 156

U
Union Grove Cemetery, 73
Union soldiers, 19, 77
United States Army, 105
United States Navy, 111

Uruguay, 112
U.S. Cavalry, 309

V
Vaden, Bob, 50
Vaden, Paul, 65
Vanderbilt, 336–37
Vanderbilt University, 220, 336–37
Vandy, 337
Vantrease, Margaret, 197
Veach, Ann, 65
Veach, Logan, 95
Veach, Morgan, 295
Victory, Lunnie, 56
Victory, Mary Lizzie, 56
Victory, Monrow, 58
Virginia, 151, 318
Virginia, state of 3, 7–8, 67, 70, 76, 79, 83
Virginia, Amherst County, 159
Virginia, Augusta County, 73
Virginia, Bedford County, 69
Virginia, Campbell County, 3, 75
Virginia, Dinwiddie County, 67
Virginia, Halifax County, 67
Virginia, Hampden Sidney, 163
Virginia, James City County, 77
Virginia, Richmond, 273
Virginia, State of, 159, 164, 172, 224, 249, 316
Virginia Buford, 62–63
Virginia line, 7
Virginia McGee, 62, 316
Vivienne Grigsby, 40, 74

W
Waddell Hollow, 349
Waddey, 172-3, 273
Waddey, Ben, 101
Waddey, Benjamin, 3, 173
Waddey, Dick, 97, 170, 294
Waddey, Emma Virginia, 172
Waddey, Ira, 172, 192, 294
Waddey, John, 172
Waddey, Kitty, 47
Waddey, Kitty Margaret, 46, 172
Waddey, Lee, 172
Waddey, Lee S., 173
Waddey, Mack, 14
Waddey, Mr., 273
Waddey, Mrs., 172
Waddey, Polly Lowe, 170
Waddey, Richard F., 47
Waddey, Richard Frank, 172–73
Waddey, Richard P., 97, 170–73
Waddey, Tom, 170

Waddey chairs, 294
Waddey family, 172, 273
Waddey, Richard P., 173
Waldon, Mary, 39
Walker, 22, 254–55
Walker, Bud, 274
Walker, Dr., 213
Walker, Jimmy, 249
Walker, J.M., 48, 54
Walker, Mr., 253
Walker, Reed, 312
Walker family, 22
Wall, Clement, 19
Wallace, 14, 284, 351
Wallace, Ella, 222
Wallace, Ellis, 62
Wallace, Jim, 58
Wallace, John, 284, 287
Wallace, Lottie, 284
Wallace, Mallie Fleming, 88
Wallace, Marvin, 46
Wallace, R.T., 62
Wallace, Thomas J., 6
Wallace, Tom, 34, 88
Wallace family, 14, 284
Wallace-Fleming-Lavender Store, 35
Wall and Mooney School, 108
Waller, Robert, 344
Wally, Watson, 308
Walter, 30
Walter, Don, 266
Walter Pyle Hospital, 126
Walters, Tom, 3
Walton, Donald Core, 43
Walton, Jack, 38–39
Walton, Jessie, 38, 40
Walton, J.L., 28–29
Walton, Mary, 38, 40
Walton, Tom, 171–72
Wampole, 235
Ware, Lizzie Knott, 103
Ware, Martha, 45, 47
Ware, Tommie Lou, 129
Ware, Tommie Lou Daniel, 131, 133
Ware, Mattie Sue 100, 102, 104
Warner, Simon, 312
War of 1812, 73
Warren, Edward, 169
Warren, Edward B., 165
Warren, Fenton, 45, 47–48, 54
Warren, Lyn, 169
Warren, Marion Grigsby, 165–69
Warren County, 8
Warren family, 23
Warren Funeral Home, 169

INDEX

Warwick, Rick, vii–ix, 99
Washington, D.C., 113
Watkins family, 288, 14
Watkins, Charles, 62
Watkins, Christine, 62
Watkins, Jerry, 314, 316, 318
Watkins, Jessie, 62
Watkins, Judy, 46
Watkins, Leslie, 62
Watkins, Lucy, 62
Watkins, Luke, 316
Watkins, Susie Lee, 315
Watson, Jack, 187
Watson, Jim, 49, 54
Watson, Pomp, 339
Watson, Ralph, 329
Watson, Vivienne Grigsby, 54, 74, 329
Watsons, the, 198
Webb, Ella Frances Grigsby, 42
Webb, Mr., 274
Webb, Samuel, 6
Webb, William S., ix, 2, 6
Webb Guards, 70
Webster, Jack, 196
Wells, Jack, 63
Wesleyan Service Guild, 169
Wesley Foundation, 210
West, Fleming, 314
West, Lee, 315
West, Malcolm, 310
West Harpeth, 109
West Harpeth River, 24, 108
West Harpeth School, 108
West Tennessee, 75
West Virginia, 314, 335
White, Leonard Strickland, 58
White, Nellie Jane, 58
White, Terry, 277
White Mule, 142
Whitfield, Raymond, 121
Whittaker, Sharon, 50
Wiley, 22
Wiley, Addie, 59
Wiley, Bill, 319–28
Wiley, Dale, 326
Wiley, Dora, 42
Wiley, Henry, 320
Wiley, Irene, 59
Wiley, James T., 6, 12
Wiley, J.W., 44

Wiley, Linda, 326
Wiley, Louise, 59
Wiley, Preston, 343
Wiley, Suedie, 343
Wiley, Susie, 59
Wiley, Thomas, 6, 12, 44
Wiley, W.H., 339
Wiley, Will, 43
Wiley, Willene, 326
Wiley, William, 8
Wiley, Willie, 59
Wiley family, 22
Wilhoite, Ben, 63
Wilhoite, Jim, 63
Wilhoite, Mabel, 63
Wilhoite, W.L., 297
Willhoit's Mill, 226
William Cicero Bond, 80, 89, 347
William Rucker Place, 9
Williams, Addie, 62
Williams, Bertha, 40
Williams, Charley, 40
Williams, Erma, 309
Williams, Ethel, 52
Williams, Frank, 40, 63
Williams, Frank, family, 103
Williams, Fred Lee, 45, 62
Williams, Helen, 4, 45
Williams, Homer, 45, 62
Williams, Hugh, 40, 45
Williams, John, 186, 233, 300, 308
Williams, Ludie, 61
Williams, Margaret Ann, 65
Williams, Morris, 33
Williams, Nell, 203
Williams, Paul, 301
Williams, Robert, 44
Williams, Sara A., 45
Williams, Sheriff Fleming, 242
Williams family, 33
Williamson County, Twelfth District, 8, 145, 156
Williamson County Bank, 212
Williamson County Bicentennial Committee, vii, ix
Williamson County Chamber of Commerce, vii
Williamson County Court, 137, 153, 156
Williamson County Court Clerk, 34

Williamson County Hospital, 326
Williamson County Road Commissioners, 5
Williamson County School Board, 3, 36
William's Store, 303
Willing Workers, 156
Wilson, 113, 204
Wilson, Ace, 91
Wilson, Goodshire, 77
Wilson, Matthew, 77
Wilson, Rev. R., 19
Wilson, Rev. R.W., 19
Wilson, Woodrow, 204
Wilson & Company, 113
Wilson family, 204
Wilson home, old, 204
Wilson House, 77
Wilson. Rev. R.W., 19
Wingo, Mr., principal, 42, 261
Women's Auxiliary, 164
Women's Society, 123
Woods, 127, 131, 180, 182, 192, 205, 221, 239, 244, 246, 277, 281, 330
Woods, Julia, 42
Woodside, Bill, 59
Woodside, Eva, 59
Woodside family, 22
Woodward, Dr., 326
Woody, Jean, 60
Wooten, Dan, 334
Works Progress Administration, 327
World War II, 169, 179, 297, 336
Wright, G.C., 41
Wright, Hazel, 63
Wright, James, 50
Wright, Veron, 63
WSM tower, 116
WWII, 150
WWI Veteran, 80
Wylie, Nora, 41
Wylie, Preston, 41
Wylie, Roy, 41

Y
Yankees, 77, 79–80, 103, 107, 160, 164
Young, Frances Chrisman, 42

[Created with TExtract]